W9-DHM-192

SCENES
OF SHAME

SUNY series in Psychoanalysis and Culture
Henry Sussman, Editor

SCENES OF SHAME

Psychoanalysis, Shame, and Writing

JOSEPH ADAMSON
and
HILARY CLARK

Editors

State University
of New York
Press

Published by
State University of New York Press, Albany

© 1999 State University of New York

All rights reserved

Production by Susan Geraghty
Marketing by Fran Keneston

Printed in the United States of America

PS
169
.S44
S34
1999

For information, address State University of New York
Press, State University Plaza, Albany, N.Y., 12246

Library of Congress Cataloging-in-Publication Data

Scenes of shame : psychoanalysis, shame, and writing / Joseph Adamson
    and Hilary Clark, editors.
        p.   cm. — (SUNY series in psychoanalysis and culture)
    Includes bibliographical references and index.
    ISBN 0-7914-3975-5 (hardcover : alk. paper). — ISBN 0-7914-3976-3
(pbk. : alk. paper)
        1. American literature—History and criticism—Theory, etc.
    2. Shame in literature. 3. English fiction—History and criticism-
    -Theory, etc. 4. Literature—Psychological aspects.
    5. Psychoanalysis and literature. 6. Psychology in literature.
    I. Adamson, Joseph, 1950–   . II. Clark, Hilary Anne, 1955–
    III. Series.
    PS169.S44S34 1998
    813.009'353—dc21   97-49913
                                                                            CIP

10 9 8 7 6 5 4 3 2 1

520799

CONTENTS

FOREWORD

There was a time when the only way you could learn about shame—someone else's shame—was by reading novels or going to the movies. Spurned passion is shame. Whoever hopes for love fears humiliation cloaked thinly in the tame word "rejection." There is nothing tame about shame, which wounds in direct proportion to the good feeling and sense of relational safety it attacks, impedes, stifles. The barroom brawl is triggered by a fantasized (shaming) insult. We keep up with the Joneses in order to reduce the possibility of invidious comparison that will bring us shame. Cosmetic surgery is image maintenance, a system through which we guide the eyes of the potentially shaming observer to what now may make us proud. Creativity, said Léon Wurmser, requires the heroic transcendence of shame; every tale of scientific or political or romantic or economic courage and success is about effort that was carried along on a wave of enthusiasm sufficient to wash away potentially stultifying shame. For ages, all this was conveyed to us by serious writers whose observations allowed us to sample shame safely much in the way we thrill to the amorous exploits that draw us to "cheaper" sources.

There was a time when you couldn't talk about your own shame with the cadre of psychotherapists trained to celebrate guilt and demean embarrassment as its vaguely indecent sibling. Pride, one polar opposite of shame, was equated with narcissism and therefore shameful. Whenever you felt too embarrassed to discuss something with the still-faced therapist, you were exposed to a grave lecture about "resistance" to the uncovering analytic process. The emotionality associated with shame was defined as a weapon in the arsenal of the "superego," an invisible and seditious army that one day landed mysteriously in the psyche of the child to provide torment for sexual wishes visible only to the analyst.

Then a troupe of brave, creative scholars outed shame and declared it the issue of our era. Independently, pioneers like Silvan Tomkins (1963), Helen Block Lewis (1971), and Léon Wurmser (1981) stood toe to toe with the entrenched establishment to which shame had always been invisible and by their work made shame salient. No longer hidden in the wings, it took center stage and became the stylish darling of a decade. Next, hucksters declared it "toxic" and an enemy of humankind, while journalists in broadcast and print drowned the public in shameless disclosures of anything that had ever been a central privacy. Nonetheless, just as Bible scholars talk of pre- and postlapsarian life in terms of the shame experienced by Adam and Eve, historians of the future will see our generation as that within which ongoing sober, sensible discussion of shame became possible and all areas of scholarship infused both with new courage and new language for human emotion.

Now this collection of essays makes us turn again to the world of literature and philosophy, examining those who allowed us to feel so deeply when we first encountered them, asking how they knew so much when we were young and innocent. Within what life experiences were Nietzsche's sophistication and Kierkegaard's vision nested? How did Hawthorne come to know so well the skills through which public humiliation could be used to punish love and destroy the human spirit? Dare we use the quaint, outmoded term "depression" to disguise the agony of Anne Sexton's chronic, unremitting, and unattended shame once we learn the matrix within which that shame was embedded? Essay after essay, this book forces new awareness of all affective experience on those who search for the sources of meaning in the writers who have moved them.

This is the time when Professors Adamson and Clark can ask psychoanalysts and literary scholars to walk hand in hand so that all of us may learn better and think more clearly about the power of great writers. Their book, this book, could not have been organized before the revolution in our understanding of shame, and will be seen as a significant part of the evolution in literary criticism made possible by it.

Donald L. Nathanson, M.D.
Executive Director
The Silvan Tomkins Institute
Clinical Professor of Psychiatry
Jefferson Medical College

ACKNOWLEDGMENTS

This book began as a somewhat tentative venture between two friends. Since then, a very congenial and generous group of scholars has come along and made it possible. We would like to thank all the contributors now for their time and care, and for the admirable quality of their efforts. They have given faith and substance to an idea.

Henry Sussman and Carola Sautter provided crucial encouragement at the early stages. James Peltz, who joined us in midstream, has proven to be a very reliable and flexible editor. We are grateful to the three anonymous readers who reported on the manuscript for the press; their observations and recommendations have been extremely helpful. The critical suggestions and guidance of all the contributors have been greatly appreciated. For their special help and commitment throughout the project, we would like to thank Jeffrey Berman, Brooks Bouson, and Barbara Schapiro.

CONTRIBUTORS

Joseph Adamson is Professor of English and Comparative Literature at McMaster University. He is the author of *Wounded Fiction: Modern Poetry and Deconstruction, Northrop Frye: A Visionary Life,* and *Melville, Shame, and the Evil Eye.*

Jeffrey Berman is Professor of English at SUNY, Albany. He is the author of *Joseph Conrad: Writing as Rescue, The Talking Cure, Narcissism and the Novel,* and *Diaries to an English Professor.*

J. Brooks Bouson is Associate Professor of English at Loyola University in Chicago; she is the author of *The Empathic Reader: A Study of the Narcissistic Character and the Drama of the Self* and *Brutal Choreographies: Oppositional Strategies and Narrative Design in the Novels of Margaret Atwood.*

Hilary Clark is Associate Professor of English at the University of Saskatchewan; she is the author of *The Fictional Encyclopedia: Joyce, Pound, Sollers.*

Philip Collington is a part-time instructor at the University of Toronto; his recently completed Ph.D. dissertation enlists Kohutian self-psychology to investigate cuckoldry anxiety as depicted in Shakespeare's plays.

Benjamin Kilborne is a psychoanalyst in private practice. He has taught at various universities and is a training and supervising analyst at the Los Angeles Institute and Society for Psychoanalytic Studies. He has worked and published extensively on the subject of shame and is currently working on a full-length study of the psychology of appearance.

Gordon Hirsch is professor of English and director of the College of Liberal Arts Honors Program at the University of Minnesota. He is co-editor (with William Veeder) of *Dr Jekyll and Mr Hyde after One Hundred Years.*

Joseph Lichtenberg is a psychoanalyst in private practice in Washington, D.C. He is Editor-in-Chief of *Psychoanalytic Inquiry,* Clinical Professor of Psychiatry at Georgetown University, and Director of the Institute of Contemporary Psychotherapy. He is the author of *"The Talking Cure," Psychoanalysis and Infant Research, Psychoanalysis and Motivation*, and co-editor (with Frank Lachmann and James Fosshage) of *The Self and Motivation Systems* and *The Clinical Exchange*.

Barbara Schapiro is Professor of English at Rhode Island College. She is author of *The Romantic Mother: Narcissistic Patterns in Romantic Poetry* and *Literature and the Relational Self*. She is co-editor (with Lynne Layton) of *Narcissism and the Text: Studies in Literature and the Psychology of Self*. Her most recent work, *D. H. Lawrence and the Paradoxes of Psychic Life*, is forthcoming from SUNY Press.

Léon Wurmser is Clinical Professor of Psychiatry at the University of West Virginia and Training and Supervising Analyst, New York Freudian Society. He is the author of *The Hidden Dimension* and *The Mask of Shame*, as well as, in German, *Flucht vor dem Gewissen, Die Zerbrochene Wirklichkeit*, and *Das Rätsel des Masochismus*.

CHAPTER 1

Introduction:
Shame, Affect, Writing

Joseph Adamson and Hilary Clark

I

The essays in this volume all explore the role of shame as an important affect in the complex psychodynamics of literary works. The significance of shame as a central human emotion has now come to be widely recognized in the fields of psychoanalysis, psychotherapy, and psychology. Literary scholars, however, have been rather slow in showing interest in the way these developments may enhance our understanding of literature, largely, it would seem, because of the current dominance of Lacanian and poststructuralist versions of psychoanalysis. Fortunately, the same cannot be said of those analysts and researchers who have been exploring shame. Again and again, they have turned to literary examples in order to illustrate or expand their knowledge about this powerful emotion. In her highly regarded pioneering study of shame, Helen Merrell Lynd features a host of literary examples, while many of the psychologists and psychoanalysts who have subsequently pursued an interest in shame, such as Léon Wurmser and Silvan Tomkins, have displayed an even greater eagerness to turn to the imaginative world of literature for evidence of compelling psychological reality.[1] The implication seems to be that the world of fiction offers a wealth of metaphors and images for understanding shame and *affective* reality in general. By the same token, our knowledge of literature may be enhanced by a deepened scientific and psychoanalytic understanding of this reality.

The relevance of the literary and mythopoeic imagination to the understanding of psychological reality is hardly a new discovery. Lionel Trilling cites the story of how Freud, when greeted on the occasion of a

1

celebration of his seventieth birthday as the "'discoverer of the unconscious' . . . corrected the speaker and disclaimed the title. 'The poets and
philosophers before me discovered the unconscious,' he said. 'What I
discovered was the scientific method by which the unconscious can be
studied'" (32). It is a commonplace that Freud repeatedly turned to literature and myth to support the discoveries that his new science was
beginning, often in a more awkward and laborious fashion, to uncover.
He clearly believed that the metaphors, images, and symbols that are the
language of literature offer an acute insight into inner reality, an insight
difficult to attain by other means.

However, as literary scholars and humanists are all too aware, the
ideology of science has for the most part tended to disregard and under-
value both the affective and the imaginative dimensions of human experience. The serious study of the imaginative realm is often dismissed as
anti-objective and antirealistic. In the same way, despite increasing
attention to the affects in popular psychology and New Age publica-
tions, there is a deep-rooted and ongoing tendency in our culture to deny
the emotions any real significance in our understanding of the world.
Perversely, this tendency has invaded the academic disciplines of the arts
and social sciences as well. In recent years literary criticism has been
dramatically transformed by the rise of radically new methodologies—
deconstruction, New Historicism, cultural criticism, race, gender, and
gay and lesbian studies—all alike in their insistence on predominantly
ideological and political understandings of culture. According to these
new "philosophies of suspicion," humanistic approaches to the understanding of literature and culture are no longer tenable. The words
"imagination" and "creativity" are now stigmatized terms in academic
scholarship; indeed, one is *ashamed* to use them any more in speaking
of literary texts. References to the complex world of affective reality and
inner experience explored by literature are viewed as hopelessly naive
and retrograde.

Affective life is thus viewed as derivative, secondary, and even
unreal and imaginary, in relation to other, superordinate factors. However, to deny the emotional complexity and richness of human life is to
ignore the variety of ways in which human beings perceive and interact
with their world. Ultimately, it is to deny oneself invaluable knowledge,
knowledge that is as relevant to our understanding of the social and
political as it is to our understanding of the personal. Current discussions in literary criticism that focus on questions of race, class, and gender would do well to give more consideration to the affective sources
and consequences of social injustice and inequalities of power. Shame
affect is particularly relevant here. Whenever a person is disempowered
on the basis of gender, sexual orientation, race, physical disability,

whenever a person is devalued and internalizes the negative judgment of an other, shame flourishes. Shame attends the process of subjection in general, as more than one essay in this volume illustrates. Brooks Bouson's essay on Toni Morrison's *The Bluest Eye* focuses on the role of shame in defining self-image in a racist society. Joseph Lichtenberg's analysis of a vignette from *Middlemarch* addresses the question of shame and gender, illustrating how shame is used coercively in a male-dominated society—by both men and women—to enforce socially approved gender roles. As Lichtenberg points out, for many young girls, like Eliot's Maggie Tulliver and Letty Garth, "a central injury is the trauma of inequality, of being valued less as a female from infancy on."

Helen Block Lewis, one of the pioneers in shame, made a point of emphasizing the link between the experience of shame and women's experience under patriarchy. Lewis suggests, indeed, that the traditional overlooking of shame affect in psychoanalytic theory and practice is due to the feminization of this affect in particular: "The neglect of shame [and the greater emphasis on guilt] in both psychiatry and in psychoanalysis reflects prevailing sexist thinking" (*Role of Shame* 4). In the predominantly "scientific atmosphere" of these institutions, drives have been emphasized over affects; even within the realm of affects, shame, associated with femininity, has been seen as a "less prestigious emotion than guilt" (11), with guilt accordingly emphasized. Francis Broucek points out that in his *New Introductory Lectures on Psychoanalysis* Freud relates "shame not so much to a need to hide and protect the genitals but to conceal genital deficiency. Shame thus became 'a feminine characteristic par excellence'" (12).

Thomas Scheff has addressed the neglect of shame as a widespread phenomenon of modern societies, though he does not link it specifically to sexist assumptions. Scheff has explored the crucial part played by shame in establishing and regulating social bonds. He starts with the assumption that a threat to attachment is always inherent in shame. As the positive affects of interest and enjoyment are particularly instrumental in the establishment of attachments and bonds with others, so shame, which brings about a partial reduction of precisely these two positive affects (and thus disturbs without destroying mutuality), is particularly instrumental in the regulation of social interaction. Scheff regards the absence of any attention to shame in the social sciences (until recently) as part of the general tendency in modern Western societies to deny the emotional content of communal bonds and ties, and the social relevance of the emotions:

> Pride and shame serve as instinctive signals, both to self and other, to communicate the state of the bond. We react automatically to affirma-

tions of, and threats to, our bonds. However, if a culture is sufficiently
insistent, it can teach us to disguise and deny these signals. If the idea
of the social bond is repressed in modern societies, then we would
expect that these two emotions would also be systematically repressed.
(*Microsociology* 15)

Scheff notes that "pride and shame could be treated openly and directly"
by scientists such as Darwin in the nineteenth century. (It is perhaps no
accident that a number of the essays gathered here concern nineteenth-
century writers—Nietzsche, Eliot, Hawthorne, Kierkegaard—who show
a particular sensitivity to the understanding and imagery of shame.)
However, in today's discussions "these two emotions [shame and pride]
have all but disappeared. . . . [O]rthodox psychoanalysis glosses over
them, and they fare little better in systematic research" (15). Scheff points
out that "the denial of shame is institutionalized in the adult language of
modern societies" (17). Writing ten years ago, Donald Nathanson, a psychiatrist, made the same observation: "Shame seems to be an emotion little discussed in our clinical work. In the 20 years I have stayed awake at
case conferences, attended lectures, professional meetings, and symposia,
I have never heard a single case in which embarrassment, ridicule, humiliation, mortification, or any other of the shame family of emotions was
discussed" (*Many Faces* viii). Despite this neglect, however, the sudden
burst of books and writing on shame, even when they were ignored, sig-
nified to Nathanson "the sort of ferment (attended by cultural denial)
that usually precedes a major shift in cultural understanding" (viii).

Broucek claims that "Freud's attitude and the attitude of later psychoanalysts toward shame was one of disrespect. Shame was viewed as
one of the major forces promoting repression and resistance to the analytic process, thus opposing insight into the sexual dynamics underlying
the various neuroses" (12). Fortunately, psychoanalysis has remained
open to change and transformation, and has inevitably moved away from
a constraining framework based on aggressive drives and sexual conflict
toward an understanding more attentive to the affects and their observable influence on the development of human personality. Over the last
two decades, detailed research into the psychological development of
infants by psychoanalysts and psychologists has greatly enhanced our
understanding of the emotional basis of human motivation in general.[2]
Psychoanalysts such as Joseph Lichtenberg now recommend attention to
the affective experience of their patients (a refinement of Heinz Kohut's
emphasis on the significance of empathy in human relations and specifically in the analytic situation): "Actions and gestures that evoke affects,
and affects themselves and their transitions, are thus the golden thread
we follow to be empathically attuned with our patients" (254). The view,
as Tomkins summarizes it, of "human beings as the battleground for

their imperious drives, which urge them on blindly to pleasure and violence, to be contained only by a repressive society and its representations within—the ego and the superego" ("Shame" 137), has largely been rejected by psychoanalysts and psychotherapists as a simplification based on scientific and ideological assumptions that no longer apply. Rather, what forms the human self, besides certain genetically inherited predispositions, is the nexus of human relationships in which the human individual is intensely engaged from birth (even prebirth) on.[3] This engagement with others, which is the basis of the deeply social nature of human beings, is primarily of an emotional or affective nature.

Many of the early "heretics" or pioneers, such as Adler and Jung, who diverged from classical Freudian psychoanalysis, seem to have been frustrated, indeed, by Freud's inability to adapt his model of the human psyche to the undeniable influence of other factors more crucial than the "drives" and the conflicts to which they give rise. The history of psychoanalysis has been the history of fully recognizing the implications of human relationships and emotional motivation for an understanding of the human psyche. Freud tended to view the affects—anxiety, anger, and love—as derivatives, as either symptoms or sublimations of libidinal or aggressive impulses and wishes ultimately conceived of in terms of the two great biological forces ruling human life, the drive to erotic union and the drive toward death. But the power that Freud lent to these impulses suggests that the instincts and drives, as he assumed them to be, include to a great extent affective elements not explicitly recognized as such. The complex emotional coloring of sexual experience and of our experience of the body's physical life made Freud lose sight of the discrete nature of the affective system. He was thus led to confuse the role of drives—hunger, thirst, elimination (of waste), sex, pain, the need to breathe—with the very distinct role of affects. As Silvan Tomkins, the founder of contemporary affect theory, observes:

> Thus, in the concept of orality, the hunger drive mechanism was confused with the dependency-communion complex, which from the beginning is more general than the need for food and the situation of being fed. In the concept of anality, the elimination drive mechanism has been confused with the contempt-shame humiliation complex, which not only is more general than the need to eliminate but also has earlier environmental roots than the toilet training situation. In the concept of the Oedipus complex, the sex drive mechanism, admittedly more plastic than a drive such as the need for air, was confused with the family romance, which involves the far more general wishes to *be* both parents and to *possess* both parents. (*Affect* 1: 109)

Thus the power of Eros in human life can be explained only if we accept that we are not simply talking about a drive to mate. Sexual pleasure is composed primarily of affective elements of excitement and joy; these are its primary motivating elements, not the wish for sex per se. In the same way, aggression and hatred cannot be adequately explained in terms of the wish to defeat a sexual or Oedipal rival, nor can they be explained in terms of some deep instinctual force mysteriously urging human beings to destruction and death. They are, rather, a powerful emotional amalgam made up primarily of the so-called hostility triad—anger-rage, contempt (dissmell), and disgust—and often propelled as well by fear.[4] This is not at all to deny the biological foundations of psychological experience; it is, indeed, to recognize that what primarily motivates human beings are not drives or instinctual life, narrowly conceived, but affects, which like drives and instincts are innate, but, unlike them, are highly adaptable and nonspecific.

Thus, in contrast to the traditional view of affects as a superfluous, irrational, and atavistic feature of human beings, Tomkins claims that the affective complexity of human beings is one of the most distinctive features of their success as a species. He goes so far as to ask if "anyone may fully grasp the nature of any object when that object has not been perceived, wished for, missed, and thought about in love and in hate, in excitement and in apathy, in distress and in joy. . . . Only an animal who was as capable as man could have convinced himself that the scientific mode of acquaintance is the only 'real' mode through which he contacts reality" (*Affect* 1: 134–35). He stresses that "the belief in the reality or irreality of affect is a derivative of the socialization process and that there has been for the past two thousand years a recurrent polarity of ideology which centers upon the reality or irreality of human affect" (135). If the perception of affect has often been ignored and left undeveloped in favor of more formal and abstract languages, one of the most important functions of literature has been to provide a privileged place of redress, a sphere of expression where emotional life can be explored and refined in ways that are discouraged elsewhere. In literature, Tomkins observes, language used "for the expression, clarification and deepening of feelings" counters "the reduction in visibility of affects, effected by language which embeds, distorts or is irrelevant to the affects and which thereby impoverishes the affective life of man" (*Affect* 1: 219). The essays presented in this volume testify precisely to this affective role of language in literature, the ways in which imaginative writers explore, clarify, and enrich our emotional life.

II

One of the great attractions of the work of Jacques Lacan for literary theorists and critics has been its emphasis on language and the signifying dimension of culture. There can be no question that Lacan's contribution to certain areas of literary and cultural studies has been indispensable. His attention to the rhetorical and metaphorical language of the unconscious has led to new, nuanced readings of texts and of other cultural media such as film and television. But at the same time, this preoccupation with the signifier has tended to steer attention away from other important developments in psychoanalysis that have taken place over the last thirty years. Much of the psychoanalytic language now prevalent in literary theory and criticism, borrowed from a thinker whose own style is oracular to say the least, verges on the impenetrable and almost completely neglects the role of the affective system. As Gordon Hirsch has written, "One reason for the importance of studies of shame in contemporary psychological research is the emphasis on observed, primary affect, and on a response to this affect which is also frequently evident on an emotional level, without an inordinate reliance on abstract psychological metatheory" (65).

At the same time, certain of Lacan's concepts are clearly better understood in terms of affect. The prevalent use of the word "desire" is a good example. "*Désir*" is not a sexual concept—as Lacan himself notes—but pertains to *recognition* by the other, and therefore to the social field and to a bond that is ultimately emotional, not sexual. In Lacan's view, a profound *méconnaissance* is at the core of neurosis, and "*désir*" is, ultimately, the wish for *reconnaissance*, for mutual and reciprocal recognition in relation to the other. This is indeed the terminal point of analysis in the cure: reciprocally to recognize and be recognized, *desire* being *desire for recognition through the other*. Drawing on Hegel, Lacan says: "Le désir même de l'homme se constitue, nous dit-il, sous le signe de la médiation, il est désir de faire reconnaître son désir" (*Écrits* 181). ["Man's very desire, he tell us, is constituted under the sign of mediation, it is the desire to have one's desire recognized."] However, with the emphasis that Lacan places on the cognitive and symbolic aspect of this recognition, as intellectually fascinating as it is, the *affective* dimension is almost completely lost from view. Theoreticians such as Daniel Stern, Joseph Lichtenberg, and Jessica Benjamin have shown that such recognition is not so much a matter of cognition as a matter of "motives and affects activated in contexts of human interaction" (Lichtenberg 299). When this interaction traumatically fails and breaks down, "the dynamics of domination and submission result" (Schapiro, *Literature* 19), just as in Hegel the dialectic of master and slave disrupts the unalienated consciousness.

Certain other affective concepts, not always recognized as such, play a predominant role in Lacan's theorizing. Shame is particularly important. In his seminars, shame is central to his fascinating discussion of the scopic drive and the complex interplay of the eye and the gaze. Lacan understands the eye as a perceptual organ, while the gaze refers to the vision of an objectively self-aware subject or self, to the double focus, in terms of the visual field, of human consciousness. Like Sartre, Lacan sees shame as the negative affect central to that defining experience of objective self-awareness, involving the alienation of self through a paralyzing self-consciousness in relation to the other. Significantly, when he makes the distinction between the eye and the gaze, he focuses on the experience of shame and cites a passage in which Sartre links desire and shame in the experience of alienation.[5] Desire, as Lacan says, is the desire of the other, or the other's desire: "Le désir de l'homme, c'est le désir de l'Autre" (*Écrits* 900). Similarly, he says of the gaze: "The gaze I encounter is not a seen gaze, but a gaze imagined by me in the field of the Other" (*Four* 84). Kilborne points out in his essay on Kierkegaard that it is not just how we appear to the other but how we *imagine* we appear to the other that is involved in shame. For Sartre and Lacan, this dependence on the other defines the negative aspects of the inescapable condition of human intersubjectivity, in which one remains inevitably alienated and estranged from oneself ("le désir de l'homme s'aliène dans le désir de l'autre" [*Écrits* 343]; ["human desire is alienated in the other's desire"]). It would be interesting to explore in more detail, as Kilborne's essay points us to, the central role of the affect shame in the elaboration of Sartre's philosophy. The same is true of the role of shame in Lacan's writings. The negative assessment by both Sartre and Lacan of human self-awareness in the social field may largely be due to the important, though hidden, role of shame in their thought.

The introduction of "affect" into the development of philosophical thought is, in a very broad sense, a legacy of Romanticism, in which *feeling* becomes the only satisfactory way to know the world. "Gefühl ist alles," as Faust says to Gretchen. This radical reevaluation of emotion is shared by thinkers such as Kierkegaard and Nietzsche, in whose work, as Kilborne's and Wurmser's papers so clearly show, deep affective or emotional conflict drives thought, as the classical relationship between an exalted "reason" and a degraded "passion" is completely overturned and even reversed. In his study of the emotions, however, Sartre's attitude to affective life continues to be dominated by his profound Cartesianism. For him, "the origin of emotion is a spontaneous and lived degradation of consciousness in the face of the world" (77). Emotions are a form of magic, a cunning way of shirking *engagement* in the world, of escaping freedom and consciousness, the onerous but morally necessary responsibilities of humankind. There is no doubt that emotions are often utilized precisely in this fashion, as indeed the entire area of *denial* and *defenses* explored by psychoanalysis demonstrates. But the ends to which certain affects are eventually put, precisely as a way of defending against *other affects*, cannot be a starting point for understanding the nature of the emotions. Furthermore, it is difficult to imagine any social or political commitment without a very significant emotional investment in that commitment; a consciousness freed from emotion would be so utterly indifferent to the world that it would be difficult to say that it perceived anything at all. Indeed, contrary to Sartre's view of the emotions as degrading consciousness, Nathanson observes that "so much is going on in the human brain that nothing can be said to gain our *attention* unless it triggers an affect. Affect is responsible for *awareness*, for only that which gains affective amplification gets into the limited channel we call *consciousness*" (*Knowing Feeling* 12).

In his study of the emotions, Sartre does not mean the examples he uses—fear, joy, sadness, anger—to be exhaustive, as his study is not a fully developed phenomenology. Indeed, he omits any discussion of shame, which, in *Being and Nothingness* and *Saint Genet*, is the indispensable mode of the self's stolen and objectified consciousness and freedom in relation to others. In the section "The Look," part of the chapter "The Existence of Others" in *Being and Nothingness*, he defines shame as "shame of *self*; it is the *recognition* of the fact that I *am* indeed that object which the Other is looking at and judging. I can be ashamed only as my freedom escapes me in order to become a *given* object" (320). This negative experience of the other as sitting in judgment, this painful double focus on the self as seen by the other, is, indeed, one of the central features of shame as an emotion. As Helen Lewis points out:

> Because the self is the focus of awareness in shame, "identity" imagery is usually evoked. At the same time that this identity imagery is registering as one's own experience, there is also vivid imagery of the self in the other's eyes. This creates a "doubleness of experience," which is characteristic of shame. . . . Shame is the vicarious experience of the other's negative evaluation. In order for shame to occur, there must be a relationship between the self and the other in which the self cares about the other's evaluation. . . . Fascination with the other and sensitivity to the other's treatment of the self render the self more vulnerable in shame. ("Shame" 107–8)

This emphasis on the other suggests, perhaps, that shame, in contrast to guilt, is an externally regulated emotion. It was according to such a conception that Ruth Benedict, in *The Chrysanthemum and the Sword*, coined the dichotomy between shame societies and guilt societies, which she applied to Eastern and Western cultures respectively. Her ideas were later fruitfully applied by E. R. Dodds in studying the role of shame in ancient Greece. This dichotomy may be legitimate in light of the *relatively* greater emphasis placed on dishonor and disgrace, on the public areas of shame and exposure, on "loss of face," in Mediterranean and Eastern societies. But as Takeo Doi observes of Benedict's argument, "it is evident that when she states that the culture of guilt places emphasis on inner standards of conduct whereas the culture of shame places emphasis on outward standards of conduct she has the feeling that the former is superior to the latter" (48). Philip Collington's essay on Faulkner's South as a so-called shame society shows some of the difficulties of maintaining such distinctions. Indeed, many of the most memorable characters in Western literature, such as Bronte's Heathcliff and Melville's Captain Ahab, are motivated by their flight from shame; their obsessive need to eradicate humiliation—whether through self-enclosure, ambition, or revenge—appears to make them immune to feelings of guilt and sympathetic concern for others. Benedict's refusal to recognize the enormous role played by shame in the West, while displacing its importance to the East, may be one more sign of the way that the human sciences, in their analysis of society and human personality, are reluctant to accord significance to shame and to emotions in general. Moreover, shame, as much as guilt, involves inner standards of conduct, since feelings of inferiority and defectiveness clearly exist in people without the presence of a ridiculing or scornful other; by the same token, "inner" feelings of guilt must be originally derived from "outward standards of conduct" embodied in judging and condemning parental figures.

The internalization of shame through identification with the "shamer" is a crucial part of the psychology dramatized by almost every author treated in the essays in this volume. Brooks Bouson's essay on Toni Morrison's *The Bluest Eye*, in particular, demonstrates the way in which the victims of racism are often forced to turn the other's contempt inward. For so many of Morrison's African-American characters, white standards of beauty and lovability form, through identification with the oppressor, part of an inner superego and create a deep conflict. There is a split in the superego between the demand that one conform to the models of the shaming other—white society—and the conflicting demand that one remain loyal to the reality of one's self. It is this internalized shame, this deeply rooted self-contempt and self-hatred that must be overcome. Such a conflict between the fear of self-loss and the fear of being shamed and punished for not disappearing or hiding oneself has been explored by Wurmser in detail throughout his writings. Indeed, Freud's doubling of the personality into an observed self and a critical observing agent (superego and ego ideal) that judges the self is clearly congruent with the notion of a shame internalized through identification with a judging other.

As that part of the ego that critically observes and passes judgment on the self, the superego induces both guilt (for moral wrongdoing) and shame (for perceived inferiority), but the very existence of such a split in the self suggests the "doubleness of experience," as Lewis calls it, induced by shame, in which "the self cares about the other's evaluation." As Lewis puts it, "[s]hame . . . involves more self-consciousness and more self-imaging than guilt. The experience of shame is directly about the self. . . . At the same time . . . there is also vivid imagery of the self in the other's eyes" ("Shame" 107). This "doubleness of experience" particularly marks the experience of women and other devalued and disempowered groups in society. It is precisely because the self cares about significant others and is concerned about rejection and loss of their love—the ultimate threat in shame—that something like a superego can be installed within the self in the first place. In the need to defend itself against the shaming disapproval of the other, the injured self may find itself locked in a struggle between a loyalty to the self and an internalized archaic agent directing shame at the self. (The term "archaic" here, in its psychoanalytic sense, refers to the earliest period of the formation of the personality in childhood.)

Adamson shows to what extent Hawthorne's work is pervaded by the imagery of an internalized judging other that condemns the self, as developed most dramatically in the relationship between Chillingworth and Dimmesdale in *The Scarlet Letter*. Hawthorne's fiction displays a particular sensitivity to the double focus in shame and to the feeling of being dangerously vulnerable to exposure. This is reflected—in his visual imagery, in his characters, and in his narrators—in an exaggerated sense of objective self-awareness and self-consciousness, in which the ego is divided between an observer and an observed, a shamer and a shamed self.

In his essay on Kierkegaard, Kilborne focuses on the importance of the concept of a discrepancy or tension between ego and ego ideal for an understanding of shame, emphasizing that the motivation in constructing a self-image is the regulation of feeling. A self, as Kilborne quotes Kierkegaard, "is what it has as a standard of measurement." But the ego ideal (a component of the superego) may be split between competing ideals of the self. The conflict that arises in Kierkegaard pits the need for self-assertion (the need to be *who one is* in the eyes of a transcendental Other, or "God") against the fear of exposure and shame in a social context. The situation of "despair" occurs when there is a conflict between the fear of self-loss and the fear of being rejected as flawed in some way by the other if one reveals that self. "Most men live their lives in quiet desperation," as Thoreau puts it in *Walden*, because they sacrifice, out of shame, the genuine self that they are to a conformist ideal. This is the danger, it seems, in Kierkegaard's view, of regarding society as a transcendental other. Only God, in his view, can serve such a role, as a genuine measure and standard for the self; in this regard, shame is a particularly important affect motivating the deepest religious life of the individual. The greatest danger for Kierkegaard, as Kilborne suggests, is not to be seen at all, to be a "disappearing who."

III

The idea that the affects form the primary motivational system of human beings is the position of Silvan Tomkins, whose fascinating theories have recently received, with the publication of Eve Kosofsky Sedgwick and Adam Frank's *The Silvan Tomkins Reader*, long overdue attention in the field of literary theory and criticism. Tomkins's massive four-volume work on affect, the result of a forty-year period of research and theorization, represents the most powerful and persuasive challenge not only to a strictly drive-based psychoanalytic theory of human motivation—a theory by now long since rejected even by most analysts—but to cognitive ("appraisal") theories and behavioral theories of human motivation as well. In Tomkins's view, the cognitive "appraisal" of a situation is not sufficient in itself to provide the urgency that is part of human motivation. This is the role of affect: affect makes certain things matter, makes them compelling, in a way that no objective assessment is capable of doing.

Psychoanalysis is an area of knowledge that, in its relatively brief history, has always had to remain sensitive to developments in psychotherapy and psychology. Rather than a threat to its essential postulates, Tomkins's work can be seen as consistent with the changes that have taken place in psychoanalysis itself over the years: precisely, the move away from many of Freud's initial assumptions toward a more extensive interest in relations, emotions, and the self. What Tomkins offers psychoanalysis is an extraordinarily precise understanding of the affects and their relation to the development of human personality.

For Tomkins, affects, like instincts and drives, are part of the innate biological apparatus of human beings and have served an essential function in the evolution of the human species. Human beings are unique in that they are *affectively* equipped, as he puts it in the simplest terms, "to want to remain alive and to resist death, to want to experience novelty and to resist boredom, to want to communicate, to be close to and in contact with others of his species, to experience sexual excitement and to resist the experience of head and face lowered in shame" (*Affect* 1: 170).

Tomkins isolates nine innate affects. There are, first of all, two positive affects. These are interest-excitement and enjoyment-joy. (The hyphenated terms reflect the range of intensity of that particular affect, from mild to extreme.) Tomkins explains affects in terms of the density of neural firing. Interest-excitement, for example, is caused by a certain increase in neural stimulation while enjoyment-joy is triggered by a sudden decrease in stimulation; this is why interest and enjoyment are often complementary affects, as in the excitement and enjoyment-joy of sexual intercourse, or the excitement of seeking a solution to a complex intellectual problem and the joy in finding it. These positive affects are of particular importance because without them human beings would show no interest in, or attachment to the world or those around them. As these are the affects that ensure the forging of bonds between infants and their caregivers, they are the very basis of strong human attachments, and therefore of social community, as well as the foundation of the positive regard for others and for oneself, and therefore of an integrated sense of personality.

The negative affects are greater in number, and they function, in general, to produce a state of urgency about certain negative states the organism finds itself in: fear-terror, distress-anguish, anger-rage, shame-humiliation, dissmell, and disgust. There is, finally, the neutral, so-called "resetting affect" of surprise-startle. Tomkins explores the nature of these affects in minute detail, and shows how what we call emotions are, in fact, complex amalgams of affects or conflicts between competing affects, according to the strategies, influenced by predisposition and history, adopted by the individual. For example, what some shame analysts call humiliated fury or shame-anger—the feeling that Heinz Kohut, the founder of self psychology, labels "narcissistic rage"—Tomkins would understand as shame affect that reaches such a painful point of overload that it triggers anger, an affect distinct from but often accompanying shame. Anger is, of course, one of the most important defenses against shame. Indeed, the particular power of shame to combine with other affects—anguish, contempt, rage, fear—is one of the things that make it such a crucial element in the emotional life of human beings.

Shame, according to Tomkins, is peculiar as a negative affect in that it is triggered by any impediment to positive affect, its function being specifically to interrupt states of interest and enjoyment that have captured the organism. Tomkins postulates that "[t]he innate activator of shame is the incomplete reduction of interest or joy. Hence any barrier to further exploration which partially reduces interest or the smile of enjoyment will activate the lowering of the head and eyes in shame and reduce further exploration or self-exposure powered by enjoyment or joy" (*Affect* 2: 123). As Charles Darwin, Tomkins's precursor in the scientific exploration of the emotions, describes the same reaction: "Under a keen sense of shame there is a strong desire for concealment. We turn away the whole body, more especially the face, which we endeavour in some manner to hide. An ashamed person can hardly endure to meet the gaze of those present, so that he almost invariably casts down his eyes or looks askant" (340).

To use an example cited in discussions of shame, we are all probably familiar with the experience of mistaking from a distance a stranger for a close acquaintance, and hailing the person with signs of affection and mutuality. After realizing one's error, embarrassment ensues—one looks away, one feels "stupid," confused, and disoriented—and any further interaction is immediately broken off. As Nathanson points out, the reaction is not something that we can consciously control: "As soon as we have seen the face of the other person our own head droops, our eyes are cast down, and, blushing, we become briefly incapable of speech" (*Shame and Pride* 135). Shame affect has thus performed its function: it has *instantaneously* reduced interest in the object by limiting positive affect, and temporarily discouraged any further attempts at communion. Tomkins suggests that the power of shame has something to do with human physical survival, and one can think of any number of situations where undue interest or pleasure in an object would be life-threatening. "Shame affect," as Nathanson summarizes Tomkins's findings, "is a highly painful mechanism that operates to pull the organism away from whatever might interest it or make it content," and thus it is "painful in direct proportion to the degree of positive affect it limits" (*Shame and Pride* 138).

It is important to note that for Tomkins shame affect does not require the presence of another person to be activated, though it is, indeed, an affect that is absolutely crucial in its social manifestations and in the development, through the interaction with others, of a sense of self and of self-image. We can observe, for example, how a child can experience shame affect in the failure to complete a particularly difficult task; when the child's exasperation reaches a certain point, the posture of shame will be induced—head dropping down, body slumping, and eyes looking away.

In shame, the reduction of positive affect is incomplete, Tomkins emphasizes, in the sense that the subject does not utterly abandon the object, does not entirely relinquish the goal of regaining the prior state of positive feeling once shame has dissipated. As a negative emotion, shame is, in mild doses, particularly well designed to allow for an ongoing, carefully regulated positive interaction and communion with one's environment. Thus, shame is particularly instrumental as a protective mechanism regulating human beings in their eagerness for communal life, in their expressiveness, perception, and interaction with others and with their environment. Shame serves to reduce without destroying the positive affects of interest and enjoyment that govern curiosity and communality, whenever these states are perceived as frustrated, undesirable, or dangerous.

Shame thus "binds" with drives and other affects, and these shame-binds, as Tomkins calls them, are particularly crucial in understanding the significance of shame in psychodynamics. Since Freud effectively ignored the distinct role of affects he focused exclusively on the binding of the drives with shame. The obtrusive and insistent life of the body—sex, elimination of waste, eating—are all particularly associated with complex feelings of shame. Shame and guilt about bodily life are, in classical psychoanalysis, the essential motivation behind the mechanism of repression. A conflict associated with a "drive," however, can emerge in the first place only through an affective conflict, for instance, the binding of sexual *excitement* with fear or shame.

Gershem Kaufman, a psychotherapist whose work, like Donald Nathanson's, has been deeply influenced by Tomkins's research, has devoted much of his thinking to the importance of such affective binds.[6] In a shame-anger bind, for example, the feeling of anger might automatically make one feel ashamed, so that bound by shame one would avoid showing anger, and thus perhaps unduly suffer from a lack of assertiveness and an inability even to express justifiable anger. In a shame-distress bind, one feels shame whenever one feels sad or distressed in some way, thus repressing and at the same time intensifying both the sadness and the shame; inasmuch as this emotional complex is mostly unconscious, the subject is left at the mercy of an unidentified but debilitating feeling-state. To take another example, fear is, through socialization, often bound by shame, especially in men, so that one may feel ashamed whenever one experiences fear, even when one is able to hide it from others or from oneself. People diagnosed with incurable diseases often deny their fear and terror, even though it would seem the most natural thing in the world at such a juncture to be afraid.

It is also the case, indeed, that the very expression of affect is itself bound by shame, the permissible extent of expression of affect varying significantly from one culture, one family, one social context to another. We all know from experience the extent to which being too emotional, or too expressive, or too loud, or too excited, or too joyous, is bound by shame. Shame, indeed, covers shame itself—it is shameful to express shame. It is here that we can see perhaps most clearly the dramatic importance of the role of art as a way of exploring the emotions; in art and literature, shame and repression are diminished, and the richness of emotional life, its stimulation and turbulence and nuance, is investigated in its complexity. As readers, we explore the excitement and joy of love, the release and liberation of laughter after great struggle, the devastation of deep loss, the searing sting of shame and humiliation, the agony and anger born from intense conflict, and the terror of death.

IV

As the preceeding discussion suggests, the excessive inhibition of emotion has damaging consequences. Thomas Scheff speaks of unacknowledged shame leading to anger or rage as the source of malignant feelings of resentment, with cataclysmic effects on individuals and societies. The inhibition of positive affect is equally injurious, since the free expression of interest and enjoyment enhances the growth of basic trust, creativity, and the capacity to form deep and lasting attachments. Among the negative emotions, shame is the emotion that functions most to discourage the expression of other affects, including itself. Thus, in light of the dangers of such inhibition, it might seem logical to advocate the adoption of a general *shamelessness* in many of the areas of human life governed by shame, and to argue that this would have a liberating and therapeutic effect on human societies.

A society without shame, however, would be a society without intimacy. One of the functions of what Carl Schneider calls "mature shame" is to protect certain sensitive areas of personal and interpersonal experience that a society considers important to keep private. What these areas are may vary dramatically among societies and cultures, and they will necessarily change and evolve in the course of history. But it is almost impossible to conceive of a society that did not protect certain aspects of human life from public invasion and exposure. If such a society existed, it would be hard to understand how it could be a healthy one.

Contemporary North American society is a case in point. Doubtless, the new openness and honesty about previously tabooed subjects, such as sex or bodily life, has significantly improved human relations. But what often passes as a refreshing frankness combating unhealthy repression may also be a symptom of what Andrew Morrison has called the "culture of shame." It could be argued that the phenomenon of shamelessness in our society is to a large degree a defense against shame, not a liberation from it. Bouson points to a perfect illustration of this, in her discussion of the behavior of Cholly in Toni Morrison's *The Bluest Eye*. Wurmser describes such shamelessness as a "reaction-formation against shame" (*Mask* 264); it is shame "displaced." The denial of shame, according to Nathanson, is reflected in the narcissism of contemporary society:

One may wonder about the fairly recent swing from privacy and modesty toward public nakedness and display; away from the seclusion of curtained windows toward glass walls that reveal interior rooms; from social acceptance of the privacy of personal grief and pain to the canonization of the intruding investigative reporter. Perhaps it is the devaluation of the affect shame that has allowed our culture to slip into its current "narcissistic" preoccupation with exposure. (*Shame and Pride* 5)

We need only think of the way that daytime television in the United States is dominated by a flaunting of the private areas of human experience in the personal lives of complete strangers. Andrew Morrison speaks of the way that shame is "broadly exposed through media attention to shame-infused incidents and relationships," for example,

the role of news coverage in representing, and on occasion leading to, the suicides and homicides that reflect shame and shame-based depressions. Further media documentation of shame's prevalence in current society comes from the themes and interviews of television talk shows like Geraldo Rivera's and Oprah Winfrey's. Frequent examples of spouse abuse, drug addictions, and other compulsive behaviors dominate these shows, where participants are eager to explain their various humiliations and to attain some degree of acceptance and relief. The immense popularity of these shows, and the broad demand from viewers to experience and participate in tales of degradations and self-abasement, document the prevalence of the shame culture in contemporary American society. (*Culture* 196)

The recent murder case surrounding the Jenny Jones show is an example of the possible consequences of the exploitation of such heedless exposure.[7]

In *Shame, Exposure, and Privacy*, Carl Schneider has written most eloquently about shame and the need for boundaries. Like many other theorists of shame such as Wurmser and Tomkins, Schneider argues that shame protects against violations of inner boundaries in the self and of sensitive areas of human life that should not be subjected to exposure. Jeffrey Berman's essay on shame and writing in the classroom is particularly relevant here. One of the dangers of revealing shame in student writing is that further shame may be induced in the student. As Berman points out, certain cautions and safeguards are crucial, such as sensitivity to the feelings of the student and a respect of "boundaries between self and other." Wurmser writes: "If one also crosses another's inner limits, one violates his privacy, and he feels shame. The transgressor himself may now feel both guilt—for the transgression of the first boundary, for having inflicted hurt—and shame, owing to identification with the exposed object. Violation of privacy tends to evoke shame in both subject and object" (*Mask* 62). When violations occur in chronic or traumatic form, then shame becomes the core of severe structures of defense in the traumatized individual or community, one such defense being the aforementioned aggressive shamelessness that has so invaded modern life. Shame, in itself, then, is one of the most indispensable guardians of human life. It is the dangerous "magnification" of shame, as Tomkins calls it, that has such a devastating effect on people and societies.[8]

It is interesting to correlate Tomkins's view of shame affect with the work on shame by Wurmser. The latter has insisted on the impact that shame and other negative affects can have on expression and perception, and how the frustration and distortion of wishes to communicate and to explore the world can damage the very core of an individual's self-concept. Freud linked shame almost exclusively to matters of sexual knowledge and exposure. He regarded shame, in a way not unrelated to Tomkins's understanding of its function, as an affective mechanism—a *Reaktionsbildung*—serving as a defense against inappropriate scopophilic and exhibitionistic drives or wishes, wishes to see and to know, to show and display oneself in a sexually intrusive manner. Thus, particularly intense wishes or fears, in a patient, centered on knowing or seeing would suggest a displacement of denied and repressed voyeuristic wishes that could be traced back to a specifically sexual trauma. No psychoanalyst today would be likely to draw quite this conclusion, unless somehow or other immured from the complex host of developments over the last several decades. Again, Freud tended to narrow the field of explanation to the area of drives—oral, anal, genital—whereas, along with Tomkins, Nathanson, and others, Wurmser understands shame as closely tied to perceptual and expressive wishes that are not sexually specific, though they may certainly become so in the course of development.

As more than one essay in this collection underscores, in traumatic or abusive situations shame, combined with other negative affects, becomes magnified and turns into a chronic experience. It then has a toxic effect on the development of healthy desires to know and discover the world and commune with others, and on the development of a confident and trusting self. "The modes of attentive, curious grasping and of expressing oneself in nonverbal as well as verbal communication are the arena where in love and hatred, in mastery and defeat our self is forged and moulded. If this interchange is blocked and warped, the core of the self-concept is severely disturbed and becomes permanently twisted and deformed" (Wurmser, "Shame" 83). One of the ways that Wurmser defines shame, then, is as "a basic protection mechanism in the areas of perception and expression, a protection in the sense of preventing overstimulation in these two areas, as well as 'drive restraint' in the form of preventing dangerous impulses of curiosity and self-exposure" ("Shame" 80–81). These impulses or "drives" are more specifically: "(1) the urges for active, magical exhibition—the wishes to fascinate; (2) their reverse: the fear to be passively exposed and stared at; (3) the urges for active curiosity; and (4) their reverse: the fear of being fascinated and overwhelmed by the spectacles offered by others" (81). The first two drives, in other words, are exhibitionistic; the last two voyeuristic, or scopophilic. These drives may be blocked when shame as a defensive mechanism against violation fails to protect the self. Shame may then become an emotion that dangerously monopolizes the subject's relations with the world. It may lead to chronic aversive responses, in the forms of withdrawal and antagonism. Fears of being overexposed, invaded, or taken over by others may be amplified to a paralyzing extent, leading to severe states of depression. Correspondingly, compulsive forms of self-assertion and the aggressive desire for power and control over others can serve as defenses and as a means of satisfying the thwarted innate wishes to show and see.

The essays in this volume attest to the importance of these perceptual and expressive wishes and fears, and the defenses and means of gratification associated with them. The imagery of looking—both seeing and being seen—is examined in Kilborne's essay on Kierkegaard, in relation to the whole question of existence as a genuine self. Bouson's essay on *The Bluest Eye* touches on a similar conflict, illustrating the use of what Wurmser calls the "magic eye" as a defense against severe shame. A fear of being exposed as unlovable is countered by an intense and compulsive looking for the consolidating admiring gaze of the other. Thus, Pecola ends up hiding in the pathetic fantasy of her blue eyes. However, the cost of defending against the fear of exposure through a counterphobic magic eye is the disappearance and tragic loss of the self. This relation between shame and visual imagery of exposure and invasion is also the focus of Adamson's essay on Hawthorne, whose work, like that of his contemporary Melville, is traversed and haunted by the theme of a shaming "evil eye."

There would seem to be, indeed, a significant link between shame, taboos on looking, and the popular folkloric belief in the evil eye. Wurmser makes this link, and Tomkins devotes a whole section of his analysis of shame affect and looking to a discussion of this widespread belief. Tomkins regards it as a classic expression of the "universal taboo on looking," which is "most severe when two individuals . . . look directly into each other's eyes at the same time" (*Affect* 2: 157). The nature of this taboo is twofold: "it is a taboo on intimacy," which is maximized by "mutual looking," and it expresses the constraints found in all cultures on the direct expression of affects (157), the face and eyes being the site of such expression. At the end of his discussion of the scopic drive in *The Four Fundamental Concepts of Psychoanalysis*, Lacan discusses the evil eye in relation to looking and mortification (i.e., searing shame): "The evil eye is the *fascinum*, it is that which has the effect of arresting movement and, literally, of killing life. At the moment the subject stops, suspending his gesture, he is mortified. The anti-life, anti-movement function of this terminal point is the *fascinum*, and it is precisely one of the dimensions in which the power of the gaze is exercised directly" (*Four* 118). Indeed, the power of such a gaze lies in its ability both to expose and to fascinate—*oculus fascinus* was the term for the evil eye in ancient Rome, the eye being considered the privileged weapon of the fascinator (Tomkins, *Affect* 2: 162)—so that escape from it seems impossible, fight as one may to ward it off. As Hilary Clark shows in her contribution on Anne Sexton, the poet struggled against a shaming evil eye throughout her adult life, resulting at least partly from the experience, as a child, of excessive invasion of self-boundaries. For Sexton, haunted by the perception of herself as defective, damaged, unlovable, this evil eye was death itself (she committed suicide in 1974), both fearful and powerfully fascinating.

The passive modes of both the wish to be seen and the wish to see are usually expressed as fears. That is, the punishment for exhibitionism, for showing oneself, is that one will be overexposed, "stared at," "overcome and devoured by the looks of others" (Wurmser, *Mask* 162). The punishment for looking is then that one will become fascinated by what one sees, to the point of being taken over and controlled by the object. Thus, *not looking* and *hiding*—"see no evil, hear no evil, speak no evil"—are two important modes of defending against searing or chronic shame; they are indeed the perceptual and expressive basis of denial and repression.[9]

Wurmser has correlated his analysis of the perceptual-attentive "drives" to Kohut's conception of a bipolar self, to the two archaic images—the grandiose self and the idealized selfobject—that Kohut views as defining the developmental basis of the self. Kohut's work, with its emphasis on the need for empathic healing as a remedy for the original empathic failure on the part of caregivers (the source of narcissistic disorders), has represented a particularly significant development in moving psychoanalysis away from drive conflict and emphasizing the role of affects in psychodynamics: shame as the primary negative affect involved in "empathic failure," as well as the positive affects of interest, excitement, and joy involved in successful empathic interactions. What Kohut calls the grandiose self corresponds to the part of the self that grows and develops as the child's grandiosity (its feelings of power and of control over its environment) and exhibitionism (its pleasure in showing itself and in being seen and admired by others) are consistently confirmed by a responsive caregiver. The idealized selfobject corresponds to the part of the self that develops through idealization of and identification with an apparently all-powerful parent.[10]

Kohut coined the term "selfobject" to refer to the way that the child perceives significant others: the mother and father, for example, are perceived as being to some degree a part of the self. Gross empathic failure by the so-called selfobject—a severe lack of cooperativeness and responsiveness, for whatever reason—floods the self with intolerable feelings of betrayal and powerlessness and causes intense humiliation leading to withdrawal or rage. The individual is thus unable to internalize structures provided by a healthy interaction with others, and fails to develop a strong sense of self; consequently, it never entirely grows out of this archaic perception of significant others. In adult life, the ego remains under the control of repressed components of this early self, and it finds itself at the mercy of unintegrated emotional reactions. The individual may, for example, repeatedly and obsessively seek affirmation and admiration by cooperative selfobjects, or she may be dominated by the "unrequited longing to be strengthened and protected when necessary by an alliance with an admired, powerful figure" (Basch 15).

Indeed, it is clear that, though Kohut himself uses the word sparingly, the most significant element in the profile of the narcissistically damaged personality is the affect shame. Narcissistic injury—the root cause of what Kohut calls narcissistic personality disorder—is more or less synonymous with mortification or humiliation. As Howard Bacal points out, Kohut associated "narcissistic rage . . . with a sense of shame" (236), while Andrew Morrison, whose approach is essentially Kohutian, goes even farther and, as Bacal summarizes his position, "underscores shame as the central affect associated with 'narcissistic rage.'" Morrison views shame and humiliation as "the quintessential reaction to the sense of helplessness in the face of the experience of selfobject failure. However, since these affects are so intolerable, they are quickly erased from consciousness and, at the same time, trigger the expression of narcissistic rage at the offending object" (Bacal 236). The case of Nick and of other victims of abuse, as Berman points out in his essay, recalls the experience recounted in many nineteenth-century novels (e.g., *Frankenstein, Wuthering Heights, Great Expectations*), in which a traumatic injury to the sense of self produces "shattered identities, heightened vulnerability, empathic disturbances, and massive rage."

Barbara Schapiro shows, for example, how in Lawrence the wish to be accepted and loved as a bodily, sensuous self expresses a wish to overcome narcissistic injury, deep woundedness, and feelings of rejection and shame about oneself, but that the desire to reveal and give oneself to the other is also inhibited by fears of being rejected as "disgusting" or "horrible," as well as fears of being invaded and controlled, of being taken over and of losing oneself. The need to assert power and control over the other, in order to preserve self-integrity, thus comes to take the place of recognition and love: if one perceives a great risk in giving oneself to the other, this perception can lead to the *noli me tangere* attitude that Schapiro analyzes in Lawrence. (The same conflict, as Berman's essay shows, is one of the psychological consequences of abuse that Nick reveals in his life writing, and it is an attitude Wurmser shows to be central in Nietzsche's work.) At the same time, the consequent feeling of isolation is defended against by fantasies of merger and fusion with powerful or idealized objects or others.

Collington's essay on Faulkner, in particular, relies on a Kohutian framework, which aligns narcissistic injury with the experience of shame. Collington analyzes the strategies of hiding and what Kohut calls narcissistic revenge in Faulkner's *Absalom, Absalom!*, primarily as they are expressed in the ambitious rise to power of Thomas Sutpen. Sutpen, a ruthless social climber, responds to shame and deep humiliation by seeking to turn the tables and exert an absolute control over his environment so as never to suffer such humiliation again. This attempt to barricade a deeply wounded self against any further injury—a strategy doomed to tragic failure—is characteristic of other characters in the novel, in particular Rosa Coldfield, who, like Miss Emily in Faulkner's short story "A Rose for Emily," in a kind of rigid fury walls up a deeply vulnerable self behind an icy fortress of outraged pride and resentful vindictiveness. In her essay on Lawrence, Schapiro remarks upon a similar emotional pattern: "Lawrence's fiction consistently portrays characters whose souls have hardened and 'crystallised' as a result of severe narcissistic injury."

Severe shame and humiliated rage arise from continual subjection to explicit forms of neglect and abuse (emotional, verbal, physical, sexual). In particular, shame as the negative side of narcissism, the preoccupation with the self as rejected by judging others, has traditionally shaped the experience of women under patriarchy. Women and others who suffer from inequality in power are particularly prone to the humiliated rage that stems from unacknowledged shame, a rage turned on the self and transformed to guilt because one does not feel entitled to it. Again, as the passive experience of being devalued and disempowered, shame is linked with low self-esteem and depression; it has been established that roughly twice as many women as men suffer from depression.[11]

Thus shame as a chronic affective experience makes the subject feel defective or flawed, and consequently has a profound impact on self-estimation and self-image. The chronic experience of shame also deeply affects one's trust in the world. As Helen Merrell Lynd describes the far-reaching effects of shame:

> Sudden experience of a violation of expectation, of incongruity between expectation and outcome, results in a shattering of trust in oneself, even in one's body and skill and identity, and in the trusted boundaries or framework of the society and the world one has known. As trust in oneself and in the outer world develop together, so doubt of oneself and of the world are also intermeshed.
>
> The rejected gift, the joke or the phrase that does not come off, the misunderstood gesture, the falling short of our own ideals, the expectation of response violated—such experiences mean that we have trusted ourselves to a situation that is not there. We have relied on the assumption of one perspective or *Gestalt* and found a totally different one. (46)

This "shattering of trust" can lead to an all-pervasive feeling of estrangement and meaninglessness, both of oneself and of one's environment. Ultimately, in Tomkins's words, shame can be "felt as an inner torment, a sickness of the soul" in which the subject "feels himself naked, defeated, alienated, lacking in dignity or worth" (*Affect* 2: 118). "If distress," he observes, "is the affect of suffering, shame is the affect of indignity, of defeat, of transgression, and of alienation. Though terror speaks to life and death and distress makes of the world a vale of tears, yet shame strikes deepest into the heart of man."

V

The distinction between shame and guilt is something that has preoccupied students of shame from the beginning. Ruth Benedict and Helen Block Lewis, for example, regarded the distinction as having a decisive value, the one relying on it to define cultural differences, the other using it to clarify the nature of particular psychological syndromes. But any ultimate distinction between guilt and shame is rejected by others. One of the difficulties with Ruth Benedict's shame/guilt dichotomy, as Takeo Doi points out, is the postulation that "guilt and shame [are] entirely unrelated to each other, which is obviously contrary to the facts. One and the same person very often experiences these two emotions at the same time, and they would seem to have a very close relationship; the person who has committed a 'sin' is very frequently ashamed of what he has done" (48). Indeed, Tomkins rejects the distinction altogether, at least as concerns the role of primary affects. For him, the innate basis of the feeling of guilt is shame-humiliation. Thus he defines guilt simply as moral shame. David Cook, whose work is informed by Tomkins's theories, deplores "the failure to understand guilt as a variant of shame" and asserts that "the investigation of guilt as a separate construct is an empirical dead-end for the study of psychopathology" (134). At the same time, however, guilt is a recognizably different feeling from what we commonly know as shame. "The core affect," Cook says, "of guilt, embarrassment, shyness, discouragement, and humiliation is shame, but the coassembly of perceptions, cognitions, and intentions into any of these emotions can be vastly different" (135). Carroll Izard, whose understanding of affect is also inspired by Tomkins, still considers it useful, in his textbook study of the emotions, to treat shame, shyness, and guilt as quite distinct in character. Wurmser, in particular, sees a distinction between shame and guilt as indispensable. Much of his conception of psychodynamics in severe neuroses, as exemplified in his essay, in this volume, on conflict in Nietzsche's thought, is based on insight into the dynamic relationship between these two distinctive emotions.

Shame-guilt dynamics are a commonly observed phenomenon. The attempt to escape shame (by asserting oneself in the form, let us say, of an ambitious drive to succeed in one's profession) may bring on guilt, particularly in women, for asserting superiority over others; however, the attempt then to make amends and atone for perceived aggressivity and harm may mean that one then falls back into the arms of shame (one feels lacking in power, weak and reduced, and thus yearns all the more to compete and assert oneself). A fundamental conflict is at play here. If shame, as in so many of the narcissistic defenses, prevents atonement for or even acknowledgment of guilt, then the feelings of guilt are often denied and stifled, and thus become unconscious. The willingness to accept guilt thus often conflicts with the narcissistic defenses against shame—grandiosity, unbridled ambition, refusal to accept limitations, selfishness, envy, rage—which are discussed in most of the essays in this volume.

It is in this important area of the defenses that Heinz Kohut's work on "narcissism" is so useful; Kohut notes that those afflicted with severe narcissistic disorders are unable to empathize and feel for others. In his essay on *Middlemarch*, Gordon Hirsch analyzes the egotistical and jealous Casaubon as an illustration of this type of character, whose need to ward off his own feelings of vulnerability and shame have atrophied his ability to care about others; in a narcissistic defense against his own feeling of lovelessness, he becomes a being incapable of intimacy and love. Kohut says that those who suffer from deep narcissistic injury "understand others only insofar—but here with the keenest empathy!—as they can serve as tools towards their own narcissistic ends or insofar as they interfere with their own purposes" (*Search* 834). Again, Faulkner's Sutpen, as Collington demonstrates in his essay, exemplifies, in a more ostentatiously violent way, the same narcissistic defense: to defend against the *perceived* rejection and contempt of others, he ends up treating other human beings as a mere means to his own grandiose ends, expendable when their purpose is fulfilled.

In his examination of conflict in Nietzsche's system of thought, Wurmser offers a compelling analysis of the crucial distinction between shame (which stems from a violation of the self) and guilt (which stems from a violation of others). Wurmser speaks of Nietzsche's "war" against shame and guilt, his feeling that guilt is something inflicted on the self by the other, out of essentially poisonous motives of *ressentiment*—and as a kind of castration, as a means of making one feel weak, powerless, submissive, and ashamed. Nietzsche's own attack on shame and guilt, however, as Wurmser so clearly demonstrates, is itself motivated by a deep, unconscious *ressentiment*, by the magnitude of his own feelings of woundedness and vulnerability, and corresponding irresolvable sense of injustice.

There is, however, a deeply creative basis of guilt that lies, not in the fear of punishment for transgression, but in the capacity to identify with the feelings of others and to experience concern and love: the terrible feeling, for example, that one has hurt another human being, and the impulse to seek atonement for wrongdoing, regardless of whether one will be caught and suffer for it. This capacity is based on empathy, which, as Vernon C. Kelly Jr. defines it, "occurs when, through affective resonance, the affect of another triggers the same affect in us. . . . Even though our biographies are different, we sense that we have been thrust into the other's shoes for a moment, and know what we would feel if we were in his or her experience" (72). Lichtenberg speaks of the developmental importance of altruistic feelings in children, based on growing "empathic sensitivity" (114). "Clear, forceful, empathic parental responses enhance the child's feelings of goodness associated with altruism and making reparations. . . . The pairing of parent and child may richly encourage the child's capacity for empathic compassion, or it may stimulate anxious, shameful, or guilty concern, or antagonism toward a victim" (115). Melanie Klein developed her theory of reparation on the basis of her observation of the guilty need, in young children, to mend an object torn apart by aggressive impulses. In her essay, Clark explores the reparative role of poetry for Anne Sexton: in *The Death Notebooks* in particular, poetic composition—as an act of reparation of and to the other—is held up, if only briefly, as a means of overcoming toxic narcissistic shame.

The word "guilt," then, as already suggested, is used quite often to refer to very different things—archaic fears of retaliation and punishment, feelings of shame about one's self and one's actions, and altruistic feelings of responsibility and concern for the person hurt.[12] Shame also has quite distinct meanings, meanings that broadly accord, indeed, with these senses of guilt. According to Wurmser, shame is first an anxiety, "the *fear* of disgrace"; second, it is "the *affect of contempt* directed against the self—by others or by one's own conscience" ("Shame" 67). The third meaning, "almost the antithesis of the second one," is "an overall character trait preventing any such disgraceful exposure, an attitude of respect toward others and towards oneself, a stance of reverence," ultimately, "a sense of awe" (67–68). The ability to admit shame, as Nathanson observes, is an indispensable part of human growth: "Shame is a response to exposure—by forcing attention to the self it protects us from narcissism, as when we are made to accept that the viewing other does not share our opinion of ourselves" (5). This is the basis of a mature sense of shame as Schneider describes it: "The ancient Greeks knew the deeply religious dimension inherent in a mature sense of shame. Their concept of *aidos* meant both shame and awe" ("Mature" 209). He concludes: "Because we know ourselves incapable of living together in a community of complete trust and openness more than momentarily, shame is and will be always in order as the mark of our vulnerability as selves both separate from and belonging to a larger whole" (209).

Northrop Frye speaks of "the novelist's total act of knowledge, the divine comprehension which has sympathy but not affection, wrath but not resentment" (no. 53) as its basis. It is this kind of knowledge that is reflected and developed in George Eliot's work; indeed, it is the core of her ethical philosophy, as Hirsch's paper shows. As exemplified in Dorothea in *Middlemarch*, "Eliot's sympathy or compassion," as Hirsch puts it, "is a means of defending against shame"—shame here to be understood in Wurmser's first and second senses, as anxiety and as self-directed contempt. This sympathizing and trusting capacity defends specifically against the destructiveness of the narcissistic defenses against shame, as exemplified in such characters as Bulstrode, Lydgate, Rosamund, and Casaubon, who use their sense of superiority to cover over and ward off gnawing feelings of shame and humiliation. In contrast to the narcissistic defense against shame, Hirsch outlines the intriguing relationship between shame and what Eliot calls ardor, between the burning of the blush and the burning ardor of a loyalty to ideals and to the values of trust, protection, and sympathy with others. Both sympathy, the ability to feel with others, and ardor, the flame of an intense if often misguided idealism, defend against the social destructiveness of the narcissistic defenses that Eliot is so adept at exposing. This same sense of shame as a preventative attitude that protects the sacred areas of human life is also, as Adamson's essay demonstrates, a central concern of Hawthorne's work as well, in the depiction of those obsessed protagonists—Aylmer, Rappaccini, Ethan Brand, Chilling-worth—whose narcissistic defenses against shame lead them to violate the private sanctity of other selves, the ultimate consequence of which is psychic destruction.

Shame and guilt thus work together in constructive ways: the ability to feel and acknowledge genuine guilt and shame, rooted in human sympathy and fellow feeling, defends against the destructive consequences of unconscious feelings of shame—manifested, for example, in the narcissistic need to extend one's power and control—that may push one to violate the other's physical or personal boundaries; the capacity to experience shame and guilt openly may serve to defend against egotism and coldness, unconscious defenses against shame that result in a betrayal of the other's trust and love. Inversely, excessive and unconscious feelings of shame and guilt, especially feelings of inferiority and unworthiness, and fears of punishment, may prevent one from necessary self-assertion, so that one remains indefinitely in a state of shame, feeling weak and powerless.

VI

Tomkins and some of the psychotherapists inspired by him, such as Kaufman and Nathanson, have focused on the relationship between affect, image, and memory, and the way that the individual builds up a personal storehouse, a data base, as it were, of imagery and scenes for which various scripts are constructed, which are then drawn on as a way of managing intolerable affects.[13] Similarly, Lichtenberg speaks of "model scenes" consisting of episodic and procedural memories that "reflect the experiences that persons have as caregivers succeed in responding, or fail to respond" to their developmental needs (261). These model or nuclear scenes and scripts are of the utmost significance to the individual in their affective intensity and magnification. As Tomkins describes them,

> they matter more than anything else, and they never stop seizing the individual. They are the good scenes we can never totally or permanently achieve or possess. If they occasionally seem to be totally achieved or possessed, such possession can never be permanent. If they reward us with deep positive affect, we are forever greedy for more. . . . If they punish us with deep negative affect, we can never entirely avoid, escape, nor renounce the attempt to master or revenge ourselves upon them despite much punishment. If they both seduce and punish us, we can neither possess nor renounce them. If they are conflicted scenes, we

can neither renounce wishes of the conflicting nor integrate them. If they are ambiguous scenes, we can neither simplify nor clarify the many overlapping scenes which characteristically produce pluralistic confusion. These are the conditions par excellence for unlimited magnification. (*Affect* 3: 96)

What is described here is precisely what Freud posed as the puzzle of the *Wiederholungzwang*, the compulsion to repeat. It is interesting, then, that Tomkins should cite the paradigms of mortality and the classical triangular scene as examples of such nuclear scenes and scripts, mortality "because it cannot be mastered, nor can it be avoided," and the triangular scene because "the male child who loves his mother excessively can neither totally possess her (given an unwanted rival) nor totally renounce her. He is often destined, however, to keep trying and, characteristically, to keep failing" (96). Each of the essays presented in this volume is an attempt to draw out such deep conflicts inasmuch as they involve shame, conflicts that are crucial to an understanding of the authors in question. Indeed, the question each essay explores is one that Tomkins, in the same passage, presents us with: "What is it which guarantees that human beings will neither master the threats to which they are exposed nor avoid situations which they cannot deal with effectively" (96)?

The one thing we have not spoken of yet—and yet most pertinent to this study—is the often compulsive relationship between shame and creativity. Shame, which is the painful feeling of exposed vulnerability, has a particularly interesting relationship to writing. As Jeffrey Berman shows in his essay on shame and writing in the classroom, writing is potentially an act of the most dangerous exposure, and thus it often becomes an artful and ingenious playing with masks, a play that is so much a part of authors such as Kierkegaard and Nietzsche. But writing, precisely because it allows one to hide and reveal oneself at the same time, also allows for an intimacy and trust to be established with another or others, perhaps, in a way that no other situation provides.

This is perhaps the great lesson of Berman's discussion. The conditions of a shared piece of personal writing in a classroom are, doubtless, different from that of the creative writer facing a seemingly faceless public; further, as a victim of abuse, Nick's self-disclosure was an act that put his vulnerability in the hands of others, an act of trust on the part of someone who, from experience, had every reason not to take the risk. But is this not ultimately this case with all writers? The writer seeks some degree of display, even when she is in hiding, and must be able to trust in an audience, in the willingness of others to see her as she is without undue fear of overexposure or invasion or rejection. This is why many writers are so sensitive to the criticism of their work, seeing it is a rejection of themselves. Winnicott writes of his patients: "Even when our patients do not get cured they are grateful to us for seeing them as they are" (138). In the same way, perhaps, to write at all, the writer must be able to assume—to use Brooks Bouson's suggestive term—an "empathic reader"; one needs to be able to trust, that one will be "seen and heard," that one's self will be given back. And isn't this, indeed—going in the other direction now—what writing offers the reader? One of the most interesting studies of shame to date is a literary one: Christopher Ricks's *Keats and Embarrassment*. Ricks makes the point that there is something quite distinctive about the intimacy that literature is able to offer us: "It is a crucial fact about the genuine mutuality and reciprocity, and indeed intimacy, of our relation to books that there is no mutuality or reciprocity of embarrassment" (189).

Tomkins's script theory suggests that writers are human beings who are deeply captured by their nuclear scenes, those scenes that "can be neither mastered nor avoided, neither possessed nor renounced." They are particularly "destined," as he puts it, "to keep trying and, characteristically, to keep failing" (96). This is because the writer seeks, through his or her capacity to communicate, nothing short of the surmounting of shame in its destructive aspects. Such a surmounting is the goal of both love and creativity. If severe feelings of shame compel us to hide and conceal inner reality from others and from ourselves, it is often countered in the writer by a creative ideal, a defiant and even ruthless decision not to turn away or to lie, a courageous and almost *shameless* will to see and to know that which internal and external sanctions conspire to keep us from looking at and exploring. Nathanson speaks of the ability of those who are able "to live with the soul naked to the light of truth," of the "courage and maturity" that it takes "to give up any defense, to stare bravely into the light" ("Denial" 53); it takes courage because, in Nathanson's words, "[t]he mental mechanisms are not some sort of refuge for the weak. They are . . . protective systems inherent to the nature of human beings, defenses accumulated through the ages of evolution, recruited even today in the life of an organism struggling for survival" (53–54). Shame and denial go hand in hand, and the apparent "shamelessness" of the creative writer, as the following pages should illustrate, is not the shamelessness that results from a denial of shame. It is, rather, an attitude allowing for the most resolute exploration of an emotion that, as Tomkins claims, strikes deepest in the human heart.

NOTES

1. Lynd, Kohut, Tomkins, and in particular Wurmser, have shown a keen and profound interest in the way that psychological reality expresses itself in the

world of culture and literature. Tomkins's application of affect theory to a variety of writers and creative thinkers includes Stendhal, Hemingway, Chekhov, O'Neill, and Tolstoy. Wurmser has written on writers such as Sophocles, Shakespeare, Balzac, Dickens, George Eliot, James, Ibsen, Nietzsche, Kafka, and Lagerkvist. Both provide models of what a criticism richly informed by a psychoanalytic understanding of the role of shame has to offer. In terms of literary form, Kohut and Wurmser have both demonstrated a deep interest in tragedy and the tragic character, and Wurmser has explored the nature of tragedy, tragic personality, and tragic conflict in its relation to archaic conflicts rooted in shame and guilt.

2. See, for example, Joseph Lichtenberg, *Psychoanalysis and Infant Research* and *Psychoanalysis and Motivation*; also, Daniel Stern, *The Interpersonal World of the Infant: A View from Psychoanalysis and Developmental Psychology*.

3. Schapiro's *Literature and the Relational Self* provides, as a framework to her reading of several literary works, a useful and stimulating introduction to the interpersonal theories of psychological development as developed by psychoanalysts such as Daniel Stern and Jessica Benjamin. See especially pp. 22–24 of the introduction to her book, where she argues for an alternative to the Lacanian emphasis on language as what we are born into. "Linguistic emphasis of Lacanian psychoanalysis has contributed to that theory's popularity with literary critics and scholars. Much of the current clinical research, however—particularly empirical work such as Stern's on the early interactions and responses of infants—would seem to belie Lacan's view of the primacy of language in the construction of subjectivity. Affective attunement precedes linguistic development and creates its own idiom" (22).

4. "Many studies of the emotion lead to the conclusion that situations that elicit anger often elicit disgust and contempt as well. When people are asked to imagine a situation that makes them angry and then to describe their feelings, the three emotions of anger, disgust, and contempt are frequently listed" (Izard 254).

5. Sartre "refers to the sound of rustling leaves, suddenly heard while out hunting, to a footstep heard in a corridor. And when are these sounds heard? At the moment when he has presented himself in the action of looking through a keyhole. A gaze surprises him in the function of voyeur, disturbs him, overwhelms him and reduces him to a feeling of shame. . . . Is it not clear that the gaze intervenes here only in as much as it is not the annihilating subject, correlative of the world of objectivity, who feels himself surprised, but the subject sustaining himself in a function of desire?" (Lacan, *Four* 85).

6. Kaufman's writings are the basis of much of John Bradshaw's popularization of shame theory, for example in *Healing the Shame That Binds You*. He has also inspired some of Robert Bly's work.

7. A man was invited to appear on the show, expecting that a woman was going to reveal that she had a crush on him (the subject was "secret admirers"); there instead was a casual male acquaintance who had just indulged the audience with his sexual fantasies about the unsuspecting guest. Two days later the victim of the trick, who had apparently been suffering from depression, shot down the admirer he apparently saw as his shamer. Lawyers for the defense

argued that the murder was triggered by the humiliation that their emotionally fragile client had undergone on the show. Indeed, the show appears to have been set up as an ambush, and the sought-for surprised or shocked reaction was clearly predicated on the knowledge that many men are still socialized to regard homosexual relations with shame, fear, and hostility. The jury convicted the man of second degree murder, a lesser charge.

8. The immeasurable consequences of a "magnification" of shame for an entire nation is illustrated by Hitler's Germany. Kohut, Wurmser, and Scheff have all pointed to the way that shame-driven feelings of resentment drove Germany into war and ultimately to mass murder. Scheff proposes that "both Hitler and his public were in a state of chronic emotional arousal, a chain reaction of shame and anger, giving rise to humiliated fury" and to "a cycle generating rage and destructive aggression since the shame component was not adequately acknowledged" (*Bloody Revenge* 120).

9. The theme of "looking" in connection with shame brings to mind the important work of Donald Winnicott, especially his essay on the mother's face as mirror ("Mirror-role of Mother and Family in Child Development"). The starting point of his essay is Lacan's concept of the mirror stage, the significance, in terms of self-perception, that Lacan gives to that stage in development when the child becomes objectively self-aware, and thus can identify herself in a mirror. Before this stage of objective self-awareness, the child's sense of self derives largely from her relationship with the mother's face, and Winnicott underscores the role of apperception—the kind of interactive looking that the interaction between mother and child exemplifies—in defining a person's sense of possessing a viable and genuine self. Winnicott then extends the implications of this to the role of the healer in her interaction with the patient. "Psychotherapy is not making clever and apt interpretations; by and large it is a long-term giving the patient back what the patient brings. It is a complex derivative of the face that reflects what is there to be seen" (138).

10. A number of literary studies have made use of Kohut's work: Barbara Schapiro's *The Romantic Mother* (1983), *Literature and the Relational Self* (1994), and, with co-editor Lynne Layton, *Narcissism and the Text: Studies in Literature and the Psychology of Self* (1986); Brooks Bouson's *The Empathic Reader* (1989); Jeffrey Berman's *Narcissism and the Novel* (1990); Henry Sussman's *Psyche and Text* (1993); and Joseph Adamson's *Melville, Shame, and the Evil Eye* (1997).

11. See Susan Nolen-Hoeksema, *Sex Differences in Depression.* Lewis notes that field-dependence (a cognitive style that emphasizes the self's "relation to significant others") is marked by sex difference: "Women, on the average, are slightly more field dependent than men" (*Role* 7), at least in communities that value independence in men, and devalue it in women. This sex difference "parallels the sex differences in proneness to depression and paranoia, especially between the ages of 15 and 35" ("Shame" 103–4).

12. Lichtenberg describes the development of altruism in the child: "The emotion that accompanies the child's prosocial acts may represent empathic arousal and altruism, or fearfulness, or self-incriminating feelings and reparative shame or guilt" (114).

13. See, in particular, Donald Nathanson's collection of essays, *Knowing Feeling: Affect, Script, and Psychotherapy*, and Gershem Kaufman's *The Psychology of Shame*.

WORKS CITED

Adamson, Joseph. *Melville, Shame, and the Evil Eye: A Psychoanalytic Reading.* Albany: State U of New York P, 1997.

Bacal, Howard and Kenneth M. Newman. *Theories of Object Relations: Bridges to Self Psychology.* New York: Columbia UP, 1990.

Basch, Michael Franz. "A Comparison of Freud and Kohut: Apostasy or Synergy." Detrick 3–22.

Benedict, Ruth. *The Chrysanthemum and the Sword: Patterns of Japanese Culture.* Boston: Houghton Mifflin, 1946.

Berman, Jeffrey. *Narcissism and the Novel.* New York: New York UP, 1990.

Bouson, J. Brooks. *The Empathic Reader: A Study of the Narcissistic Character and the Drama of the Self.* Amherst: U of Massachusetts P, 1989.

Broucek, Francis J. *Shame and the Self.* New York: Guilford P, 1991.

Cook, David R. "Empirical Studies of Shame and Guilt: The Internalized Shame Scale." Nathanson, *Knowing Feeling* 132–65.

Darwin, Charles. *The Expressions of the Emotions in Man and Animals.* London: John Murray, 1901.

Detrick, W. Douglas and Susan P. *Self-Psychology: Comparison and Contrasts.* Hillsdale, N.J.: Analytic P, 1989.

Doi, Takeo. *The Anatomy of Dependence.* Trans. John Bester. Tokyo: Kodansha International, 1973.

Frye, Northrop. Notebook 3. Pratt Library. Victoria University. University of Toronto.

Hirsch, Gordon. "Shame, Pride and Prejudice: Jane Austen's Psychological Sophistication." *Mosaic* 25.1 (1992): 63–78.

Izard, Carroll E. *The Psychology of the Emotions.* New York: Plenum P, 1991.

Kaufman, Gershem. *The Psychology of Shame: Theory and Treatment of Shame-Based Syndromes.* New York: Springer, 1989.

Kelly, Vernon C. "Affect and the Redefinition of Intimacy." Nathanson, *Knowing Feeling* 55–104.

Kohut, Heinz. *The Analysis of the Self: A Systematic Approach to the Psychoanalytic Treatment of Narcissistic Personality Disorders.* Madison, Conn.: International Universities P, 1971.

———. *The Search for the Self.* Vol. 2. Madison, Conn.: International Universities P, 1978. 4 vols. 1978–90.

Kosofsky Sedgwick, Eve and Adam Frank, eds. *Shame and its Sisters: A Silvan Tomkins Reader.* Durham, NC: Duke UP, 1995.

Lacan, Jacques. *Écrits.* Paris: Éditions du Seuil, 1966.

———. *The Four Fundamental Concepts of Psycho-Analysis.* Ed. Jacques-Alain Miller. Trans. Alan Sheridan. New York: Norton, 1978.

Layton, Lynne and Barbara Ann Schapiro, eds. *Narcissism and the Text: Studies in Literature and the Psychology of Self.* New York: New York UP, 1986.

Lewis, Helen Block, ed. *The Role of Shame in Symptom Formation.* Hillsdale, N.J.: Lawrence Erlbaum, 1987.

———. "Shame and the Narcissistic Personality." Nathanson, *Many Faces* 93–32.

Lichtenberg, Joseph. *Psychoanalysis and Motivation.* Hillsdale, N.J.: Analytic P, 1989.

Lynd, Helen Merrell. *On Shame and the Search for Identity.* New York: Harcourt Brace, 1958.

Morrison, Andrew. *The Culture of Shame.* New York: Ballantine, 1996.

———. *Shame: The Underside of Narcissism.* Hillsdale, N.J.: Analytic P, 1989.

Nathanson, Donald L. "Denial, Projection, and the Empathic Wall." *Denial: A Clarification of Concepts and Research.* Ed. E. L. Edelstein, D. L. Nathanson, and A. M. Stone. New York: Plenum, 1989. 37–55.

———, ed. *Knowing Feeling: Affect, Script, and Psychotherapy.* New York: Norton, 1996.

———, ed. *The Many Faces of Shame.* New York: Guilford P, 1987.

———. *Shame and Pride: Affect, Sex, and the Birth of the Self.* New York: Norton, 1992.

Nolen-Hoeksema, Susan. *Sex Differences in Depression.* Stanford, Calif.: Stanford UP, 1990.

Ricks, Christopher. *Keats and Embarrassment.* London: Oxford UP, 1974.

Sartre, Jean-Paul. *Being and Nothingness: An Essay on Phenomenological Ontology.* Trans. Hazel E. Barnes. New York: Washington Square, 1966.

———. *The Emotions: Outline of a Theory.* Trans. Bernard Frechtman. New York: Philosophical Library, 1948.

Schapiro, Barbara Ann. *Literature and the Relational Self.* New York: New York UP, 1994.

———. *The Romantic Mother: Narcissistic Patterns in Romantic Poetry.* Baltimore: Johns Hopkins UP, 1983.

Scheff, Thomas J. *Bloody Revenge: Emotions, Nationalism, and War.* Boulder, Color.: Westview P, 1994.

———. *Microsociology: Discourse, Emotion, and Social Structure.* Chicago and London: U of Chicago P, 1990.

Schneider, Carl. *Shame, Exposure, and Privacy.* New York: Norton, 1992.

———. "A Mature Sense of Shame." Nathanson, *Many Faces* 194–213.

Sexton, Anne. *The Death Notebooks.* Boston: Houghton Mifflin, 1974.

Stern, Daniel. *The Interpersonal World of the Infant: A View from Psychoanalysis and Developmental Psychology.* New York: Basic Books, 1985.

Sussman, Henry. *Psyche and Text: The Sublime and the Grandiose in Literature, Psychopathology, and Culture.* Albany: State U of New York P, 1993.

Tomkins, Silvan. *Affect, Imagery, Consciousness.* Vol. 1: The Positive Affects. New York: Springer, 1962.

———. *Affect, Imagery, Consciousness.* Vol 2: The Negative Affects. New York: Springer, 1963.

————. *Affect, Imagery, Consciousness.* Vol. 3: The Negative Affects (Anger and Fear). New York: Springer, 1991.

————. "Shame." Nathanson, *Many Faces* 133–61.

Trilling, Lionel. *The Liberal Imagination: Essays on Literature and Society.* Garden City, N.Y.: Anchor Books, 1950.

Winnicott, D. W. *Playing and Reality.* Harmondsworth, U.K.: Penguin, 1974.

Wurmser, Léon. *The Mask of Shame.* Baltimore: Johns Hopkins UP, 1981.

————. "Shame: The Veiled Companion of Narcissism." Nathanson, *Many Faces* 64–92.

CHAPTER 2

The Disappearing Who:
Kierkegaard, Shame, and the Self

Benjamin Kilborne

The biggest danger, that of losing oneself, can pass off in the
world as quietly as if it were nothing: every other loss, an arm, a
leg, five dollars, a wife, etc. is bound to be noticed.
—Søren Kierkegaard (*The Sickness unto Death* 62–63)

Søren Kierkegaard, the Danish philosopher of the early nineteenth century (he died in 1855), focused extensively on the nature of the self and
of the individual, and on the shame (for Kierkegaard, the "sin") that
defines the human condition. By so doing, he raised questions of ethical
responsibility and of the limitations of logical systems, questions
avoided by Hegel and Nietzsche. More fundamentally still, by wrestling
with the nature of the self, Kierkegaard influenced the course of subsequent psychological/philosophical investigations, influencing, for example, both Freud and William James.

While Kierkegaard has often been interpreted to have emphasized
guilt when speaking of sin, I will propose a different interpretation:
namely, that it is the concept of *shame* that lies at the core of
Kierkegaard's concept of sin and also of his concept of dread, that terrible "sickness unto death" that threatens the self. For the purposes of this
paper we will provisionally define shame as involving discrepancies
between the way one wants to be seen and the way one feels or imagines
one is being looked at, a failure to conform to an ideal (in psychoanalytic terms, a profound conflict involving the ego ideal). These discrepancies together produce efforts to control the way one appears. And,
more importantly still, every effort to control the way one appears is
simultaneously an effort to regulate one's feelings. Therefore, shame can
give rise to obsessive efforts to control appearances, so as to control

what one feels. However, the effort to control who one is and how one feels through the way one is seen is an effort doomed to failure. Depending on others for a sense of who one is often leads to more shame and greater efforts to conceal the fear of dependence on what others see.

In *The Phenomenology of the Spirit* (1806), Hegel described self-reflection as a process whereby one understands how the thinking self can be conscious; he thereby framed questions of consciousness to be taken up by Kierkegaard and, later, the existentialists and phenomenologists. Neither static nor finite, the Hegelian dialectical process of understanding (and the sense of identity with which it is associated) is *dynamic*, and comes about through the forever incomplete efforts at grasping who we are.[1] If for Descartes the one thing that cannot be doubted is doubting itself, for Hegel, the one thing that cannot be negated is the process of negation itself.[2] And for Kierkegaard, the self is "a relation which relates to itself. . . . The self is not the relation but the relation's relating to itself" (*Sickness* 43). In other words, the self is a *process* of relating, just as self-consciousness for Hegel is a *process* of negation.

While Kierkegaard built upon Hegel, he also departed significantly from the latter's definition of self-consciousness as dependent upon a logic-driven dialectics of negation and alienation. For example, in *The Concept of Dread* Kierkegaard criticizes Hegel for a logical system that pretends to be dynamic, but that, by its very nature, can never produce change or respond to responsibility. Because Kierkegaard's self can never fully *be* itself, and must *become* itself (in part by being what it is not), the self is always subject to despair (*Sickness* 60).

In this paper I will draw upon Kierkegaard's notions of the self, sin, and despair as developed in *The Sickness unto Death* to elucidate contemporary experiences of shame and identity confusion, and also use my work as a clinician to bring contemporary concerns about shame dynamics to bear on a reading of Kierkegaard.

WHAT IS DESPAIR?

A sequel to the work published five years earlier, under the title, *The Concept of Dread* (also translated as *The Concept of Anxiety*),[3] *Sickness Unto Death* set out to describe an anxiety so intense that other forms pale by contrast and can therefore be more easily borne. Generally speaking, before the nineteenth century, works of philosophy dealt primarily with ideas, not feelings. In this respect *The Concept of Dread*,[4] *Fear and Trembling*, and *Sickness unto Death* broke fresh ground by making feeling states the object of philosophical investigation.

Kierkegaard composed *The Sickness unto Death* in the first five months of 1848, but deliberated for more than a year before deciding to publish it under a pseudonym, an interesting fact over which much ink has been spilled. It did not appear until July 13, 1849. Kierkegaard's basic argument in *Sickness unto Death* is that despair (the sickness unto death) is a sickness of the spirit and therefore of the self, a "self disorder."[5] For Kierkegaard despair has three forms: (1) unconscious despair in which one is not conscious of having a self in despair; (2) "not wanting in despair to be oneself"; and (3) "wanting in despair to be oneself" (43).

In explaining what despair is, Kierkegaard compares the first kind to an illness that has not yet manifested itself, like measles before the spots. Next comes the declared despair. When a young girl despairs over losing a love, either to death, misfortune or a rival, what she is really pained about is not being able to lose herself in him, having made herself conscious of how her own self is an embarrassment. "This self, which should have been her richesse—though in another sense just as much in despair—has become, now that 'he' is dead, a loathsome void. . . . To despair over oneself, in despair to want to be rid of oneself is the formula for all despair" (50).

To be ashamed is, as I noted above, to experience a discrepancy between the self one feels oneself to be and the self that one needs to be either for oneself or for others ("to want to be rid of oneself"). For Kierkegaard, despair over one's identity leads to hiding, not being able to tolerate the embarrassment of oneself, not being able to lose oneself in another. "The self which, in his despair, he wants to be is a self he is not (indeed, to want to be the self he truly is, is the very opposite of despair)" (50).

For Kierkegaard, this essential dread or despair, this existential crisis of identity, is what connects us with the "divinity," by which I take him to mean what makes us conscious and confirms the experience of the "spirit" in us. It is the scale and intensity of this anxiety that distinguishes it from all others, and that, for Kierkegaard, requires an act of the imagination beyond the powers of human understanding. At this point, Kierkegaard, like Descartes, invokes God. However, it is altogether possible to acknowledge a debt to Kierkegaard for having contributed to defining an important psychological dynamic, without necessarily subscribing to any religious belief in the existence of God.

Kierkegaard, like Descartes and Hegel, builds upon the Socratic maxim that the unexamined life is not worth living. "The only life wasted is the life of one who so lived it, deceived by life's pleasures or its sorrows, that he never became decisively, eternally, conscious of himself as spirit, as self" (57). However, such consciousness is acquired at the price of considerable pain and shame, since the human impulse is to hide our despair, even from ourselves. He speaks of "the horror of this most dreadful of all sickness and misery, namely its hiddenness. Not just that someone suffering from it can wish to hide it and may be able to do so, not just that it can live in a person in such a way that no one, no one at all, discovers it. No, but that it can be so concealed in a person that he himself is not aware of it" (57).

THE SHAME OF DESPAIR

The despair of which Kierkegaard speaks at such length is at once an inability to be oneself and a fear that this inability will be seen and recognized. Thus, there is a shame reaction to feelings of despair. Shame leads to despair and despair to shame, in a vicious circle.

Stepping outside the world of Kierkegaard for a moment, let us consider shame as (1) exhibited in behavior, (2) felt subjectively, (3) thought about while one is behaving, and (4) reacted to by the real or fantasized other, in terms of whose reactions one "knows" or does not know what one is feeling. Since shame is at bottom shame about the self, felt in interaction with an other, I am ashamed as I imagine I appear to you. But there is more. Shame deals not only with appearances (i.e., how I appear to the you), but also with *imagined* appearances (i.e., how I *imagine* I appear to you). We may well ask: How much can I know about my own appearance in your eyes? How *do* I appear to you? To what extent and in what ways is that truly knowledge of me? How can I control my appearance and to what ends? This brings us back to the idea adumbrated at the outset of this paper, that attempts to control one's appearance are attempts to control one's feelings. Shame always entails attempts at the regulation of feelings.

As Sartre (for whom hell was other people) notes, shame allows me to realize that I am that object that another is looking at and judging. What dialectically I can understand of myself depends upon another person.[6] Self-recognition derives from shame and dread, as does recognition of others. As Sartre writes: "I realize [the other] through uneasiness" (251). "It is shame or pride which reveals to me the other's look and myself at the end of that look" (237).

Unlike Kierkegaard, whose focus is the individual and for whom despair reveals the self, Sartre explicitly relates self-knowledge and knowledge of others.[7] Whereas, like Descartes, Kierkegaard invokes God to guarantee the search for the self and to validate the quest for self-consciousness, Sartre has self-consciousness depend upon the existence, not of God, but rather of others.[8] This very Durkheimian idea[9] (that society is God and others are required for self-consciousness) rather sharply distinguishes Kierkegaard and Sartre, although the dynamics of their systems are similar: both deal with shame states and identity. For Kierkegaard, self-consciousness and despair depend upon the notion that God is looking. For Sartre, they depend upon what one can know, imagine, and feel of others, who are also looking. For Sartre, shame has three correlates: *I* am ashamed of *myself* in front of *others*. In order to be ashamed, I must feel (and be self-conscious about my feelings of) myself, the other, and myself as I view myself through what I imagine (and experience) to be the eyes of the other. In the final analysis, then, it may not make much difference who is looking on, whether God or Society. What matters is that there is a presence looking on in whose eyes one is being judged and before whom one can never fully be oneself.

DESPAIR AND IDENTITY

Never a static property of the self, self-consciousness can exist only in being acknowledged by others. But others can never know of us what we know. And so the always incomplete and dialectical process of trying to know ourselves necessarily produces shame over discrepancies between views and versions of who we are.[10]

For Kierkegaard the pain of these discrepancies prompts not only self-consciousness, but, what for him is the same thing: a consciousness of one's spirit. But such a consciousness must, for him, include the powers of the imagination, since his definition of a self includes what is not yet (i.e., potentiality). Since the self can never be itself, and that is a source of continuous despair, identity depends upon the imagination. Following Fichte, Kierkegaard notes: "what feelings, understanding and will a person has depends in the last resort upon what imagination he has—how he represents himself to himself, that is, upon imagination. . . . The self is reflection and the imagination is reflection, the self's representation of itself in the form of the self's possibility" (60–61).

Discrepancies between ways of appearing and ways of being, as it were, animate the world, since they are forever making appearances unstable. Kierkegaard takes this Hegelian notion[11] and redefines it as inspiring a feeling of dread and shame over the instability of the world of appearances. "Imagination is the infinitizing reflection" (61). Imagination (imagining how we appear to others) can lead either to greater (spiritual) awareness or to loss of self. "The fantastic is, generally speaking, what carries a person into the infinite in such a way that it only leads him away from himself and thus prevents him from coming back to himself"

(61). Since shame entails embarrassment over the person one is seen to be, because one is helpless to present the self one feels others need to see, shame can be, as it were, a sort of malfunction of the imagination.

For Kierkegaard, since the self contains both what is and what is not yet, shame and despair lead to consciousness, and consciousness leads to spiritual salvation. However, this sequence does not come about by itself, since the self must steer a course between imagining itself and recognizing necessity and limitation. It can be knocked off course if it lacks "the strength to obey, to yield to the necessary in one's self, what might be called one's limits" (66–67), or gives in to "fantastically reflecting itself in possibility" (67). In other words, it must navigate between a blind stab into the infinite (in which case it loses itself in fantasy) or a reliance on others (doing itself out of existence). In the latter case, the person "dares not believe in himself, finds being himself too risky, finds it much easier and safer to be like the others, to become a copy, a number, along with the crowd" (64).

DESPAIR, FUTILITY, AND ILLUSION

For Kierkegaard, there are two ways of losing oneself. One is "the wishful," and the other is "the melancholic." In the first case one runs on hope; in the second on fear or dread (67). The two are equally futile. One either loses oneself in wishful thinking, which is like an infant's efforts to articulate words (68), in which case all is imagination and the self is lost. Or one loses oneself in dread, as though all were consonants and one cannot speak, and one "perishes in the dread, or perishes in what it was he was in dread of perishing in" (67). The determinist, the fatalist, is necessarily in despair, "like the king who starved to death because all his food turned to gold" (70).

Unconsciousness of despair bears great similarities to the unconscious of which Freud spoke. "To arrive at the truth one has to pass through every negativity [layers of negation and repression]; it is just as the old story says about breaking a certain magic spell: it won't be broken unless the piece is played right backwards" (74). Freud's psychoanalytic method, which he sometimes presents as scientific (something Kierkegaard never does), seeks to undo the spell of repression by "playing the piece backwards" to restore to the individual an essential sense of identity. In a further correspondence, not only is the very term *psychoanalysis* related to the soul, as Bruno Bettelheim has pointed out, but the Greek root "psuche" means at once breath and soul. Kierkegaard explicitly equates prayer with breathing, an implicit reference to the meanings of the Greek word.[12]

Kierkegaard's emphasis on the individual also allows him to give a central place in his concept of the self to selfishness, something that Hegel and the social determinists (e.g., Durkheim) avoid.[13] For Kierkegaard, as for Freud, a person's "natural qualifications," such as human "drive and inclination" are always and necessarily selfish. Indeed, "naturally there is nothing a man clings to so tight as to his self-ishness—which he clings to with his whole self" (qtd. in Elrod 91).[14] Moreover, since the self's quest to become itself is essentially selfish, when Kierkegaard speaks of love he takes a position not so far from that of Freud—and of Sartre, who in *Being and Nothingness* argues that to love is to want to be loved (474–84). In short, for Kierkegaard, the notion of a self implies at once a need for others and selfishness.[15]

The notion of illusion and its functions that one finds in Kierkegaard shows up in Freud's notions of the functions of dreams and defenses. Kierkegaard speaks of hope and wishes as driving the attempt not to despair (as Freud sees wish fulfillments as the key to dream interpretation). He also speaks of the illusions of the old. "An older woman who has supposedly left all illusion behind is often found to be fantastically illuded, as much as any young girl, in her own recollections of herself as a young girl, of how happy she was then, how beautiful she was, etc. This *fuimus* [we have been], which we so often hear from older people, is just as great an illusion as the younger person's illusions of the future; they lie or invent, both of them" (*Sickness* 89). This passage is of particular interest not only for the history of Freud's seduction theory, but also for the history, within psychoanalysis and clinical work, of the nature of memory and distortion, leading straight to the current controversies over the false memory syndrome and Freud's abandonment of the seduction hypothesis. There is thus an emphasis both in Kierkegaard and in Freud on the imagination. Shame dynamics depend upon the imagination, and give rise to fantasies of false personae, an insight that provides an interesting perspective on the pseudonyms Kierkegaard used in writing his books.[16]

For Kierkegaard, "through the eternal the self has the courage to lose itself in order to win itself" (98), a notion analogous to that of psychoanalysis, which aims to give the self courage to engage in the regression (fear of losing itself) as a result of which it will in the end "win itself." But the quest for the self always runs up against impossibility, for "at a whim," as he writes in *The Concept of Dread*, "it can dissolve the whole thing into nothing."[17] Like the self, thought "becomes another thing, and attains a dubious perfectibility by being able to become anything at all" (*Concept* 9). The reason for such evanescence Kierkegaard attributes to "something the Christian would call a cross, a basic fault, whatever that may be" (*Sickness* 101). Interestingly, the psychoanalyst Michael Balint would write a book entitled *The Basic Fault*.

The conundrum of feeling ashamed of a basic fault while needing to communicate it reappears, for example, in the work of Pirandello. In *Six Characters in Search of an Author*, Pirandello himself, the imaginary author, cannot get his characters to communicate what he wants them to. The characters rebel against him; but, since they depend upon actors to express themselves, and these actors have their own preoccupations, the characters cannot represent themselves adequately. The entire situation recalls the following passage in which Kierkegaard speaks of the dilemma of the despairer. It is "as if a writer were to make a slip of the pen, and the error became conscious of itself as such—perhaps it wasn't a mistake but from a much higher point of view an essential ingredient in the whole presentation—and as if this error now wanted to rebel against the author, out of hatred for him forbid him to correct it, and in manic defiance say to him: 'No, I will not be erased, I will stand as a witness against you, a witness to the fact that you are a second-rate author'" (*Sickness* 105).

In speaking of envy, Kierkegaard hits upon the feelings of contempt that have come to be recognized as the hallmark of shame defenses. "Envy is concealed admiration. A man who admires something but feels he cannot be happy surrendering himself to it, that man chooses to be envious of what he admires. He then speaks another language. In this language of his the thing he admires is said to be nothing, something stupid and humiliating and peculiar and exaggerated. Admiration is happy self-surrender; envy is unhappy self-assertion" (*Sickness* 118).

All the above forms of "not-seeing" or illusion hide the pain and conflict inherent in the self-consciousness of being ashamed,[18] and thereby fundamentally deny something essential about the self. Such denial leads to deep feelings of imposture, of not knowing who one is.[19]

DESPAIR, LOOKING, AND AFFECT REGULATION

Looking as wanting to be seen (and fearing to disappear if I am not) becomes a source of shame if it leads to loss of control over appearance and my feeling of self. If I look at you, then you become for me "that object in the world which determines an internal flow of the universe, an internal hemorrhage" (Sartre 233). The "drain hole" look of the Other sucks out who I am for myself, reconstituting it through the perception of one who is not myself.[20]

One may respond to shame (or sin) by either looking or not looking. Looking behaviors express feelings of shame as well as the efforts to conceal them. And fantasies of being seen often give rise to behaviors of not looking, as a magical protection against being seen (if one does not look, one cannot be seen). Feelings of vulnerability, of being caught off guard, appear to be essential to the shame experience. But intensifying the shame experience even more is the experience of being seen to feel ashamed, and being seen by one who cannot be seen (so that there is no way of shaming him back). Sartre writes that shame is driven by the perception "that I cannot in any case escape from the space in which I am without defense—in short, that I am seen" (235). While for Kierkegaard, implicitly if not explicitly, such an experience can be associated with religious awe, for Sartre it is purely individualistic, and therefore unavoidably humiliating.[21] One of the unforgettable features of Oedipus is the force of his shame at realizing that he did not see his own fate, and was ignorant of the process of his own undoing. Indeed, so blind was he that he unwittingly engineered his own demise. It is worth underlining the intractability of the dilemma of shame, dialectical self-consciousness, and negation and dependency on others; the more ashamed one is, the more *ipso facto* one depends on the idea one has of the ways one is being seen—and on those who are doing the seeing.

A fundamental danger in living, despite all the accoutrements of success and substance, is to forget, not to notice that one lacks a self. "Such things cause little stir in the world; for in the world a self is what one least asks after, and the thing it is most dangerous of all to show signs of having" (*Sickness* 62). From this we can infer that one cannot be too ashamed of one's self without losing it, and that, conversely, an ability to tolerate having one's self seen is a necessary part of having a self to hold on to. In other words, too much shame leads to a loss of the self.

Kierkegaard continues: "The biggest danger, that of losing oneself, can pass off in the world as quietly as if it were nothing: every other loss, an arm, a leg, five dollars, a wife, etc. is bound to be noticed" (62–63). The unconscious shame over being blind to so basic a loss makes us so dependent upon what others see of us (and/or what we imagine others see of us) that we can easily lose our "selves." Interpolating, we have to be willing to reveal our selves and have the faith both that we are able to do so, and that doing so is worth while. As Kierkegaard notes, whether or not the individual driven by "sickness unto death" goes under depends upon whether he or she has faith (a notion upon which William James and others will expand later). Faith to Kierkegaard contains an element of some belief in possibility.

It is worth pausing for a moment to consider Kierkegaard's critique of Hegel. Kierkegaard held that the Hegelians would in fact like to assume a role with respect to human history given only to God. James Collins notes, with reference to Kierkegaard's critique:

> What John Dewey has so often castigated as the Aristotelian spectator-theory of knowledge and the Christian view of contemplation, is in fact

this world-historical viewpoint of the Hegelians. It severs the individual from his empirical relations, robs him of personal freedom and
responsibility and saps the initiative from human planning under genuinely contingent circumstances. This is the consequence of converting
the Christian theory of history into a philosophical doctrine. (135–36)

Hegelian philosophy strikes at the heart of what Kierkegaard regards as
the freedom of the personal individual-God bond. It "suffers from the
perspectival illusion of viewing history as the freedom of necessity"
(Collins 136), simply because it is already and cannot be changed.
"From our previous study of becoming, however, it is clear that the historical process, like every other instance of becoming, remains contingent, and offers further opportunity for the growth of human freedom
and the working of divine providence. These are considerations which
lie beyond the System" (136). In Kierkegaard's eyes, Hegel was wrong
when, in reaction to Kant, he essentially equated thought and being, and
Kant was right in "stressing the cleft between thought and being, phe-
nomenal object and noumenon" (124).

Collins summarizes Kierkegaard's three criticisms of Hegel found in
the introduction to *The Concept of Dread*:[22] the meaning of history cannot ever be contained in any philosophical science ("a logical system is
possible; an existential system is impossible" [121]), existence can never
be described by an idealistic dialectic (174), and ethical responsibility
(i.e., change) can never be accounted for within the Hegelian (or any
logical) system.[23]

SIN, SHAME, AND BEING SEEN

Being seen by one whom one cannot see (or not being seen by one who
can see) is threatening—and shameful. This, of course, is the situation in
the Garden of Eden, which has often been "overlooked." Not only are
Adam and Eve ashamed of being found out to have been disobedient,
they are ashamed of being seen to know what they know.

When Kierkegaard equates "belief" (in God) with self-consciousness (i.e., the presence of self), he relates sin to the absence of self. Belief
in God for Kierkegaard creates an ideal, a standard (i.e., God) against
which one is nothing, and, equally important, a "being" in whose eyes
one can imagine oneself. Sin is "before God, or with the conception of
God, in despair not wanting to be oneself, or wanting in despair to be
oneself." The key here is "before God." "What made sin so terrible was
its being before God" (*Sickness* 112). For Kierkegaard, God is not external at all. Rather the idea (and ideal) of God functions as that part of
the self that generates feelings of shame, wanting to hide (as in the case

of Adam and Eve) because its standards are so much loftier than anything one can manage. "What really makes human guilt into sin is that
the guilty person was conscious of being before God" (112).

Despair depends upon consciousness of the self. But the self depends
upon the standard by which the self measures itself, and infinitely so
when God is the standard. The more conception of God, the more self;
the more self, the more conception of God (*Sickness* 112). Again, compare this to Freud: "Where id was there let ego be." The more consciousness of the Unconscious, the more self, and the more self, the more
consciousness of the Unconscious. Also, Freud and psychoanalysts speak
of the ego ideal, an ideal of the self that can generate shame. Listen to
what Kierkegaard, in *Either/Or*, has to say about the psychological functions of ideals: "This self which the individual knows is at once the
actual self and the ideal self which the individual has outside himself as
a picture in likeness to which he has to form himself, and which, on the
other hand, he nevertheless has in him since it is the self" (*Either/Or* 2:
263, qtd. in Connell 142).

When anyone feels he or she has fallen miserably short of the ideal,
there is a great sensitivity to being shamed by others. At this point in
Sickness unto Death, Kierkegaard imagines the tale of the mightiest
emperor who summoned the poor farmhand, who was so astonished
that his existence could be noticed that he was ashamed and fearful of
being mocked, being made a fool of in the eyes of everyone, even though
the emperor wanted to make the farmhand his son-in-law.

But there is one thing worse than being made a fool of in the eyes of
everyone: being made a fool in the eyes of no one, so there is nobody
who can see the shame of feeling foolish. Because Kierkegaard can imagine that God sees the shame of Adam and Eve, they are protected from
the chaos, fragmentation, disorientation, and annihilation of self that
would result if there were no God to recognize the shame. So while
much attention has been focused on how painful it is for Adam and Eve
to have been caught and thrown out of the Garden of Eden, not enough
attention has been paid to not having a Garden of Eden to be thrown
out of, not having a God (or any imaginary being) who can see the
shame. Strangely, then, belief in God, such as Kierkegaard proposes,
actually saves us from endless shame, by bringing into existence a being
in whose eyes shame can be imagined to be recognized.[24]

The opposite of sin is not virtue but rather faith. This point is driven
home in the following passage from *The Concept of Dread*, in which
Kierkegaard links sin and anxiety with repentance gone wild:

> Sin advances in its consequence; repentance follows it step by step, but
> always a moment too late. It forces itself to look at the dreadful, but

> like the mad King Lear . . . it has lost the reins of government, and it has retained only the power to grieve. At this point, anxiety is potentiated into repentance. The consequence of sin moves on; drags the individual along like a woman whom the executioner drags by the hair while she screams in despair. . . . Sin conquers. Anxiety throws itself despairingly into the arms of repentance. . . . In other words, repentance has gone crazy. (Qtd. in Connell 174)

In other words, "[d]read is the possibility of freedom" (*Concept* 139), "the dizziness of freedom which occurs when the spirit . . . gazes down into its own possibility, grasping at finiteness to sustain itself. In this dizziness freedom succumbs. . . . Psychologically speaking, the fall into sin always occurs in impotence" (*Concept* 55). This fall into sin is a fall away from faith.

Why should Kierkegaard think it useful to consider Adam's fall and original sin as part of a philosophical treatise? In part because it represents to him a kind of malfunction of the imagination about which we spoke earlier. "The history of the human race acquires a fantastic beginning, Adam was fantastically put outside, pious sentiment and fantasy got what it desired, a godly prelude, but thought got nothing" (*Sickness* 23). In other words, the entire Genesis myth has been misunderstood. Any adequate explanation must account for Adam as an individual.[25] For Kierkegaard one cannot arrive at original sin through the negation of innocence, an observation that strikes at Hegelian dialectics. Kierkegaard redefines original sin as ignorance (not knowledge), thus reestablishing the Socratic maxim "know thyself" as a goal. In so doing Kierkegaard redefines the meaning of innocence, which he believes can never be anything but illusion. "Innocence is not a perfection one ought to wish to recover; for as soon as one wishes for it, it is lost, and it is a new guilt to waste time on wishes."[26]

The human being is a synthesis of soul and body. "But a synthesis is unthinkable if the two are not united in a third factor . . . the spirit. In the state of innocence man is not merely an animal, for if at any time of his life he was merely an animal, he never would become a man. So then the spirit is present, but is in a state of dreaming" (*Concept* 39). This means that a state of innocence depends upon potentiality only.

"The sexual itself is not the sinful," Kierkegaard observes, demonstrating how sophisticated his notion of innocence is. "Real ignorance of the sexual, when nonetheless it is present, is reserved for the beast, which therefore is enthralled in the blindness of instinct and acts blindly. . . . Innocence is a knowledge which means ignorance" (*Concept* 61). In clinical work, not seeing, attempting to present oneself as innocent as a way of "not knowing" what one in fact knows, crops up frequently—and, as I mentioned, lies at the heart of the tragedy of Oedipus.

Kierkegaard's emphasis on sexuality, selfishness, and the self places him within the orbit of what today might be defined as psychology. During his own lifetime Kierkegaard's idea of the individual drew much attention ("bitter notoriety" [Collins 175]), and provided a model for Ibsen's Dr. Stockmann in *An Enemy of the People*. What is perceived as excessive individualism grows in part out of Kierkegaard's notion of the individual's relation to God. His dialectic of "Thou and I" was later to be taken up by Buber, Berdyaev, and other personalists. In treating the other as "thou" one responds to him or her with all that is most intimate and personal (Collins 199), a position, particularly in the light of Kierkegaard's emphasis on the human being as a creature of passions, reminiscent of Freud's notions of transference.[27]

Despair over sin feels empty, since in sin the self is conscious "of its having nothing whatever to live on, not even a self-image" (*Sickness* 143). Kierkegaard quotes, from Shakespeare's *Macbeth*, the lines pronounced by Macbeth when he has murdered the king:

> . . . for from this instant
> There's nothing serious in mortality.
> All is but toys. Renown and grace is dead.
> (Act 2, Scene 3, Lines 94–96)

Such a lack of seriousness—"all is but toys"—translates a profound sense of disorientation at the core of the sense of self. "I can't take myself, anything I want or anyone I know seriously," commented one patient when speaking of shameful feelings. This patient was ashamed of feeling so much like a toy, ashamed that others seemed "real" but not she.

And so one layer of shame covers another. Not taking oneself seriously can be seen as the result of sin, producing dread and anxiety, in which case reliance upon God can provide something to grasp so as not to be hurled into the abyss of seemingly endless shame.

> He who goes astray inwardly . . . soon discovers that he is going about in a circle from which he cannot escape. . . . I can imagine nothing more excruciating than an intriguing mind, which has lost the thread of its continuity and now turns its whole acumen against itself, where conscience awakens and compels the schemer to extricate himself from this confusion. It is in vain that he has many exits from his foxhole; at the moment his anxious soul believes that it already sees daylight breaking through, it turns out to be a new entrance, and like a startled deer, pursued by despair, he constantly seeks a way out, and finds only a way in, through which he goes back into himself. (*Either/Or* 1: 304)

In other words, shameful feelings of being "toylike" can result in still more shame over being so stigmatized, so different from others, who are "real," in which case there may be no orienting oneself, since there is no self to orient and no selves from which to get one's bearings. In this case, out of shame, the loss goes unrecognized. The self has been, as it were, murdered without a struggle and without a trace of there ever having been anything to miss.

This brings us, in closing, to the fundamental notion that "a self is what it has as a standard of measurement" (*Sickness* 147). Without a standard of measurement, a self cannot recognize itself.[28] For Kierkegaard, God functions as the internalized standard of measurement with respect to which one can recognize one's self—and by so doing avoid the state of dehumanizing and irreversible dread and shame which the unrecognized loss of self brings on.[29]

NOTES

1. As Wurmser, in *The Mask of Shame*, has pointed out, shame has everything to do with dialectical processes.

2. "And experience is the name we give to just this movement, in which the immediate, the inexperienced . . . becomes alienated from itself and then returns to itself from this alienation" (Hegel 21).

3. *The Concept of Anxiety*, ed. and trans. R. Thomte (Princeton, N.J.: Princeton UP, 1980).

4. Walter Lowrie, the translator and editor of the edition of the *Concept of Dread* on which I have relied, has several interesting things to say about the book. First, its style is unlike the other pseudonymous works, showing the greatest unevenness of style of all his works. Kierkegaard was aware of this book's difficulty, and accompanied it with a frivolous companion piece called *Prefaces*, a book that focused on trivial details in the little world of Copenhagen. Interestingly, the pseudonym he chose for this work was Virgilius Haufniensis, or the watchman of Copenhagen. This is pertinent inasmuch as looking and being seen play so crucial a role in his concepts both of dread and of despair.

5. Since Kohut and the self psychologists, this notion of a self disorder has come into the psychoanalytic/psychotherapeutic vocabulary. But there are no footnotes to Kierkegaard in Kohut or the self psychologists, although there are clearly religious overtones to their positions.

6. "Beyond any knowledge which I can have, I am this self which another knows" (237), writes Sartre.

7. When I feel myself to be the object of your gaze, I may well be uncomfortable not knowing myself as you know me. I cannot understand my object status all alone. As Sartre writes, "the Other does not constitute me as an object for myself but for him" (251).

8. Shame, writes Sartre, "supposes a me-as-Object but also a selfness which is ashamed" (252).

9. See Durkheim's *Elementary Forms of Religious Life* for a brilliant and altogether indispensable analysis of Society as God.

10. In a sense, the phenomenologists in general attempt an analysis of self-experience that by definition defies Cartesian (and Hegelian) logic. Hegel and Sartre attempt to define self-consciousness as a feeling, not simply as "objective" knowledge, but both aim at describing phenomena beneath rationalization. Both believe that truth belongs to what is known of the self not in isolation (e.g., Kant) but rather in relationship to others.

11. This is why, notes Hegel, the Greeks thought of the void as the principle of motion, although they did not go so far as to identify the negative as the self. Hegel writes: "The disparity which exists in consciousness between the 'I' and the substance which is its object is the distinction between them, the *negative* in general. This can be regarded as the *defect* of both, though it is their soul, or that which moves them. That is why some of the ancients conceived the void as the principle of motion, for they rightly saw the moving principle as the negative, though they did not as yet grasp that the negative is the self. Now, although this negative appears at first as a disparity between the 'I' and its object, it is just as much the disparity of the substance with itself. Thus what seems to happen outside of it, to be an activity directed against it, is really its own doing, and Substance shows itself to be essentially Subject" (21).

12. Compare these lines from Kierkegaard: "To pray is also to breathe, and possibility is for the self what oxygen is for breathing" (*Sickness* 70).

13. Elsewhere (Kilborne, "The Vicissitudes of Positivism") I have examined the religious origins of the social sciences, and the extent to which faith influenced the concept of a "social science" (like a "Christian science"). An emphasis on the unity (and health) of the self, so clear in the writings of Kierkegaard, can be seen in part as a reaction to the French Revolution and as part of the movement of religious revival and Romanticism.

14. Kierkegaard closely follows Aristotle on this point. The natural man is one who "loves himself selfishly" (Elrod 91).

15. "The existence of what Kierkegaard called the natural man requires the existence of the other. So closely aligned are the natural man and social existence that one cannot exist without the other" (Elrod 119).

16. "The pseudonyms sought to rescue the individual from the objectifying mentality of the Hegelian metaphysic by employing a variety of devices to enable the reader to discover that the subjective life could not be expressed, understood or fulfilled in any abstract system of thought" (Elrod xii).

17. "What it [the self] understands itself to be is in the final instance a riddle; just when it seems on the point of having the building finished, at a whim it can dissolve the whole thing into nothing" (*Concept* 46).

18. Compare Sartre, who suggests that shame is in what one fantasizes to be the recognition (or nonrecognition) of others. I can deny that you are seeing the object that I fear you are making me into, believing in effect that the object I fear you make me into is not "me" (the person you are making ashamed is not me). Or I can deny that I am an object at all, and try instead to look at you and make *you* ashamed.

19. Shame, observes Sartre, is "the consciousness of being irremediably what I always was: 'in suspense'—that is, in the mode of the 'not-yet' or of the 'already-no-longer'" (Sartre 277).

20. "What sort of relations can I enter into with this being which I am and which shame reveals to me?" (Sartre 237)

21. Sartre defines shame as "the original feeling of having my being outside, engaged in another being and as such without any defense, illuminated by the absolute light which emanates from a pure subject. . . . Pure shame is not a feeling of being this or that guilty object but in general of being an object, that is, of recognizing myself in this degraded, fixed and dependent being which I am for the Other. Shame is the feeling of an original fall, not because of the fact that I may have committed this or that particular fault, but simply that I have 'fallen' into the world in the midst of things and that I need the mediation of the Other in order to be what I am. I am ashamed not only of the discrepancy between what you know me to be as your object and what I feel myself as subject to be, but I am also ashamed of feeling ashamed of such feelings" (254).

22. Kierkegaard levels criticism at Hegel's concept of being. He focuses on modes of being, that of God and that of existing individuals, and criticizes Hegel's notion of abstract necessity as the force driving being. God's being is not abstract and dialectical, and neither is that of the individual. Characterizing Kierkegaard's critiques of Hegel, Collins notes: (a) that Hegel does not understand that existence "can never be subsumed within a system of finite thought, no matter how broad and inclusive its principles and method"; (b) that Hegel is inept in dealing metaphysically with the basic notions of being and becoming because of "his failure to distinguish between these concepts in their logical status and as representative of objects, which are themselves nonconceptual"; (c) and, finally, that Hegel's theory of world history is "inimical to man's ethical life as a responsible individual" (Collins 119–20).

23. *Either/Or*, as Stendahl understands it, presents three different approaches to the possibility of change: (1) aesthetics (which manipulates but does not believe in change), (2) ethics (which sees change in commitment), and (3) religion (which sees change in conversion) (114).

24. "Because the self is not a static essence but a relation that relates (or misrelates) itself to itself and that also relates (or misrelates) itself to God, sin is not an individual action or series of individual actions or 'sins' but an ongoing misrelationship" (Kirmmse 361).

25. "To explain Adam's sin is therefore to explain original sin, and no explanation is of any avail which explains original sin and does not explain Adam" (*Sickness* 26).

26. "Innocence is not an imperfection with which one cannot be content to stop but must go further; for innocence is always sufficient unto itself, and he who has lost it (lost it, that is to say, in the only way it can be lost, i.e., by guilt, and not in the way it perhaps pleases him to have lost it)—to that man it will not occur to boast of his perfection at the cost of innocence" (*Concept* 34).

27. In his emphasis on the individual, Kierkegaard draws upon the tradition of Augustine and Luther. Kierkegaard takes up the Thomistic notion that man is a finite, body-soul complex, but he revises his definition to include man as a creature of passions (for Kierkegaard the will is a major natural passion).

28. Compare Sartre: I cannot "make myself be for myself as an object; for in no case can I ever alienate myself from myself" (250–51).

29. Compare William James in the following passage: "There are innumerable consciousnesses of emptiness, no one of which taken in itself has a name, but all different from each other. The ordinary way is to assume that they are all emptinesses of consciousness, and so the same state. But the feeling of an absence is *toto coelo* other than the absence of a feeling. It is an intense feeling. The rhythm of a lost word may be there without a sound to clothe it; or the evanescent sense of something which is the initial vowel or consonant may mock us fitfully, without growing more distinct. Every one must know the tantalizing effect of the blank rhythm of some forgotten verse, restlessly dancing in one's mind, striving to be filled out with words" (43).

WORKS CITED

Balint, Michael. *The Basic Fault*. London: Tavistock, 1968.

Collins, James. *The Mind of Kierkegaard*. 1953. Princeton, N.J.: Princeton UP, 1983.

Connell, George. *To Be One Thing*. Macon, Ga.: Mercer UP, 1985.

Durkheim, Émile. *The Elementary Forms of Religious Life*. New York: Free Press, 1965.

Elrod, John W. *Kierkegaard and Christendom*. Princeton, N.J.: Princeton UP, 1981.

Hegel, G. W. F. *Phenomenology of Spirit*. 1807. Trans. A.V. Miller. Oxford: Oxford UP, 1977.

James, William. *The Writings of William James*. Ed. John J. McDermott. Chicago: U of Chicago P, 1977.

Kierkegaard, Søren. *The Sickness unto Death*. 1849. Trans. Alistair Hannay. London: Penguin, 1989.

———. *The Concept of Dread*. 1844. Trans. Walter Lowrie. Princeton, N.J.: Princeton UP, 1944.

———. *Either/Or*. 1843. Trans. Walter Lowrie. 2 vols. Garden City, N.Y.: Doubleday, 1959.

———, Ed. Trans. R. Thomte. *The Concept of Anxiety*. Princeton, N.J.: Princeton UP, 1980.

Kilborne, Benjamin. "The Vicissitudes of Positivism: The Role of Faith in the Social Sciences." *Journal of the History of the Behavioral Sciences* 28 (1992): 352–70.

Kirmmse, Bruce H. *Kierkegaard in Golden Age Denmark*. Bloomington: Indiana UP, 1990.

Sartre, Jean-Paul. *Being and Nothingness*. Trans. Hazel Barnes. New York: Citadel, 1964.

Stendahl, Brita K. *Søren Kierkegaard*. Boston: Twayne, 1976.

Wurmser, Léon. *The Mask of Shame*. Baltimore: Johns Hopkins UP, 1981.

CHAPTER 3

Guardian of the "Inmost Me": Hawthorne and Shame

Joseph Adamson

"Be true! Be true! Be true! Show freely to the world, if not your
worst, yet some trait whereby the worst may be inferred!"
—Nathaniel Hawthorne (*The Scarlet Letter* 260)

In each of the prefaces to his novels—*The Scarlet Letter* (1850) and the
three romances that follow—Hawthorne expresses a wish for a cooperative audience, a wish that reflects a fear of showing his inner self, or
inmost me. In the introductory section of *The Scarlet Letter*, for example, he speaks ironically of having "inexcusably" favored the reader with
his writings—"for no earthly reason, that either the indulgent reader or
the intrusive author could imagine" (3). The phrases "indulgent reader"
and "intrusive author" are consistent enough with prefatory conventions, but in Hawthorne's case they coincide with a more than common
sensitivity to the infringement of the proper boundaries between oneself
and others. On the surface, what is expressed is a fear of intruding on
the reader. This fear, however, clearly masks another: that in showing
oneself and giving oneself to the other one may suffer rejection or, even
more significant perhaps, risk losing a certain inner sovereignty.

To counter these fears, Hawthorne conceives of an ideal private circle in which intimacy and communion would not be blocked by the fear
of one's boundaries, or the other's, being violated. Mark Van Doren
observes that Hawthorne "made much of an 'invisible audience' of 'cog-
nate minds' for whom, and only for whom, one writes what was near-
est to one's heart" (64). In a way that recalls the ethic of the *happy few*
cherished by Stendhal, an author equally prone to such defensive considerations, Hawthorne insists upon the rights of a certain reserve, and
envisions a discriminating mode of communication separating the sym-

pathetic few from the uncomprehending many: "The truth seems to be, however, that, when he casts his leaves forth upon the wind, the author addresses, not the many who will fling aside his volume, or never take it up, but the few who will understand him, better than most of his schoolmates and lifemates" (3).

Shame here, then, appears to be a reaction formation against an impulse to show oneself. For Hawthorne, self-display is only possible if there exists a "true relation with his audience." "But—as thoughts are frozen and utterance benumbed, unless the speaker stand in some true relation with his audience—it may be pardonable to imagine that a friend, a kind and apprehensive, though not the closest friend, is listening to our talk" (4). Elizabeth Peabody describes her future brother-in-law on one his first visits to the house, as looking "almost fierce with his determination not to betray his sensitive shyness, which he always recognized as a weakness. But as he became interested in conversation, his nervousness passed away" (qtd. in Van Doren 54). The fear that the other cannot be trusted if one shows oneself leads to a freezing ("thoughts are frozen and utterance benumbed") that blocks all efforts at self-revelation. Hawthorne is thus careful, in his preface, to outline those very particular conditions in which he can speak his intimate feelings without risk. The balance between a certain distance and a certain intimacy is of the utmost importance, and only when we feel we are in the presence of a nonthreatening "genial consciousness," a friend though not the closest, can "a native reserve [be] thawed" and then "we may prate of the circumstances that lie around us, and even of ourself, but still keep the inmost Me behind its veil. To this extent and within these limits, an author, methinks, may be autobiographical, without violating either the reader's rights or his own" (4).

This anxiety may well have played a crucial part in the intense but apparently short-lived friendship between Melville and Hawthorne, as the former's reference to his old friend as the "shyest grape" in the poem "Monody" would seem to suggest. Edwin Miller, in his biography of Melville, proposes that the latter transgressed the boundaries of privacy with Hawthorne, which led to a sudden cooling in the relationship. One of his pieces of fictional evidence is the scene in The Blithedale Romance (1852) in which the overbearing Hollingsworth "proposes" to Coverdale, who is then put in the position of having explicitly to refuse the offer—it is more like an ardent demand—that he enter into a mergerlike bond with his friend.

One of the major themes of Hawthorne's novels and stories seems to be the danger of such intrusions directed at the self, or directed by the self at others. As such, his work poses in particularly evocative ways the question of "the cardinal role," as Léon Wurmser puts it, "that (mainly visual) perception and expression play in the conflicts leading to the emergence not only of shame, but of the inner private area of the self and the core of identity, of basic trust and a balance between narcissistic investment and object relations" (*Mask* 65). In discussing the function of shame in the social field, Wurmser proposes the existence of "an area of inwardness and interior value that should not be violated by any agent from outside or even by other parts of one's personality." Here shame performs an almost sacred role as "the guardian of inner reality" (64); it "guards the separate, private self with its boundaries and prevents intrusion and merger. It guarantees the self's integrity. . . . More specifically, it shields the self against overexposure and intrusive curiosity" (65). Wurmser points out that, reciprocally, "if one . . . crosses another's inner limits, one violates his privacy, and he feels shame." The violation of this innermost core of the self may result in the sort of rage that Heinz Kohut has classified as "narcissistic," but which might be better understood in terms of what some psychologists and psychoanalysts have called humiliated fury or shame-anger, anger that serves to defend against intense shame: "If this area of integrity and self-respect is infringed upon, shame and often violent rage ensue" (62).

Hawthorne's work illustrates in the most interesting ways this function of shame in guarding the self from invasion and unprotected exposure. In light of this I will try to show how this particular shame-anxiety can also be linked to the singular quality of guilt in Hawthorne: guilt in his writings is often about transgressing or violating the other's boundaries; but it is also about not giving of oneself, about selfishly denying oneself to the other. These are the two "unpardonable sins" in his moral universe.

Hawthorne's interest in the erotic theme—his depiction of the tragic destinies of Hester Prynne and other female protagonists in his fiction— invariably involves what I would describe as *a scene of shame*, most often staged as a public scene of judgment in which a woman incurs deep shame under the gaze of an accusing male protagonist or patriarchal society or group. In each case, her "inmost Me," as it were, is violated by intrusive and unsympathetic judges, who err, it seems, because they put reason over emotion. Of the Puritan authorities who condemn and shame Hester at the beginning of *The Scarlet Letter*, the narrator says that "out of the whole human family, it would not have been easy to select the same number of wise and virtuous persons, who should be less capable of sitting in judgment on an erring woman's heart" (64).

An interesting version of this paradigm is the short story "The Birthmark" (1843), which features quite explicit shame imagery as well as

Hawthorne's typical threatening male protagonist, an obsessed character of probing scientific intellect who manipulates and controls a humiliated female character. The same theme runs through other stories, such as "Rappaccini's Daughter" (1844) and "Ethan Brand" (1850), and is incidentally observable in *The Scarlet Letter* in Chillingworth and Hester's relationship. It can also be found in *The Blithedale Romance*, in the complex relations among Zenobia, Priscilla, Hollingsworth, and Westervelt; in *The House of the Seven Gables* (1851), in the mesmerizing of Alice Pyncheon by the vindictive Matthew Maule; and finally in *The Marble Faun* (1860), in the casting out of the criminal but persecuted Miriam (though in this case the judge is a woman—the severe and puritanical Hilda). In "The Birthmark" the humiliating takes the form of Aylmer's growing obsession to remove at any cost the birthmark on his wife's face. The birthmark becomes, for him, an essential flaw, an immeasurable defect, ultimately a hideous deformity, and his wife Georgiana responds to his obsessive scrutiny with a growing self-consciousness and deepening, chronic shame.

A prominently visible and shame-inducing *stigma* that singles out and isolates a character from his or her community is a repeated detail in Hawthorne's work. In both "The Birthmark" and *The Scarlet Letter*, the stigma seems somehow impossible to remove: Hester tries and fails in the forest; Pearl forces her to sew it back on, and she never tries to remove it again, even when the community encourages her to do so. A similar stigma is attached to Beatrice Rappaccini, in the nonvisible form of a deadly poison; like Georgiana, in trying to extirpate the stigma she loses her life. The veil that Reverend Hooper mysteriously wears in "The Minister's Black Veil" (1835), which he does not even remove on his death-bed, plays a related role. In the case of Beatrice, Georgiana, and Hester, the stigma is associated with a "stain" of female sexuality that is the projection of a ruling male ideology.

The theme of the stigmatized woman is a recurrent motif in romance, as Northrop Frye has pointed out: "The removal of some stigma from the heroine figures prominently in romance as in comedy, and ranges from the 'loathly lady' theme of Chaucer's Wife of Bath's Tale to the forgiven harlot of the Book of Hosea" (*Anatomy* 193). What is involved in such stories is a testing of the strength of the hero's love, and it appears to turn on what Winnicott means by creative looking, in which "what I apperceive I also perceive" (134). Winnicott speaks of that "complex derivative of the face that reflects what is there to be seen" (137). To clarify the difference between a shame-inducing looking and the creative looking that strives toward seeing and being seen, he uses the analogy of an individual's capacity for love, and puts it in romantic terms: "So the man who falls in love with beauty is quite different from the man who loves a girl and feels she is beautiful and can see what is beautiful about her" (133). The only thing, in other words, that might remove the stigma—that is, the *feeling of being scrutinized*—from Georgiana's face is the conviction that her husband feels "she is beautiful and can see what is beautiful about her." At one point Aylmer, referring to his plans to remove the mark, compares himself to Pygmalion: "Even Pygmalion, when his sculptured woman assumed life, felt not greater ecstasy than mine will be" (*Mosses* 41). Pygmalion created a statue, a work of art, which his love was strong enough to bring to life; in contrast, Aylmer inhumanly treats the person he loves like a work of art, as something that should be flawless and perfect. Love and creativity are sacrificed here to a wish for power and control, a wish that has become absolute and has taken the obsessive form of an impossible narcissistic demand for perfection. (It should be noted that this is a conflict apparent in the uncertainty of Hawthorne's own attitude to Aylmer; as he writes in a notebook entry: "A person to be the death of his beloved in trying to raise her to more than moral perfection; yet this should be a comfort to him for having aimed so highly and holily" [184].)

Finally, Georgiana herself begins to hate the mark on her cheek—"Not even Aylmer now hated it so much as she" (48)—and she convinces him at last to give her the antidote. "There is but one danger," she tells him, "that this horrible stigma shall be left upon my cheek!" (52). The same situation, it is worth noting, occurs at the end of "Rappaccini's Daughter," when Beatrice determines to take the antidote, after Giovanni, in a rage, blames her for having poisoned him through her love, and turns on her, telling her how hateful and hideous he finds her. Both these stories explore the failure of love and creativity—the tragic need to have power and control over others and the inability to give of oneself in love—that is one of the most devastating consequences of shame and the narcissistic defenses used to ward it off.

In commenting on shame anxiety, the fear associated with the experience of exposure in shame, Wurmser comments: "One fears one will be punished by 'shaming' procedures after the exposure. What these procedures have in common is the affect tone of contempt, a specific type of rejection, regardless whether this shaming consists of looks, words, certain tones of speech, or outright pillorying" (*Mask* 52). The fear of exposure and of the shaming procedures associated with it is central to *The Scarlet Letter*, Hawthorne's masterpiece, and the work in which shame is perhaps most thoroughly explored. The three central characters are all defined by their relationship to a particularly "punishing" experience of shame: Hester is publicly humiliated and ostracized; Dimmes-

dale lives in a state of debilitating apprehension that he will be exposed
and suffer the same or worse punishment; and Chillingworth exemplifies the density of the narcissistic defenses (against shame) while acting,
in his relationship with Hester and particularly Dimmesdale, as a punishing figure that associates him with an archaic experience of shame,
with the fear of being invaded and controlled by a contemptuous other.

HESTER

The novel opens with Hester's punishment by shaming, in which she is
displayed for the public gaze without any hope of hiding or covering.
Very specific "shame imagery" enters into the first description of her as
she emerges from the darkness of the prison into the glaring light of day.

> When the young woman—the mother of this child—stood fully
> revealed before the crowd, it seemed to be her first impulse to clasp the
> infant closely to her bosom; not so much by an impulse of motherly
> affection, as that she might thereby conceal a certain token, which was
> wrought or fastened into her dress. In a moment, however, wisely judg-
> ing that one token of her shame would but poorly serve to hide
> another, she took the baby on her arm, and, with a burning blush, and
> yet a haughty smile, and a glance that would not be abashed, looked
> around at her townspeople and neighbours. (52)

First, Hester instinctively tries to cover herself with her baby, but she is
only, as it were, covering one shame with another (which is often, in a
more complex way, how shame works). Unable to conceal or hide her
shame, she is left exposed and reacts "with a burning blush." Her only
way of defending herself is "a haughty smile, and a glance that would
not be abashed." In other words, instead of surrendering to the instinctive impulse in shame to drop her head and avert her gaze, she defiantly
smiles and raises her head and looks directly at the crowd. Haughtiness
is a classic defense against shame, and Hester remains to the end of the
novel, to a large extent, defiant in the face of her shamers. As she walks
to the scaffold, she is followed by a group of staring children who run
ahead, "turning their heads continually to stare into her face and at the
winking baby in her arms, and at the ignominious letter on her breast."
Hester attempts to fight back through her haughty demeanor, while
undergoing "an agony from every footstep of those that thronged to see
her, as if her heart had been flung into the street for them all to spurn
and trample upon" (55).

   In this opening passage the narrator takes a moment to describe a
penal machine whose particular power to humiliate and mortify is in
fact spared Hester. But the description gives the flavor of the possibili-

ties that exist in such a world. It is a diabolical contrivance, the machine being "so fashioned as to confine the human head in its tight grasp, and thus hold it up to the public gaze. The very ideal of ignominy was embodied and made manifest in this contrivance of wood and iron. There can be no outrage, methinks, against our common nature,—whatever be the delinquencies of the individual,—no outrage more flagrant than to forbid the culprit to hide his face for shame" (55). Hester is spared this particularly searing punishment, but "[k]nowing well her part, she ascended a flight of wooden steps, and was thus displayed to the surrounding multitude, at about the height of a man's shoulders above the street" (55–56). The effect of such a public display, the narrator concludes, "was not without a mixture of awe, such as must always invest the spectacle of guilt and shame in a fellow-creature, before society shall have grown corrupt enough to smile, instead of shuddering, at it" (56).

The connection between searing shame and exposure of a visual nature is particularly underlined in this opening scene of the novel. "The unhappy culprit sustained herself as best a woman might under the heavy weight of a thousand unrelenting eyes, all fastened upon her, and concentred at her bosom. It was almost intolerable to be borne" (56–57). The feeling of intense shame is captured here in a fundamental fashion (indeed, this passage is cited by Wurmser in the context of his discussion of archaic forms of shame [*Mask* 99, 139]). In "the whole scene" Hester is "the most conspicuous object" (57), and to defend herself against the agony of this consciousness her mind wanders, only to come back with a shock: "Lastly, in lieu of these shifting scenes, came back the rude market-place of the Puritan settlement, with all the townspeople assembled and levelling their stern regards at Hester Prynne,—yes, at herself,—who stood on the scaffold of the pillory, an infant on her arm, and the letter A, in scarlet, fantastically embroidered with gold thread, upon her bosom!" (58) Shame is quite precisely this "intense consciousness of being the object of severe and universal observation" (60).

Hester's ordeal, of course, does not end on the scaffold. It defines her entire relationship to her community afterwards. Shame of this magnitude involves a fundamental *transfiguration* of the person in relation to the world, and this aspect is extensively explored in the novel. In the opening description of Hester's shaming, the narrator describes the way that her relations with her society are radically altered by her badge of shame: "It [the scarlet letter] had the effect of a spell, taking her out of the ordinary relations with humanity, and inclosing her in a sphere by herself" (54). Hester Prynne is a perfect example of a *pharmakos*, an outcast or scapegoat figure, like the biblical Cain. The mark on her, the mark of Adultery, is described as being "more intolerable to a woman's heart than that which branded the brow of Cain" (84). Hawthorne describes with the greatest accuracy the way in which the relations of the person stigmatized by shame are dramatically changed: "Every gesture, every word, and even the silence of those with whom she came in contact, implied, and often expressed, that she was banished, and as much alone as if she inhabited another sphere, or communicated with the common nature by other organs and senses than the rest of human kind" (84).

The work of Franz Kafka comes to mind here. Kafka's fiction abounds in images of transfiguration and metamorphosis that express the deep sense of isolation and alienation that define the experience of chronic shame. Die Verwandlung is, of course, the supreme achievement in this regard. The experience of a human being transformed into a monstrous insect is merely an exaggerated image of the same sense of isolation and alienation that we find in Hester Prynne. Hester has been transformed into an object of fear or "horrible repugnance," of the "bitterest scorn" (84). These are the affects or emotions that define the community's attitude to her, by which they convey her utterly reduced position in society, a position "brought before her vivid self-perception, like a new anguish, by the rudest touch upon the tenderest spot" (84). Even the poor "often reviled the hand that was stretched forth to succor them" (84). (As the imagery in this passage makes clear, the two primary affects behind the contempt and scorn that are heaped on the ostracized Hester are what Tomkins calls disgust and dissmell/contempt.) Those of wealthier rank often used more malicious expressions of scornful rejection, "that fell upon the sufferer's defenceless breast like a rough blow upon an ulcerated wound" (85). "Continually, and in a thousand other ways, did she feel the innumerable throbs of anguish that had been so cunningly contrived for her by the undying, the ever-active sentence of the Puritan tribunal. . . . She grew to have a dread of children; for they had imbibed from their parents a vague idea of something horrible in this dreary woman" (85). Children call out "Adulteress" as she passes, and the shame she feels is such that "[i]t seemed to argue so wide a diffusion of her shame, that all nature knew of it" (85). Finally, there is, again, the omnipresence of the gaze:

> Another peculiar torture was felt in the gaze of a new eye. When strangers looked curiously at the scarlet letter,—and none ever failed to do so,—they branded it afresh into Hester's soul; so that, oftentimes, she could scarcely refrain, yet always did refrain, from covering the symbol with her hand. But then, again, an accustomed eye had likewise its own anguish to inflict. Its cool stare of familiarity was intolerable. From first to last, in short, Hester Prynne had always this dread-

ful agony in feeling a human eye upon the token; the spot never grew callous; it seemed, on the contrary, to grow more sensitive with daily torture. (86)

Hawthorne's description perfectly captures the "freezing" or "burning ('searing'), numbing quality" of shame on its victim, as well as the terrible experience of estrangement and exposure, as Wurmser summarizes it:

Shame anxiety . . . is accompanied by a profound estrangement from world and self, present and past. All eyes seem to stare at the shamed one and pierce him like knives. Everyone seems full of taunts and mockery; everyone undoubtedly knows about his profound disgrace. This tendency for shame anxiety to spread from one situation to all situations makes it akin, even if not causally related, to paranoid ideas. (*Mask* 53)

The victim of such dense and chronic shame often turns her face into an expressionless mask (*Mask* 210, 305). For such victims, it is a common means of veiling reality. Indeed, Wurmser cites Hester Prynne as a prime example of this defense against exposure (54). Her face, in the novel, is described as having a "marble coldness" (164), or a "marble quietude" (226). It is "like a mask; or rather, like the frozen calmness of a dead woman's features" (226). The face, as Tomkins insists, is the site of emotion, and thus such a lifeless and impassive expression protects against seeing and feeling, as the freezing or numbing quality of shame is used to defend against shame itself: "It was a sad transformation. . . . [T]here seemed to be no longer any thing in Hester's face" (163). The enduring of such severe and chronic shame, the narrator observes, has the power to transform one's very identity, to the point of de-sexing and robbing a woman of the tenderness of her "feminine character and person," crushing it "so deeply into her heart that it can never show itself more" (163–64).

CHILLINGWORTH

The acute sensitivity to unfavorable self-exposure, which appears at every turn in Hawthorne's work, is perhaps most dramatically revealed in the crime or unpardonable sin associated with so many of his villains: the shameless intrusion by one person into the innermost sanctum of another self. Just before she catches sight of Chillingworth on the outskirts of the crowd, Hester has been casting back her mind to her unhappy marriage to the man she now believes dead. The most notable part of the description of this aged scholar is the "strange, penetrating power" of his bleared eyes "when it was their owner's purpose to read the human soul" (58). As he discovers her on her pedestal of shame, "his look became keen and penetrative" (61). This penetrating look—that is, to *be exposed to such a look*—is clearly expressive of the most frightening aspects of an archaic experience of shame.

Chillingworth's ability to penetrate into the recesses of people's souls and scrutinize aspects of themselves that they are terrified will be exposed can be understood in two ways: first, in terms of the structure of Chillingworth's own personality, as a potent narcissistic defense against shame, through an aggressive power and control over others; and secondly, in terms of a figure who embodies a certain archaic fear, as a dramatic expression of the fear of exposure, the anxiety that one will be subjected to such a piercing look. Chillingworth's gaze has a frightening fascinating power that threatens to devour its victim. Hester's look is drawn to him, as she turns against her will "still with a fixed gaze towards the stranger; so fixed a gaze, that, at moments of intense absorption, all other object in the visible world seemed to vanish, leaving only him and her" (63). She is horrified by the prospect of an interview alone with him. Indeed, Chillingworth's look has such a disturbing effect that Hester finds herself in the ironic dilemma of being forced to protect herself from one shame by embracing the other, as she uses the less toxic form of public exposure and humiliation, only moments before almost intolerable to be borne, as a shield to ward off the unbearable intrusiveness of her husband's penetrating gaze:

> Such an interview, perhaps, would have been more terrible than even to meet him as she now did. . . . Dreadful as it was, she was conscious of a shelter in the presence of these thousand witnesses. It was better to stand thus, with so many betwixt him and her, than to greet him, face to face, they two alone. She fled for refuge, as it were, to the public exposure, and dreaded the moment when its protection should be withdrawn from her. (63–64)

The Satanic qualities of Chillingworth are obvious. However, one of the things that makes Hawthorne's apparently simple and often schematic allegories so intriguing is his ability to draw out the psychological core of such archetypes. The figure of Satan, as an aspect of the human personality, can be linked to both Freud's superego—in its demonic and repressive aspect—and Jung's shadow. One of the traditional roles of Satan, besides that of the tempter, is the accuser. As Frye observes, the Jungian shadow "can only be the diabolos or accuser, the agent of the moral law" (Notebook 3, 152]. The moral law enforced by the Puritan community in *The Scarlet Letter* is based on a false polarity, all false polarities, as Frye specifies, being "founded on the good-and-evil one of Genesis, which in turn is founded on shame, or erotic repression" (Notebook 27, 182). The ultimately demonic nature of a moral knowledge disastrously "attached to a sense of shame and concealment about sex" (Frye, *Words* 194) is a central theme in Hawthorne and is invariably associated with the theme of the expulsion from the Garden.

"The May-Pole of Merry Mount" (1836) is a perfect example of this theme. The neurotic moral judge, Governor Endicott, intrudes upon the spring festival and the marriage of the the Lord and Lady of the May, a young couple who have been joined together outside the confines of the law. He accuses them of "shameful" activity and casts them and their companions out of the garden; in the face of this shaming, the man and woman nobly try to intercede for one another, which is what Hester does for Dimmesdale at the beginning of *The Scarlet Letter*. They show, in other words, the genuine meaning of love to the accusor, who can only understand things in the polarized terms of good and evil. It is, of course, the woman who suffers most particularly in such a society, as Hester does, through man's projection of a repressed sexuality onto her. Frye observes of such a patriarchal moral order: "The moralist, of course, wants to create as many categories of crime as he can, and reduce sin to crime wherever possible. . . . Making adultery a crime is usually a part of the anxiety of male domination . . . & so is part of the sado-sexual set-up" (Notebook 27, 513). This is a perfect description of the Puritan society as Hawthorne portrays it.

The outer judge—delegate of the social moral order—has an inner and demonic counterpart. The sketch "The Haunted Mind" (1834) offers the prototype of this inner accuser:

> A sterner form succeeds, with a brow of wrinkles, a look and gesture of iron authority; there is no name for him unless it be Fatality, an emblem of the evil influence that rules your fortunes; a demon to whom you subjected yourself by some error at the outset of life, and were bound his slave forever, by once obeying him. See! those fiendish lineaments graven on the darkness, the writhed lip of scorn, the mockery of that living eye, the pointed finger, touching the sore place in your heart! Do you remember any act of enormous folly, at which you would blush, even in the remotest caverns of the earth? Then recognise your Shame. (*Twice-Told Tales* 307)

As Hester's own dilemma suggests, torn as she is between two sources of shame, Chillingworth's personality reflects a pathological form of superego functions—observing and condemning—that appear in the society in a milder, less destructive form. His penetrating look that judges and makes Hester shudder with fear (shame anxiety) is a demonic version of the gazing and condemning Puritan society and its leaders. In his interview with Hester, Chillingworth's intrusive look is emphasized again: "With calm and intent scrutiny, he felt her pulse, looked into her eyes,—a gaze that made her heart shrink and shudder, because so familiar, and yet so strange and cold" (72). It is a "familiar" look, one that she knows, and yet strange and cold in the sense that she cannot see herself in it, in Winnicott's sense of one's self not being given back: she has become an indifferent or inhuman thing in his gaze. Chillingworth's look, as his name suggests, "freezes" its victim and induces a feeling of deadly mortification that is the counterpart of the "searing" effect of the scarlet letter on Hester ("it [the scarlet letter] seared Hester's bosom so deeply" [88]).

As noted, the qualities of freezing and searing are often associated with acute forms of shame. Hawthorne's use of such imagery suggests the severity and archaic nature of the experience described. In the same chapter, Chillingworth touches the scarlet letter on Hester's bosom: "'Even if I imagine a scheme of vengeance, what could I do better for my object than to let thee live . . . so that this burning shame may still blaze upon thy bosom?'—As he spoke, he laid his long forefinger on the scarlet letter, which forthwith seemed to scorch into Hester's breast, as if it had been red-hot" (73). Her punishment is to be the magnitude of her shame: he tells her to live and "bear about thy doom with thee, in the eyes of men and women" (73).

Chillingworth's evil eye turns up elsewhere in Hawthorne's work. In *The House of the Seven Gables*, for example, there is Holgrave, a daguerreotypist, who appears to exercise uncanny powers of observation and to exert, when he wants, a hypnotic influence on others. Holgrave's ancestor is Matthew Maule, the wizard who hypnotizes Alice Pyncheon and turns her into a puppet he controls. Seeking revenge for the dispossession and death of his grandfather, Matthew Maule uses his magical power to humiliate the daughter of his enemy until she, quite literally, dies of shame—*mortified*. Hawthorne rightly relates this shame-inducing power of the eye to the proverbial evil eye of folklore:

> There was a great deal of talk among the neighbours, particularly the petticoated ones, about what they called the witchcraft of Maule's eye. Some said that he could look into people's minds; others, that, by the marvellous power of this eye, he could draw people into his own mind, or send them, if he pleased, to do errands to his grandfather, in the spiritual world; others, again, that it was what is termed an Evil Eye, and possessed the valuable faculty of blighting corn, and drying children into mummies with the heartburn. (189–90)

In *The Blithedale Romance*, there is the mesmerist Westervelt who exercises a vaguely sinister power over women, to which Priscilla, as the Veiled Lady, falls victim, while Chillingworth's invasiveness is echoed in the prying and inquisitiveness of Coverdale's "shameless" looking. Coverdale, who is also the narrator of the story, is a spectator-observer, a voyeur, and an ogler.[1]

In his fascinating study of Hawthorne's "mad scientists," Taylor Stoehr has demonstrated the significance of Hawthorne's interest in mesmerism and other popular pseudoscientific phenomena of the period. Sophia Peabody used mesmerism to cure her headaches, and both Elizabeth Peabody and Margaret Fuller were interested in its possible therapeutic value. A dentist and mesmerist by the name of Dr. Fiske, whom Stoehr speculates may have been a possible model for Westervelt and Holgrave (Westervelt is a mesmerist with false teeth, while Holgrave is a mesmerist who has dabbled in dentistry), treated Sophia with mesmerism, as did later a Mrs. (Cornelia) Thomas Park. Sophia also showed an interest in the spiritualist aspects of mesmerism: somnabulistic states and clairvoyance.

Mesmerism seems to have crystallized for Hawthorne his fear of spiritual violation and psychic intrusion. In a letter he cautions Sophia:

> Supposing that this power arises from the transfusion of one spirit into another, it seems to me that *the sacredness of an individual is violated by it*; there would be an *intrusion into thy holy of holies*—and the intruder would not by thy husband! Canst thou think . . . of any human being coming into closer communion with thee than I may?—than either nature or my own sense of right would permit me? (Qtd. in Stoehr 42; my emphasis)

Hawthorne points out that, since Sophia and he are one person, Mrs. Park's influence over her means that she is bringing her fiancé into an equally intimate relation with the mesmerist: "And, sweetest, I really do not like the idea of being brought, through thy medium, into such an intimate relation with Mrs. Park!" (qtd. in Stoehr 43). At the beginning of the letter, Hawthorne uses terms that recall the decision by Holgrave, in *The House of the Seven Gables,* not to exercise the magical power of his eye over Phoebe: "I am unwilling that a power should be exercised on thee. . . . If I possessed such a power over thee, I should not dare to exercise it" (qtd. in Stoehr 42). Hawthorne closes the letter by exclaiming that "Love is the true magnetism." Love, in which a unique intimacy is possible, is a guardian that protects us from shame. For love is first of all reverence toward the person's dignity and individuality. Shame, in Wurmser's words,

> is an indispensable guardian of privacy and of inner reality, a guardian that protects the core of our personality—our most intense feelings, our sense of identity and integrity, and above all our sexual wishes, experiences, and bodily parts. Without this covering of shame one feels

robbed of dignity—unless one deliberately relinquishes it, in order to
be blessed with the greater and more complete dignity of love. (*Rätsel*
457; my translation)

The Unpardonable Sin in Hawthorne's fiction is the violation of this dignity. "The Unpardonable Sin," he writes in his notebook, "might con-
sist in a want of love and reverence for the Human Soul; in consequence
of which, the investigator pried into its dark depths, not with a hope or
purpose of making it better, but from a cold philosophical curiosity,—
content that it should be wicked in whatever kind or degree, and only
desiring to study it out" (251).

Accordingly, Chillingworth's evil eye is the visual mode of the other
theme associated with him: the ability to know, to reveal what is hidden, to dig and expose that which is buried and concealed in the depths,
and which the frightened and panic-stricken self fears will come to light.
As he says to an onlooker when he first sees Hester on the scaffold:
"Thus she will be a living sermon against sin, until the ignominious letter be engraved upon her tombstone. It irks me, nevertheless, that the
partner of her iniquity should not, at least, stand on the scaffold by her
side. But he will be known!—he will be known!—he will be known!"
(63). In his interview with Hester, he says: "Never know him! Believe
me, Hester, there are few things . . . few things hidden from the man,
who devotes himself earnestly and unreservedly to the solution of a mystery. Thou mayest cover up thy secret from the prying multitude. Thou
mayest conceal it, too, from the minister and magistrates. . . . But as for
me, I come to the inquest with other senses than they possess. I shall
seek this man, as I have sought truth in books; as I have sought gold in
alchemy" (75). Very clearly depicted here, in symbolic and allegorical
terms, are the archaic aspects of the fear of being invaded and seen,
known, penetrated in the inviolable core of oneself: "The eyes of the
wrinkled scholar glowed so intensely upon her, that Hester Prynne
clasped her hands over her heart, dreading lest he should read the secret
there at once" (75).

The same kind of imagery is prominent again in the two chapters (9
& 10) that describe Chillingworth and his relationship with Dimmesdale. Chillingworth wishes to keep Dimmesdale alive, in order to torture
him with unconscious shame and guilt. He recognizes that Hester's fate
is preferable. Her shame is in the open, and can be experienced as an
ordeal that she may well overcome in the end. But Dimmesdale lives in
fear at his shame will be dragged into the light, and it is this that pro-
gressively destroys him. The conflict in Dimmesdale is between two
irreconcilable poles: the wish to reveal himself, to stand on the scaffold

in broad daylight and bare his breast in confession, to be seen by others for who and what he is—*to be recognized*—and, in absolute opposition to this, the terrible *fear of exposure*, of being met with an unsympathetic and condemning gaze. Chillingworth is the very projection and embodiment of this fear.

The relationship between the two, shamer and shamed, exposer and exposed, seer and seen, is suggested by a number of Hawthorne's early notebook entries: "A perception, for a moment, of one's eventual and moral self, as if it were another person,—the observant faculty being separated, and looking intently at the qualities of the character. There is a surprise when this happens,—this getting out of one's self,—and then the observer sees how queer a fellow he is" (178). "The strange sensation of a person who feels himself an object of deep interest, and close observation, and various construction of all his actions, by another person" (183). This doubleness is the situation, if we transpose the relation into inner reality, of the self's relationship to the superego, that agency within the ego that has as its function the intense and impersonal supervision of the self. Van Doren quotes an English biographer: "[Hawthorne] seemed, in fact, to be two men; and the one was constantly in the attitude of watching and commenting on the other" (54). It is this doubleness that is reflected in the pairing of Chillingworth and Dimmesdale, who coexist and feed off one another in a horrible struggle of shame and guilt. As the minister's physician and closest confidante, Chillingworth

> strove to go deep into his patient's bosom, delving among his principles, prying into his recollections, and probing every thing with a cautious touch, like a treasure-seeker in a dark cavern. Few secrets can escape an investigator, who has opportunity and license to undertake such a quest, and skill to follow it up. A man burdened with a secret should especially avoid the intimacy of his physician. . . . [T]hen, at some inevitable moment, will the soul of the sufferer be dissolved, and flow forth in a dark but transparent stream, bringing all its mysteries into the daylight. (124)

The figure of Chillingworth, in his uncanny ability to look and know, brings to mind, precisely as a projected and dreaded superego figure, the fears associated with the power of the analyst or therapist. As Lynd writes, "there can be no doubt of the extent to which shame operates in the analytic hour, nor of the intensification of shame if there is a lack of understanding, or any sign of contempt, on the part of the analyst" (31). This is an outcome, as Lynd emphasizes, "not only of exposing oneself to another person but of the exposure to oneself of parts of the self that one has not recognized and whose existence one is reluctant to admit" (31). This exposure to the other and to oneself is the very crux of Dimmesdale's relationship to Chillingworth. In his discussion of the need for the analyst to be sensitive to the threat of shame in his patients and not to betray that trust, Carl Schneider notes that there is good reason for feeling vulnerable "to the psychoanalytic eye and ear . . . one is constantly being led into further disclosure than one has chosen or consented to" (*Shame* 102) The practice of psychoanalysis is "a field marked by the dynamic interplay between covering and uncovering, between the tacit and the explicit" (Schneider, "Mature Sense" 209). Schneider quotes the following passage from Freud:

> When I set myself the task of bringing to light what human beings keep hidden within them, not by the compelling power of hypnosis, but by observing what they say and what they show, I thought the task was a harder one than it really is. He that has eyes to see and ears to hear may convince himself that no mortal can keep a secret. If his lips are silent, he chatters with his finger-tips; betrayal oozes out of him at every pore. And thus the task of making conscious the most hidden recesses of the mind is one which it is quite possible to accomplish. (Qtd. in Schneider, *Shame* 102)

If "exposure to oneself is at the heart of shame" (32), it is the exceptional qualities required to look at oneself *through one's shame*, as it were, that make Hawthorne's own penetration and acute novelistic powers of observation such a remarkable feature—a power, as Van Doren puts it, "to analyze the conditions of the soul which most men, if they admit them at all, are too confused to consider calmly" (58).[2] Part of the mystery of *The Scarlet Letter* is, according to Van Doren, Hawthorne's astonishing impassiveness—"how merciless a moralist Hawthorne keeps on being, how relentlessly he lets truth punish these very people for whom his pity is so complete" (145). As Richard Fogle observes, he "holds his characters to the highest standards, for he literally brings them to judgment at the bar of eternity as immortal souls," and even his "gently humorous character portraits are murderous, not from malice or heat, but from judgment and icy cold. . . . He combines sympathy with a classic aloofness, participation with cool observation" (4–5).

What happens when observation is not combined with sympathy is, of course, one of Hawthorne's great themes. The fate of the scientist or healer—Aylmer, Rappaccini, Ethan Brand, Chillingworth—whose wish for disclosure and knowledge is perverted in the service of power, control, and revenge, is a constant in Hawthorne's work. Ethan Brand is the model of this perversion. The unpardonable sin sought throughout the world by the protagonist turns out to be his own unholy prying into the human soul to find the unpardonable sin; it has turned into a violation and manipulation of others and of the most intimate aspects of their inner lives. One of Brand's psychological experiments is on an innocent and vulnerable young woman (whose name, Esther, is, interestingly, the same name as Hester Prynne's), whose soul, in the process, he has heedlessly "wasted, absorbed, and perhaps annihilated" (*Snow-Image* 94). At the beginning of his quest, a "simple and loving man," he "looked into the heart of man" with "reverence," "viewing it as a temple divine, and, however desecrated, still to be held sacred by a brother"; with "awful fear" he prayed that "the Unpardonable Sin might never be revealed to him" (98). Then "ensued the vast intellectual development" that eventually "disturbed the counterpoise between his mind and heart" (98–99). His heart had perished, ceasing "to partake of the universal throb. He had lost his hold of the magnetic chain of humanity" (99). As a pryer into souls—Schneider's criticism of Freud's inattention to the threat of shame in analysis comes to mind here—Ethan Brand lacked the one essential thing that anyone sharing in the secrets of others cannot do without: human sympathy. "[H]e was now a cold observer, looking on mankind as the subject of his experiment, and, at length, converting man and woman to be his puppets, and pulling the wires that moved them to such degrees of crime as were demanded for his study" (99).

Similarly, in Chillingworth, the genuine wish to know and uncover, which is the scientist's, turns into something obsessive and destructive. "He had begun the investigation, as he imagined, with the severe and equal integrity of a judge, desirous only of truth," but

> as he proceeded, a terrible fascination, a kind of fierce, though still calm, necessity seized the old man within its gripe, and never set him free again, until he had done all its bidding. He now dug into the poor clergyman's heart, like a miner searching for gold; or, rather, like a sexton delving into a grave, possibly in quest of a jewel that had been buried on the dead man's bosom. (129)

Chillingworth conducts a "long search into the minister's dim interior. . . . He groped along as stealthily, with as cautious a tread, and as wary an outlook, as a thief entering a chamber where a man lies only half asleep,—or, it may be, broad awake,—with purpose to steal the very treasure which this man guards as the apple of his eye" (130).

The unpardonable sin committed by Ethan Brand and Chillingworth is a form of *soul-murder*, the annihilation of another person's *psyche* through the hidden control and manipulation of that person and the violation of his/her inmost core. This is an unpardonable sin because it is a violation of a person's deepest sense of privacy and personal integrity. In this sense, shame, as a preventative attitude, has a sacred function, especially for the healer, whose "proper therapeutic stance," as Schneider writes, "is finally one of awe and deep respect, for we stand on holy ground—we engage in an encounter that involves doubleness—the experience of both mystery and revelation, of reticence before the indescribable and of the revelation of that which was concealed" ("Mature Sense" 209).

DIMMESDALE

Dimmesdale—victim of both Chillingworth and his own pitiless conscience, of the relentlessness of his superego—is introduced during the public shaming of Hester by his colleague John Wilson as being of the opinion that "it were wronging the very nature of woman to force her to lay open her heart's secrets in such broad daylight, and in presence of so great a multitude" (65). Dimmesdale's personality is largely determined by the most painful sensitivity to exposure. It is this acute sensitivity which, as I have already suggested, is a source of his feelings of guilt, his "moral shame," as Tomkins would put it: not just for something he did, but also for something he did not do; not just for his transgression, but also for his cowardice and weakness, in selfishly refusing to reveal and give of himself in honesty and love. Lynd perspicuously says that Hawthorne's great novel, "an unfolding of shame, does not fail to note that the deepest shame is not shame in the eyes of others but weakness in one's own eyes" (31). When Dimmesdale comes forth and expresses himself in his sermons, however, it is with an astonishing freshness and "purity of thought" that affects people "like the speech of an angel" (66). The conflict between these poles in his personality, between the fear of exposure and his gifts of self-expression, defines his singular relationship to his community. He is the ultimate hypocrite and liar who hides the secret of a "polluted self" from the people, but at the same time, in his deep wish to show his feelings, he is an inspiring and charismatic figure who, speaking to their hearts, brings them together and makes them one.

The first aspect—living a lie—is reflected emblematically in the tapestry that is draped on the wall of his apartment: "The walls were hung round with tapestry said to be from the Gobelin looms, and, at all events, representing the Scriptural story of David and Bathsheba, and Nathan the Prophet, in colors still unfaded, but which made the fair woman of the scene almost as grimly picturesque as the woe-denouncing seer" (126). In the biblical story (2 Samuel 11 and 12), David has an adulterous relationship with Bathsheba, the wife of Uriah, who is killed in battle when David arranges to have him sent into the forefront of the fighting. "Thou art the man," Nathan the prophet proclaims, publicly exposing and denouncing the king. Thus, we have the trio of The *Scarlet Letter*: in David, the young leader who hides a guilty secret; in Bathsheba, the adulterous woman; in Nathan, the older prying *seer*. But we also have an image of the unmistakable triangle that recurs throughout Hawthorne's work: the weak and cowardly young man fearful of exposure (and who fails the test of genuine love)—Dimmesdale, Giovanni, Coverdale, Aylmer; the shamed "dark lady"—Hester, Esther, Beatrice, Zenobia, Georgiana; and the Jungian "shadow" figure—Chillingworth, Rappaccini, Westervelt, Aylmer—who embodies an archaic superego, a vindictive and cruelly shaming and punishing conscience.

The first thing we learn about Dimmesdale is, in fact, his paralyzing shame-anxiety:

> Notwithstanding his high native gifts and scholar-like attainments, there was an air about this young minister,—an apprehensive, a startled, a half-frightened look,—as of a being who felt himself quite astray and at a loss in the pathway of human existence, and could only be at ease in some seclusion of his own. Therefore, so far as his duties would permit, he trode in the shadowy-by-paths, and thus kept himself simple and childlike. (66)

The source of Dimmesdale's name would seem to be the word "dim," which suggests the muffling and cloaking of his inner life from observation (e.g., "Then, after long search into the minister's dim interior . . ." [130]). Dimmesdale is also associated, as in the passage just quoted, with what Tomkins would call the affect surprise-startle, his "startled" look being noted a number of times. For example: "But old Roger Chillingworth, too, had perceptions that were almost intuitive; and when the minister threw his startled eyes towards him, there the physician sat; his kind, watchful, sympathizing, but never intrusive friend" (151). Surprise or startle is an affect often accompanying shame and shame-anxiety. Dimmesdale's nervous temperament, the fact that he is so sensitive to the presence of others, is the sign of a someone who has something to hide, and who is afraid of being caught at his most vulnerable or revealing. As Helen Merrell Lynd observes, "[m]ore than other emotions, shame involves a quality of the unexpected. . . . Whatever part voluntary action may have in the experience of shame is swallowed up in the sense of something that overwhelms us from without and 'takes us' unawares. We are taken by surprise, caught off guard, or off base, caught unawares" (32). Dimmesdale dreads that what he feels is his inner pollution and hideousness will be dragged into the light of day: he fears the experience, and he fears the punishment that will follow, which will involve more shame and more exposure. In conversation with Chilling-worth, he says of sinners, and therefore in defense of himself and his own cowardice: "guilty as they may be, retaining, nevertheless, a zeal for God's glory and man's welfare, they shrink from displaying them-selves black and filthy in the view of men" (132). "They fear to take up the shame that rightfully belongs to them" (133), the unsympathizing Chillingworth responds, putting the same point in terms of a cold cen-suring of moral weakness and of any justification of hypocrisy and lying.

It is worth casting back at this point to the opening two paragraphs of the novel in which, as discussed at the beginning of this paper, the author directly addresses the possibility of a "true relation with his audi-ence." He imagines a friend sympathetic but detached, "a friend, a kind and apprehensive, though not the closest friend," to whom one may speak of things and of oneself but "still keep the inmost Me behind its veil" (4). In such a case, neither the reader's nor the writer's rights to privacy will be violated. This concern is repeated, in a tragic form, in Dimmesdale's failure to find a true relation with his community and with those around him. As Dimmesdale explains to Hester in the forest, in a way that echoes the author at the beginning of the novel: "Had I one friend,—or were it my worst enemy!—to whom, when sickened with the praises of all other men, I could daily betake myself, and be known as the vilest of all sinners, methinks my soul might keep itself alive thereby. Even thus much of truth would save me. But, now, it is all falsehood!—all emptiness!—all death!" (192). Chillingworth is such an "enemy," in secret, while openly purporting to be such a friend and con-fidant. The author's expression of desire, in the preface, for both close-ness and distance ("a friend . . . though not the closest friend") and for a certain withholding of his "inmost Me," indicates a mistrust of com-plete intimacy, of any unconditional giving of himself. The role of Chill-ingworth, who has invaded and violated the intimacy of his friend and patient, "violated in cold blood the sanctity of a human heart" (212), speaks to that fear in the most graphic way possible. When Dimmesdale discovers the truth about the physician, he laments "the horror of this thing! And the shame!—the indelicacy!—the horrible ugliness of this exposure of a sick and guilty heart to the very eye that would gloat over it!" (195). Expressed here in such stark terms is not only the horror of exposure to an external observer. There is also the crushing and helpless feeling of exposure to a kind of archaic conscience or superego, to a cold and hostile, condemning, scornful, contemptuous look or eye, to a gloating evil eye—an inner, ultimately, and not an outer, eye. "Public exposure," Lynd remarks of The Scarlet Letter—and we can recall Hes-ter's turning away from Chillingworth to the shaming crowd at the beginning of the novel—"may even be a protection against this more painful inner shame" (31).

In their moment in the forest, the intimacy between Hester and Dimmesdale represents, in contrast, a moment of looking and being looked at in which the threat and fear of shame is absent, and it is depicted as a joyous moment of relief: "Else, I should long ago have thrown off these garments of mock holiness, and have shown myself to mankind as they will see me at the judgment-seat. Happy are you, Hester, that wear the scarlet letter openly upon your bosom. Mine burns in secret. Thou too knowest what a relief it is, after the torment of a seven years' cheat, to look into an eye that recognizes me for what I am" (192). This is the ultimate wish of all human beings perhaps: to *be recognized for what one is*, by a loving eye from which the need to hide or cover oneself, with all one's flaws and defects, imagined or otherwise, is absent, without the fear of judgment or shame. "And yet they lingered. . . . Here, seen only by his eyes, the scarlet letter need not burn into the bosom of the fallen woman! Here, seen only by her eyes, Arthur Dimmesdale, false to God and man, might be, for one moment, true!" (195–96). One of the signs of psychological and emotional health is to be capable of intimacy, and one of Hawthorne's central themes is the barrier that shame puts up between the self and the other, thus estranging us not only from other human beings, but from our genuine selves.

"Thy heart must be no longer under his evil eye" as Hester says to Dimmesdale, to which he replies that "It were far worse than death, but how to avoid it" (196). At this point they contemplate the possibility of seeking refuge through flight: "Is there not shade enough in all this boundless forest to hide thy heart from the gaze of Roger Chillingworth?" (197). Flight, concealment, and covering are, of course, the most simple responses to shame, and thus they dream of running and hiding, to get beyond "his power and knowledge." However, the cowardice and falsity of Dimmesdale's situation and his relation to his community lead only more inexorably into more intense feelings of self-loathing and self-contempt.

> He had striven to put a cheat upon himself by making the avowal of a guilty conscience, but had gained only one other sin, and a self-acknowledged shame, without the momentary relief of being self-deceived. He had spoken the very truth, and transformed it into the veriest falsehood. And yet by the constitution of his nature, he loved the truth, and loathed the lie, as few men ever did. Therefore, above all things else, he loathed his miserable self! (144)

Shame, as Wurmser defines it, is essentially contempt directed at the self, either from outside or from within. Dimmesdale ends up feeling the most debilitating self-contempt, disgusted as he is at his own falsity and hypocrisy and cowardice in not confessing, out of fear of shame; hiding out of shame leads to deeper shame. The fear of shame thus leads Dimmesdale to hide, which leads to increased shame and guilt, and increased fear of exposure, and thus to a state of paralysis, in which the flight from shame is no longer possible.

We can draw some conclusions now about the nature of shame and guilt dynamics in Hawthorne. Shame and guilt are inseparable. Guilt, indeed, is often associated with weakness, cowardice, lying, and selfishness, due to the fear of exposure. In Hawthorne's fiction, those who commit acts of aggression—the violation of another's boundaries in pursuit of control, power, or revenge—are guilty of the crime of soul-murder, their own and others, and may come to feel morally responsible for the terrible harm done to others. But there is another source of guilt in Hawthorne. The psychological and moral consequences of lying, hypocrisy, and self-concealment interested Hawthorne early on. There is, for example, the following notebook entry: "Insincerity in a man's own heart must make all his enjoyments, all that concerns him, unreal; so that his whole life must seem like a merely dramatic representation. And this would be the case, even though he were surrounded by true-hearted relatives and friends" (166–67). The experience of oneself and the world around one as unreal is the consequence of such insincerity, which is often rooted in shame and the fear of self-revelation.

Thus, when someone feels guilty in Hawthorne, such as Dimmesdale in *The Scarlet Letter* or Reuben Bourne in "Roger Malvin's Burial" (1832), it is often a consequence of a withholding motivated by narcissistic defenses against shame.[3] The theme of the *first lie*, so brilliantly developed in the latter tale, one of Hawthorne's earliest pieces, is an indispensable key here. In this story, Reuben Bourne is forced, through no fault of his own, to abandon his dying friend and future father-in-law in the forest and then proceeds to conceal the true nature of his actions, which in themselves are neither heroic nor morally reprehensible, so that they appear noble and praiseworthy. This first lie to his wife is out of the reluctance to show himself in a reduced light, as cowardly, weak, and selfish, and thus it leads inexorably to lying, hypocrisy, and concealment—and thus to guilt, and then to more cowardliness, weakness, selfishness, lying, and increased shame and guilt as long as he remains silent about the truth. The phrase from "The Haunted Mind"—"a demon to whom you subjected yourself by some error at the outset of life, and were bound his slave forever, by once obeying him"—is a perfect depiction of what we find here: a fatal duplicity of the self, motivated by the fear of exposure, that has put one under the power of a haunting inner judge. The guilt here is very close to, and inextricably intertwined with shame: one feels guilty for selfishly not spelling out the complete truth, out of the fear of being seen as less than strong and brave.

This is the nature of the guilt in Dimmesdale as well; selfishness and cowardice lead to a whole "dim" web of lies and concealments about the self, in which one feels an ever increasing shame and guilt for not being honest about who one is. Dimmesdale is originally afraid of being looked upon as a filthy and polluted sinner—of being exposed as dirty and weak—and for this reason weakly and selfishly lies about who he is; this fateful concealment adds to the first shame an even worse and growing shame and guilt.[4] Hester's role in concealing the identity of Chillingworth from Dimmesdale is part of the same dynamic. When she first recognizes Chillingworth he raises a finger to his lips, and she later swears, conjoined by him, to keep his identity secret, the result of which is to place Dimmesdale completely under Chillingworth's power and thus intensify his debilitating feelings of shame and guilt (thus "the sufferer's conscience had been kept in an irritated state, the tendency of which was . . . to disorganize and corrupt his spiritual being" [193]).

This dynamic, it seems to me, explains Hawthorne's famous preoccupation with Dr. Johnson's act of contrition for a guilty act of disobedience and wrong done to his father. In an early notebook entry, Hawthorne, over a decade before he writes *The Scarlet Letter*, observes: "Dr. Johnson's penance in Uttoxeter Market. A man who does penance in what might appear to lookers-on the most glorious and triumphal circumstance of his life. Each circumstance of the career of an apparently successful man to be a penance and torture to him on account of some fundamental error in early life" (180). Once, as a boy, Johnson refused, out of selfish pride—that is, out of shame for his father, a bookseller who sold his wares in the marketplace—to accompany his father to market in Uttoxeter; later in life, he made atonement for his guilt by an act of public humiliation:

> "Once, indeed, [said he,] I was disobedient; I refused to attend my father to Uttoxeter-market. Pride was the source of that refusal, and the remembrance of it was painful. A few years ago I desired to atone for this fault. I went to Uttoxeter in very bad weather, and stood for a considerable time bareheaded in the rain, on the spot where my father's stall used to stand. In contrition I stood, and I hope the penance was expiatory." (Boswell 578; Ashbourne, August 12, 1784)

In *Our Old Home* Hawthorne describes the bas-relief at the base of the statue of Dr. Johnson in Uttoxeter that depicts the scene: "He stands bareheaded, a venerable figure, and a countenance extremely sad and woe-begone, with the wind and rain driving hard against him, and thus helping to suggest to the spectator the gloom of his inward state" (132). Hawthorne devotes almost an entire chapter to the episode, calling it "as beautiful and touching a passage as can be cited out of any human life" (137). We can recognize in Johnson's act of contrition a particularly poignant version of the many scenes of shame that recur in Hawthorne's fictions.

It is interesting to consider the reasons for the dominance of shame in Hawthorne's work.Throughout his life, Hawthorne seems to have suffered from shame and depression, along with a defensive reserve—manifested, for example, in his "strong aversion to public speaking" (Stewart 17)—and a tendency to seclusion. His "low spiritedness," according to Randall Stewart, was "partly a temperamental affliction from which, like most sensitive persons, he was to suffer at intervals throughout his life" (24). Stoehr quotes a passage (from the English notebooks) which Hawthorne wrote at the height of his success, when he had "more wealth and fame and ease than he had ever known" (133). It concerns a "singular dream" that he has the impression of having dreamed "ever since I have been in England":

> I am still at college—or, sometimes, even at School—and there is a sense that I have been there unconscionably long, and have quite failed to make such progress in life as my contemporaries have; and I seem to meet some of them with a feeling of shame and depression that broods over me, when I think of it, even at this moment. This dream, recurring all through these twenty or thirty years, must be one of the effects of that heavy seclusion in which I shut myself up, for twelve years, after leaving college, when everybody moved onward and left me behind. How strange that it should come now, when I may call myself famous, and prosperous!—when I am happy, too!—still that same dream of life hopelessly a failure! (Qtd. in Stoehr 133)

The dream may evoke as well the period as a boy when a serious leg injury confined him to the house for three years, another period of "heavy seclusion" and of depressing inactivity in his life, at least from the point of view of practical affairs. This feeling of being a hopeless failure is one of the symptoms of shame-induced depression, the sign, in psychoanalytic terms, of the predominance of an accusing and shaming conscience or superego.

Certain circumstances in Hawthorne's life may be of particular significance. His mother and her three children lived with her family and remained dependent on them for support even into Hawthorne's adult years. It is curious that Hawthorne is so remarkably silent about the Manning family, in spite of their apparent indulgence in supporting and educating their nephew. The influence of his mother's brothers, who belonged to the world of practical affairs, social responsibility, and economic independence, may have made him resentful of the male world of social authority and its shaming judgment of the "weak" and "feminine" artistic sensibility. An "artist of the beautiful" like his character Owen Warland, Hawthorne clearly identified with his female protagonists and their taste for the gorgeous and the beautiful. As a sensitive and imaginative young man with "a feminine cast of mind," to use Emerson's words (qtd. in Van Doren 55), who wished to reveal himself and his feelings but was afraid and distrustful, and as someone indulged from his earliest years by his mother and sisters, he was deeply sympathetic to the situation of women under the humiliating control of patriarchal authority. At the same time, the author of *The Scarlet Letter* saw much amiss in Hester's independence of spirit and moral wandering. Hawthorne's attitude to his female protagnoists reflects the deep ambivalence, that mixture of instinctive sympathy and reactive anxiety, with which he regarded the plight of women and their struggle for emancipation. He was capable of recognizing the injustice done to them, but could not always accept them as fully independent agents; psychologically and emotionally, like so many men of his time (and our own), he needed to see them first of all as mothers, lovers, and helpmates.

A more compelling factor to consider perhaps is the apparent coldness and formality of his relations with his mother, an awkwardness that seems to have masked intense feelings that remained unexpressed. At the same time, he felt an enduring sense of obligation toward her. In his biography, Edwin Miller claims that "by whatever means—her seeming weaknesses may have caused the children to believe they had to protect her—she retained, probably without even consciously trying, such a hold that only Hawthorne dared to venture, after years of vacillation, into marriage and separate himself from this closely knit unit" (31). For "despite her self-effacing, unempathic ways [Hawthorne's mother] was in the eyes of her children a powerful presence or image, even if because of her passivity and her chilled emotional responses not a wholly satisfying one" (31).

This chilled responsiveness may explain Hawthorne's own adamantine emotional composure. It was shattered, as Hawthorne later recalled, on the occasion of reading "the last scene of *The Scarlet Letter* to my wife, just after writing it—tried to read it rather. . . . But I was in a very nervous state then, having gone through a great diversity of emotions, while writing it, for many months. I think I have never overcome my own adamant in any other instance" (qtd. in Van Doren 143). However, as Van Doren points out, "another such instance had occurred, just six months earlier," at the death of his mother (144). This event is doubtless one of the sources of the "great diversity of emotions" to which he refers. Before describing, in his notebook, his emotional collapse as he sat at the side of his dying mother, he depicts their relationship:

> I love my mother; but there has been, ever since my boyhood, a sort of coldness of intercourse between us, such as is apt to come between persons of strong feelings, if they are not managed rightly. I did not expect to be much moved at the time—that is to say, not to feel any overpowering emotion struggling, just then—though I knew that I should deeply remember and regret her. Mrs. Dike left the chamber, and then I found the tears slowly gathering in my eyes. I tried to keep them down; but it would not be—I kept filling up, till, for a few moments, I shook with sobs. For a long time, I knelt there, holding her hand; and surely it is the darkest hour I ever lived. (429)

The coldness that Hawthorne speaks of as coming between the two suggests a defense against intense affect. Hawthorne and his sister Elizabeth, according to Miller's biography, both observed "that their mother could not cope with feelings and demonstrations of affection" (32–33). Miller suggests that Hawthorne's emphasis, in his writings, "upon repression, non-communication, and the absence and fear of tactile contact and gratification" (33) can be traced back to his "mother's failure" (33) as a responsive caregiver. This empathic failure is consistent with the way in which, in his work, the wish for communion and intimacy comes into conflict with the fear of being invaded or rejected by the other. Thus, the substitute for intimacy is spectatorship, intimacy at a distance—looking in from outside: "As everybody testified and his behavior illustrated, he was reclusive and often melancholic and like his fictional characters a spectator with the coolness and distance provided by such a stance" (Miller 33). A good example of this conflict in his fiction is Coverdale in *The Blithedale Romance*, a compulsive "looker" who is unable to connect with others because of a narcissistic self-protectiveness that masks, perhaps, the fear of self-loss. Or there is the protagonist of *Wakefield* who abandons his wife simply out of curiosity— in order to be able to observe himself and his life from outside.

Hawthorne's emotional life was clearly stimulated and deepened in his relationship with Sophia Peabody, a relationship that, as Walter Herbert's biographical look at their marriage has shown, was a sexually fulfilling and genuinely loving one. It is after meeting Sophia that a distinctive erotic element enters his writing. For one thing, the "garden" imagery of his stories, clearly associated with sexual love, becomes notable; the imagery is attached, in particular, to Beatrice, Hester and

Pearl, Phoebe, and Zenobia. His marriage to Sophia seems to have resulted in an emotionally difficult separation from his mother and his sisters. The need to distance himself from them in forging his new relationship may have awakened old feelings of guilt, feelings, however, that, in the form of the theme of penance, certainly haunt Hawthorne's work from the beginning. The experience of genuine intimacy with Sophia may also have made him acutely aware of the witholding, narcissistic aspects of his own personality, and of the tragic nature of the conflict between love and selfishness.

A plot he returned to was that of the woman who finds her sincere love betrayed by a weak and self-absorbed man, whose defensive narcissism and *basic mistrust*, to use Erik Erickson's term, destroys intimacy and genuine relationship. One of the most striking depictions of this theme is "Egotism; or, the Bosom Serpent." The snake that gnaws at Roderick Elliston's bosom "seemed the symbol of a monstrous egotism to which everything was referred, and which he pampered, night and day, with a continual and exclusive sacrifice of devil worship" (*Mosses* 274). Similarly, Goodman Brown's doubts isolate him from Faith. The Reverend Mr. Hooper witholds love and intimacy from his wife. Giovanni savagely repudiates Beatrice. Dimmesdale disowns Hester. This self-isolation is already apparent in the very early "Roger Malvin's Burial": Reuben Bourne lies and hides from his wife, after he feels guilty for leaving her father behind in the forest to die alone. At the end of the story, Reuben breaks down, like Hawthorne weeping uncontrollably at the bedside of his dying mother: "Then Reuben's heart was stricken, and the tears gushed out like water from rock" (*Mosses* 360).

The creative influence of Hawthorne's relationship with Sophia can be seen in the writing that culminates in *The Scarlet Letter*. But there was also a conventional and repressive aspect to their marriage. It is reflected, for example, in the censoring, superego role carried out by female characters such as Phoebe and Hilda. Sophia herself censored certain passages of *The Blithedale Romance* that she regarded as too frank and open. After *The Scarlet Letter* Hawthorne's work, for whatever reason, was never to achieve again the same intensity and power. Nevertheless, his entire body of work remains testimony to Tomkins's view that the imaginative writer uses language "for the expression, clarification and deepening of feelings" and thus enriches "the affective life of man" (219). What Hawthorne did to reveal his feelings in his writing has left us with one of the most psychologically profound bodies of work in literature. It has deepened our knowledge of the emotions and of the role of shame in particular, both destructive and creative, in shaping the human personality.

NOTES

1. Hawthorne's own penetrating look is worth noting here. Henry Murray, for example, speculates that Plinlimmon's prying stare in Melville's *Pierre* may indeed have been modeled on Hawthorne's "silent steady gaze," which seems to have been "embarrassing or distressing to some people" (lxxviii). "Wonderful, wonderful eyes," one observer commented. "They give, but receive not" (Frederika Bremer, qtd. in E. H. Miller 240)—an observation that, however enthusiastic in its admiration, might suggest that his look could, indeed, put others on the defensive. Elizabeth Peabody—Sophia Hawthorne's sister—describes the "piercing, indrawing gaze" with which he first regarded her sister on their first meeting (qtd. in Van Doren 52).

For an intriguing discussion and analysis of the imagery of the "gaze" in Hawthorne's work, from a phenomenological and poststructuralist viewpoint, see John Dolis, *The Style of Hawthorne's Gaze: Regarding Subjectivity* (Tuscaloosa, Ala: U of Alabama P, 1993).

2. Compare Lynd's remarks: "In reviewing Stendhal's Diaries, Auden expressed surprise that Stendhal found it hard to admit certain things to himself and asked, 'How can admitting anything to oneself be daring?' In raising this remarkable question Auden reflects the extent to which many people at present have become insensitive to the experience of shame and to the deep ambiguities in human nature in which it is rooted" (32).

3. Vernon Kelly makes the distinction between narcissism and healthy self-ishness: "True narcissism shuts out others in order to protect a damaged self. Healthy selfishness allows a temporary focus on the inmost self out of love and respect for the needs of the self and in order to enhance one's capacity for positive intimate interaction" (87).

4. It is worth noting the relevance of the recent film *Quiz Show* to these issues of shame and guilt, particularly since I cite throughout this paper the work of Mark Van Doren, whose biography of Hawthorne appeared in 1949. The film is centered on the role of Van Doren's son Charles in the quiz show scandal at the end of the 1950s. Charles Van Doren finds himself, after the "first lie"—he allows himself to be trapped into the use of rigged answers in his first appearance on the show—caught in a false position akin to that of Roger Malvin and Dimmesdale. He is gradually enveloped in a tightening web of hypocrisy and deceit that makes him feel guilty, but that his conflicting wish to shine and be admired leads him to accept. At the core of everything is the corrosive power of the lie about who he is, a lie he allows himself partly in his oedipal struggle to compete with, and gain the approval of, his highly successful father (Mark Van Doren). When he finally brings himself to confess his involvement, his situation is even more reminiscent of Dimmesdale's. Just as Dimmesdale's confession at the end of the novel is lost and misunderstood by the crowd in the emotion and turmoil of the moment and taken to be yet another sign of his sanctity, so Charles Van Doren's eloquent confession of shameful wrongdoing and wilful deception is taken by a number of the senators at the hearing as a further index of his honor and praiseworthy character. In this quite remarkable film the issue of shame plays an even larger role than I have outlined here, and on a number of fronts. It is worth a paper of its own.

WORKS CITED

Boswell, James. *The Life of Dr Johnson.* Vol. 2. London: J. M. Dent & Sons, 1960.

Fogle, Richard. *Hawthorne's Fiction: The Light and the Dark.* Norman: Oklahoma UP, 1964.

Frye, Northrop. *Anatomy of Criticism.* Princeton, N.J.: Princeton UP, 1957.

——. *Notebooks.* Pratt Library. Victoria University. University of Toronto.

——. *Words with Power: Being a Second Study of "The Bible and Literature."* Harmondsworth, U.K.: Penguin, 1990.

Hawthorne, Nathaniel. *The American Notebooks.* Vol. 8 of The Centenary Edition of the Works of Nathaniel Hawthorne. Ed. Claude M. Simpson. Columbus: Ohio State UP, 1972.

——. *The Blithedale Romance* and *Fanshawe.* Vol. 3 of The Centenary Edition of the Works of Nathaniel Hawthorne. Columbus: Ohio State UP, 1964.

——. *The House of the Seven Gables.* Vol. 2 of The Centenary Edition of the Works of Nathaniel Hawthorne. Columbus: Ohio State UP, 1965.

——. *Mosses from an Old Manse.* Vol. 10 of The Centenary Edition of the Works of Nathaniel Hawthorne. Columbus: Ohio State UP, 1974.

——. *Our Old Home.* Vol. 5 of The Centenary Edition of the Works of Nathaniel Hawthorne. Columbus: Ohio State UP, 1970.

——. *The Snow-Image and Uncollected Tales.* Vol. 11 of The Centenary Edition of the Works of Nathaniel Hawthorne. Columbus: Ohio State UP, 1974.

——. *The Scarlet Letter (and Selected Tales).* Vol. 1 of The Centenary Edition of the Works of Nathaniel Hawthorne. Columbus: Ohio State UP, 1962.

——. *Twice-Told Tales.* Vol. 9 of The Centenary Edition of the Works of Nathaniel Hawthorne. Columbus: Ohio State UP, 1974.

Herbert, Walter T. *Dearest Beloved: The Hawthornes and the Making of the Middle-Class Family.* Berkeley: U of California P, 1993.

Kelly, Vernon C. "Affect and the Redefinition of Intimacy." Nathanson, *Knowing Feeling* 55–104.

Kohut, Heinz. *The Search for the Self.* Vol. 2. Madison, Conn.: International Universities P, 1978. 4 vols. 1978–90.

Lacan, Jacques. *The Four Fundamental Concepts of Psycho-Analysis.* Ed. Jacques-Alain Miller. Trans. Alan Sheridan. New York: Norton, 1978.

Lynd, Helen Merrell. *On Shame and the Search for Identity.* New York: Harcourt Brace, 1958.

Miller, Edwin Haviland. *Melville.* New York: George Braziller, 1975.

——. *Salem Is My Dwelling Place: A Life of Nathaniel Hawthorne.* Iowa City: U of Iowa P, 1991.

Murray, Henry. Introduction to *Pierre or, The Ambiguities.* New York: Hendricks House, 1962: xii–ciii.

Nathanson, Donald L. *Shame and Pride: Affect, Sex, and the Birth of the Self.* New York: Norton, 1992.

——, ed. *Knowing Feeling: Affect, Script, and Psychotherapy.* New York: Norton, 1996. 55–104.

——, ed. *The Many Faces of Shame.* New York: Guilford P, 1987.

The New Oxford Annotated Bible. Revised Standard Version. Ed. Herbert G. May and Bruce M. Metzger. New York: Oxford UP, 1973.

Schneider, Carl. *Shame, Exposure, and Privacy.* New York: Norton, 1992.

————. "A Mature Sense of Shame." Nathanson, *Many Faces,* 194–213.

Stewart, Randall. *Nathaniel Hawthorne: A Biography.* New York: New York UP, 1948.

Stoehr, Taylor. *Hawthorne's Mad Scientists: Pseudoscience and Social Science in Nineteenth-Century Life and Letters.* Hamden, Conn.: Archon, 1978.

Tomkins, Silvan. *Affect, Imagery, Consciousness.* Vol. I: The Positive Affects. New York: Springer, 1962.

Van Doren, Mark. *Nathaniel Hawthorne.* New York: Viking, 1957.

Winnicott, D. W. *Playing and Reality.* Harmondsworth, U.K.: Penguin, 1980.

Wurmser, Léon. *The Mask of Shame.* Baltimore: Johns Hopkins UP, 1981.

————. *Das Rätsel des Masochismus: Psychoanalytische Untersuchung von Über-Ich-Konflikten und Masochismus.* Berlin: Springer, 1993.

————. "Shame: The Veiled Companion of Narcissism." Nathanson, *Many Faces,* 64–92.

CHAPTER 4

Ardor and Shame in Middlemarch

Gordon Hirsch

Usually readers of George Eliot's *Middlemarch* stress the sociological and ethical aspects of the novel rather than the psychological. Certainly the title of the book, which refers to the fictional town in or near which the characters live, and its subtitle, "A Study of Provincial Life," point to the book's social dimensions. The book's ethical focus is also evident. The narrative propels its characters through one set of ethical dilemmas and choices after another, in order to develop a thematic argument demonstrating the need for "sympathy" and fellow-feeling in a modern era increasingly dominated by a divisive individualism and "egoism." Still, Eliot is clearly fascinated by emotions and individual psychology as well as by her social and ethical themes, and she makes a very serious effort to understand both the power of affects and their connections with the structures of her society.[1]

Eliot is in fact a remarkable student of the points where emotion, society, and ethical thought intersect, documenting both the socially disruptive and the socially binding aspects of important affects such as shame, which she repeatedly links to her central thematic concerns. Shame is connected with individuals' quests for "vocation" in the novel—for a career, profession, something to do. Shame is associated as well with their idealism, which Eliot calls "ardor," but also with their shortcomings, disillusionment, and despair when that idealistic vision fails to be realized for one reason or another. Characters try to defend against shame by developing their narcissism and grandiosity, by becoming what Eliot would call "egoists," armoring themselves against the judgments and opinions of others.

In other words, Eliot paints a complicated portrait of shame: it knits society together in a web of shared values, yet it may also be coercive. It promotes idealism, but may bring on depression and despair when idealism is frustrated. There is perhaps an evolutionary, Darwinian subtext to all of this: shame is a nonviolent way of binding together the social group, the community, but it can be an instrument of oppression and conformity as well, as the community identifies and persecutes its scapegoats. It is an intensely personal and private feeling, but also the quintessentially interpersonal emotion, the one most likely to function as a social regulator. George Eliot's insight into the role of affects generally and shame in particular is thus subtle and complex. She relates individual psychology both to questions of personal ethics and to forms of social organization.

SHAME AND NARCISSISM

The operations of shame in *Middlemarch* are clearest, as Alexander Welsh has noted, in the melodramatic Bulstrode subplot.[2] John Raffles is aware of the banker Bulstrode's shady past in London, where as a kind of pawnbroker Bulstrode likely trafficked in stolen goods, and where, though a strict Evangelical, he nevertheless suppressed news of the discovery of the runaway daughter of the wealthy woman to whom he proposed marriage. The daughter's whereabouts remain hidden. Bulstrode marries, inherits his first wife's fortune upon her death, and, after convincing himself that the source of his wealth and position is immaterial, becomes a leading citizen and moral lantern of Middlemarch, persuaded that he now deploys his wealth as an instrument of divine providence. Raffles suddenly appears on the scene, however, functioning as Bulstrode's "incorporate past" (523), and tries to extort money from him. Whereas the first part of *Middlemarch* registers Bulstrode's position of power and authority in the community, the last half details Raffles's blackmail of Bulstrode and the latter's fear of exposure and disgrace.

Other characters represent similar, though perhaps more complicated, cases where narcissism and grandiosity serve as defenses against shame.[3] Among the more interesting examples are Tertius Lydgate and his wife, Rosamond Vincy. Lydgate is a medical man, new to the town, whose central characteristic is his ambition of becoming a hero of medical science. Though born to the gentry, Lydgate is of limited means for that social class, and his medical practice tends as a matter of course to compromise his social status. At the same time, however, any compromise of his professional ideals for the sake of money is equally threatening to his sense of self-esteem. Lydgate, then, is vulnerable on two fronts—socially and professionally. Eliot carefully details his defensive pride by noting his "conceit" and "benevolent contempt" for the Middlemarchers he has come to join, and this pride, Eliot notes, is his "spot of commonness," his moral shortcoming, the chink in his moral armor (149–50). He is someone who bears himself "with the careless politeness of conscious superiority," who always "seemed to have the right clothes on by a certain natural affinity, without ever having to think about them" (167). Fred Vincy, for example, picks up on this attitude and considers Lydgate "a prig, tremendously conscious of his superiority" (672). Eliot makes it very clear that Lydgate alienates his medical colleagues by assuming his superior knowledge and shaming them for their misdiagnoses, for their old-fashioned treatment regimens, and particularly for dispensing and directly charging for their own prescriptions, which Lydgate recognizes invites a conflict of interest. Just as Lydgate shames his fellow practitioners for their scientific backwardness and provinciality, so he shames his rival for the affections of Rosamond Vincy, the unfortunate Ned Plymdale, when Ned shows interest in the fashionable literary annual *Keepsake*. Yet, as Eliot suggests, Lydgate's shaming of others merely underlines his own spot of commonness and vulnerability—his need to believe in his superiority.

It is only when Lydgate marries Rosamond Vincy, whose narcissism (which Eliot calls "egoism") is as unreflecting as his own, that he encounters an intractable object that cannot be subordinated to himself. As the genteelly educated daughter of a Middlemarch manufacturer, Rosamond has a social status she would prefer to rise above. She has in fact been trained throughout her life and schooling to concoct a narcissistic "romance" about how a gentleman will marry her and carry her away from Middlemarch. An early impression of Rosamond's narcissistic self-alienation is communicated through the image of Rosamond as "an actress of parts; . . . she even acted her own character, and so well, that she did not know it to be precisely her own" (117). Eliot magnificently depicts the somewhat condescending tenderness that Lydgate feels toward Rosamond, which is based on his sexist assumption that "the innate submissiveness of the goose" will beautifully correspond "to the strength of the gander" (356). When Lydgate is frustrated by Rosamond's resistance, his "tenderness . . . , which was both an emotional prompting and a well-considered resolve, was inevitably interrupted by . . . outbursts of indignation either ironical or remonstrant" (702). His condescension spills over into rage and contempt: by the end of the novel, Lydgate is calling Rosamond "his basil plant; and when she asked for an explanation, [he] said that basil was a plant which had flourished wonderfully on a murdered man's brains" (835).

Their entire relationship is in fact shamed-based: Lydgate feels Rosamond undercuts him through her want of openness, which may go so far as duplicity (666)—as when she countermands his instructions for letting their house, or when she secretly writes to his uncle, a baronet, to appeal for funds. Lydgate tries to shame Rosamond into compliance, but in this context she is in fact shame-less and sees herself as the victim of his want of proper solicitude, as the aggrieved party. Eventually, through her "negations" of his wishes and actions, through her passive and not-so-passive aggression, Rosamond, much to Lydgate's astonishment and horror, "had mastered him" (667).[4]

When the couple falls deeply into debt, Lydgate's continued pride, born of a fear of shame—"the pride which made him revolt from exposure as a debtor, or from asking men to help him with their money" (648)—isolates him. He particularly resents "the humiliation of asking" for financial assistance since he has prided himself on his independence (678). Lydgate's marriage to Rosamond and his sinking into debt produce in him a sense of "pleasureless yielding to the small solicitations of circumstance" (782–83) that will result in the abandonment of all of his old, proud ideals. When he turns briefly to gambling in hopes of finding a way out of the financial morass, Fred Vincy observes in Lydgate the "excited narrow consciousness" of a gambler as opposed to his habitual "air of self-possessed strength" (671). Although Lydgate once possessed "strength and mastery" (764), now "people think [him] disgraced" (757), believing that he has accepted a bribe from Bulstrode to keep from probing too deeply into Raffles's suspicious death. Lydgate feels shame when he is discovered gaming by Mr. Farebrother, and the "humiliations" Lydgate's pride suffers at this point in the novel, the "disgust with himself" he feels (677), appear in the book beside the various humiliations Bulstrode suffers as the disgraceful "past facts" of his life become known (686). As always in Eliot, this kind of contiguity and parallelism invites comparison and connection[5]—in this case between Lydgate's humiliation and Bulstrode's.

Another of the most fully realized depictions of narcissistic defenses against shame in *Middlemarch* is to be found in Dorothea's first husband, Edward Casaubon. Eliot shows in great detail how this pedant hopes to furnish the world with his magnum opus, a "Key to all Mythologies," which will show how "all the mythical systems or erratic mythical fragments in the world were corruptions of a tradition originally revealed" (24). At the same time, Eliot demonstrates that beneath the surface Casaubon has no real confidence in his work, and she pokes a great deal of fun at his sensitivity to the sneers of his critics—all named after fish—Carp, Tench, and Pike.

Even more importantly, after Dorothea Brooke marries him—as an

expression of her need to be married to a worthy, estimable husband—
once her disillusion sets in Casaubon feels especially bitter at what he
takes to be her criticism:

> Poor Mr. Casaubon! This suffering was harder to bear because it
> seemed like a betrayal: the young creature who had worshipped him
> with perfect trust had quickly turned into the critical wife. . . . To his
> suspicious interpretation Dorothea's silence now was a suppressed
> rebellion; a remark from her which he had not in any way anticipated
> was an assertion of conscious superiority; her gentle answers had an
> irritating cautiousness in them; and when she acquiesced it was a self-
> approved effort of forbearance. (418)

All of Dorothea's responses are now, in the context of their marriage,
interpreted by Casaubon as judgments on himself. Although Dorothea
does indeed have reason at this point to doubt the usefulness and validity of Casaubon's scholarship, she has in fact studiously censored her
critical thoughts about her husband. Instead, Eliot makes clear,
Casaubon is largely projecting his self-doubt onto his wife, so that she is
felt to be a "cruel outward accuser," giving voice to "those confused
[inward] murmurs which we try to call morbid, and strive against as if
they were the oncoming of numbness" (200). Before marriage,
Casaubon's self-doubts had been easier to set aside: "But Dorothea, now
that she was present—Dorothea, as a young wife, who herself had
shown an offensive capability of criticism, necessarily gave concentra-
tion to the uneasiness which had before been vague" (360).

Casaubon grows jealous, too, of the friendship between Dorothea
and his young cousin, Will Ladislaw, whom Casaubon knows to be critical of his scholarly work, but Eliot consistently locates the principal
source for Casaubon's feelings in his own anxiety, characterizing his jealousy as "a blight bred in the cloudy, damp, despondency of uneasy egoism" (243). He is "too doubtful—too uncertain of himself" (364–65).
His sense of self-worth is fragile, despite his presentation of himself to the
world as an important scholar. His pride in his public image is brittle,
and a corroding sense of vulnerability and shame lie just beneath the surface. Eliot offers a splendid image drawn from the world of classical
drama to express this discrepancy between public persona and inward
feelings of shame: "Doubtless some ancient Greek has observed that
behind the big mask and the speaking-trumpet, there must always be our
poor little eyes peeping as usual and our timorous lips more or less under
anxious control" (314). Less elegantly, perhaps, modern psychologists
have termed this phenomenon "the impostor syndrome" (Clance and
Imes); Casaubon's professional and scholarly grandiosity papers over a
deep conviction of his worthlessness and inadequacy.

In the section of the novel titled "The Dead Hand," Casaubon even tries to control Dorothea after his death—"from what is called fatty degeneration of the heart"! (423)—by attempting to mobilize her shame to prevent her remarriage to Will Ladislaw. At first the dying Casaubon hopes to extract a general, unspecified promise from Dorothea. The way he haltingly phrases his ambiguous request is "that you will let me know, deliberately, whether, in case of my death, you will carry out my wishes: whether you will avoid doing what I should deprecate, and apply yourself to do what I should desire" (477). Dorothea protests that "it is not right—to make a promise when I am ignorant what it will bind me to" (478). In fact, unaware of the intensity of Casaubon's jealousy of Will, she believes that her husband is attempting to yoke her to pursuing his mythological researches after his death. After hours of resistance and internal conflict, Dorothea is finally prepared to agree to Casaubon's cryptic request, but he dies before they meet again. The "dead hand," however, is expressed in the codicil to Casaubon's will that would deprive Dorothea of her late husband's property if she marries Ladislaw. Dorothea has no great need for the income from Casaubon's property, so the codicil is partly an effort publicly to shame Will and Dorothea into compliance.

The language Eliot uses to communicate Dorothea's uneasy resolve, prior to Casaubon's death, to submit to his demands is fascinating:

> She simply felt that she was going to say "Yes" to her own doom: she was too weak, too full of dread at the thought of inflicting a keen-edged blow on her husband to do anything but submit completely. . . . Neither law nor the world's opinion compelled her to this—only her husband's nature and her own compassion, only the ideal and not the real yoke of marriage. She saw clearly enough the whole situation, yet she was fettered: she could not smite the stricken soul that entreated hers. If that were weakness, Dorothea was weak. (481)

Dorothea's preparation to accede involves no active choice, but rather one into which she falls: "She simply felt that she was going to say 'Yes.'" The quality of that submission, based on a reluctance to cause injury, is conveyed by the passive agency in which Dorothea's thoughts are framed, by the imagery of containment and control that is contrasted with the imagery of a dreaded violent attack, and by the evasive, conditional narrative commentary that concludes the passage ("If that were weakness, Dorothea was weak").

After Casaubon dies and his will is read, however, Dorothea no longer feels bound by such "duteous devotion" to her husband. In fact, she is shocked at the way Casaubon has brought shame upon them both by making his unworthy fears and suspicions public:

The living, suffering man was no longer before her to awaken her pity: there remained only the retrospect of painful subjection to a husband whose thoughts had been lower than she had believed, whose exorbitant claims for himself had even blinded his scrupulous care for his own character, and made him defeat his own pride by shocking men of ordinary honor. (493)

The "dead hand" of the codicil is one last expression of Casaubon's narcissism and need to control, through the use of shame and the threat of financial penalty, but it fails utterly. In fact, Casaubon's effort to bind Dorothea after his death has the effect of liberating her, demonstrating that her husband was unworthy in a way she had never fully grasped.

SHAME AND VOCATION

Critics have long suggested that the issue of "vocation," what work the men and women will find to do, is a crucial one in this novel.[6] Lydgate's struggles with his medical career have already been touched upon, and many of the book's other characters—including Dorothea Brooke, Mr. Brooke, Mary Garth, Caleb Garth, the Rev. Camden Farebrother (who would have preferred becoming a naturalist rather than a cleric)—exemplify this theme in one way or another. In Fred Vincy and Will Ladislaw, particularly, the relation of vocation to shame is most fully worked out.

Fred Vincy is in some respects a rather minor character in the novel, yet thematically he is very important because of the light he casts on this matter of vocation. Fred, Rosamond's brother, is the child of an upper-middle-class manufacturer, and, indeed, his father has attained such important positions in the town of Middlemarch as alderman and mayor. Fred was sent off to "Omnibus College," but failed his examination and dropped out before obtaining his degree, which would have qualified him for a gentleman's career in the church. He spends much of the novel being rebuffed by Mary Garth, his admirable childhood sweetheart, on grounds that he has proved himself "to be fit for nothing in the world that is useful" (255). The only career Fred can visualize for himself is in the church, though Mary, who can see he has no true religious vocation, declares that she will not accept him if he chooses that path. Instead, she thinks his courtship of her ought to wait "until he has done something worthy," found some fitting work: "I should like better than anything to see him worthy of every one's respect. But please tell him I will not promise to marry him till then; I should shame and grieve my father and mother. He is free to choose some one else" (517). Meanwhile, Fred gambles, is repeatedly denounced by his father for his idle and spendthrift ways, and suffers the embarrassment of falling into debt and defaulting on that debt, with the result that his co-signer Caleb Garth, Mary's father, is liable. Mary's mother retaliates and tries to shame Fred by alluding to the Reverend Camden Farebrother's romantic interest in Mary; Farebrother is considered by Mrs. Garth and by most Middlemarchers to be a much more admirable and worthy man than Fred.

In essence, then, Fred's difficulty in finding a vocation involves shame; the woman he loves, her parents, and his own parents all try to shame him. He internalizes their judgments that he is foolish, ridiculous, and worthless because he can find no career.[7] Eventually Mary's father takes pity on Fred and brings him into his business of managing estates, though not before denouncing him for having developed a gentlemanly but illegible style of handwriting—one that is totally inappropriate for a man of business who must keep accurate records. Fred Vincy, then, represents the possibility that one might fail utterly at one's vocation, or even at discovering one's vocation. He manifests a young person's sense that his self is flawed and inadequate (cf. Morrison 86), and as such Fred represents the shameful obverse of that vocational grandiosity with which characters like Bulstrode, Casaubon, and Lydgate present themselves to the world.

Vocation is also a crucial issue for Will Ladislaw, who starts out as a dilettantish painter, imagines for a time he might become a poet or perhaps a journalist, and eventually finds his metier in politics. In the beginning Will is dependent on his cousin, Mr. Casaubon, for financial support, and yet he clearly is sensitive to Casaubon's feelings that he will never amount to much. In fact, Eliot hints that some of Will's attack on Casaubon's erudition is motivated by the feeling that his own perseverance and accomplishments are being criticized by his cousin (207). Will's attacks on Casaubon's competence, in other words, partly reflect his own feelings of inadequacy and self-reproach. Like Casaubon, Will sometimes interprets Dorothea's most innocuous remarks as expressions of criticism; when she pleads her ignorance about Will's drawing and about art in general, Will "took her words for a covert judgment, and was certain she thought his sketch detestable" (80). Later Eliot records Will's sense that he is "making a fool of himself" (468) by hanging around Middlemarch and working for Mr. Brooke, and she dramatizes this by meticulously documenting Will's embarrassing attempt to catch a glimpse of Dorothea in Lowick Church. Before this fiasco ends, Will is "utterly ridiculous, out of temper, and miserable" (473). After Casaubon's death, Will is motivated by "his proud resolve to give the lie beforehand to any suspicion that he would play the needy adventurer seeking a rich woman" (547), and his "pride became a repellent force, keeping him asunder from Dorothea" (546). Later in the novel, too, his pride defends against feelings of shame when he forbids himself to express his love for Dorothea so long as he lacks fortune and position. Similarly, he spurns Bulstrode's offer of money to repair the wrong once done Will's mother on the grounds that his mother had originally refused money gotten from the same tainted source and in the belief that Dorothea would think less of him for accepting Bulstrode's offer.

The worst crisis in Will's life develops when Dorothea discovers him with Rosamond in what appears to be a romantic scene, and Will feels ashamed at himself and angry at Rosamond, whom he considers the cause of his disgrace in Dorothea's eyes. In the meantime, the Middle-marchers believe there is indeed a scandal brewing between Rosamond and Will, as they had earlier suspected that there must have been a rela-tionship between Dorothea and Will while Casaubon still lived; Mrs. Cadwallader, in particular, steps up her attacks on Will as "the grand-son of a thieving Jewish pawnbroker" (772) and the son of "a rebellious Polish fiddler or dancing master" (819). Society, in other words, seeks to shame Will and thrust scandal upon him, while Will struggles to maintain his independence and reputation while at the same time trying to discover his life's work. The key question for Will throughout is what Dorothea will think of him, how she will judge him, and the critical arena for this judgment is in the context of vocation, what he will become. Will's quest for a vocation and respectability, then, is a con-stant struggle against a vulnerability to shame.

MINOR CHARACTERS, SHAMEFUL SCRIPTS, AND CANDOR

Shame is an issue for a very great number of minor characters in the novel. For example, Mr. Brooke, Dorothea's uncle and guardian, puffs himself up into a political figure, purchases a newspaper, and runs for parliament. Eventually these bids for admiration crumble, particularly when an effigy of Brooke is used to mock him at a campaign rally, an event that rapidly deteriorates as the candidate is pelted with rotten eggs. A telling point against Brooke is that he cannot truly be a "reform" candidate while he exploits all the tenants living on his estate and the estate itself goes to rack and ruin. These are issues that Brooke's genteel friends, Sir James Chettam and Mrs. Cadwallader, repeatedly try to raise with him, in anticipation of the efforts of his political enemies to shame and discredit him.

Sir James Chettam himself suffers shame when Dorothea Brooke rejects him as a suitor in favor of Casaubon. Chettam's injured pride causes him to turn romantically toward Dorothea's sister, Celia, after Mrs. Cadwallader works on his injured sensibility by suggesting that

Celia has always been interested in him. As the narrator comments, "Pride helps us, and pride is not a bad thing when it only urges us to hide our own hurts and not to hurt others" (62). Later on, both Sir James and his wife, Celia, repeatedly attempt to shame Dorothea in an effort to dissuade her from any plan of marrying Will Ladislaw.

Peter Featherstone uses shame to control his relatives. He forces Fred Vincy, for instance, to obtain a note from Bulstrode certifying that Fred has not been advanced any money based on expectations of an inheritance from Featherstone. By allowing these imputations to stand unanswered, Fred's father explains to Bulstrode in requesting such a letter, "you might as well slander Fred" (130). Shame is the means by which Featherstone gains power and control over all those around him, playing one set of relations off against another; and, in part, it is the way many of his relatives, whom Eliot terms "the Christian carnivora" (331), seek to control him, as they remind him of their family connection, which they hope he will honor in his will. After Featherstone's death, he continues to exercise power over his greedy relatives through another exercise of the "dead hand," by leaving his property to his illegitimate son, Joshua Rigg, an act that expresses both Featherstone's defiance of his family and his desire to shame the lot of them.[8]

Sarah Dunkirk, who is not strictly speaking a character at all but part of the book's prehistory, exists largely because of her proud rejection of shame. She is Will Ladislaw's mother, and the only thing the reader is told about her is that she ran away from the family of Bulstrode's first wife because their wealth derived from pawning stolen property.

Perhaps the character who most directly embodies conventional, genteel opinion is Mrs. Cadwallader, whom Eliot employs to exemplify the use of shame as a social sanction in the novel. The verse epigraph that Eliot places at the head of the chapter in which Mrs. Cadwallader is introduced clearly points to her character: "My lady's tongue is like the meadow blades,/ That cut you stroking them with idle hand./ Nice cutting is her function" (52). In the chapter proper she is described as having "a turn of tongue that let[s] you know who she was, . . . a lady of immeasurably high birth, descended as it were, from unknown earls" (53). Speaking from this position of social eminence, she is quick to tell Mr. Brooke exactly "what people say of you, to be quite frank" and to let him know when he is only mouthing "a piece of clap-trap you have got ready for the hustings" (54). Later in the novel, she spreads gossip to Dorothea about Ladislaw, who "is making a sad dark-blue scandal by warbling continually with your Mr Lydgate's wife, who they tell me is as pretty as pretty can be" (628). In a very telling, extended metaphor, soon after Mrs. Cadwallader is introduced into the novel, Eliot turns a "microscope" on a hypothetical microorganism to find that "a stronger lens" reveals "certain tiniest hairlets which make vortices for [its] victims while the swallower waits passively at his receipt of custom. In this way, metaphorically speaking, a strong lens applied to Mrs. Cadwallader's matchmaking will show a play of minute causes producing what may be called thought and speech vortices to bring her the sort of food she needed" (83). This is Eliot's metaphorical portrait, then, of her foremost example of snobbery, matchmaking, gossip, scandal, and the operations of shame in the book. More than anyone else, Mrs. Cadwallader is the voice of Middlemarch society.

In yet another striking figure Eliot embodies the operation of all of these strong social pressures in her personification of the "Candor" that makes a Middlemarch wife aware "that the town held a bad opinion of her husband. . . . To be candid, in Middlemarch phraseology, meant, to use an early opportunity of letting your friends know that you did not take a cheerful view of their capacity, their conduct, or their position; and a robust candor never waited to be asked for its opinion" (741). Thus Harriet Bulstrode does not have long to wait before she learns of her husband's disgrace. "Candor" in Middlemarch directly expresses the town's censure, explicitly marking an individual's shame and fall from grace.

ARDOR AND DISILLUSION

The other side of the coin of shame is, as has already been suggested, the "ardor" manifested by a number of Eliot's young idealists. To Eliot, this word suggests an ambitious idealism, fervor, zeal, passion. The word itself derives from the Latin *ardere*, meaning "to burn." In a sense, the fire of ardor is the obverse of blushing, which is a shameful burning. Ardor is the pride of achievement and accomplishment, to which the intensity of youthful idealism might lead.

Although much of *Middlemarch* concerns itself with ardor, the fear of failure, of not accomplishing one's goals, is very much present as well. Eliot's "Prelude" to the novel emphatically introduces the theme of "ardor" by citing the case of Saint Theresa of Avila, founder of a religious order, and by describing "her flame" and her "passionate, ideal nature [which] demanded an epic life" (3). Eliot insists, however, that "the social lot of women" constrains them, and in modern times one frequently encounters a young woman whose ardor can find no socially acceptable expression: "Here and there is born a Saint Theresa, foundress of nothing, whose loving heart-beats and sobs after an unattained goodness tremble off and are dispersed among hindrances, instead of centering in some long-recognizable deed" (4). The novel's "Finale" returns to the example of Saint Theresa; however, it more positively iterates the themes and images of the "Prelude," implying that even the "unhistoric acts" of an ardent woman may be "incalculably diffusive" on those around her (896), rather than, as the "Prelude" would have it, merely "dispersed among hindrances." Diffusion, in other words, carries a very different weight than dispersal. The entire book, from its very beginning to its final words, chronicles this oscillation between achievement and failure, between ardor and disappointment, between pride and shame.

Nor does the book foreclose the possibilities of an ironic kind of "success" at the end. Tertius Lydgate becomes "what is called a successful man," with a medical practice among the well-to-do, "alternating . . . between London and a Continental bathing place. . . . But he always regarded himself as a failure: he had not done what he once meant to do" (834–35). Eliot ironically interweaves success and failure: though the world thinks Lydgate has succeeded, he regards himself as having failed. Yet what Lydgate has actually achieved might—given his social background and personal limitations—be regarded as more realistic than his grandiose scheme of becoming a hero of medicine, an outcome available to relatively few.

One other way of gauging the downside of ardor and the idealistic quest for vocation is to note that perhaps the novel's most memorable moment is Dorothea Brooke's fall into deep despair during her honeymoon visit to Rome. Casaubon has buried himself in the Vatican library to do research, and Dorothea feels the crushing (if still inarticulable) weight of her disillusion with the ideals of her marriage as she confronts the visible decay of Rome, seeing "ruins and basilicas, palaces and colossi, set in the midst of a sordid present, where all that was living and warm-blooded seemed sunk in the deep degeneracy of a superstition divorced from reverence." The city itself is a "vast wreck of ambitious ideals, sensuous and spiritual," an image of ideals smashed and left in fragments, drained of all vitality. This passage culminates in the remarkable description of "the red drapery which was being hung [in St. Peter's] for Christmas spreading itself everywhere like a disease of the retina" (193–94), perhaps the most striking image of unhappiness and disillusion to be found anywhere in fiction.[9]

The core affects in *Middlemarch* oscillate, then, between an idealistic hopefulness and somber disillusion, between ardor and depression. The obverse of all the proud hopefulness in the novel is a profound sense of failure and despair.

DOROTHEA'S SYMPATHY AND WOMEN'S ROLES

At a critical point early in *Middlemarch*, Eliot asks a rhetorical question that has become famous in the history of the novel, "But why always Dorothea?" (278). It is a question that, one third of the way into the novel, deflects our attention from the consciousness of the book's heroine and invites us to engage with the thought processes of other, perhaps less central and less admirable characters, in order that we may see things from their points of view and understand their behaviors as well. The question is Eliot's quintessential demonstration in the narrative itself of the need for "sympathy" rather than "egoism," if we are ever to understand one another and function ethically in a social milieu.

However, since this essay has largely put Dorothea to one side in its discussion of shame, it seems appropriate to bring her back to center stage in order to consider how Eliot's crucial theme of "sympathy" relates to the emotion of shame. The crisis of Dorothea's story occurs when she suddenly comes upon Will Ladislaw and Rosamond Vincy in what appears to be an intensely romantic moment. Will's response is shame and embarrassment at being discovered in what looks like a compromising situation, and Dorothea's initial response is "jealous indignation and disgust," "burning scorn":

> But the base prompting which makes a woman more cruel to a rival than to a faithless lover, could have no strength of recurrence in Dorothea when the dominant spirit of justice within her had once overcome the tumult and had once shown her the truer measure of things. All the active thought with which she had before been representing to herself the trials of Lydgate's lot, and this young marriage union which, like her own, seemed to have its hidden as well as evident troubles—all this vivid sympathetic experience returned to her now as a power: it asserted itself as acquired knowledge asserts itself and will not let us see as we saw in the day of our ignorance. She said to her own irremediable grief that it should make her more helpful, instead of driving her back from effort. (788)

Dorothea is aware of her injury, but she overcomes her jealousy by a conscious, willed sympathy—or empathy, since she is able to identify the difficulties of the Lydgates' marriage with her own earlier marital problems with Casaubon. Dorothea subsequently returns to Rosamond's house to offer financial and emotional support, and as a result prompts Rosamond's acknowledgment that Dorothea has misinterpreted the earlier scene and that Will is not in love with Rosamond. The narrator offers this commentary on Dorothea's extraordinary efforts to assist the Lydgates: "It is given to us sometimes even in our everyday life to witness the saving influence of a noble nature, the divine efficacy of rescue that may lie in a self-subduing act of fellowship" (803).

Despite the fact, then, that Middlemarch exists in a secular universe of social judgments and sanctions, a world governed largely by the shaming of Mrs. Cadwallader and the community's "Candor," there are other values that may be invoked. Eliot insists on the unity of society, its organic relations: this novel is not titled "Dorothea Brooke," as it might well have been, but "Middlemarch." Dorothea's essential virtue, from Eliot's point of view, is her desire to protect individuals from calumny, from false or distorting accusations that shame. A crucial aspect of Dorothea's character is her readiness to trust people, unless or until that trust is proven to be misplaced. Thus she continues to feel the obligations of her marriage to Casaubon, almost to the point of pathology, even after she has learned the limits of his affection for her and has come to doubt the value of his intellectual pursuits: "It seemed as if she must quell every impulse in her except the yearnings of faithfulness and compassion" (592). Similarly, Dorothea absolutely refuses to suspect Will Ladislaw of any unworthy pursuit of herself while Casaubon is alive, and trusts in his integrity after Casaubon's codicil is disclosed, even though Will himself feels "I have been grossly insulted in [Dorothea's] eyes and in the eyes of others. There has been a mean implication against my character" (631). Finally, Dorothea is absolutely loyal in defending Lydgate's probity when the townfolk by and large believe he has been influenced by Bulstrode's "bribe"; Dorothea is readier publicly to defend Lydgate against these suggestions of improper influence than Lydgate is in his own mind. This is how she expresses the radically self-sacrificing loyalty she acts upon: "Mr. Lydgate would understand that if his friends hear a calumny about him their first wish must be to justify him. What do we live for, if it is not to make life less difficult to each other?" (733–34). "I believe that people are almost always better than their neighbors think they are," Dorothea notes, and the narrator adds: "Some of her intensest experience in the last two years had set her mind strongly in opposition to any unfavorable construction of others" (733).

Eliot's point is the very Victorian one that her world is threatened by fragmentation and atomism. Individuals, left to their own devices, may act entirely out of "egoism," without any shared set of values. Because egoistic individuals still live in a society, there may be social sanctions, but they are likely to be applied without a sound ethical basis. They will be based on a struggle for personal power and ascendancy, and they will be founded upon presumptions of guilt, rather than an empathic generosity. Eliot presents "sympathy" or compassion as a means of defending against shame. It invokes belief, trust, and loyalty to individuals to whom one has grown attached—regardless of whatever accusations and imputations are abroad. It mobilizes a resistance to conventional social judgments, to what "the world believes" (738).[10] Dorothea's energies, her passion and ardor, resist shame and disillusion. The shame of the blush is transformed into the idealizing flame of ardor, and a certain naivete is preferable to suspicion too readily deployed:

> While [Dorothea] was full of pity for the visible mistakes of others, she had not yet any material within her experience for subtle constructions and suspicions of hidden wrong. But that simplicity of hers, holding up an ideal for others in her believing conception of them, was one of the great powers of her womanhood. (772)

One of the reasons Eliot is so interested in depicting resistance to shame is that she perceives it as something to which women are particularly vulnerable. Much of *Middlemarch* is concerned with the question of what it is that women can do in a society in which men are predominant,[11] and, as Gershen Kaufman declares, "Shame is the affect of inferiority" (17). The best-known and most pointed expression of this sense of limitation occurs in the book's "Finale," where Dorothea's marriage to Will Ladislaw is described. Ladislaw will eventually enter Parliament, where he can work for reform, and Dorothea will provide "wifely help":

> Many who knew her, thought it a pity that so substantive and rare a creature should be absorbed into the life of another, and be only known in a certain circle as a wife and mother. But no one stated exactly what else that was in her power she ought rather to have done. (836)

This popular opinion is still a kind of shaming of Dorothea, a corroding skepticism. Eliot knows that, rather than ideal conditions, we live in "an imperfect social state, in which great feelings will often take the aspect of error, and great faith the aspect of illusion" (839). She insists, however, that it is preferable to live in trust and belief in one another, even though that might risk "the aspect of illusion" and even occasional error, than to live in a society dominated by shame and skeptical disbelief.[12]

NOTES

1. One classic discussion of "the presentation of feeling" in *Middlemarch* is Barbara Hardy's "*Middlemarch* and the Passions." Hardy notes that Eliot places her passionate moments in a densely social world: "The characters relate to each other's emotions, and are changed by the relation" (10).

2. Welsh is one of the few critics to allude to shame in *Middlemarch*, but he focuses primarily on Eliot's complex representation of the pursuit of knowledge,

showing how one aspect of this is represented by the acquisition of information that results in blackmail, scandal, and exposure. Welsh's emphasis finally is on themes related to knowledge and accountability rather than on affect.

3. Helen Block Lewis ("Shame and Guilt" 248) and Léon Wurmser (28), are among the modern psychiatrists who explore the role of narcissism and grandiosity as defenses against shame and self-hatred.

4. Léon Wurmser closes his book with a wonderful description of such shame-based relationships, one which could apply almost word for word to the Lydgates: "Where the other is *used*, partially or fully, emotionally or physically, unconsciously or consciously, love flees and shame enters. This happens where part of the other is disregarded, where calculation and envy, comparing, competing, and accounting take over, where the growth of the other is put down, where stinginess enters and the demand for one's rights and dues is thrown up, where 'I am hurt' is more important than 'what may I have done wrong?' Most of all, shame demolishingly takes over when one has given all of oneself only to be responded to by a selfish, calculating demand, by duplicity, a cold stare, a sarcastic comment. There is no greater humiliation than giving oneself trustingly and absolutely and being countered with selfishness and betrayal. Then privacy protected by the walls of shame becomes the only refuge in such a stunted relationship. Shame thus is . . . the night side of love" (309).

5. Barbara Hardy (*Novels* 78–134) and David Carroll, for example, stress the way Eliot uses repetition, parallels, and contrasts.

6. Alan Mintz offers the most complete discussion of the importance of this subject to George Eliot.

7. Gershen Kaufman considers the relation between "failure in vocation" and shame (53–54), and Andrew Morrison notes that rather than speaking explicitly about shame, his patients generally "speak instead of feeling foolish, ridiculous, pathetic, insignificant, invisible, or worthless" (196), which is very much the way Fred Vincy judges himself.

8. Gershen Kaufman offers a good, brief description of the way in which "scripts that aim at maximizing power over others and maintaining control . . . constitute [a] strategy for protecting the self against shame" (101). Featherstone is basically a mass of such power scripts.

9. Helen Block Lewis is among the clinicians who argue that "shame is a central component in depression. . . . Depressed people feel helpless to affect their destiny at the same time that their (helpless) self seems to them the appropriate target of hostility" ("Shame and Guilt" 250–51). See also Lewis, "The Role of Shame in Depression over the Life Span."

10. In a more skeptical modern age, Léon Wurmser argues that such unqualified and idealized love can itself be a defense against shame, a means of undoing a fundamental sense of deprivation and unlovability in oneself (199–200).

11. Helen Block Lewis has written tellingly about shame as a particular problem for women in Western societies (*Sex* 203–19).

12. I wish to thank my spouse, Louella Elizabeth Hirsch, for her many valuable editorial and interpretive contributions to this essay.

WORKS CITED

Carroll, David R. "Unity through Analogy: An Interpretation of *Middlemarch*." *Victorian Studies* 2 (1959): 305–16.

Clance, Pauline R., and Suzanne A. Imes. "The Impostor Phenomenon in High Achieving Women: Dynamics and Therapeutic Intervention." *Psychotherapy: Theory, Research & Practice* 15 (1978): 241–47.

Eliot, George. *Middlemarch*. Ed. Rosemary Ashton. New York: Penguin, 1994.

Hardy, Barbara. "*Middlemarch* and the Passions." *This Particular Web: Essays on Middlemarch*. Ed. Ian Adam. Toronto: U of Toronto P, 1975. 3–21.

———. *The Novels of George Eliot: A Study in Form*. New York: Oxford UP, 1967.

Kaufman, Gershen. *The Psychology of Shame: Theory and Treatment of Shame-Based Syndromes*. New York: Springer, 1989.

Lewis, Helen Block. "The Role of Shame in Depression over the Life Span." *The Role of Shame in Symptom Formation*. Ed. Helen Block Lewis. Hillsdale, N.J.: Lawrence Erlbaum, 1987. 29–50.

———. *Sex and the Superego: Psychic War in Men and Women*. Rev. ed. Hillsdale, N.J.: Lawrence Erlbaum, 1987.

———. "Shame and Guilt in Human Nature." *Object and Self: A Developmental Approach*. Ed. Saul Tuttman, Carol Kaye, and Muriel Zimmerman. New York: International Universities P, 1981.

Mintz, Alan. *George Eliot and the Novel of Vocation*. Cambridge, Mass.: Harvard UP, 1978.

Morrison, Andrew P. *Shame: The Underside of Narcissism*. Hillsdale, N.J.: Analytic P, 1989.

Welsh, Alexander. *George Eliot and Blackmail*. Cambridge, Mass.: Harvard UP, 1985.

Wurmser, Léon. *The Mask of Shame*. Baltimore: Johns Hopkins UP, 1981.

CHAPTER 5

George Eliot and
Dilemmas of the Female Child

Joseph D. Lichtenberg

Great creative artists apply their empathic sensitivity to the depiction of dilemmas of human development and, thereby, call our attention to problems that years later scientists may study by more laborious means. This statement is so well authenticated in literary criticism that by now it has become a cliché. Nonetheless, each reiteration of the evidence for it opens new pathways of understanding. I shall use one tiny incident in *Middlemarch* to illustrate this thesis once again.

Middlemarch, unarguably one of George Eliot's best novels, takes up, among many other matters, the fate of women born, living, and dying in the England of the nineteenth century. A brilliant creative writer who found it necessary to publish under a male pseudonym would gravitate naturally to depicting the struggle of women for self-realization against the background of male dominance. *Middlemarch* takes up the fate of four young women. Celia is attractive, conventional, and practical. From an upper-class family, she marries well, cares for others, and is extravagant only in her infatuation for her baby. Mary Garth is likewise a competent pragmatist, comes from the rising middle class, and acts as the counterbalance to the immaturity and improvidence of her childhood lover. The two main characters are Rosamond and Dorothea. Rosie is blessed or cursed with stunning good looks, and, as other Eliot beauties, is totally self-centered and obstinately devoted to getting her way. In the adversity of her husband's failures, she learns little that humanizes her egotism.

Dorothea is endowed with the same burden as her creator—vision, creativity, ambition, and brilliance—and no opportunity to learn how to use those gifts. Full of energy, she lurches into several mistaken efforts to lead a useful life. Like Mary Ann Evans, Dorothea finally perseveres, but not as a George Eliot. Eliot makes clear the nature of Dorothea's accomplishment and its limitation: being "absorbed into the life of another, and . . . only known in a certain circle as a wife and mother" (764). Eliot explains: "But no one stated exactly what else that was in her power she ought rather to have done" (764). The "determining acts of her life . . . were the mixed result of a young and noble impulse struggling amidst the conditions of an imperfect social state. . . . For there is no creature whose inward being is so strong that it is not greatly determined by what lies outside it" (765–66). As her consolation to the women of her time for accepting Dorothea's solution, Eliot adds "the growing good of the world is partly dependent on unhistoric acts" (766).

The story of the Brooke sisters, Celia and Dorothea, Rosamond Vincy, Mary Garth, and their families and husbands provides the complex interwoven tapestry of the novel. In addition, *Middlemarch*, like the novels of its time, is enriched immeasurably by vignettes that offer the author's observations on a host of matters. I have chosen one vignette that I believe provides an underpinning to the basic structure of the novel. This brief episode dramatically portrays determining conditions for what lies within and outside a growing female child's power, and demonstrates the scorching impact of maternal shaming on the daughter's sense of self-worth.

Mrs. Garth is making apple puff pastry while giving a lesson in grammar to young Ben and his sister Letty. Ben is protesting, "I hate grammar. What's the use of it?" Letty, with an air of superiority, defends her mother's position only to have her mother undercut her defense as referring to pronunciation, not grammar. Mrs. Garth returns to her focus on Ben, chiding him for eating an apple peel and challenges him that if he doesn't learn to make people understand him they would turn away from him as a tiresome person. What would he do then? she challenges.

> "I shouldn't care, I should leave off," said Ben.
> "I see you are getting tired and stupid, Ben," said Mrs. Garth, accustomed to these obstructive arguments from her male offspring. Having finished her pies, she moved towards the clothes-horse, and said, "Come here and tell me the story I told you on Wednesday about Cincinnatus."
> "I know! He was a farmer," said Ben.
> "Now, Ben, he was a Roman—let *me* tell," said Letty, using her elbow contentiously.
> "You silly thing, he was a Roman farmer, and he was ploughing."
> "Yes, but before that—that didn't come first—people wanted him," said Letty.

"Well, but you must say what sort of a man he was first," insisted Ben. "He was a wise man, like my father, and that made the people want his advice. And he was a brave man, and could fight. And so could my father—couldn't he mother?"

"Now, Ben, let me tell the story straight on, as mother told it to us," said Letty, frowning. "Please, mother, tell Ben not to speak."

"Letty, I am ashamed of you," said her mother, wringing out the caps from the tub. "When your brother began, you ought to have waited to see if he could not tell the story. How rude you look, pushing and frowning, as if you wanted to conquer with your elbows! Cincinnatus I am sure, would have been sorry to see his daughter behave so." (Mrs. Garth delivered this awful sentence with much majesty of enunciation, and Letty felt that between repressed volubility and general disesteem, that of the Romans inclusive, life was already a painful affair.) (222–23)

Eliot expresses her meaning unmistakably. The mother is accustomed to obstructive arguments from her male offspring. She provides him with a ready excuse—he is getting tired. Toward her female offspring her tone differs totally. Where the reader recognizes a bright eager girl who absorbs information and desperately wants to satisfy the hunger of her curiosity about the world, Mrs. Garth sees a child who *is* rude, pushing, frowning, and aggressive. Mrs. Garth does not see Letty as *behaving* in a frustrated manner as a consequence of her inability to get her superiority of information confirmed. She cannot recognize that instead of being shamed and humiliated, were Letty to be appreciated, she would become more calm and civil about her intelligence. Mrs. Garth sees Letty only as a rude, out-of-control *person*. Where Ben can lay claim to his father by conflating him with Cincinnatus, Letty's mother tells her she is a sorry example of a daughter. Letty learns it is Ben's learning, not hers that Mrs. Garth cares about. The shaming that Letty is subjected to has a depersonalizing, objectifying effect and a predictable consequence: a disesteem that makes life "a painful affair."

The vignette I have quoted occupies but one page in a long book. The textural significance is incontrovertible, but how much weight did Eliot mean to give it? Neither Ben nor Letty is important in any of the main plots. Eliot provides an answer in her finale. She reviews the fate of each of the four principal women, their spouses and progeny. And alone of any of the other many characters, she recalls Ben and Letty and repeats the theme of the vignette:

Ben and Letty Garth, who were uncle and aunt before they were well in their teens, disputed much as to whether nephews or nieces were more desirable; Ben contending that it was clear girls were good for less than boys, else they would not be always in petticoats, which showed how little they were meant for: whereupon Letty, who argued much from books, got angry in replying that God made coats of skins for Adam and Eve alike—also it occurred to her that in the East the men too wore petticoats. But this latter argument, obscuring the majesty of the former, was one too many, for Ben answered contemptuously, "The more spooneys they!" and immediately appealed to his mother whether boys were not better than girls. Mrs. Garth pronounced that both were alike naughty but that boys were undoubtedly stronger, could run faster, and throw with more precision to a greater distance. With this oracular sentence, Ben was well satisfied, not minding the naughtiness; but Letty took it ill, her feeling of superiority being stronger than her muscles. (761–62)

This oracular pronouncement was delivered by a mother who took pride in *her* knowledge and was a dedicated educator.

Two questions arise that lie outside the purview of the creative artist: Does similar biased positive treatment of boys and negative of girls by mothers occur frequently? Besides the pride-shattering effect on girls can other less obvious effects occur? I turn to development research[1] and clinical experience with adult analysands for answers.[2]

The immediate problem these anecdotes present lies in the different responses of Mrs. Garth to the behavior of Ben and Letty—both of whom acted in ways that were aversive to her. Were these differential responses idiosyncratic to Eliot's characters or representative of a cultural bias that the artist intuitively recognized?

Universally we recognize that life begins with the gender distinction as paramount. "It's a boy!" "It's a girl!" No other designation announces a birth with such evocativeness. Not birth weight, assurances of health, lusty cry, or even the state of the mother will satisfy the curiosity of parents and family members. Each parent is poised between two fantasy elaborations—one for his or her "boy," and one for his or her "girl." The sex of the newborn leads each important caregiver (parents, grandparents) to cycle-in their conscious and unconscious expectations of the boy or girl. When these expectations are incompatible, the child develops in a world of conflicting pulls that will affect his or her gender role and under very aberrant conditions his or her gender identity.[3]

Babies are not, however, passive, helpless victims, their genital anatomy alone determining their destiny. Each baby girl and boy has biological givens that affect the unfolding of their gender identity and role. Sensory responses are generally well organized in girl newborns. Girls have greater responsiveness to taste, greater mouth activity, and more tongue involvement during feeding, as well as greater overall tactile sensitivity (Korner). Thus, a mother may find that the optimal arousal for her girl baby comes with gentler handling and that she responds especially well to oral comforting. Female infants at twelve weeks of age are more sensitive to auditory signals than are boys. Moss found that girls are talked to more than boys. Females who were touched, vocalized with, smiled at, and played with scored higher on the Bayley MDT, whereas boys with very actively interactional mothers scored more poorly.

Mothers have a greater tendency to maintain physical closeness with six-month-old girls than with same-age boys (Goldberg and Lewis). By the end of the first year, femininity and masculinity are well established in the reciprocal social interplay of infant and family (Fast). Girls spend more time than boys in actual physical contact with their mothers in free-play situations (Fisher 71–72). When separated from mother by an artificial barrier, the boy's solution is to explore means to go around or climb over, the girl's solution is to signal distress by crying with arms up in a gesture of appeal (Korner).

Within the first year, mothers can be observed to favor their son's more autonomous *activity* and their daughter's greater sensitivity in their *interrelatedness*. By fourteen months, girls are more likely to remain closer to their mothers and less apt to be involved in conflicts over will than boys. By eighteen months, sons indicate they value more highly their mother when she is less directive and intrusive while daughters show a more positive response to their mother when she involves herself and directs the play. By twenty-four months, boys withdraw from a negatively expressive mother while girls are relatively unaffected. During the toddler period, girls are more inclined to remain within an aversive engagement, increasing their skills in close encounter struggles with their mother. Girls get a complex dual message from their mothers: they are rewarded with positive affect when they can themselves move away from mother and look after themselves, but get indications of mother's more sensitive attachment when they maintain good emotional and behavioral control and are closely attentive to mother's emotions. These studies provide strong indications that within the first few years of life distinctly different values are set for what mothers prize in their sons and daughters and for what sons and daughters prize in their mother's responses to them.

Lewis found that positive specific attributions were higher for three–year-old boys and negative specific attributions were higher for girls. Lewis relates these findings in studies of toddlers to the finding that in response to academic performance "[w]omen are socialized to blame themselves for their failures, but not to reward themselves for their successes; the reverse is true for men" (103). In addition, women are likely to make internal attribution for their failures and external attribution for their successes. Lewis reports a finding that dovetails exactly with Eliot's vignette of Letty and Ben: "When a female child shows anger, parents use a variety of techniques, including direct punishment and love withdrawal, to inhibit her behavior. But when a male child exhibits aggressive behavior, his parents make little or no effort to inhibit his behavior; indeed, they may even actively encourage such behavior" (100). Women are thus more apt to experience shame in response to both problem-solving failure and the expression of anger.

In films on moral development, Emde demonstrated gender differences in responses to the task of finishing a story containing a moral dilemma. One story involved a mother and two children. The mother doll tells the children she is going out and they should be good and not go into the shelves when she is gone. The mother doll is then placed in a box near the table. The dilemma develops from the younger sibling cutting him or herself and needing a bandaid resting on the shelf. The girl responded with great distress, saying, "Mother said not to go on the shelf." She wishes for mother to return; and, before the interviewer can intervene, she runs around the table and retrieves the mother doll. She finishes the story by having Mother reassure her that she is a good girl for coming to get her and that she will get the bandaid for the cut. The little boy finishes the story differently. He has the boy doll climb up and get the bandaid for his brother. He has mother return and tell him she is angry with him. He replies defiantly, "I don't care."

Another story involves dolls portraying a boy, his same-age friend, and his younger brother, or the same combination of three girls. Through the interviewer, the friend tells the boy or girl, "I won't play with you unless you get rid of your younger brother" (or sister). The child is then to complete the story with the dolls. The story the little girl makes up resolves the problem by talking with the friend urging her to be nice, and all three end up playing together. In contrast, the little boy sends his brother away. He tells the interviewer that he had to send him away because he and his friend were wearing the same kind of shirt while his little brother wasn't. Emde's films add dramatized confirmation to the by-now universal distinction that girls are cultured to place their highest values on relational caretaking concerns while boys place higher value on independence, direct instrumental solutions, and assertiveness.

To this point, the emphasis has been on mother-daughter or parent-daughter influences. In a society where males are more dominant, the forces that shape male beliefs about women directly affect women's views of themselves (Lichtenberg and Lazar). Women, who focus more on relationships, have an awareness of and a tendency to accommodate to the preferences, attitudes, fears, and hostilities of the males with whom they are involved. A man's experiences of intimacy with women resonate with memories of his first intimacy with his mother, which if hurtful or humiliating, will predispose to a self-protective, dehumanizing hostility in his treatment of women. In Ben's view, Letty and all girls then can be viewed as dehumanized "spooneys" who wear petticoats and by implication are physically inferior. In her choice of "spooney," Eliot has Ben contemptuously call girls silly, sentimental fools.

Eliot alludes to the fact that for Letty and many other young girls a central injury is the trauma of inequality, of being valued less as a female from infancy on. Letty understandably views herself as much less valued than her male brother. Despite her quick wit, and learning, the devaluing view of her mother diminishes her view of herself as a unique person with a right to separateness, autonomy, and the pride of personal agency, intelligence, and competence. Benjamin, Person, Stoller, Dinnerstein, and others document the pressure on girls to submit to a view of themselves as a passive object of man's desires, an "it" instead of an "I."

What are possible outcomes of this deprivation of support for a girl's individuality, subjectivity, skills, and talents? She may develop a guilt-laden hunger for the absent mirroring of her own unique sense of personal agency, coupled with rage and a sense of despair about achieving this mirroring in a patriarchal world. This grouping of hunger, rage, shame, and despair is a neglected source of female masochistic behavior and various forms of hostile erotic fantasies (Lichtenberg and Lazar).

This assault on her self-esteem and positive feelings can lead a woman to submission to a powerful male who is consciously viewed as an idealized source of respect and happiness. Unconsciously, the relationship with the man may provide the woman with a much needed vicarious exhilaration of power as construed in a masochistic fantasy. In a straightforwardly pragmatic way, Mary Anne Evans's subterfuge of submergence into "George Eliot" is a symbolic abandonment of self in the quest for the opportunities her talents deserved (as in her way Letty's also deserved).

In an earlier similar sister-brother pair, involving Maggie Tulliver, a natural scholar, and Tom, a reluctant student, in *The Mill on the Floss*, Eliot reveals another outcome. Despite Tom's overt contemptuous view of girls and his painfully cruel treatment of her, Maggie dotes on him. With all of the characteristics of a young girl's crush,[4] she makes gaining Tom's affection and attention a central source of her happiness. His rejection and abandonment of her sends her to risk her life with gypsies in her desperation to be appreciated.

I may have been drawn to Eliot's portrayal of Letty, Ben, and Mrs. Garth by my knowledge of Nancy, whose psychoanalysis is described in detail in *The Clinical Exchange*. Matt, her older brother, was verbally, physically, and sexually abusive to Nancy. Their mother ignored and denied the abuse and blamed the disturbances in the household on Nancy for following Matt around and pestering him rather than playing alone with her dolls. A "model scene" depicting Nancy, Matt, and their mother occurred when Nancy was about four years old. The mother lifted Matt up on the table so that he could sing to her as she worked in the kitchen. Nancy then begged for her turn to be lifted and sing only to be told she was silly, *she* couldn't sing. Years later in elementary school, Nancy joined the class choir. One day on coming home, she announced excitedly that she had been asked by the teacher to sing a solo. Nancy remembered her mother's scoffing laugh: "Oh but you can't sing, Matt is the singer in our family." Confused and shattered, Nancy, as she did on many occasions, incorporated her mother's negative verdict of her worth into her being and dropped out of the choir. Equally damaging to her development, Nancy followed her mother's lead about Matt's worth. She idolized him and maintained so deep a crush on him that until years later well into her analysis no other man could measure up to the glow mother and she portrayed Matt to have despite powerful contradictory evidence.

In contrast to the outcomes of such prolonged painful, submissive eroticized attachments to abusive partners, a woman who feels confirmed in the value of her gender and in the worth and uniqueness of her self will have the flexibility for tenderness and intimacy in her relationship with either gender and in her erotic life.

What does Mrs. Garth expect and want from Ben and Letty? From her son she has come to expect that the independence and assertiveness she supports will lead him to distance himself from her point of view and to regard her request-demands as unwelcome intrusions. She accepts that she will have to use persuasion and pressure to get him to do as she wants. And what she wants at the moment is for him to accept her pedagogy. Eliot in her wrap-up chapter has Mary Garth state that she too wanted her children to learn, but never forced grammar on them. From the vignette we get no indication of whether Mrs. Garth expects Letty to learn or whether it makes any difference to her that Letty is able to be so quick and retentive. We are told that unlike Ben's obstreperousness, which she took with relative equanimity, her daughter's using her elbows to compete infuriates her. We sense that when a female's dealing with a male is involved, Mrs. Garth is unable to distinguish between an intention of assertiveness and aggressive antagonism. Neither are to be a desirable component of femininity. Alternatively, both are to be expected from boys who run and throw better—an odd but not unusual confabulation. (It is noteworthy that Mary Ann Evans's own brother was often cruel and disrespectful to her and refused to help their impoverished widowed sister and her children.) Letty's primary crime may not have been that she was competing with Ben, or showing him up, or interfering with Mrs. Garth's efforts to control and teach him. From the research on mother-daughter expectations, we can infer that Mrs. Garth's primary wish was for Letty to place relational goals before any other. To be a proper girl, Letty should express kindness and helpfulness to her brother. Above all, Letty should want to be close to her mother in sensitivity, empathy, and intent, that is, Letty's point of view, cares, and concerns should automatically be attuned to those of her mother. Letty violated that major basis for mother-daughter harmony and was made to experience scorching shame as punishment.

Thus shame, humiliation, and embarrassment are often weapons parents use to prevent lapses in gender-based responses. When intensely and unfairly applied to a developing child they can leave the bitterness Eliot recreated in Letty Garth and Maggie Tulliver.

NOTES

1. Reviewed in Lichtenberg, *Psychoanalysis and Motivation*; Lichtenberg, Lachmann, and Fosshage, eds., *The Self and Motivational Systems*; and Lichtenberg and Lazar.
2. See Lichtenberg, Lachmann, and Fosshage, *The Clinical Exchange*.
3. See Stoller, *Perversion* and *Presentation of Gender*.
4. After shutting down her budding sexuality in adolescence through religious fanaticism, Mary Ann Evans developed a series of intense crushes on unavailable or unresponsive men until her passionate turbulent "marriage" to George Lewes (Taylor).

WORKS CITED

Benjamin, Jessica. *The Bonds of Love*. New York: Pantheon, 1988.
Dinnerstein, Dorothy. *The Mermaid and the Minotaur*. New York: Harper & Row, 1976.
Eliot, George. *The Mill on the Floss*. 1860. New York: Bantam, 1990.
———. *Middlemarch*. 1871–72. New York: Bantam, 1992.
Fast, Irene. "Developments in Gender Identity: Gender Differentiation in Girls." *International Journal of Psychoanalysis* 60 (1979): 443–53.
Fisher, Seymour. *The Female Orgasm*. London: Lane, 1973.
Goldberg, Susan and Marc Lewis. "Play Behavior in the Year Old Infant: Early Sex Differences." *Child Development* 40 (1969): 21–31.
Korner, Anneliese. "Sex Differences in Newborns with Special Reference to Differences in the Organization of Oral Behavior." *Journal of Child Psychology and Psychiatry* 14 (1973): 19–29.

————. "The Effect of the Infant's State, Level of Arousal, Sex, and Autogenetic Stage of the Caregiver." *The Effect of the Infant on Its Caregiver.* Ed. Michael Lewis and Leonard Rosenblum. New York: Wiley, 1974. 1005–21.

Lewis, Michael. *Shame: The Exposed Self.* New York: Free P, 1991.

Lichtenberg, Joseph. *Psychoanalysis and Motivation.* Hillsdale, N.J.: Analytic P, 1989.

Lichtenberg, Joseph, Frank Lachmann, and James Fosshage, eds. *The Clinical Exchange.* Hillsdale, N.J.: Analytic P, 1996.

Lichtenberg, Joseph, Frank Lachmann, and James Fosshage, eds. *The Self and Motivational Systems.* Hillsdale, N.J.: Analytic P, 1992.

Lichtenberg, Joseph and Susan Lazar. "Sensual Enjoyment, Sexual Excitement, and Femininity: Appreciating the Female Sexual Response." *Psychoanalytic Inquiry* (forthcoming).

Moss, Howard. "Sex, Age and State as Determinants of Mother-Infant Interaction." *Merrill Palmer Quarterly* 13 (1967): 19–36.

Person, Ethel. "The Construction of Femininity: Its Influence throughout the Life Cycle." *The Course of Life.* Vol. 5. Ed. George Pollock and Stanley Greenspan. Madison, Conn.: International UP, 1993.

Stoller, Robert. *Perversion: The Erotic Form of Hatred.* New York: Pantheon, 1975.

————. *Presentation of Gender.* New Haven, Conn.: Yale UP, 1985.

Taylor, Ina. *The Life of George Eliot: A Woman of Contradictions.* New York: Morrow, 1989.

CHAPTER 6

"Man of the Most Dangerous Curiosity": Nietzsche's "Fruitful and Frightful Vision" and His War Against Shame

Léon Wurmser

VALUE POLARITIES: THINKING IN TERMS OF CONFLICT

Let me begin with a few statements by this psychologist who is so much more than just a psychologist:

Soul as multitude of subjects . . . soul as a social structure of drives and affects . . . (*Jenseits* 12)[1]

. . . one who is, in contrast to the metaphysicians, happy not to shelter within "an immortal soul," but *many mortal souls.* (*Menschliches* 2.17)

. . . *those dangerous shudders of cruelty turned against the self.* (*Jenseits* 229)

. . . for us the law "Everyone is most distant from himself" applies to all eternity—with respect to ourselves, we are not "men of insight." (*Genealogie,* "Vorrede" 1)

Actions are *never* what they appear to be to us. (*Morgenröte* 116)

All instincts that are not discharged outwardly *are turned inward*—this is what I call the internalization of man. . . . Hostility, cruelty, the pleasure in persecution, in attack, in change, in destruction—all this turned against the possessors of such instincts: *this* is the origin of the "bad conscience." (*Genealogie* 2.16)

But to eliminate the will altogether, to unhinge all the affects, sup-
posing we were capable of this—what about this? Wouldn't that mean
to *castrate* the intellect? (*Genealogie* 3.12)

. . . the real "*conflict of motives*":—something entirely invisible
and unconscious for us (*Morgenröte* 129)

The triumph of the ascete over himself, his eye turned inward
which sees *man split into one who suffers and one who observes*, and
from now on only watches the outside world in order to gather as it
were wood for his own fire-pile, this last tragedy of the drive for excellence where there is only *one* person left who incinerates himself,—this
is the worthy conclusion belonging to the beginning [that of the cruel
barbarian inflicting with greatest pleasure pain upon the other]: in
both cases an unspeakable happiness in front of torture. (*Morgenröte*
113)

The psychoanalyst finds himself at home in these profound revelations and questionings, these new and often strikingly poetic images for
self-examination and self-deception. In fact, there is hardly a statement
in Nietzsche's writings whose deep psychological truth does not directly
appeal to the psychoanalyst's listening and knowing mind—and yet also
hardly one where this insight is not put in the service of a new, specific,
and ultimately deeply troublesome value priority, a new menacing
superego command. Statement of *descriptive* truth is subtly altered into
prescriptive claim and into *proscriptive* scorn. Implacable insight is used
for equally implacable condemnation, in behalf of a very specific absolute value: *strength = power = life = good.*

Before we study this fateful turn in Nietzsche's thinking, we need to
study the foundation that makes him even today such absorbing and
utterly important reading, especially for analysts: *his consistent thinking
out of the consciousness of inner conflict, including unconscious inner
conflict.* In that sense it is only appropriate if Thomas Mann calls this
implicitly, by applying the term to Schopenhauer, already psychoanalysis ("Schopenhauer" 232).

For psychoanalysts there is another especially relevant point of reference for such a rethinking of Nietzsche: many aspects of C. G. Jung's
teachings are based on an uncritical taking-over of the most iconoclas-
tic thoughts of Nietzsche, which are translated into therapeutic action,
without taking into account the horrendous ethical implications of this
appropriation. In fact, it strikes me as hardly more than a shallow aping
of what is in Nietzsche the profoundest questioning of conventional
morality, a doubt born out of pain and the deepest probing.

There were of course innumerable other such cut-rate Nietzsches.
One of them was Hitler, whose "Hintertreppenmythus" ("backstair

myth"), as Thomas Mann called it, was based on a half-understood Nietzsche, that is, the sadistic-paranoid half, distilled from hidden burning resentment.

"Those who know Nietzsche's significance for Germany can easily find the bridge that spans the abyss between the 'before' and 'after.' It is indeed impossible to understand the development of Germany without this last German philosopher. His influence within the boundaries of Germany was—and still is—boundless. . . . Like Luther, he is a specifically German phenomenon—radical and fatal" (6), we read at the beginning of Karl Löwith's autobiographical account *My Life in Germany before and after 1933*, which was completed in 1940 during his exile in Japan and only published in 1986.

One of the questions raised precisely by this, however, is the following: How is it that Nietzsche's philosophy had, together with that of Marx, this uncanny power *for paranoid abuse and violence* that determined in very particular ways the history of the twentieth century? Albert Camus poses the problem most dramatically:

> In the history of the intelligence, with the exception of Marx, Nietzsche's adventure has no equivalent; we shall never finish making reparation for the injustice done to him. Of course history records other philosophies that have been misconstrued and betrayed. But up to the time of Nietzsche and National Socialism, it was quite without parallel that a process of thought—brilliantly illuminated by the nobility and by the sufferings of an exceptional mind—should have been demonstrated to the eyes of the world by a parade of lies and by the hideous accumulation of corpses in concentration camps. The doctrine of the superman led to the methodical creation of submen—a fact that doubtless should be denounced, but which also demands interpretation. (76)

Can we let Nietzsche off for what has been done in his name? "Great men, like great epochs, are explosives in which an immense force is stored up" (*Götzendämmerung*, "Unzeitgemässen" 44).

THINKING OUT OF CONFLICT, BREAKING APART IN CONFLICT

Wherever we look in examining the work of Nietzsche it is a *philosophy of inner conflict* that makes the manifest aphorisms and essays understandable and coherent—not just a *psychology of inner conflict*, but in the full sense *a philosophy* trying to understand *the essence of man, human history and culture, and most of all man's comprehension of the world and of himself, including science, including all valuation, includ-*

ing all art, on the basis of inner conflict. This is a philosophical revolution of the first order, adumbrated by only a few: Plato and Augustine (both of whom he criticizes often with acrid contempt), Shakespeare and Goethe (both of whom he mostly admired, but not without reservations), and then of course, Schopenhauer.

Nietzsche speaks of the "martial history of the individual" ("Zur Kriegsgeschichte des Individuums") (*Menschliches* 1.268), where various cultures, ages and generations are in the most ferocious battle within the individual, of the thinker treating his thoughts as if they were persons with whom he has to fight, whom he has to protect, nourish, join, whose tyranny he wants to defy, whose faltering he meets with pity, whose power he fears, whom he gives the authority to honor the self, to praise or to chide it and to treat it with contempt—"that we deal with them as with free spiritual individuals, independent powers, equal to equal—this is the root of the curious phenomenon that I have called 'intellectual conscience'" (*Menschliches* 2.26).

Under the title "Morality as Self-Division of Man": "Is it not evident that in all these examples man prefers *one part of himself*, a thought, a desire, a creation, over *another part of himself*; that he therefore *splits up* his being and sacrifices one part to another? . . . In morality, man treats himself not as an 'individuum,' but as a 'dividuum'" (*Menschliches* 1.57).

One cardinal observation needs to be made here that I have not encountered elsewhere: the most radical shift in Nietzsche's epistemological and metaphysical revolution consists in the attempt to reexamine all the basic philosophical questions from a vantage point in psychology, specifically from that of a psychology of multiple, contradictory, fighting parts within the subject, his emphasis on the multiplicity of the subject and its inner conflict. The former, namely the "subject as fiction," that "there is neither a subject of knowing nor a subject of the will, neither an I nor a soul nor generally in any individual a stable centre" (*Nachgelassene* 658), has been noted by Colli in his commentary to volume 13 of the collected works; the latter aspect, that of inner conflict as *philosophical* starting point (not merely as a precursor of the psychoanalytic understanding of mental processes), I have not seen. Psychology, and a radically new psychology at that, is being used as cornerstone for a new philosophy; it is being counted upon to reveal to us what is deepest and most relevant for an understanding of human nature, of human insight into the universe, of history and culture, of art, and of course of religion and morality. How early this formed Nietzsche's consciousness is shown by his notes of 1864 (when he was twenty): "Or how often sleeps the will, and only the drives and inclinations are awake? . . . Struggle is the continuous nourishment of the soul, and it knows how to draw from it enough sweetness and beauty" (Janz 1: 119).

This is the revolution which even today makes Nietzsche the pioneer of an entirely new, highly relevant, profoundly inspirational philosophy.

A SELF-DESPISING CREATURE

"There should be a being which would have blocked a self-despising creature as I am from coming into existence" (qtd. in Löwith, *Nietzsches* 232). Nietzsche's thinking was a hidden battle against weakness, an overt attempt to transform suffering into creativity and triumph. His kinship in this with Schopenhauer is evident; the answers were to be opposite.

For Schopenhauer, redemption from the incessant conflict within the Will lies in the *Intellekt*, "the intellect torn away from the will and turned into pure and innocent insight" (Mann, *Essays* 3: 206), especially as shown in art and in saintliness.

In the progress of his own thinking Nietzsche reverses this valuation, or rather he vacillates between two opposite stands: the later his work, the more strongly "Geist," intellect, thinking, turn into an enemy, though never one combated with the same vehemence as the guilt-based conscience, while life is unconditionally affirmed. Fascinatingly, we find early evidence of this value reversal in a letter he wrote at the age of twenty-two to his friend Gersdorff: "What was man to me and his restless wanting! What to me the eternal 'Thou shalt,' 'Thou shalt not'? How different is the lightning, the storm, the hail, free powers, without ethics! How happy they are, how forceful, pure will, without clouding by the intellect!" (Janz 1: 98).

Yet this was not to remain true for all of his writings. The battle, his own inner conflict, seems to remain far more evenly poised. There are many works where intellect, reason, understanding, the "unconditional pursuit of truth," are being treated as the culmination of life: "The same life that has its peak in old age also has its peak in wisdom, in that mild sunshine of a constant spiritual joyfulness" (*Menschliches* 1.292).

THE THREE STATIONS OF THE MYTHICAL WAY
AND THE FRACTURED SYNTHESIS

Löwith dramatically describes Nietzsche's system as a movement of thought, marked by three stations: the *death of the Christian God, man confronted with nothingness,* and *the will for eternal return*—as a way that goes from the "thou shalt" to the birth of the "I will," and then to

the rebirth of the "I am" as the "first movement" of an eternally returning existence within the natural world of all existing things (*Nietzsches*
40).

For example, first the spirit becomes the *camel*, one "who has previously subjected himself to the discipline of tradition," "humbled himself, carried the heavy and the heaviest burden" (Kaufmann 4). Then,
secondly, he turns into the defiant *lion*:

> What is the great dragon which the spirit will no longer call lord
> and God? "Thou shalt" is the name of the great dragon. But the spirit
> of the lion says, "I will."
>
> "Thou shalt" lies in his path, sparkling like gold, a beast covered
> with scales; and on every scale glitters a golden "Thou shalt."
>
> Values, thousands of years old, glitter on these scales, and thus
> speaks the mightiest of all dragons: "All the value of things—glitters on
> me.
>
> "All value has long been created, and I am all created value. Ver-
> ily, there shall be no more 'I will'." Thus speaks the dragon. . . .
>
> To create freedom for oneself and a sacred "No" even to duty: for
> that, my brothers, the lion is needed. ("Verwandlungen," *Zarathustra*)

Thirdly, he becomes the *child*: "The child is innocence and forget-
fulness, a new beginning, a game, a self-propelling wheel, a first movement, a sacred 'Yes'—that is, all symbols for the new philosophy of the
eternal return of the same.

The old conscience, the old morality, is indeed the core of Nietzsche's rejection. "*Dead are all gods: now we want the Superman to
live*—let this be one day at the great noontide of our will!" (at the end
of part 1; see also "Vom höheren Menschen"; quoted in Löwith, *Nietzsches* 47). The precondition for this is the radical destruction of traditional morality, the rule of the "*Thou shalt*": "This long plenitude and
sequence of demolition, destruction, ruin and cataclysm that now stands
ahead—who could sufficiently guess this today and thus become the
teacher and foreteller of this monstrous logic of terror, the prophet of a
darkness and solar eclipse the like of which has never occurred on
earth?" (*Wissenschaft* 343)

"Morality, insofar as it *condemns* in itself, and *not* out of regards,
considerations, purposes of life, is a specific error with which one should
have no sympathy, an *idiosyncrasy* of the degenerate which has caused
untold harm!" (*Götzendämmerung*, "Moral" 6). Morality is called "the
true poisoner and slanderer of life" ("Irrtümer" 6). He wants to eradicate "the instinct for *wanting to punish and judge*," and, in a resolute
reversal, to "remove the concept of guilt and punishment from the
world" (7).

The image evoked is that of *castration*: "The Church fights against

passion by excision [*Ausschneidung*] in every sense of the word: its practice, its 'cure' is *castration*. It never asks: 'How can one change desire
into something spiritual, beautiful, divine?'—it has at all times put the
emphasis of its discipline on extirpation (of sensuality, of pride, of the
desire for power, of greed, of vindictiveness). But attacking the passions
at their roots means attacking life at its roots. . . . The radical enmity,
the deadly enmity against sensuality remains a serious symptom"
("Moral" 1, 2).

"Sacrificing God for the nothing—this paradoxical mystery of ultimate cruelty has been vouchsafed for the generation that is now coming" (*Jenseits* 55).

The anthropological postulate of nihilism points to the elementary
"will" to power; in Löwith's words: "Life itself is being understood as
universal 'will' to power, and thus Nietzsche's basic distinction of phenomena according to strength and weakness is related to the strength
and weakness of the will that is grounded in life" (Löwith, *Nietzsches*
57). "[F]or the will, as the affect of command, is the decisive mark of
sovereignty and strength" (*Wissenschaft* 347; qtd. in Löwith 54).

In this philosophical revolution he sees, as his own central distinction, the antithesis between life as growing and as declining ("Aufgang
und Niedergang"), between rich life and impoverished life ("das
Lebensvolle vom Lebensarmen"), between the healthy and the degenerate ("das Wohlgeratene vom Mißratenen").

> The one richest in the fulness of life, the Dionysian god and man, can
> allow himself not only the view of what is terrible and questionable,
> but even the terrible deed itself and every luxury of destruction, disso-
> lution, negation; for him, it seems as if what is evil, absurd, and ugly
> were permissible, owing to an exuberance of procreative, fertilizing
> energies that are able to create out of every desert a luxuriant fruit gar-
> den. (*Wissenschaft* 370)

In its most poignant, crispest formulation, in "Antichrist":

> What is good?—Everything that heightens in man the feeling of power,
> the will to power, power itself.
> What is bad?—Everything that stems from weakness.
> What is happiness?—The feeling that power *is growing*-that a
> resistance is overcome.
> *Not* contentment, but more *power*; *not* peace at all, but war; *not*
> virtue, but capability (virtue in the Renaissance style, *virtù*, virtue free
> of moralic acid).
> The weak and infirm should perish: first proposition of *our* phi-
> lanthropy. And one should even help them to do so.
> What is more harmful than any vice?—Active pity for the infirm
> and weak—Christianity. (*Antichrist* 2)

The turn around from the Will to Nothing into the Will to Eternal Return is based on this main distinction.

Persuasively, Löwith points to the inner fracture in Nietzsche's "ideal sequence": "His doctrine breaks apart because the will for the *eternalization of the modern ego*, whose existence had been thrown into Being, cannot fit with the contemplation of an *eternal circle of the natural world*" (*Nietzsches* 126). He (alias Zarathustra) predicts the absolute harmony, the overcoming of all divisions in a highest kind of Being, whereby man's being "in contradiction with the Universe," in which "natural life in the existence of man as knowing is divided" (Löwith, *Nietzsches* 101), would be transcended. Yet this insight into the universal harmony of nature can only be attained by a supreme act of "self-conquest," the decision in favor of the "will to power," the most massive self-transcendence and claim for one's own will: "*This world is the will for power—and Nothing besides!* And you yourselves also are this will for power—and Nothing besides!" (qtd. in Löwith 95). "My strongest attribute is self-overcoming. But I also need it most—I always stood by the abyss" (qtd. in Löwith 96).

"The *problem* with the doctrine of return is that of the *unity* of this *split* between the human will for an aim and the aimless circling of the world" (Löwith 67); "the real difficulty consists in bringing the vision of the eternally circling universe in accord with the purposeful will of man towards the future" (74). "Thus the doctrine presents itself: first as the setting of an ideal goal for the man of will—and with that it replaces the Christian belief in immortality by the will to self-eternalization—and second as the observation of a physical fact in the unwilled Being-so-and-not-otherwise of the physical world—and with that it replaces the ancient cosmology by modern physics. This twofold interpretability as an *atheistic* religion and as a *physicalistic metaphysics* shows that the doctrine as a whole is the *unity of a split*, between the *nihilistic* existence of man who had gotten rid of God and the *positivistic* presence of physical energy. As scientist of nature Nietzsche is however a philosophical dilettante, and as the founder of a religion a 'hybrid of illness and will for power'" (87).

Thus he puts the doctrine of the eternal return both as an *ethical imperative* and as a *theory of natural science* (Löwith 92). This attempt to reconquer a lost world and its unity fails singularly; it breaks critically apart "in the irreconcilable double meaning of a practical-moral postulate and of a theoretical claim" (92). "*The cosmic meaning stands in conflict with the anthropological [meaning]* so that the one turns into the nonsense of the other" (64).

Similarly to Löwith, Giorgio Colli concludes: "Finally we face a will to power that is at the same time valuation and being: almost a mystical sum-mary in which the metaphysical substance, 'Being,' represents itself at the same time as judgment and as will, i.e. as rational and as irrational. The threads get inextricably entangled. The theoretical search for the inconceivable conditions of consciousness, for the falsification of consciousness, driven so far into the depths, somersaults, gets stuck and finally peters out without finding this time its adjustment [settlement] in skepticism; this torment cannot be stilled" ("Nachwort," *Nachgelassene* 660).

What can we add as psychoanalysts to this philosophical finding? Specifically, the fractured results of the philosophical *procedere*, of this daring philosophical tightrope walking, this thinking in extremes, are these not something with which we are somewhat acquainted, and about which we may have something to say?

"A LAUGHING-STOCK OR A PAINFUL EMBARASSMENT": NIETZSCHE'S WAR AGAINST SHAME

As the founder of an atheistic religion, Nietzsche is, to use his own words, "a hybrid of sickness and will to power" ("Vorwort," *Ecce* 4); yet the whole depth of this split is revealed when he writes:

> I know my fate. One day my name will be tied to the recollection of something immense—a crisis the likes of which has never been seen on earth, the *most profound collision of conscience*, a decision conjured up *against* everything that had hitherto been believed, demanded, sanctified. I am no human being, I am dynamite. ("Warum ich ein Schicksal bin," *Ecce* 1; qtd. in Löwith, *Nietzsches* 113; first emphasis added)

It is this "most profound collision of conscience," or as we would say, this *conflict within the superego*, which is for us the psychoanalytically relevant center point of the problem faced by Nietzsche and all those deeply influenced by his revolutionary thinking.

Duties, reverence (*Ehrfurcht*), guilt have to be abolished in this "transvaluation of all values" ("Umwertung aller Werte") that liberates from the "Thou shalt": "Being ashamed of one's immorality: that is a step on the ladder at the end of which one also becomes ashamed of one's morality" (*Jenseits* 95).

What then lies at the core of this transvaluation? The killing of God—of authority, of the father? The removal of guilt? Can it simply be coerced into the oedipal schema? Surely, it is all that in some way. Yet it seems to me, it is *Nietzsche's relentless battle against weakness (weakness of will, of control, of being oneself), a desperate fight against feeling ashamed*. All obligation, all guilt is finally a burden that makes weak and invites the abysmal humiliation that his entire fight against Western morality tries to eradicate.

I teach you the overman [superman]. Man is something that should be overcome. What have you done to overcome him?

What is the ape to man? A laughing-stock or a painful embarrassment [literally: a shame]. And man shall be just that for the overman: a laughing-stock or a painful embarassment.

You have made your way from worm to man, and much in you is still worm. Once you were apes, and even now man is more ape than any ape. ("Vorrede," *Zarathustra* 3)

In the sharpest formulation it appears at the end of Book 3 of *The Joyful Wisdom*:

268
What makes one heroic?—To go and meet at the same time one's highest suffering and one's highest hope.

269
What do you believe in?—That the weights of everything need to be calibrated anew.

270
What does your conscience say?—"You shall become who you are."

271
Where lie your greatest dangers?—In pity.

272
What do you love in others?—My hopes.

273
Whom do you call bad?—One who always wants to put to shame.

274
What is for you the most humane thing?—Sparing someone shame.

275
What is the seal of freedom attained?—No longer being ashamed in front of oneself.

Let us look at the antitheses (or word-pairs): of pride and shame; of respect (or honor) and contempt (or derision, jeering, scorn); of courage and cowardice; of sincerity and guileful, insidious deception; of open revenge and resentment as vindictiveness without strength and courage; of purity (cleanliness) and impurity (uncleanliness); of power (self-control) and decadence; of nobility and being part of the herd (the much too many, the superfluous). All these form, as it were, a kind of "counterpoint" in most of his work. Most emphatically this is true for the "symphony" of his master poem, *Also sprach Zarathustra*. They all belong to the *spectrum of shame conflicts*, they all express his own struggle against fearing to be exposed, "ashamed"—as the physically and emotionally, *deeply* suffering and lonely man he really was and as the weak human being he dreaded to be. "One does not kill by anger but by laughter" ("Vom Lesen," *Zarathustra*), and he speaks of "the horrible torture of offended honor" (*Menschliches* 1.61), which may represent more suffering than life is worth. Therefore the refrain: "Man is something that should be overcome"—man as a weak, shameful, suffering being, burdened by conscience and an animal of the flock ("Herdentier"), contemptible and resentful.

What is meant by "shame"? To define the concept of shame, I will quote from an earlier work:

[T]he word shame really covers three concepts: Shame is first the *fear* of disgrace, it is the *anxiety* about the danger that we might be looked at with contempt for having dishonored ourselves. Second it is the feeling when one is looked at with such scorn. It is, in other words, the *affect of contempt* directed against the self—by others or by one's own conscience. Contempt says: "You should disappear as such a being as you have shown yourelf to be—failing, weak, flawed, and dirty. Get out of my sight: Disappear!" One feels ashamed for *being exposed*. . . . Third, shame is also almost the antithesis of the second one, as in: "Don't you know any shame?" It is an overall *character trait* preventing any such disgraceful exposure, an attitude of respect toward others and toward oneself, a stance of reverence—the highest form of such reverence being called by Goethe (1829) "die Ehrfurcht vor sich selbst," reverence for oneself. This third form of shame is discretion, is tact, is sexual modesty. It is respect and a sense of awe—a refusal 'to touch, lick and finger everything, a nobility of taste and tact of reverence,' as Nietzsche calls it in *Beyond Good and Evil*. In short, we can discern *three forms of shame: shame anxiety, shame affect as a complex reaction pattern, and shame as a preventive attitude.* (Wurmser, "Shame" 67–68)

My point is that Nietzsche's most intimate concern is the fighting off of the exposure of weakness, the categorical avoidance of shame in the second meaning, as complex shame affect: of feeling ashamed, of being shamed, humiliated, disgraced, and of accepting such a verdict. When I say Nietzsche is waging war against shame, I mean it strictly in the first two ways of understanding; his main defensive attitude is shame in the third sense, and that is actually also how he usually employs the word "Scham." All the outrageous, proto-Nazi demands, all those defiantly sadistic outbursts appear like a last ditch fight of spite, of defiance and scorn against this pervasive sense of inner shame, or rather the pervasive fear of being shamed, of being discovered as weak—a defense by reaction formation.

"The darkening of the sky above man has always prevailed in proportion to how much man's shame *before man* has grown" (*Genealogie* 2.7). It is the "noble man" ("der vornehme Mensch"), living in the "*pathos of distance*" (*Jenseits* 257), who exploits and conquers the others and is full of contempt against the coward, the weakling, the liar, the herdlike animal, against the one who allows himself to be mistreated, to be the frightened, the one out for narrow utility. His moral is that of "self-glorification" ("Selbstverherrlichung"): "The noble human being honors the powerful within himself" (*Jenseits* 260).

This is my point: *the whole new morality and metaphysics of Nietzsche stands in the service of this fight against the sense of shame*—the freedom of a "man to whom nothing is forbidden, except it be *weakness*, whether that weakness be called vice or virtue" ("Unzeitgemässen," *Götzendämmerung* 49). It is the advocacy of a value system built on ruthless strength, self-control, will power, an absolute avoidance of any vulnerability, of any exposure, of any weakness—in a crescendo of power.

It is the precedence of this fight against feeling ashamed and against shaming others, a fight at times approaching "shamelessness" ("Unverschämtheit"), which gives us the key to so much that appears "at first blush" enigmatic and paradoxical, often shocking in Nietzsche's morality—a morality, though, built by somebody who at the same time is determined and permeated by a deep sensibility of honor, of dignity, and dedicated to the relentless search for truth.

This value system, built on the battle against shame, culminates in the adoration of beauty, beauty being understood as the expression of strength of will, as the freedom from any restraints that could weaken such will, the "audacity [super-courage] of the superman" ("[den] Übermut des Übermenschen"), as Löwith calls it (*Nietzsches* 63). "In what is beautiful man sets himself up as the measure of perfection. . . . Man really mirrors himself in things; he sees as beautiful everything that gives him back his own reflection. . . . The man in this condition transforms things until they mirror his own power—until they are reflections of his perfection. This *compulsion* to transform into the perfect is—art" ("Unzeitgemässes," *Götzendämmerung* 19, 9).

Beauty is based on "appearance," even on "seeming"—to being seen with admiration; the value of beauty is thus intimately related to the spectrum of the affects of shame and the battle against shame. Is beauty not the ultimate, though transient victory over shame? "[A]rt in which precisely the *lie* is sanctified, in which the *will to deception* has good conscience on its side, is much more fundamentally opposed to the ascetic ideal than is science" (*Genealogie* 3.25). In this ideal opposed to shame, *purity* is important: "What most deeply separates two people is a different sense and degree of cleanliness" (*Jenseits* 271); the highest instinct of cleanliness leads to holiness—and utterly isolates. And this description again turns into prescription when he adds later on, again in the context of the analysis of nobility ("Vornehmheit"): "For solitude is a virtue for us, as a sublime tendency and urge for cleanliness which guesses how the contact between man and man—'in society'—is inevitably unclean. Any community, somehow, somewhere, sometime, makes 'base'" (*Jenseits* 284). He speaks of the "perfectly uncanny sensitivity" of his "instinct for cleanliness" ("Warum ich so weise bin," *Ecce* 8); everywhere he can sense "the hidden filth." "*Disgust* in man, in the 'rabble,' was always my greatest danger"; "I perish under unclean conditions." Thus his humanity requires constant self-overcoming. "All prejudice stems from the intestines" ("Warum ich so klug bin," *Ecce* 1).

Thus one can say that this "new" superego is one that is deeply rooted in categories of "anality"—purity, control, willfulness, defiance, horror of all shame and submission, and with that characteristically "split" into absolute extremes of judgment, always in fact judging, with a bitter resentment underneath (what I have studied in regard to Lagerkvist's *Dvärgen*).[2]

We may call this "new" ideal "narcissistic" or "anal" or "a war against shame" or "preoedipal"—all this is correct. Yet is it sufficient?

"RESSENTIMENT": "THE SLAVE-REVOLT IN MORALITY"—A "DISGRACE OF MAN"

With the last phrase of the above title I refer to the passage in the *Genealogy of Morals*: "all these instincts of reaction and *ressentiment* . . . these 'instruments of culture' are a disgrace of man" (*Genealogie* 1.11). I already mentioned the poisonous stream of resentment flowing out of the core weakness. It is now exactly about this subject of the resentment, "das Ressentiment," that Nietzsche has a lot to say of the very greatest relevance, and much more to express that is not directly put into words.

He ascribes it to "the priestly people of the Jews," how "out of powerlessness the hatred in them grows into something monstrous and uncanny, into something that is most spiritual and most poisonous"; "they get satisfaction against their enemies and conquerors in the end only by a radical transformation of their enemies' values, that is to say, by an act of the *most spiritual revenge*" (*Genealogie* 1.7). They replaced the aristocratic *value equation of good = noble = powerful = beautiful = happy = loved by God* with its opposite, an opposite that now would be clenched "by the teeth of the most abysmal hatred (the hatred of impotence)," namely that "only those who are wretched are good, the poor, powerless, lowly alone are good; the suffering, deprived, sick, ugly alone are the pious ones, the only ones loved by God, only for them is their blessedness" (*Genealogie* 1.7). With this value revolution "*the slave revolt in morality* begins."

Soon thereafter there comes a passage that seems to me particularly revealing for the double message of resentment expounded by this great and dangerous thinker, a double message that, I believe, somewhat answers the question of why his philosophy came to develop an effect of such horrendous "brisance" and destruction:

> This Jesus of Nazareth, the incarnation of the gospel of love, this "Savior" bringing blessedness and victory to the poor, to the sick, to the sinners—was he not precisely this seduction in its uncanniest and most irresistible form, the seduction and the detour to just those *Jewish* values and renovations of the ideal? Hasn't Israel just by way of the detour through this "Savior," through this ostensible adversary and dissolver of Israel, *attained* the ultimate goal of its sublime vindictiveness? Doesn't it belong to the black art of a truly *great* policy of revenge, of a far-sighted, subterranean, slowly grabbing, and premeditated revenge that Israel would, in front of the world, deny its real instrument of revenge as if it were some deadly enemy and nail it to the cross, so that "all the world," i.e. all the enemies of Israel, would without hesitation swallow this bait? And on the other side, could anyone, in all the refinement of his mind, devise an altogether more *dangerous* bait? Anything that could equal the tempting, intoxicating, numbing, corrupting power of that symbol of the "holy cross," that ghastly paradox of a "God on the Cross," that mysterium of an unimaginable, ultimate, and extreme cruelty and self-crucifixion of God *for the sake of man?*
>
> What is certain at least is that *sub hoc signo* Israel, with its revenge and transvaluation of all values, has hitherto triumphed again and again over all other ideals, over all the more *noble* ideals. (*Genealogie* 1.8)

This is, on the one side, a most trenchant analysis of the pernicious effect of resentment—an "analysis" not so much only of the "Jewish" resentment: its real target is the resentment hidden within Christian ethics and metaphysics, and even beyond that, the entire old morality, the traditional conscience altogether. Untruthfulness, inner and outer deception and, most of all, a passive outward orientation, all born out of pervasive weakness and impotence ("Ohnmacht"), carried by a vicious spirit of relentless but insidious revenge, and couched in terms of poison, dissolution, decay, and narcosis—these are the shameful attributes of the "Mensch des Ressentiments," this countertypus to the man of nobility.

Yet, on the other side, it is also a statement that itself shows all the influence of resentment: it is a bitter accusation of an insidious poisoning of the Western world by a Jewish conspiracy of more than 2,000 years duration, of a most cunning, skillful, and success-crowned emasculation of "noble man," the degradation of "tragic man," the sapping of the strength of the enemy, in short, his humiliation and defeat, by the most elegant means of revenge, the self-castration with the help of a magic symbol. It is the accusation of the power of resentment by the very means of a magic exerted by the appeal to everybody's own deeply buried sense of unfairness.

Doesn't it obviously also apply to himself what he says about the law-breaker ("Verbrecher") and then specifically about the reformer, literally the "renewer of the spirit" ("Neuerer des Geistes"): "Almost every genius knows as one of his developments the 'Catilinarian existence,' a feeling of hatred, revenge, and revolt against everything that already *is*, that is no longer *becoming*. . . . Catiline—the form of pre-existence of *every* Caesar" ("Unzeitgemäßes," *Götzendämmerung* 45).

This is what I mean by Nietzsche's *philosophy of resentment* at its purest, over and beyond his most intelligent *descriptive analysis* of resentment. The description given before applies, I believe, to Nietzsche's own reasoning in this crucial context—that of the overthrow of "Christian" (= Jewish = anti-aristocratic = antinoble = shame and guilt evoking) morality. This philosophical overthrow of traditional values ("superego") by a thorough and ongoing analysis and destruction of the attitude of resentment and its pernicious effects represents the first pillar of that threefold arch of Nietzsche's thinking, as outlined by Löwith, the pillar of the defiance against the "thou shalt" ("du sollst").

This then is the new ethic, this is the new antithesis, this is the inner conflict conjured up by Nietzsche in ever new images and proclamations, in steady shifts back and forth between most skillful *description* and equally skillful, yet ultimately extremely dangerous *prescription*—a prescription followed eagerly by all those prompted exactly by that very resentment so masterfully drawn here by a magician of the language.

A CENTRAL DENIAL

Nietzsche's resentment is, as mentioned, most centrally directed against Christianity and the conscience built upon guilt and self-punishment, but it also showers scorn and venom over the mass culture ("the herd," "die Herde"), over everything bourgeois or socialist. Special arrows are ready for two: rationalism and economical thinking (more generally, utilitarianism).

However, both the concept of resentment and the affect of resentment cannot be understood without the underlying concept of justice and the deep sense of unfairness: "I have not been treated justly"; concept and affect presuppose this. Yet this notion of injustice is completely left out by Nietzsche. This means that psychologically resentment hangs in the air; it becomes the last supposedly explanatory element used to explain all the rest, treated as if it were the main enemy. Yet, in fact, it is itself quite analyzable and in need of further explanation.

Analyzing it we find that both the sense of not having been treated fairly in regard to respect, recognition, honor, and dignity, "being seen and heard," that is, if one feels shamed, and the sense of not having been treated justly in regard to love, tenderness, possession, sensuality, warmth—that both lead to the affect of resentment. The common denominator is: the sense of justice or fairness has been violated.

In short, what is by and large a statement about the pervasiveness and perniciousness of the resentment, itself turns out to be, if allowed to resonate in the listener, permeated by that gnawing feeling of injustice, powerlessness, and wish for revenge marking resentment. Furthermore it is being hypostatized into a broad tool of explanation and condemnation without Nietzsche's acknowledging its derivative character and pushing his analysis to the end.

This again represents a deep fracture in Nietzsche's argument. Can this be generalized? Conditionally, yes: this is one pole of his thinking— a line leading from shame and suffering to resentment to revenge in the form of the destruction of all values and the creation of a new world of values, a world beyond weakness and shame. It is based on the overthrow of the old superego and its replacement by one totally reversed.

Yet what is the other pole? It is self-discipline, even self-torment, on behalf of an equally absolute wish for truthfulness, for selfless analysis, as unconditional a pursuit as the venomousness of that resentment and the war against shame have been. How can he wage this two-front war at the same time—the war against lie and error, and the war against shame and resentment?

To this quest for truth and its own inner break we turn now.

THE "ABSOLUTE WILL NOT TO DECEIVE ONESELF"

Nobody who reads Nietzsche's works with an impartial interest fails to be deeply struck by the fervor of the search for truth, and in fact by the profound truth of so much that it unveils. Truth is never treated by him as absolute, but the search for truth is; for example, he speaks of the *"unconditional [i.e. absolute] inquiry into what is true"* (*Menschliches* 2.13). He says it about Zarathustra—not about the work, but his own alter ego: "His teaching, and it alone, has truthfulness as its highest virtue—this means the opposite of the *cowardice* of the 'idealist' who flees from reality. . . . The self-overcoming of morality out of truthfulness; the self-overcoming and transformation of the moralist into his opposite—into *me*—this is what the name of Zarathustra means in my mouth" ("Warum ich ein Schicksal bin," *Ecce* 3).

"But we can draw no conclusions from Nietzsche except the base and mediocre cruelty that he hated with all his strength, unless we give first place in his work—well ahead of the prophet—to the clinician" (65), says Camus. Isn't it rather, though, that this is one of the creative tensions in his work—*his* creative "agon"? Throughout I have been noting the sly back and forth between *description* and *prescription*, if not *proscription*. This stylistic doubleness, this conflict in rhetorical means, is however nothing else than expression of the deeper conflict between the attitude of the clinician or therapist and that of the revolutionary prophet. The first wants the truth in order to demonstrate the deception and to heal the suffering caused by it; the second wants revenge for his powerlessness and shame, and needs the power to redress the balance of unfairness, to heal his own resentment.

These two are never reconciled for good, they only seem so. The fracture in the reasoning pointed out by Löwith is one outcome of this. It seems to me that both lines of motivation are most powerfully at work in Nietzsche, and the immense doubleness of his cultural and political effect is a result, writ in the largest letters on the backdrop of the historical stage.

Thus there is that other side—the ethos of implacable truthfulness, with its inherent cruelty, especially against the self:

> It is *this* will to appearance, to simplification, to the mask, to the cloak, in short, to the surface . . . *against* which that sublime inclination of the one seeking insight is working—the one who takes things in their profundity, in their multiplicity, in their foundation, and *wants* to takes them that way: as a kind of cruelty of the intellectual conscience and taste, which every courageous thinker will recognize in himself, assuming that he has properly hardened and sharpened his eye for himself and is accustomed to strict discipline, as well as strict words. (*Jenseits* 230)

He speaks—in regard to the "bad conscience"—of "this uncanny and horrifyingly pleasurable work of a soul that is willingly torn apart, which inflicts suffering on itself out of the desire to inflict it" (*Genealogie* 2.18).

Thus in another formulation, one that gives deeper justice to the method of conflict analysis, specifically here in the sense of the inquiry into value polarities, we should notice: There is a conflict between an absolute ethos of truthfulness and an equally absolutely set ethos of will and power, the avoidance of exposed weakness, that is, of shame. His work appears to be torn between these two ethical postulates, both being held absolutely. While he is a master in working out conflict at its sharpest, in setting up the opposites as absolutes (as *extremes*), he is torn by them, and every attempt at reconciliation keeps falling apart again, even the ultimate attempt in the form of the synthesis of human life and cosmic being—"will to power" versus "the eternal return of the same." The fracture remains, the heroic effort fails, illness and destruction tear this most wonderful work asunder.

LOVE AGAINST LONELINESS

Still deeper: behind that consuming yearning for truthfulness lies a devouring craving for *love*, for *belonging*. "You fool, hide your bleeding heart in ice and scorn" ("Vereinsamt," *Gedichte*).

"*Love* is the danger for the most solitary man, love of anything *if only it is alive*! Indeed, my foolishness and modesty in love is laughable!" ("Der Wanderer," *Zarathustra*).

He says of Zarathustra's "Night Song": "the immortal lament of being condemned not to love, by the overabundance of light and power, by his *sun*-like nature" ("Zarathustra," *Ecce* 7).

In *Beyond Good and Evil*, he writes: "Do not remain attached to a person: and be it the most loved—every person is a prison, also a corner. . . . One has to know how *to preserve onself*; the hardest test of independence" (41).

Since the unveiled expression of love itself would be a sign of weakness, it can express itself only in an endless stream of the most entrancing symbols of beauty, of "heroic idylls" of Nature. He keeps coming back to the "*pathos of distance*." One's neighbour has to be kept at a distance, and yet sought on a thousand paths of lonely scorn and ecstasy.

Time and time again *Erkenntnis* (insight, understanding, recognition, knowledge) appears as the highest good, the purpose of life: "This goal is for oneself to become a necessary chain of rings of culture . . . to see the bottom in the dark well of your being and knowing . . . [to learn] that no honey is sweeter than that of knowledge" (*Menschliches* 1.292).

This absolute ethos of truthfulness dictates the thorough *skepsis* that became so much the knifelike edge of all genuine psychological analysis influenced by, or akin to Nietzsche's; the title "Human, All Too Human" ("Menschliches, Allzumenschliches") is equated with "psychological observation" (*Menschliches* 1.35). "Man himself has an unconquerable inclination to let himself be deceived," he says in "On Truth and Lying." "Man is *very well defended against himself*, against his own spying and laying siege; usually he cannot perceive of himself more than his outer bulwarks. The fortress itself is inaccessible to him, even invisible, unless friends and enemies turn traitor and lead him in by a secret path" (*Menschliches* 1.491).

DOUBLE FACE—DOUBLE VISION

Yet on the other side, painfully, Nietzsche realizes that "only in love, shaded by the illusion of love, is man *creative*" (Mann 246). This dangerous illusion needs to be destroyed, in favor of "the adoration of the strong and beautiful life . . . a heroic estheticism, under the protectorate of the God of tragedy, Dionysos. It is just this Dionysian aestheticism that makes the later Nietzsche the greatest critic and psychologist of morality known in the history of the mind" (247). The need for lying and the ascetic desire for the painful unmasking of the truth stand side by side.

This contradiction is already present in the opposition of the "Apollonian" and the "Dionysian" elements in his first book, with his preference for the latter. The conflict is sharpened even more when we find at the beginning of *Beyond Good and Evil* (1886): "In spite of all the value that might belong to the true, the truthful, the selfless—it may be that a more fundamental value, one that is higher for all of life, might have to be ascribed to appearance, to the wish to deceive, to selfishness, and to desire" (2). Thus a most astute psychological *description* changes into a *prescription* in terms of an extreme ethical pragmatism and utilitarianism, with the ascription of value and the implicit absolutizing of life as value.

The same shortly thereafter: "The falseness of a judgment is for us still no objection against a judgment; in this our new language might sound strangest. The question is, rather, to what extent does it promote life, preserve life, preserve the species, perhaps even improve the species through breeding. . . . To concede that untruth is a condition of life—that really means dangerously resisting the accustomed value feelings; and a philosophy that dares to do this already puts itself by that beyond good and evil" (*Jenseits* 4).

Yet the crucial statement of the insight at issue is this, in Nietzsche's own words:

> The conception of the world forming the background to this book is peculiarly dark and unpleasant: under all the types of pessimism that have become known so far none appears to have reached that degree of maliciousness. The *opposition of a true and an apparent world is lacking*: there is only one world, and this one is false, cruel, contradic-

tory, seductive, *without meaning.* . . . A world like this is the true world. . . . *We need [the] lie* in order to gain victory over this reality, this "truth," i.e., in order to *live.* . . . [The fact] itself that the lie is necessary in order to live belongs to this frightening and questionable character of existence. (*Nachgelassene* 193)

Thus, adds Giorgio Colli, "*the philosophy of power becomes the philosophy of the lie*" ("Nachwort," *Nachgelassene* 661). The conflict between the will for truth and the will for power ends in an unsolvable supreme paradox.

Camus speaks of the preponderance of the clinician. Is this really true? My own impression is that, especially in his later works, the prophet more and more subverts the clinician, cruelty and vindictiveness pervert curiosity and the impassioned search for truth, hatred infiltrates all interest, the sense of loss of love and of loneliness cries through the protests of strength and power.

In our distant view of his work, these contradictions and paradoxes, emerging from that double quest for truth and for strength, converge and form an ever deepening rift within.

THE TWO NIETZSCHES: THE DOUBLENESS— "IT WAS AT NOON, THAT ONE BECAME TWO"

Let us take together what we have found so far: There is the fierce denunciation of resentment and of its pernicious consequences—yet at the same time there is the unmistakable poison of that same feeling pouring out in his scorn.

There is the radical rejection of guilt and punishment, of remorse and pangs of conscience, their banishment from the new ethics; there is the ferocious rejection of any ethics built upon the "thou shalt"—yet it is hard to imagine a writer or thinker who is more condemnatory and critical, more judgmental and punishing, more corrosive in his contempt and ridicule. As I have said, the prophet, no matter how much denied, always wins out over the skillful psychologist and clinically subtle diagnostician in the constant shift from description to prescription and from that to proscription.

Then there is the duality of thinker and poet, both being of the greatest brilliance and depth, both of enormous power—and yet forced together and again breaking apart.

And there is something else. It has been said many times that Nietzsche was no anti-Semite. Yet there are many passages that are as vitriolic as the worst from any anti-Semitic tract; for example, in *The Twilight of the Idols*, where he extols "*Aryan* humanity" of "'pure blood'" and "nobility" against the *"anti-Aryan* religion *par excellence,"* a religion of hatred. I also find a passage like this particularly hard to stomach: "The history of Israel as a typical history of the *denaturalization* of the natural values" with its "radical *falsification* of all nature, of all naturalness, of all reality, of the entire inner world" (*Antichrist* 24–35).

But then there also are beautiful passages about the Jews; for instance, in *Human, All Too Human*:

> [T]he Jew becomes as useful and desirable an ingredient [in a European mixed race] as any other national remnant. There are unpleasant, even dangerous attributes in every nation, in every man; it is cruel to demand that the Jew should be an exception. I would like to know how much one should, in the total account, forgive a people which, not without guilt on all our parts, has had the most painful history of all peoples, and to whom we owe the most noble human being (Christ), the purest sage (Spinoza), the most powerful book, and the most effective moral law in the world. Furthermore, during the darkest periods of the Middle Ages, when the Asiatic pall was lying heavily over Europe, it was Jewish free thinkers, scholars, and physicians, who, under the harshest personal constraint, held fast to the banner of enlightenment and intellectual independence and defended Europe against Asia; it is owing to their efforts not least, that a more natural, more rational, and in any case non-mythical explanation of the world could eventually triumph again, and that the ring of culture linking us to the enlightenment of Greco-Roman antiquity remained unbroken. If Christianity has done everything possible to orientalize the Occident, then Judaism has helped essentially to occidentalize it again and again: which, in a certain sense, is to say that it made Europe's task and history into a *continuation of that of Greece*. (*Menschliches* 1.7)

The same is true about nationalism; he calls it "this sickness and unreason that is the most hostile to culture there is" ("Wagner," *Ecce* 2), and yet he continually uses ethnic stereotypes.

And in a similar vein, in *The Twilight of the Idols* he makes a remark for which I myself feel the most heartfelt gratitude: "I distrust all systematizers and avoid them at all costs. The will to a system is a lack of honesty" ("Sprüche" 26). And yet, while his teaching is no system in a real sense and so many of his aphorisms and sentences seem to emerge featherlight out of the keenest perceptions, still the pervasive judgmentalness is grounded in rigid, perpetually repeated categories—in a one-sidedness, a *pars pro toto* absoluteness that keeps perverting its truth value and leads less to a true aporia than to self-contradictions and paradoxes that are not always of the greatest philosophical dignity.

Isn't this perhaps just the point: that he is *both*—a virulent anti-Semite, and a friend and lover of the Jews; categorical about everything, yet despising the categories others use and abuse; full of contempt and of respect, of hatred and of love? That there is again this extreme polarity and duality in him that he tries to reconcile, and yet cannot.

Another overarching contradiction: *justice* keeps coming up as one of the most important virtues. Very correctly, though in an historizing onesidedness (as opposed to a primarily psychological understanding), I believe, he develops it as emerging from the need for equilibrium, specifically in the archaic community: "*Equilibrium* is therefore a very important concept for the oldest teaching of law and morality; *equilibrium is the basis of justice*" (*Menschliches* 2.22).

The decisive issue is his recognition of the basic nature of justice on the basis of some original concept of equality—an equality of rights, of opportunities, not necessarily of results. While it may be traced back to allegedly deeper reasons of advantage and utility (hence a utilitarian explanation of the value of justice) or of pleasure, the fundamental quality of that equation for any kind of social life is maintained. Thus, by the grounding of justice in equality (equilibrium) the appeal to justice throughout his writings on so many levels—even on those of highest sublimation, of the "intellectual conscience" and creativity—is effectively and convincingly supported. He does use the notion of "justice" ("Gerechtigkeit") not infrequently, says even that "it wants to give everything its due" (*Menschliches* 1.636) and adds: "We want to kneel down in front of Justice as the only Goddess we recognize above ourselves" (1.637).

Yet then, much to the contrary, we keep hearing the opposite message sounded with great vehemence:

> . . . you who make souls whirl, you preachers of *equality*. To me you are tarantulas, and secretly vengeful.
>
> But I shall bring your secrets to light; therefore I laugh in your faces with my laughter of the heights.
>
> Therefore I tear at your webs, that your rage may lure you out of your caves of lies and your revenge may leap out from behind your word "justice."
>
> For *that man be delivered from revenge*, that is for me the bridge to the highest hope, and a rainbow after long storms. . . .
>
> For to *me* justice speaks thus: "Men are not equal." ("Taranteln," *Zarathustra*)

His hatred and scorn of the socialist gospel of justice on the basis of human equality or of the democratic pronouncements of equal rights keep breaking through, and with that the claim that the concepts of guilt and punishment have been "invented against knowledge [science]."

He states the contradiction himself that human beings needed equality for safety's sake, but as something that ran profoundly counter to their individual nature, something forced upon them, and concludes that there is neither natural law nor natural injustice ("Es gibt weder ein Naturrecht, noch ein Naturunrecht").

Seeing it as a fundamental conflict between two basic needs—that of the will to overpower the other and that of living together for safety's sake (or other deep motives)—would state the quandary in terms of basic conflict. To take the one, the will for power, as primary nature, and the other, the linkage of safety = community = justice, as against nature, appears to me to beg the question. Why would one be *for* nature, the other suddenly *against* nature, as he rightly states toward the end of *Human, All Too Human*: "We speak of nature, but forget that we are part of it: we ourselves are nature, in spite . . ." (*Menschliches* 2.327).

And finally a conflict and contradiction, one that is for the future most important and might be seen as growing out of the previously mentioned polarity between his rigid categorizations and his acerbic scorn against any philosophical systematization, ultimately against metaphysics altogether: I mean that slowly intensifying, ultimately fateful clash between rationality and myth that was destined to become the signal of action for those philosophical and political leaders of the coming paranoid catastrophe who were drawn to see in him their grand inspiration and philosophical guarantor.

It is easy to dismiss much of this doubleness and contradictoriness simply and only as part of pathology. On the contrary, I think that some of this belongs precisely to Nietzsche's deepest insights and prophetic anticipations. Later on it became in fact relevant for the philosophy underlying the "Complementarity Principle" as a basic epistemological tool, and it has by no means been fully integrated into our own psychoanalytic thinking.

He himself describes and justifies this doubleness of acknowledgment and denial (which we know of course well from Freud's writings about the "ego split") in an aphorism in the second volume of *Human, All Too Human*, under the heading *"Twice Unfair"*: "Sometimes we enhance the truth by a double injustice, namely when we see and present, one after the other, both sides of a matter, which we cannot see together [at the same time], yet in a way that each time we mistake [misunderstand] or deny the other side, deluding ourselves that what we see is the entire truth" (*Menschliches* 2.1)

And yet it would also be in his own spirit of relentless questioning and probing to go an extra step beyond and ask ourselves: Is this doubleness and self-contradiction not *also* part of the underlying conflict? Has it not been, as a tool of thought, used for its self-destruction, its self-abolition? And how? Is it not used, in addition to its epistemological credentials, for a purpose that stems from what Nietzsche himself has called his "suffering and deprivation"? And what would this suffering, in the current context, be due to? The biographer points repeatedly to his *"double, inauthentic existence"* (*"eine doppelbödige, unaufrichtige Existenz"*) (Janz 1: 406; emphasis added)—to unsolvable conflicts in which he more and more resorted to illness, to physical suffering, in order to have the decision "between seeming and being" (409) made for him; he himself uses the expression, "living in a peculiar conflict," referring to his need to think deeply, philosophically, and without disturbance versus his professional obligations (398ff.).

And finally, before ending this section, I have to bring up one very strange, very enigmatic remark in an "autobiographical note" from 1868 or 1869 (at the age of 24 or 25), and reported in the biography by Blunck and Janz: "What I dread is not the horrible figure behind my chair, but her voice; also not the words, but the ghastly unarticulate and inhuman tone of the figure. Yes, if it but talked like human beings" (Janz 1: 266). The biographers wonder whether other evidence for *hallucinations* of this kind may have been excised by his sister. It surely is evidence of a most radical form of doubling, of splitting the self into parts.

AN INTERPRETATION OF THE IDENTITY SPLIT

From all the unreconciled "splits" I select one I consider fundamental and decisive for a further understanding: Nietzsche speaks so much and so well about the cruelty of conscience, but his own conscience is pitiless, especially when it is turned against others, so that it endows those who take it over with the right to commit all violence without mercy. It was his conscience turned outward, his brand of archaic superego, his ferocious judgmentalness, his peculiar eloquence of contempt and ridiculing, and most of all his power to shame others by the very vehemence of his own resentment that lent its immense impetus, its mythopoetic force to a historical movement he would have abhorred had he encountered it. (I think something very similar might very well be true for Marx.)

Does not his appeal lie precisely in this doubleness of judgment and overthrow of conscience, in the doubleness of a superego based on the systematic prevention of being shamed and the elimination of those superego features having to do with guilt and punishment? I mean, an appeal rooted in just such a juxtaposition where the yoke of conscience is thrown off, yet the severity of judgment, the most pervasive judgmentalness is maintained.

Perhaps I can be more specific still. So much of life appears to be "cut out"—the depth of love, the intricacy of human relations, the questions of tenderness and attachment, and especially, as noted, the issue of justice without which no social system can endure and which forms such a very deep part of human nature. I noted above his increasingly shrill denunciation of the basis of justice in any concept of equality and the related dismissal of the ethics of guilt. As much as one has to profoundly agree with him that man's judgmentalness is one of the greatest banes in human relations and one of the most powerful poisons in the inwardness of the soul, and as much as one may wonder with him about the ultimate source of the concept of justice—the concept of justice cannot simply be removed by pointing to its abuse by vindictiveness or by demolishing the quest for equality.

What it eventually all comes down to is a resolute *"revolution against conscience,"* that is, against a specific form of conscience—at first simply the "feeling of 'sin' as a transgression against divine order," yet with that automatically also against guilt and remorse altogether: "the displeasure of remorse, the sharpest sting in the feeling of sin, is broken off" (*Menschliches* 1.133). Eventually guilt and conscience become a crime against mankind. With this imposition "*one has committed the greatest crime against mankind. Sin, . . .* man's way of self-dishonoring par excellence, has been invented to make science, culture, every kind of elevation and nobility of man impossible; the priest *rules* by means of the invention of sin" (*Antichrist* 49).

Furthermore, it is astonishing how he derives human nature again and again from external factors, from society and history, also from direct heredity of acquired traits. Justice has become entirely reduced to external utility, to a simple matter of punishment and reward; the feeling of fairness, the sense of justice as something very fundamental to human nature, is entirely dismissed. Thus it is not astonishing that the part of the superego that would be based on the sense of guilt, for having violated the rights of others, hence infringing upon the basic value of justice, can so easily and peremptorily be abolished by self-confident fiat: since it simply has been imposed historically by some malicious priests, aided and abetted by a conspiracy of that powerful race of the Jews, since it is, in other words, not part of any intrinsic human nature at all, the prophet's exhortations will declare it null and void.

Furthermore, the structure of the subject dissolves; all inner structure becomes determined from the outside, all inner conflict turns into a mere result of outside conflict, namely the conflict about power, eventually, the conflict between different centers of the "will to power" (cf. Colli, "Nachwort," *Nachgelassene*). Humanity has become *dehumanized*!

Hence it becomes one of his main messages, his main demands: to convict the old "Jewish" conscience of its mendacity and to abolish it. It is a deed of "therapeutic" liberation from conscience by externalizing it as an evil demon; after this externalization it can be killed, should be killed—and eventually will be killed—as such "vermin of conscience" ("Gewissens-Wurm") (*Antichrist* 25) should be eradicated: Nietzsche has been taken at his word.

All this seems to me a logical consequence of the basic denial of the value of justice as an independent ethical postulate of greatest force and one inextricably tied to some concept of *balance*, of equality—and, more generally, of the necessity of *human-relatedness, love* in the largest sense.

Nietzsche does not see, ot rather cannot accept, that suffering under evil is a basic human given, intrinsic to human nature, not just a psychological weakness to be proudly "made inoperative," "overcome," not merely an invention of the rabbis and priests of asceticism. He fails to note that such suffering cries for an explanation and coping, be it in the form of the various systems of cosmic justice; be it as attempts to alleviate suffering, each other's suffering, by that main target of his opprobrium, "Mitleiden"—"suffering with, pity, charity"; be it in the form of systems of social and legal justice.

This involves one giant myth—that such deep aspects of human nature are *created* from the outside, in this instance the malignant cunning of some power-greedy priests, led by that mythical Israel. It is, for such a skillful psychologist, a remarkably naive view of human nature: that it is shaped in its depths and to such considerable uniformity by external forces of a mythical character. This sort of *blaming* is the real ideological precursor of the totalitarian state—of what I have called "the three *paranoid catastrophes*" of this century—the totalitarian systems of Hitler, Stalin, and Mao Ze Dong.

What else can we call this attitude of blaming such human nature on sinister outside forces but a basically paranoid attitude of externalization, projection, and denial? The cause of weakening lies on the outside, or in a basic degeneracy ("weakness") of nature, and must be extirpated. In this way inner conflict is dealt with by global denial—the solution of Lagerkvist's *Dvärgen*.

THE DEFENSE AGAINST SHAME

I did speak of shame's third form as a reaction formation against being shamed for (wishes for) exposure and curiosity and against the traumatic sense of shame anxiety. There are countless examples in Nietzsche's writings of this attitude of shame, and the necessity of hiding, of disguise, of silence, of veiling oneself—as a protection. To give just one example, the killing of God has to eliminate the eye that saw everything; the "ugliest man" commits the deed of murdering God because the man who obeys the "thou shalt" does not want to command himself.

> He—*had* to die. He looked with eyes which saw *everything*—he saw man's depths and reasons, all his concealed disgrace and ugliness. His pitying knew no shame: he crawled into my dirtiest corners. This most curious, overintrusive, overpitiful one had to die. He always was seeing *me*: I wanted to have revenge on such a witness—or to cease living. God who saw everything, *also* saw Man: this God had to die! Man could not *endure* that such an witness live. ("Der Haßlichste Mensch," *Zarathustra*)

This deed, from now on, spares man the shame: "'How poor man is after all!' he [Zarathustra] thought in his heart; 'how ugly, how wheezing, how full of hidden shame!'"

The whole "second Nietzsche," his entire transvaluation of values, seems to me based on this magic of the reaction formation against shame, especially in the sense of a character and superego defense against the content of shame. There are also certain affects that serve as affect defenses against shame and may be used as precursors to the reaction formation: pride and vanity, spite and defiance, scorn and contempt.

Subsidiary to this is the magical undoing of suffering by creativity and beauty—a particularly lasting form of power proving that unworth had been transformed into highest and enduring worth, that "man had indeed been overcome," meaning that his shame has been wiped out, once and for all.

Another aspect of this defense against shame has to be *denial.* Wouldn't we have to say that the massive denial of wide and important areas of life mentioned, such as love and justice, might be dictated by that peculiar superego stance, that of the war against being shamed, and hence against the need to be resentful, as clinical experience shows? Yet wouldn't it also have to be a denial sustained by a constant battle against the old conscience, an opposite superego figure? Wouldn't we have to say that the player's jugglings and the shamer's dazzlings and the high-wire act are clearly only half of the truth, that this forced weightlessness that yearns at the same time to fly and to be grounded, to dance and to find the point of gravity, has to disguise some crushing heaviness and hide the deep suffering behind a courageous laughter and play?

WHO IS THE RELENTLESS ENEMY?

What is this other half? It seems to me to be this: that Nietzsche himself appears to be a man who is himself burdened by a *monstrously crush-*

ing conscience, that all his thinking is one incessant attempt to prove that this is not so anymore, that he has killed, "overcome" that inner enemy, that he has wagered his life and sanity, his reputation and companionship on its overthrow—yet without ever succeeding for more than "intoxicating" ("rauschhafte") moments of inspiration. He is burdened by a conscience that is as much fraught by guilt as by shame (in the sense of being ashamed), and accompanied by pain, helplessness, anxiety.

His whole creative life appears to be a *compulsive repetition of the shaking off of such an overbearing conscience*—the message being: "That bane of the Protestant ethic, that Christian superego of duty and categorical imperative, does not exist anymore; I have really killed it, haven't I? killed it for good, made it ridiculous forever as the malicious inner dwarf that it really always has been. Just look at me, how light I am, how unburdened of that dwarf! Look!" Parallel with such denial, however, there is the resurgence of what had been denied in the form of *projection and externalization*.

Thus we see, side by side, the greatest opposition: deepest insight into inner conflict, under the leadership of the *absolute ideal of truthfulness*, and the *paranoid externalization accompanying the denial of vast areas of inner conflict*, namely of all those having to do with the "old conscience"—guilt, remorse, responsibility toward others and, most of all, being ashamed—under the leadership of *an ideal, posed as equally absolute*, that of *strength and power*. The tension between these two absolute ideals or superego figures—of truthfulness versus power—is never resolved. It is the basic split that fractures all of Nietzsche's philosophy and underlies the doubleness: the division into a prophetic-apocalyptic, anti-shame-resentment philosophy and into a clinical-diagnostic philosophy of psychological truth and analysis. These two, I claim, stand in an irreconcilable combat. The former demands a paranoid solution, the second accepts conflict as something basic in the nature of human beings. The first is historically and culturally devastating, the second often evokes our enthusiastic admiration and assent, capable of teaching us a great deal even today, after 100 years of psychoanalysis. Nietzsche may have come closest to a convergence of the two, a partially successful synthesis, in *Zarathustra*, a work more poetic than philosophical. Otherwise the Nietzsche of truthfulness stands in "sheer oppugnancy" to the Nietzsche obsessed with the fight against weakness, his unsuccessful "war against shame and resentment." This fracture between truthfulness and strength, betweeen honesty and power underlies the fracture in his doctrine between the anthropological "will to power" and the cosmological "myth of the eternal return (recurrence) of the same," observed by Karl Löwith.

There is no doubt in my mind that Nietzsche has given all of us questions and answers that have not lost their truth value by the fact that they were taken one-sidedly and at the cost of massive denial and projection—and that he claimed for himself an inner freedom and a truthfulness that is at least open to question.

THE BASIC TRAUMA

We have seen how on the basis of a number of dubious equations conclusions are drawn that lead to the rejection and elimination of vast areas of ethics. I pull together some of those equations and their implications:

- Determinism = lack of responsibility, hence of guilt, remorse ("worm of conscience" ["Gewissenswurm"]) and of the justification of punishment
- Guilt feelings and responsibility = imposition of sanctions by God, alias by the priests, alias by Jewish-Christian tradition
- Conscience = resentment rooted in weakness and vindictiveness turned against the self
- Reasonable = advantageous or pleasurable
- Sense of justice = equality imposed by society against nature, to compensate for the weakness of the individual by an equilibrium of power
- True justice = inequality (of opportunity as well as of result)
- Life = implacable cruelty, mercilessness
- Having a true or honest conscience ("intellektuales Gewissen"), after the transvaluation of values = not to have to feel ashamed = not to be weak = not to be a "sacrificial animal" = to be proud and strong
- Will to truth = part of will to power = will to lie

In all these instances issues central to human existence are addressed often in a very novel, very perspicacious way, as long as they are put in terms of "will against will," "drive against drive," as a conflict of motivation—intrapsychically, intrasocietally, intraculturally. The error, I believe, enters, time and again, when one part of such a conflict falls under the verdict of evil and is being derided or, later on, ferociously condemned, usually as a force impinging from the outside of whatever system he is investigating—when, in other words, mythical categories of

"Either-Or" polarizations into absolute Good or Evil supersede the sober analysis of conflict, particularly when he deploys the mythical category of *pars pro toto* reasoning. Yes, life (or nature) is implacable and merciless, but human life is part of nature, as he rightly states, and while cruelty is part of it, caring and sympathy are part of it also. Pity shames and may be carried by resentment, hence hidden revenge; however, pity is also caring and identification with the other as suffering, in the knowledge that we can only hope for help if we are willing to render caring and help to others. Yes, human life "by nature" is the wish for self-preservation, is combat, is war, is the wish for ascendancy and power and glory—it needs the "pathos of distance," it wants the strength in individuality and separateness; yet human life "by nature" is also the wish for dependency and protection, for belonging, for closeness, even for merging, not only with the universe, but with another human being; it needs the "*pathos of intimacy*" just as much as it craves for the "pathos of distance."

To see all the time this crucial doubleness of human nature, this fundamental "being in conflict" whereby the opposite forces are ultimately complementary makes it possible to address causally what mythical thinking tries to make into an "Either-Or" of absolutes. What I have singled out as *Nietzsche One* was able to elaborate conflict as nobody before, "thinking out of conflict," as I put it. *Nietzsche Two* took the sword and cut the Gordian knots of those conflicts. His need for action overcame his dispassionate contemplation of the opposites. His deep abhorrence of passivity made him a spiritual Alexander and Caesar instead of a Freud.

Yet there is something deeper in this "cutting out" of one part, at the damage of the "totum." I select the one most glaring excision that has kept coming up in these considerations.

We have recognized that the upshot of Nietzsche's new ethics is the disregard of the primacy and original importance in human nature of two motivational forces: the needs to belong, to love, to care and to be cared for; and the needs to be treated with justice or fairness and hence to treat others fairly too. More and more the sole repository of motivation is being seen in the strivings for power, and that means the power of bringing about that which is advantageous and pleasurable to the individual or to the species as a whole, hence to confirm the individual's strength or the strength and force of life as a whole (as a mythical entity) and hence, as derivatives, to uphold the values of honor and nobility, namely as an expression of respect for and fear of this power.

This excision of love and especially, built upon that, of justice, in the sense of some form of equality, as fundamental components of the ethical system in general—more importantly, as part of what we would call the superego as inner authority—has very dramatic philosophical implications.

First of all, one might wonder, why this curious excision of justice as fundamental? Why then the entire excision of the part of conscience oriented toward guilt?

Nietzsche was the oldest of three children, the only one who still was close to the father. The youngest brother died less than a year after the father (in Nietzsche's sixth year of life). Mother's caring was focused now mostly upon the boy, it appears, much more so than upon the twenty-month younger sister; in a letter she called him the "Hausgötze," "the idol of the house." The sister was intensely loyal, adoring, submissive toward the older, rather despotic brother; yet she showed later on deep jealousy and hostility toward him.

The construct makes complete sense: that he struggled all his life with the conflict between wanting to be the adored child whose inequality in the direction of specialness remained safeguarded and feeling guilt about such preference, especially when this, a kind of Oedipal victory, had been bought at the price of the double death, the "double murder" of father and brother. Was not he thus the "ugliest man" who had to kill God because he, God, had been snooping in the most intimate recesses of his conscience? Was not it thus imperative to trample down the "worm of conscience" in order to mute the voice crying out in behalf of injured justice?

This is an interpretation combining our clinical experience with a large amount of what we derived from the fractured nature of the material. Yet this explanation accounts well for the "narcissistic" aspects of Nietzsche's phenomenology; it does not take in account the depth of suffering he tried to overcome.

However there is a second, I believe deeper way of interpreting the data, one that only *seems* to be contradictory, but in truth complements the first. Here the biographer opens a deeper view to us: "That death should be an expiation for an inherited [primal] guilt, for the inherited sin of Adam, is for him an entirely impossible thought. His father was and remained for him one of the most deeply revered human beings. His reverence fought against [the thought] that this kindly and pious man should have suffered early death like a punishment, as somebody 'guilty' and as a sinner. This Christian-dogmatic series of causality could and should not be true for him. . . . He opposed to it his tragic-Dionysian insight that he later on formulated as the 'Innocence of Becoming'" (Janz 1: 435).

Thus the suffering, the pain he keeps struggling with and tries to overcome, would then have one very essential root in the deep grief, the unending mourning *over* his father—clearly repeated in the never conquered hurt and grief about the break with Richard Wagner and his wife Cosima.

His fury against Christianity and against the concept of guilt and sin would be the rage against the loss of the one he truly had loved and adored (much more so than his cold and stingy, possessive and intrusive mother). His excision of the primacy of justice would reflect his unabating indignation, his own unstilled resentment about the failure of retributive justice: "How could God be fair if he allowed the untimely death of this upright man? My revenge against my innocent father's death is the proclamation: God is dead!—and the resurrection of Man-God as the dismembered Dionysos-Zagreus, and as 'overman'!" His double campaign against the Christian God and against a conscience based on guilt and sin could thus be seen as a vehement protest against the injustice of that early loss, the myth of the eternal return its undoing. The steady emphasis on joy, strength, life, becoming would be an incessant antithesis (a reaction formation as affect defense) against the underlying suffering and sadness, the pain of illness and decay witnessed in the father, and reinforced by the brother's death. His will to life and power would be a constantly proclaimed victory over the death and helplessness faced by the one he had loved most and whom he sought again and again in idealized father figures (Schopenhauer, the Greeks of antiquity, Vischer, Burckhardt, and especially Wagner).

Yet it must also be clear from the profound *ambivalence* toward all these "transference figures" that this reverence and adoration was not unmixed. The double argument given up to now also does not explain the profundity and centrality of his "war against shame," the ferocity of his contempt against weakness, victimhood and defectiveness. Is this his contempt against the father as sick, as victim of an inexorable process of decay, and as one visibly damaged? Is his own battle against shame rooted in a profound identification with the father as victim of the son's "merciless" scorn and contempt—shame being of course contempt directed against the self?

We might derive something else from our clinical experience: I have been very impressed by the severity and cruelty of the superego in cases with severe traumatization of any kind. It is as if the whole brutality of the trauma—be it physical or emotional abuse, be it massive loss or persecution, be it physical (somatic) suffering—had become part of the inner world in the form of cruelty of conscience, of self-beratement and self-punishment, in the form of overwhelming guilt and shame. One may also turn it around and say that one's own rage about the helpless surrender and terror during the trauma had been turned against the self. I think that again both understandings are complementary and need to be interpreted clinically.

In Nietzsche's case we may well assume that the slow destruction and then the loss of the father, at the age of 4 and 5, was such a protracted and yet also violent and shocking jolt to this highly gifted, sensitive child that he always carried the monster of the trauma as part of an overwhelming, harsh, menacing conscience. As we saw, part of it had to be denied, part of it was turned around 180 degrees—by turning passive into active. Passivity, victimhood, weakness were so profoundly abhorrent that he became as fiercely condemning and polemical as that inner demon was against him. Still there was such a dwelling on being the victim and on accepting and loving fate—*amor fati*—that it is hard to escape the conclusion that the outwardly demonstrated *sadistic* traits were really already a superficial manifestation of the overwhelming *masochistic orientation.* This masochistic attitude would have arisen under the "hammer beats" of trauma, developed toward "fate" (and toward a doting, but also rather aggressive, financially very withholding mother and quite early on toward the tyrannical school in Pforta), developed above all toward his own "inner judge" (the superego), and finally would have been shown toward women, shown also in his unlimited and uncanny ability to destroy whatever he had built up professionally, socially, and in his intimate relationships.

> You are going to women? Do not forget the whip! [Du gehst zu Frauen? Vergiß die Peitsche nicht!] ("Weiblein," *Zarathustra*)

> What does life mean?—Life—that means: continually ridding oneself of something that wants to die; life—that means: being cruel and implacable against everything that becomes weak and old in us, and not only in us. Life—that means therefore: being without pity towards the dying, the miserable, the old? Always to be murderous?—And yet old Moses said: "Thou shalt not kill!" (*Wissenschaft* 26)

In the first quote we observe the nakedly sadistic side motivated by fear: "Let man fear woman when she loves. . . . Let man fear woman when she hates" ("Weiblein," *Zarathustra*). In the second quote we see, side by side, the aggression first directed against the self, specifically in behalf of that superego part that wants to eradicate everything weak, that is, that wages "the war against shame," then this very same superego-led aggression turned outward, against everything weak in the outside world, and finally the quizzical, ironic, perhaps sarcastic reminder of the old, guilt-oriented superego figure, Moses.

There seems to me to be further, very strong evidence for the pathogenic importance of such overwhelming traumatization: the attempt to build up a second world of denial parallel to the first world of the trauma. Nietzsche is intoxicated by that Dionysiac world of fantasy and of art, he is fascinated by the power of deception or the lie, he keeps searching for a world that would be radically opposite to the world of pain and shame, of guilt and death, of injustice and suffering and victimhood: the world dominated by the fantasy of rebirth—the eternal recurrence. This would be a world where indeed "man would be overcome." Such a second world of denial is a counterworld to the world of resentment—and here I mean Nietzsche's own resentment, which he so bravely tried to transcend—yet in vain.

All these conjectures give us a comprehensive model that accommodates all the available data fairly well. They cannot give us scientific certainty, nor do I believe that they are sufficient; they only evince some plausibility (especially in regard to the derivation of the "war against shame" there are probably other very important factors the knowledge of which eludes us).

THE APOCALYPTIC RESULT

Historically, it is decisive that in none of these works is there an elimination of the superego. Quite to the contrary, we witness its massive reinforcement, although in profoundly altered form—from our clinical view, we would say in deeply regressive form.

To return to Nietzsche's new, ever more radical superego: the "second Nietzsche," the ideal of "Zarathustra" and his conscience, became one leading superego figure for Germany, in fact for much of Europe— with the most devastating consequences. The graver the humiliations were, especially after the First World War, the more that new superego fighting with all its weapons against the inner and the outer shame, assumed mythical proportion and power in reality—as historical, political, military, and finally murderous force. And Nietzsche anticipated this force—hoping to "overcome" it in general terms, yet deceiving himself in that he decisively helped to bring it about in its most horrible form—by his own pervasive judgmentalness in sarcasm and reproach and by his own drenching, yet denied resentment: "Verily, a monster is the power of this praising and censuring" ("Ziele," Zarathustra).

By reducing the guilt-oriented conscience to a matter of shame, to some external imposition of sanctions that leaves the individual helpless and passive, he accomplishes the entire "transvaluation of values." May it not be precisely his doubleness, the claim that all great insight requires the "Doppelblick," "the double view," combined with the depth of insight, the brilliance of language and the art of metaphor, that has endowed his message with such an enormous echo and appeal, with such a following? And further, is it not precisely this doubleness of rebellion and loyalty in his "double sight" that has such a disastrous mass appeal because of the severity of superego conflicts at a time when old securities are shaken and the allegiances of the past have been overthrown?

Nietzsche's importance consists in having drawn our attention to an ethic built upon categories of shame, and in the fact that, with extreme consistency, he developed such a morality, stressed its own truth and value, its autonomy, and put in front of us its huge significance as part of our own inner nature, its validity for us. However he made the fundamental mistake of putting it as an Either-Or, that is, he posed the categories absolutely, he reduced the guilt categories to those of shame, the factors of human nature to those of external, historical imposition, and he left out the centrality of the need for justice in human nature and as the causal issue behind the corrosive power of resentment.

Yet he could not have made those mistakes if he had not been the foremost explorer of inner conflict, and with that of the "laws" of human nature, prior to Freud. His errors honor his genius as much as his discoveries.

NOTES

This paper was originally presented to the History of Psychiatry Section, Cornell University Medical Center, 16 December 1992.

1. Please note that in the parenthetical citations to Nietzsche's texts, the number, or the last number given, refers to the section, not the page. All translations are by the author. The following English versions of Nietzsche's work have been consulted: *Beyond Good and Evil*, trans. Walter Kaufmann (New York: Vintage, 1966); *Thus Spake Zarathustra*, trans. R. J. Hollingdale (Harmondsworth, U.K.: Penguin, 1969); *The Gay Science*, trans. Walter Kaufmann (New York: Vintage, 1974); *On the Genealogy of Morals and Ecce Homo*, trans. Walter Kaufmann (New York: Vintage, 1967); *Twilight of the Idols* and *The Anti-Christ*, trans. R. J. Hollingdale (Harmondsworth, U.K.: Penguin, 1969); *Human, All Too Human*, trans. Marion Faber, with Stephen Lehmann (Lincoln: U of Nebraska P, 1984); *Daybreak*, trans. R. J. Hollingdale (Cambridge: Cambridge UP, 1982).

2. See *Die Zerbrochene Wirklichkeit*, 128–83.

WORKS CITED

Camus, Albert. *The Rebel: An Essay on Man in Revolt*. Trans. Anthony Bower. New York: Vintage, 1956.

Janz, Curt Paul. *Friedrich Nietzsche: Biographie*. 3 Vols. Munich, Vienna: C. Hanser, 1978.

Kaufmann, Walter. "Translator's Notes." *Thus Spoke Zarathustra*. New York: Viking, 1966.

Löwith, Karl. *My Life in Germany before and after 1933: A Report.* Trans. Elizabeth King. Urbana and Chicago: U of Illinois P, 1994.

——. *Nietzsches Philosophie der ewigen Wiederkehr des Gleichen.* Stuttgart: Kohlhammer, 1956.

Mann, Thomas. "Nietzsches Philosophie in Lichte unserer Erfahrung." *Essays.* Volume 1. Frankfurt: Fischer, 1978. 235–64.

——. "Schopenhauer." *Essays.* Volume 3. Frankfurt: Fischer, 1978. 193–234.

Nietzsche, Friedrich. *Die Geburt der Tragödie aus dem Geiste der Musik.* 1871. Stuttgart: Kröner, 1976.

——. "Über Wahrheit und Lüge im außermoralischen Sinne." 1873. *Unzeitgemässe Betrachtungen.* Stuttgart: Kröner, 1976.

——. *Menschliches, Allzumenschliches.* 1878, 1879, 1880. Stuttgart: Kröner, 1978.

——. *Morgenröte.* 1881. Stuttgart: Kröner, 1976.

——. *Die fröhliche Wissenschaft.* 1882. Stuttgart: Kröner, 1976.

——. *Also sprach Zarathustra.* 1883–85. Stuttgart: Kröner, 1988.

——. *Jenseits von Gut und Böse.* 1885. Stuttgart: Kröner, 1976.

——. *Zur Genealogie der Moral.* 1887. Stuttgart: Kröner, 1976.

——. *Götzendämmerung.* 1888a. Stuttgart: Kröner, 1964.

——. *Der Antichrist.* 1888b. Stuttgart: Kröner, 1964.

——. *Ecce Homo.* 1888c. Stuttgart: Kröner, 1964.

——. *Nachgelassene Fragmente.* Vol. 13 of *Sämtliche Werke.* Ed. Colli and Montinari. Berlin: de Gruyter, 1980.

——. *Gedichte.* Bern: Alfred Scherz, 1948.

Wurmser, Léon. *The Mask of Shame.* 1981. New York: Jason Aronson, 1994.

——. *Die Zerbrochene Wirklichkeit.* Heidelberg: Springer, 1989.

——. "Shame: The Veiled Companion of Narcissism." *The Many Faces of Shame.* Ed. Donald L. Nathanson. New York: Guilford P, 1987.

CHAPTER 7

"The Dread and Repulsiveness of the Wild": D. H. Lawrence and Shame

Barbara Schapiro

Biographers of D. H. Lawrence have noted a curious irony. The author of *Lady Chatterley's Lover*, the writer best known for his celebration of sexuality and uninhibited bodily expression in his art, was in many respects quite puritanical and fastidious in his life. Lawrence disliked being touched or caressed, hated being kissed on the mouth, made his wife, Frieda, wear austere, starched underwear, and once chided a female houseguest for entering the sitting-room in her ankle-length petticoat—"He disapproved," he told her, "of people appearing in their underclothes." As Jeffrey Meyers quips, "He could be a prude as well as a priest of love" (125).[1]

A careful look at Lawrence's art, I believe, can uncover the irony lurking there as well. Beneath the urgent promotion of spontaneous sensual expression in the texts is a profound sense of shame over bodily, passionate life and a concomitant narcissistic rage. As sexuality is bound up with such shame and rage for Lawrence, it can prove to be a source of terror, of dread and repulsiveness, while simultaneously representing the locus for narcissistic repair, for idealization and salvation of the self.

Lawrence's fiction indeed instructs us on how affects are inextricably entwined with the body; it also teaches how sexuality is far more deeply involved with emotional and relational issues of self and other than it is with the pleasurable release of tension. "The central motivational construct" for contemporary psychoanalysis, Robert Stolorow and George Atwood assert, has shifted "from drive to affect" (26).[2] Shame is an affect receiving particular attention because of its essential role in the most prevalent, perhaps definitive, pathology of our time: narcissism. Andrew Morrison argues that shame is central to narcissistic disorders in the same way that guilt is central to the Oedipal and neurotic problems on which Freud focused (7).

Any serious reader of Lawrence knows that the author's real concern is not with sex but with identity and relationship. Lawrence "never writes about sex," observes Robert Langbaum, "without writing about identity" (251). For Lawrence, sex involves profound issues of self that go well beyond castration anxieties and guilt over incestuous and aggressive wishes.[3] Sexual relationships in Lawrence's fiction often threaten loss of boundaries and disintegration of self; shame, rather than guilt, is the underlying affect, along with a subjective sense of unreality and emptiness. Lawrence's subject, in Heinz Kohut's terms, is less Guilty Man than Tragic Man (*Restoration* 132); the core anxiety extends beyond a self conflicted to that of the tragic dilemma of not having a self at all.[4]

Lawrence's preoccupation with identity centers primarily on the self's experience of authenticity, on *feeling* fully alive and real. His work reveals how affects and the body are deeply implicated in the subjective experience of authenticity. Current psychoanalytic theorists understand affects as both interpersonal and intrapsychic: certain affects may be innate, as Silvan Tomkins argues, but they are also molded and developed in the matrix of interpersonal relationships, ultimately becoming embedded in unconscious psychic structures.

According to psychoanalyst Daniel Stern, the most crucial factor in the development of a sense of subjective reality or authenticity is what he calls "affect attunement"—a sharing or communing between infant and caregiver of internal affect states. Such matching of feeling states is our first and most important form of sharing subjective experiences, and it serves to authorize our experience of ourselves, to validate our very being. Disruptions or defects in affect attunement can have the opposite effect; if the child's spontaneous, affective self-expression is met with a nonattuned response, the experience for the child is one of negation or rejection of self—a profound narcissistic wound.[5] It is here that shame may take root in determining character structure.

The following discussion hopes to show how shame is a determining factor in the structure of Lawrence's fiction. His art represents a "masking" of shame, to use Léon Wurmser's term, as it works to heal the wound to the self by exposing what was hidden and celebrating what was denied. Ocular imagery—seeing and being seen—also figures prominently.[6] The roots of shame in self-other attunement problems are evident as well.

Much has been made in Lawrence criticism of the author's rage toward his strong, domineering mother. Of equal importance, however, is Lawrence's deep empathy and identification with his mother's shame. For all his misogyny, Lawrence understood female shame in a patriarchal culture in a deep and visceral way. His fiction in fact demonstrates how the reality of the mother's shame—her wounded narcissism—precipitates the child's fantasy of her devouring omnipotence.

John Worthen's recent biography of Lawrence's early years offers a portrait of Lawrence's mother, Lydia, that suggests some possible sources for the shame at the heart of her son's fiction. According to Worthen, Lydia's most remarkable feature was not her domineering nature but her extreme reticence, her shyness and emotional reserve. She was indeed nicknamed "The Mouse" as a child. Worthen quotes Lawrence's younger sister Ada describing Lydia "as having 'a rather quiet, reserved and ladylike nature. . . . She was never effusive or demonstrative in any way'" (15). Above all, the sense of Lydia that emerges in Worthen's account is that of a thwarted life, a life constricted on several levels and disappointed at all stages.

Lydia's emotional constriction was likely due, at least in part, to her strict, puritanical upbringing. She was also constrained by her family's reduced economic situation (her father's family had been relatively well-off, but due to a collapse in the lace industry, they had lost almost everything). Lydia's parents were acutely sensitive to their loss of social position and esteem. When her father was later injured in an accident at work, the family was forced to depend on the support of relatives. Worthen believes that Arthur Lawrence, whom Lydia met in her early twenties, may have represented her best opportunity for escape from her family's demeaning circumstances.

Though Arthur was only a collier, a miner's wages in those days were relatively high. There is also evidence to suggest that he may have misrepresented his position to her. "While it is impossible to be certain about what Arthur Lawrence told Lydia," Worthen concludes, "or what she may have wanted to hear, it is important that she came to believe that she had been deceived" (15). Her dashed expectations compounded a pattern in her family history of loss and humiliating disappointment.

In addition, when Lydia married Arthur, she was forced to leave her family's community and move to Eastwood. Worthen emphasizes her almost complete isolation. She "had relatively few friends in Eastwood, where she lived for twenty-six years. . . . To be more exact, she never accepted that Eastwood was her community" (23). Lawrence—or "Bert" as he was known to the family—was the fourth child born to this isolated and apparently bitter and depressed mother. In *Sons and Lovers*, as I will discuss, the mother's wounded narcissism, her shame and depression, are key factors in her son Paul's identity and relational problems.

For Lydia, Arthur most likely represented an escape not only from poverty, but quite possibly from her cramped emotional life as well. From all accounts Arthur was an exuberant, highly sensual man, who drank and danced with abandon. Lydia's initial attraction to these qualities, however, soon gave way to her bitterness at being deceived and a growing antagonism toward both Arthur and the whole mining community. The marriage thus proved to have the opposite emotional effect; far from liberating her, it served only to rigidify her defenses, to increase her inwardness, isolation, and need for control. "She became sterner as she got older," Worthen notes, "and forgot her original reaction to her husband's charm and good humour" (18). Her children, as *Sons and Lovers* makes clear, became her allies and her refuge. The mother's overinvestment in her children and the shackling quality of her love are a direct product of the paucity of her life. The imperiousness and pride for which she was known may have been her best defense against a much deeper sense of injury and shame; and it is the mother's shame, not really her power, that is the legacy her son wrestled with most profoundly in his fiction.

Quoting from Lawrence's letters, Worthen maintains that we can see in the young Lawrence "a child's version of his mother's feelings; he grew up with a 'distaste for being caressed (except on occasions),' with a strong sense of untouchableness which was his 'sort of pride'" (59). The writer who came to champion bodily, sexual expression was struggling against his own heavy sense of shame and deeply ingrained inhibitions. "Loving Lydia Lawrence meant not only remaining a responsible son and becoming a salary earner," Worthen suggests, "it meant inhibiting his own carelessness, impulsiveness, anger and (in particular) sensuality" (156). In Lawrence's life, and later in his fiction, his father came to represent everything that was denied and repressed: instinctive physicality, sensuality, and spontaneous emotional expression.

Lawrence's idealized father-figures, particularly the strong, dominating male characters who figure so prominently in the novels of his so-called leadership period, are essentially idealized self-projections. Such idealization is always a defense; it is a reaction to loss and deficiency. Wurmser sees idealization as one of the preeminent masks of shame: it functions "as a powerful counterpoise to, and 'healing' of, the core of unlovability" (296). The idealization defense, however, is invariably threatened by the shame and envy that initiated it. The empty, deficient self dreads being overwhelmed by the very power and vitality it has projected outward, onto the other. These psychodynamics contribute, I believe, to the intense ambivalence bound up with homosexual love in Lawrence's work.[7] While loving another man is connected in the fiction with an infusing male potency, it is also tangled up with profound, unconscious shame, with self-contempt, and with a terror of dissolution and absorption.

As Lawrence's letters reveal, homosexual love was associated in the writer's mind with swamps, "marsh gas," and beetles. After meeting the economist John Maynard Keynes and his Cambridge homosexual set, Lawrence describes his overpowering feelings of disgust: the "smell of rottenness, marsh-stagnancy" and the "horrible sense of frowstiness, so repulsive, as if it came from deep inward dirt—a sort of sewer. . . . I feel as if I should go mad, if I think of your set. . . . It makes me dream of beetles" (quoted in Meyers 165–66).

What Lawrence craves, in other words, he also deeply dreads. Worthen describes Lawrence's extremely conflicted reaction to watching Sarah Bernhardt perform onstage. In a letter, Lawrence refers to Bernhardt as "the incarnation of wild emotion," and discusses his extraordinary fascination with her performance: "I could love such a woman myself, love her to madness; all for the pure, wild passion of it. Intellect is shed as flowers shed their petals" (147). He also describes rushing from the theater in terror lest he become "enslaved" to such a woman. As Worthen states, "He was fascinated by the idea of being enslaved, and of having his own intellectual detachment stripped from him. And he did not know if he wanted it, or if he wanted to run away from it. That was the excitement of Bernhardt" (147). That is also the excitement that inspires much of the tension and dynamics of Lawrence's fiction.

Worthen sees Lawrence's detachment from his own feelings as the most traumatic aspect of his young life. Underlying such detachment is a smoldering sense of shame connected with emotional and bodily expression. As Worthen also discusses, Lawrence was excruciatingly sensitive throughout his early years to feeling exposed and humiliated. His weak lungs and the many physical illnesses that plagued him from the time he was two weeks old contributed significantly to the problem, exacerbating his sense of deficiency and bodily shame. The rage that inevitably accompanies such shame became increasingly apparent when Lawrence entered his early twenties. The emotional constraint and the seeming gentleness and asexuality of his manner were periodically giving way to violent outbursts and angry, irrational fits. These were frequently directed at Jessie Chambers, the model for Miriam in *Sons and Lovers* and with whom Lawrence had an intensely ambivalent attachment. It wasn't until he met Frieda Von Richthofen Weekley, who was as impulsive and as sensually and emotionally uninhibited as his father, that Lawrence found a relationship that, though still perpetually conflicted, was genuinely liberating.

Sons and Lovers (1913) is a moving testament to Lawrence's conflicted but deeply empathic identification with his mother, particularly with her buried sense of shame. The first three chapters of the novel focus explicitly on the mother's wounded narcissism, on her thwarted subjectivity. The narrative immediately establishes Gertrude Morel's lack of "I-ness," her sense that she has no self, no individual agency or authentic being in her own right:

> And looking ahead, the prospect of her life made her feel as if she were buried alive.
>   . . . She seemed so far away from her girlhood, she wondered if it were the same person walking heavily up the back garden at the Bottoms, as had run so lightly on the breakwater at Sheerness, ten years before.
>   "What have I to do with it!" she said to herself. "What have I to do with all this? Even the child I am going to have! It doesn't seem as if I were taken into account."
>   Sometimes life takes hold of one, carries the body along, accomplishes one's history, and yet is not real, but leaves one's self as it were slurred over. (14)

Because the mother does not feel herself "real," the discovery of reality for the child she carries will prove to be exceedingly difficult. Lack of faith in the mother's independent reality and the concomitant sense of one's own insubstantiality or hollowness constitute the core problem for Paul.

Lawrence is astutely aware of the social and economic circumstances contributing to the mother's narcissistically impaired state. Gertrude's economic dependency in a loveless marriage keeps her powerless, angry, and resentful. As a woman, her options for self-realization and expression are limited to her role as mother and to a vicarious experience of achievement through the lives of her sons:

> The world seemed a dreary place, where nothing else would happen for her—at least until William grew up. But for herself, nothing but this dreary endurance—till the children grew up. And the children! She could not afford to have this third. She did not want it. The father serving beer in a public house, swilling himself drunk. She despised him, and was tied to him. The coming child was too much for her. If it were not for William and Annie, she was sick of it, the struggle with poverty and ugliness and meanness. (13)

By presenting Mrs. Morel's perspective, the narrative displays an empathic understanding of the mother's resentment of her fetus, Paul. This is rather remarkable given the autobiographical nature of the novel and the authorial identification with Paul. The fact that Mrs. Morel "did not want," indeed "dreaded this baby" (50) is repeated several times in the opening chapters. We are also told of her great guilt over feeling such antipathy toward her baby, and we will certainly see Paul suffer the consequences. As Jeffrey Berman points out, Gertrude is an "alternately overloving and underloving" mother (205). The narrative identification with the mother's anguish in this first part of the book, however, resists a simplistic interpretation of the novel that "blames" Gertrude Morel for her failures as a mother.[8]

Sons and Lovers dramatizes Mrs. Morel's rigidity and lack of sensuality, but it also allows the reader to see the mother herself as the beleaguered child of a cold, harsh parent—her overbearing father, George Coppard: he is described as "proud in his bearing, handsome, and rather bitter; who preferred theology in reading, and who drew near in sympathy only to one man, the Apostle Paul; who was harsh in government, and in familiarity ironic; who ignored all sensuous pleasure" (18). Though we are told Gertrude preferred her mother and "hated her father's overbearing manner towards her gentle, humorous, kindly-souled mother" (15–16), it is her father's emotional legacy that she bears: "She was a puritan, like her father, high-minded, and really stern" (18). If one is assigning blame, in other words, one must look to Lawrence's explicit representation of the oppressively puritanical, patriarchal culture of which Gertrude is a product.

The narrator also informs us that before meeting Walter, Gertrude had loved a young man, John Field, whom she was prevented from marrying by economic constraints and by Field's own rigid, autocratic father. When Field tells her he would like to go into the ministry, Gertrude responds, "Then why *don't* you—why don't you? . . . If *I* were a man, nothing would stop me" (16). Field replies, "But my father's so stiff necked. He means to put me into the business, and I know he'll do it" (16). Field's father loses the business, but Field pursues neither the ministry nor Gertrude: he becomes a teacher and marries an elderly woman with property. "And still," the narrator asserts, "Mrs. Morel preserved John Field's bible . . . [She] kept his memory intact in her heart, for her own sake. To her dying day, for thirty-five years, she did not speak of him" (17).

The portrait of Gertrude that emerges in the novel's first chapter allows the reader to understand her brittleness. The hard, affectless surface or shell protects against deep disappointment and personal diminishment, against the emotional rejection she suffered as a daughter and a woman in a father's world. After marrying Walter, she again experiences humiliation and betrayal when she learns that the house she believed was her husband's does not actually belong to him: "Gertrude sat white and silent. She was her father now. . . . She said very little to her husband, but her manner had changed towards him. Something in her proud, honorable soul had crystallised out hard as rock" (21).

Lawrence's fiction consistently portrays characters whose souls have hardened and "crystallised" as a result of severe narcissistic injury. A shameful feeling of rejection—rejection of her feeling, desiring self—underlies Mrs. Morel's proud, impenetrable surface; such shame indeed underlies Lawrence's many schizoidlike characters. It also contributes to the intense power dynamics in love that so distinguish Lawrence's fiction. "Lovelessness," as Wurmser states, "is powerlessness" (97); shame is inevitably entangled with issues of power in personal relationships.

Gertrude was originally attracted to Walter because he represented precisely what she (and her father) lacked—spontaneous, emotional, and sensual expressiveness: "the dusky, golden softness of this man's sensuous flame of life, that flowed from off his flesh like the flame from a candle, not baffled and gripped into incandescence by thought and spirit as her life was, seemed to her something wonderful, beyond her" (18). As Lawrence came to recognize so clearly, however, another person can never complete or fill the void in the self. Selves can only balance and complement one another. The empty or fractured self may typically seek to absorb or devour the other in an attempt to compensate for the deficiency, but Lawrence shows again and again how that sort of relationship is doomed.

Because Gertrude "had no life of her own," the narrator explains, "she had to put her own living aside, put it in the bank, as it were, of her children. She thought and waited for them, dreamed what they would do, with herself behind them as motor force, when they grew up. Already William was a lover to her" (44). *Sons and Lovers* is indeed the quintessential oedipal novel; it demonstrates exactly how the oedipal fantasy becomes bloated and inflamed by the mother's wounded narcissism, by her shame and depression. Paul's experience of his mother as emotionally withdrawn and withholding excites acute narcissistic shame and rage; it also exacerbates the oedipal desire to penetrate, merge with, and possess her.

The novel shows Paul even as an infant as heir to his mother's stunted life, to her sadness and shame. Mrs. Morel notes "the peculiar heaviness of its [the baby's] eyes, as if it were trying to understand something that was pain. . . . It had blue eyes like her own, but its look was heavy, steady, as if it had realised something that had stunned some point of its soul" (50). She decides to call him Paul, "she knew not why" (51). The name, however, echoes her father's affinity with the cold, harsh Apostle Paul "who ignored all sensuous pleasure." The mother cannot help but bequeath to her son her own puritanical, affectively impoverished heritage. Gertrude's lost contact with her own authentic emotional and bodily life will make it difficult for her to recognize or affirm the passional life of her sons.

Mrs. Morel's depression is mirrored in her child who, the narrator tells us, trotted after her "like her shadow" and "would have fits of depression" that were particularly unsettling for his mother: "It made her feel beside herself. . . . She would plump him in a little chair in the yard, exclaiming, 'Now cry there, Misery!'" (64). Because Mrs. Morel has defensively warded off her own deep sadness and shame, she is unable to tolerate or empathize with her son's negative affects—his feelings of grief and anger—as well. Throughout his life Paul is unable to tell his mother about any of his failures or disgraces: "he never told her anything disagreeable that was said to him, only the nice things, trying always to make her believe he was happy and well-liked, and that the world went well with him. . . . He brought her everything, except his small shames and ignominies" (135).

Due to his mother's nonattunement—her inability to respond to his negative affects, to the full expression of his passionate, bodily being—Paul never feels himself fully recognized or realized. Only his mother holds the power to confer reality and authenticate his experience of himself.[9] For the children, "Nothing had really taken place in them, until it was told to their mother" (87). For Paul, "There was one place in the world that stood solid and did not melt into unreality: the place where his mother was. Everybody else could grow shadowy, almost non-existent to him, but she could not. It was as if the pivot and pole of his life, from which he could not escape, was his mother" (261). The mother's dependence on her children—particularly her sons—to provide her own missing self-esteem makes it difficult for her children to discover their own independent selves, and thus they remain resentfully dependent, unable to "escape" her orbit. The mother will assume gigantic, fearsome proportions in fantasy precisely because of the belittlement and self-suppression she suffered in reality.

Paul's internal world, finally, mirrors his mother's. Gertrude Morel's narcissistically wounded condition, the lack of recognition and the consequent shame and rage she suffered are reproduced in her son. The subjective experience of emptiness and the detachment from affective, bodily life are passed down relationally from mother to child. Paul battles against his identification with his depressed mother as he seeks to assert himself and to realize his own authentic life. The battle is one that Lawrence continually waged himself throughout his life and his art. In his best work, the identification with the mother's shame is cast off without a wholesale repudiation of maternal ties.

Shame and the psychodynamics that defend against it are also central to a number of Lawrence's short stories. In the New Mexico–set "The

Princess" (1924) shame both determines the lives of the main characters and defines the peculiar nature of the descriptive imagery. Dollie Urquhart is the prized child of a man whom the narrator calls "just a bit mad." The most striking features of Colin Urquhart are his "vague blue eyes," eyes that seemed "to be looking at nothing," and his lack of physicality or somatic reality: he is described as a "spectre," an "echo . . . a living echo! His very flesh, when you touched it, did not seem quite the flesh of a real man" (159–60). After three years of marriage to this man, his wife, the narrator suggests, withers and dies from his very lack of substance. The child becomes his special doll—"My princess," he calls her.

The situation contains familiar Lawrencian features. A child is attached to and dependent on an other who is not "all there," who is disembodied and incapable of "seeing" or recognizing the child in her separate, real, and embodied self. The child grows up with an "inward coldness" and an incapacity for intimacy. As her father's narcissistic object, she suffers from both his grandiosity and his isolation. He tells her that they are the last of a "royal race," that they harbor royal "demons" within that set them apart from ordinary, vulgar people. Despite her coldness and arrogance, however, there is that in Dollie which yearns for human contact, for erotic expression and relationship that would bring her into being and make her real.[10]

After her father dies, she visits a ranch in New Mexico and meets the Indian guide Domingo Romero. She catches a "spark in his eye" and immediately recognizes his "fine demon." The narrator describes "an inter-recognition between them, silent and delicate" (170). Like Dollie, Romero is narcissistically wounded, arrogant, and isolated. His family had once been the owners of the ranch and the surrounding land, but they had now lost all to the white man. Romero's eyes are described as black, "half alive," "fatal," and hopeless, but at their center "a spark of pride. . . . Just a spark in the midst of the blackness of static despair" (168). Though both Dollie and Romero are only "half alive," existing in a state of frozen despair, that "spark" of potential life remains. Their attuned recognition provides the last chance for igniting desire and emerging into life for them both.

Dollie convinces Romero to take her into the mountains: "She wanted to look over the mountains into their secret heart. . . . She wanted to see the wild animals move about in their wild unconsciousness" (172–73). She wants to discover in "the core of the Rockies," in other words, what's missing at the core of her own being—authentic, uninhibited bodily and emotional expression. Inevitably, however, her search for self in the other—in the mountains and in Romero—is overpowered by her own inner deficiency, by a paralyzing shame and fear.

Desire thus turns into dread and repulsion. Described from her perspective, the mountains are "massive, gruesome, repellent" (181) and the wilderness is "squalid": "The strange squalor of the primitive forest pervaded the place, the squalor of animals and their droppings, the squalor of the wild. The Princess knew the peculiar repulsiveness of it" (184).

Dollie feels "hypnotised," furthermore, by a distant bob-cat's eyes, by its "demonish watching," which makes her shiver "with cold and fear. She knew well enough the dread and repulsiveness of the wild" (185–86). She knew well enough, in other words, the dread and repulsiveness—the deep shame—of self-exposure. For Dollie, the spontaneous, "wild" expression of one's being, particularly the expression of one's passionate, erotic physicality, is demonic and dreadful.

The same external projection of inner shame is repeated in relation to Romero. Having made camp, they lie down to sleep and Dollie dreams of being buried alive in the snow: "She was growing colder and colder, the snow was weighing down on her. The snow was going to absorb her" (187). The lapse into white, frozen nothingness is another familiar motif in Lawrence's fiction; it recalls Mrs. Morel's swooning into the white lilies in *Sons and Lovers* as well as the snowy deaths of Gerald in *Women in Love* and Cathcart in "The Man Who Loved Islands." A part of Dollie, however, struggles against such schizoid numbness and retreat—"she was so cold, so shivering, and her heart could not beat. Oh, would not someone help her heart to beat?"—and she calls to Romero to make her warm. Once again, however, she is stricken with a paralyzing dread:

> As soon as he had lifted her in his arms, she wanted to scream to him not to touch her. She stiffened herself. Yet she was dumb.
> And he was warm, but with a terrible animal warmth that seemed to annihilate her. He panted like an animal with desire. And she was given over to this thing. (188)

The scene suggests nothing short of rape: she feels assailed and annihilated by the overpowering, animal, and erotic presence of the other. Yet Dollie had felt an irresistible inner compulsion to submit to this presence in the first place. The narrator states repeatedly that "she had *willed* that it should happen to her" (italics his, 188). Masochistic submission is indeed a recurrent strain in Lawrence's work. According to Wurmser, masochism is another of the masks of shame: "It is an attack on the horrid self that quite generally wants to take away from others what they own. It is thus a kind of reaction formation" (41).

For Dollie, sexuality is bound up with her "demonic" core experience of self—with the narcissistic shame and rage associated with a passionate "letting go"—and thus she dreads what she also craves. The

story reflects one of the most primitive fantasies involved with shame—
the fantasy, in Wurmser's words, that "[m]y body and mental self are
filled with dangerous, demonic forces evoking severe disgust" (193). Sex
with Romero is agonizing "[b]ecause, in some peculiar way, he had got
hold of her, some unrealised part of her which she never wished to
realise" (193). Intimacy reactivates shame; it is experienced as an intrusion, making the self vulnerable to the original trauma of rejection.
Though Dollie's father had loved her as a "doll" or selfobject—an
extension or projection of the self (Kohut, *Analysis* xiv)—he had utterly
denied her as a feeling, desiring, fully embodied subject in her own right.

The narrative also gives us Romero's point of view, and his experience of Dollie's rejection replays the profound narcissistic wounding—
the rejection "in one's inmost area" (Wurmser 63)—at the experiential
heart of the story. When Dollie tells him that she had not liked their sexual encounter—"'I don't care for that kind of thing'" (190), Romero is
stunned: "A blank sort of wonder spread over his face, at these words:
followed immediately by a black look of anger, and then a stony, sinister despair" (190). Lawrence is a master at tracking the silent, internal
progression of affects in any given relational moment. Romero experiences Dollie's rejection as an acute narcissistic blow: shock, anger, and
finally, "sinister despair" follow. Such despair leads to sadistic, control-
ling behavior—he destroys Dollie's clothes and holds her captive—and
ultimately to his death. Romero shoots at the approaching Forest Service officers and is killed by their return fire.

Even before Romero's death, however, the narrator declares that both
he and Dollie "were two people who had died" (193). Lawrence understood well the psychic death that results from the rejection of one's being
at its affective, bodily core. Dollie tells the officers that Romero "had gone
out of his mind" (195), and the narrator reports that Dollie "too was now
a little mad" (196). Years later she refers to the episode as follows: "Since
my accident in the mountains, when a man went mad and shot my horse
from under me, and my guide had to shoot him dead, I have never felt quite
myself" (196). Horses always represent a primal sensuality in Lawrence's
fiction, and they can provoke both desire and dread.[11] Dollie cannot tolerate this level of sensual, bodily experience because of the original rejection
and the consequent shame she suffered. For her, relaxing her mental
defenses means mental disintegration—madness—and death. Romero and
the horse are connected in her mind, and both must be denied.

An earlier story, originally titled "The Miracle" and later published
as "The Horse-Dealer's Daughter" (1922), also concerns two characters
who surrender their mental defenses and encounter one another on a
primal level beneath the rational surface of their lives. Here too the characters are confronted with their own deep sense of shame—externalized

again in the natural imagery—but in this story, unlike "The Princess," both characters struggle to love in the face of their shame. In this case the sense of dread and repulsiveness associated with one's inmost self is not projected and denied, but owned and acknowledged. The possibility that one can yet be loved at the core of one's shame (which is felt to be at the core of one's being) is the miracle the story movingly conveys.

Like Miriam in *Sons and Lovers*, Mabel Pervin is forced to live under the oppressive rule of her sensual but shallow brothers, who alternately neglect and ridicule her. "They had talked at her and round her for so many years," the narrator states, "that she hardly heard them at all" (139). Lawrence once again displays an unusual sensitivity to the pain and humiliation of being female in a brutal, male-dominated world. The Pervin brothers, however, are themselves in a demeaning state of loss and disgrace as the story opens. Their widowed father has died, leaving the family's horse-dealing business in severe debt. The horses are being sold, and the family is dispersing. For one brother, Joe, "The horses were almost like his own body to him. He felt he was done for now" (138). Joe is engaged to be married, and the narrator adds, "He would marry and go into harness. His life was over, he would be a subject animal now" (138). The other brother, Fred Henry, "was master of any horse. . . . But he was not master of the situations of life" (138).

The story thus begins with a state of loss and shameful self-diminishment, and that state, as usual, is connected with the loss or suppression of bodily, sensual life (represented by the typical Lawrencian horse symbolism). Though Mabel has lived on the horse farm amidst her horsey brothers, their scorn and rejection have served to close her off long ago from that primal level of experience. Having lost contact with her sensual, feeling life, Mabel, like so many Lawrence characters, has erected a psychic wall of proud reserve. "So long as there was money," the narrator states, "the girl felt herself established, and brutally proud, reserved" (142). Money and the memory of her mother "who had died when she was fourteen, and whom she had loved" (142) had provided her only sense of self-worth, her sole reasons for living. Now that the money was gone, only the memory of the dead mother remains, and Mabel devotes herself to tending to her mother's grave. The narrator describes how, when visiting the grave, "she seemed in a sort of ecstasy to be coming nearer to her fulfilment, her own glorification, approaching her dead mother, who was glorified" (143).

Wurmser discusses the "drives for union" associated with shame (115). Mabel's desire to merge with her "glorified" dead mother is indeed rooted in her painful sense of loss and self-degradation; the narrative also associates her visits to the churchyard grave with fear of self-exposure and a schizoidlike retreat:

There she always felt secure, as if no one could see her, although as a matter of fact she was exposed to the stare of everyone who passed along under the churchyard wall. Nevertheless, once under the shadow of the great looming church, among the graves, she felt immune from the world, reserved within the thick churchyard wall as in another country. (143)

For Mabel, as for Dollie, the retreat from affective life, along with regressive, merging fantasies, defend against the underlying pain of rejection and humiliation. Their lives, as a result, are marked by a subjective sense of emptiness and inauthenticity. "The life she [Mabel] followed here in the world," the narrator remarks, "was far less real than the world of death she inherited from her mother" (143).

Mabel's retreat into the world of death is interrupted, however, by the country doctor, Jack Fergusson. The doctor too is a divided soul, alienated from his innermost being. He is initially described as having "tired" eyes and as being "muffled up" in overcoat, scarf, and a cap which "was pulled down on his head" and "which he did not remove" (140). As Mabel has erected a dense wall of emotional reserve, the doctor has muffled and suppressed his sensual, feeling life beneath the protective garb of his professional identity. Nevertheless, he continues to feel the tug toward revived contact with affective life, apparent in his "craving" for contact with the "rough, inarticulate, powerfully emotional" working people:

> Nothing but work, drudgery, constant hastening from dwelling to dwelling among the colliers and the iron-workers. It wore him out, but at the same time he had a craving for it. It was a stimulant to him to be in the homes of the working people, moving, as it were, through the innermost body of their life. His nerves were excited and gratified. . . . He grumbled, he said he hated the hellish hole. But as a matter of fact it excited him, the contact with the rough, strongly-feeling people was a stimulant applied direct to his nerves. (144)

One afternoon, Fergusson spies Mabel walking "slowly and deliberately" toward the center of a pond, ultimately disappearing into its depths. He hastens down the path to rescue her. The description of Fergusson's descent into the water emphasizes the pond's deathlike nature, and particularly its "foul," "hideous," and "repellent" aspects:

> He slowly ventured into the pond. The bottom was deep, soft clay; he sank in, and the water clasped dead cold round his legs. As he stirred he could smell the cold, rotten clay that fouled up into the water. It was objectionable in his lungs. Still, repelled and yet not heeding, he moved deeper into the pond. The cold water rose over his thighs, over his loins, upon his abdomen. The lower part of his body was all sunk in the hideous cold element. And the bottom was so deeply soft and uncertain, he was afraid of pitching with his mouth underneath. (145)

At one point when reaching for Mabel's body, the doctor loses his balance and goes under, "horribly, suffocating in the foul, earthy water." At last he succeeds in lifting her and staggering on to the bank, "out of the horror of wet grey clay" (146).

Clyde de L. Ryals argues from a Jungian perspective that this scene "is a careful working out of the rebirth archetype, embodying the rite of baptism, the purification and revivification by water" (155). The foul, slimy, and repugnant aspects of the pond, he maintains, are "symbolic of the repressed contents of the mind of neurotic persons" (155). Quoting Jung, he adds that the image of "'slime out of the depths' . . . contains not only 'objectionable animal tendencies, but also germs of new possibilities of life'" (156). Questions remain, however, as to what exactly has been "repressed" and why "animal tendencies" should be so "objectionable," especially since renewed contact with one's animal nature is precisely what the story affirms; it is indeed what makes rebirth possible. The Jungian interpretation misses, I believe, the rich particularity of the symbolic imagery and the tension of unresolved ambivalence that drives the story throughout.

The doctor's hesitant descent into the "foul, earthy water" certainly reflects, as Ryals notes, the characteristic Lawrencian horror of regressive merging or refusion with the mother. In order to understand the peculiar repulsiveness of the imagery, however—the emphasis on the rotten smell, and the repetition of the words "cold" and "foul"—we need to consider the symbolic presence of shame. The swamp imagery recalls the repugnant, foul-smelling marsh images associated in Lawrence's letters with homosexual love. The imagery suggests not only a fear of refusion or absorption, but an unrestrained anality and profound self-contempt buried beneath the surface defenses.

If the infant's physical, sensual self-expression was originally met with coldness and rejection, then that internalized response will continue to define the self's experience of its own sensuality and bodily processes. Letting go of one's mental restraints means bodily release and thus exposing one's "objectionable," smelly, bodily products. The horrible "wet grey clay" of the pond reflects the anal imagery that is one of the most frequent symbolic manifestations of unconscious shame.

Mabel and the doctor have both abandoned their mental defenses, sunk "in overhead," and surrendered to their shameful bodily selves. When Mabel regains consciousness, she asks him, "Was I out of my mind?" and he replies that perhaps she was for a moment. The threat of madness, of losing all mental control, scares them both. Stronger than that fear, however, is the powerful, vitalizing magnetism they feel toward one another. For Fergusson, "It was as if she had the life of his body in her hands, and he could not extricate himself. Or perhaps he did not want to" (147–48). When Mabel discovers that he had undressed her—thus having had the life of her body in his hands—she asks directly, "'Do you love me then?'" She falls to passionately embracing him, "indiscriminately kissing his knees, his legs, as if unaware of everything," and "yearning and triumphant and confident," she murmurs, "'You love me. I know you love me, I know'" (148).

To be seen in one's true nakedness—in one's undefended bodily being—is to be recognized, affirmed, indeed loved. For both Mabel and the doctor, however, shame and fear compete with their emerging faith in self and other and in the possibility of real intimacy. Fergusson

> looked down at the tangled wet hair, the wild, bare, animal shoulders. He was amazed, bewildered, and afraid. . . . It was horrible to have her there embracing his knees. It was horrible. He revolted from it violently. And yet—and yet—he had not the power to break away. (148)

The narrative states repeatedly that he had "no intention of loving her," that he had rescued her out of professional duty, and that he is "horrified" by this "personal element" (148–49). As in "The Princess," intimacy reactivates shame, threatening the terror of rejection, loss of control, and utter powerlessness. The doctor "had a horror of yielding to her," yet "something in him ached also. . . . He wanted to remain like that for ever, with his heart hurting him in a pain that was also life to him" (149). By warding off the deep pain of rejection and insulating themselves from all feeling, Mabel and the doctor had each been living a mechanical, nonauthentic existence. To reexperience pain is thus to reexperience life.

Shame remains, however, an unrelenting threat. In the midst of their embrace, Fergusson looks down at Mabel's damp hair: "Then, as it were suddenly, he smelt the horrid stagnant smell of that water" (149). Mabel pulls away from him with "terrible wistful, unfathomable" eyes. The doctor feels "ripped open," and thinks, "'How they would all jeer if they knew!'" (150). The story indeed concludes with the consciousness of acute shame. As Fergusson kisses her, Mabel murmurs, "'My hair smells so horrible. . . . And I'm so awful, I'm so awful! Oh, no, I'm too awful,' and she broke into bitter, heart-broken sobbing. 'You can't want to love me, I'm horrible'" (152).

The story's final lines express the profound ambivalence that loving inevitably entails for Lawrence's characters:

> "I feel awful. I feel awful. I feel I'm horrible to you."
> "No, I want you, I want you," was all he answered, blindly, with that terrible intonation which frightened her almost more than her horror lest he should not want her. (152)

Like Dollie, Mabel is terrified of being destroyed by the very expression of animal desire she craves. The hope in this story though, as opposed to "The Princess," lies in the characters' willingness to open themselves to the painful consciousness of their shame, to tolerate their wrenching ambivalence, and to trust blindly that one might yet be loved in all one's "horrible" animality.

An awareness of the role of shame in Lawrence's fiction can also help to illuminate those scenes in *The Rainbow, Women in Love,* and *Lady Chatterley's Lover* that celebrate heterosexual anal intercourse. Critics have interpreted these episodes either as expressing sublimated homosexual desires or as exemplifying the enraged need to dominate women,[12] but it is also possible that they represent the need to accept shame, one's own and the other's, as an essential component of love. In *Women in Love* we are told that Birkin had taken Ursula "at the roots of her darkness and shame—like a demon, laughing over the fountain of mystic corruption which was one of the sources of her being, laughing, shrugging, accepting, accepting finally" (304). The creative inspiration for so much of Lawrence's work is this driving need to be accepted, accepted "finally," at the roots of one's being. For Lawrence, as for all of us, those roots lie in the powerful physicality of infant life, in our primal, bodily needs and passions as we experience them in relation to the others on whom we depend.

The shame Lawrence experienced in relation to his depressed, affectively nonattuned mother helped to fuel his misogynistic rage. Nevertheless, he was equally sensitive to the roots of his mother's shame and was deeply cognizant of her pain. When women are disallowed full expression of their own subjectivity, when they have been denied their sexuality, their anger, and aggression, then as mothers, their attunement to those experiences in their children will be vitally impaired. The results, Lawrence's fiction warns, can be tragically destructive for everyone, men and women alike.

NOTES

1. For these and other examples of Lawrence's puritanical behavior, see John Worthen 59; Jeffrey Meyers 125, 236, 291–92; and Brenda Maddox 137.

2. Otto Kernberg is considered one of the pioneers of affect theory. In *Object Relations Theory in Clinical Psychoanalysis* he argues that affects precede instinctual drives and are bound in units with internalized self and object representations. For a good synthesis of current perspectives on the role of affect in psychic development, see Charles Spezzano.

3. While psychoanalytic criticism of Lawrence was originally dominated by classical Oedipal interpretations (see Daniel Weiss), the emphasis has shifted in

recent years to a pre-Oedipal and object relational focus. See Daniel Dervin; Judith Ruderman; Margaret Storch.

4. Stephen Mitchell is helpful in addressing the postmodern contention that there is no such thing as a "core" or "true" self. He suggests that we think about the self in temporal rather than spatial terms, as a matter of experience in time rather than of reified structures. When psychoanalysts talk about a true or core self, he argues, they are really referring to the subjective *experience* of authenticity, to the degree to which the experience of oneself in time *feels* meaningful and authentic (130–31). My psychological discussion of the nature of selfhood in Lawrence's fiction assumes this perspective: it focuses on felt experience. To the person who experiences some vital lack or deficiency, who feels empty and unreal, the theoretical debate about whether a real or core self actually exists matters little—it is irrelevant to the person's subjective experience of emptiness and fragmentation.

5. Affect attunement is similar to the mother's empathic mirroring function that both Kohut and Donald Winnicott describe. Intersubjective theories like those of Stern and Jessica Benjamin, however, place much more emphasis on the mother's own complex subjectivity in relation to the child: she is not just an object, a function, or a mirror to be used by the child. They stress the mutual influence in mother-infant interaction.

6. Visual dynamics are so salient to Lawrence's work that Linda Williams applies psychoanalytic feminist film theory to an analysis of his fiction. Her intriguing study focuses on the female gaze and the spectacle of male bodies as they represent shifting positions of gender and power in his novels.

7. Using Kohut's self-psychological framework, James Cowan also sees the homoerotic element in Lawrence's fiction as rooted in idealization problems—specifically, unsatisfied idealizing merger needs in relation to the father. "Lawrence's homoerotic feelings were not a primary psychological configuration," he argues, "but 'disintegration products,'" reflecting "the unmet developmental need to merge with the greatness of an idealized omnipotent paternal selfobject" (198).

8. Judith Arcana has traced what she sees as a tradition of "wholesale mother-blaming" in *Sons and Lovers* criticism. She believes this phenomenon reflects an "oedipalized mother-blaming" in our culture at large (139).

9. When children are cared for by two parents, then, as Kohut has argued, they have two chances relationally to build the psychic structures they need. Although Lawrence's father was physically present, he was psychologically unavailable because of Lawrence's emmeshment with his mother and her utter rejection of the father. Arthur Lawrence's violent temper also made identification with him deeply problematic for his sensitive son.

10. Barbara Smalley uses Karen Horney's theories to argue a similar perspective on this story. She too sees Dollie's essentially schizoid character structure as conditioned by her relationship with her "neurotic" father. He taught her "that she is basically unlovable, that she cannot be esteemed if she removes her Princess mask" (187).

11. The scene toward the end of *The Rainbow* in which Ursula is overcome by an approaching herd of horses captures this ambivalence most powerfully:

"Her heart was gone, her limbs were dissolved, she was dissolved like water. All the hardness and looming power was in the massive body of the horse-group," in "their awful, blind, triumphing flanks" (452–53).

In *Fantasia of the Unconscious* Lawrence writes: "a man has a persistent passionate fear-dream about horses. He suddenly finds himself among great, physical horses, which may suddenly go wild. Their great bodies surge madly round him, they rear above him, threatening to destroy him. . . . [T]he horse-dream refers to some arrest in the deepest sensual activity in the male. . . . The spontaneous self is secretly yearning for the liberation and fulfilment of the deepest and most powerful sensual nature" (199–200).

Here Lawrence identifies the horse imagery as representative of a specifically male sensuality. In his fiction, however, horses can symbolize a threatening upsurge of sensual, bodily desire in female as well as male characters. The intense shame that such an upsurge invariably triggers is symbolically captured in Loerke's statue in *Women in Love* of the small, naked girl, "her face in her hands, as if in shame and grief," sitting astride the "massive, magnificent stallion, rigid with pent-up power" (429).

12. See, for instance, Meyers ("D. H. Lawrence and Homosexuality") 146; Gavriel Ben-Ephraim 232; and Storch 168–69.

WORKS CITED

Arcana, Judith. "I Remember Mama: Mother-Blaming in *Sons and Lovers* Criticism." *D. H. Lawrence Review* 20 (1989): 137–51.

Ben-Ephraim, Gavriel. *The Moon's Dominion: Narrative Dichotomy and Female Dominance in Lawrence's Earlier Novels.* Teaneck, N.J.: Associated University Presses, 1981.

Benjamin, Jessica. *The Bonds of Love: Psychoanalysis, Feminism and the Problem of Domination.* New York: Pantheon, 1988.

Berman, Jeffery. *Narcissism and the Novel.* New York: New York UP, 1990.

Cowan, James. "Blutbruderschaft and Self Psychology in D. H. Lawrence's *Women in Love.*" *The Annual of Psychoanalysis.* Vol. 20. Ed. Chicago Institute for Psychoanalysis. Hillsdale, N.J.: Analytic P, 1992.

Dervin, Daniel. *A 'Strange Sapience': The Creative Imagination of D. H. Lawrence.* Amherst: U of Massachusetts P, 1984.

Kernberg, Otto. *Object Relations Theory in Clinical Psychoanalysis.* New York: Aronson, 1976.

Kohut, Heinz. *The Analysis of the Self.* New York: International UP, 1971.

———. *The Restoration of the Self.* New York: International UP, 1977.

Langbaum, Robert. *The Mysteries of Identity: A Theme in Modern Literature.* New York: Oxford UP, 1977.

Lawrence, D. H. *Lady Chatterley's Lover.* Harmondsworth, U.K.: Penguin, 1960.

———. *Fantasia of the Unconscious, & Psychoanalysis of the Unconscious.* New York: Viking, 1960.

———. "The Horse-Dealer's Daughter." *England, My England and Other Stories.* Ed. Bruce Steele. Cambridge: Cambridge UP, 1990. 137–52.

———. "The Princess." *St. Mawr and Other Stories*. Ed. Brian Finney. Cambridge: Cambridge UP, 1983. 159–96.

———. *The Rainbow*. Ed. Mark Kinkead-Weeks. Cambridge: Cambridge UP, 1989.

———. *Sons and Lovers*. Ed. Helen Baron & Carl Baron. Cambridge: Cambridge UP, 1992.

———. *Women in Love*. Ed. David Farmer, Lindeth Vasey & John Worthen. Cambridge: Cambridge UP, 1987.

Maddox, Brenda. *D. H. Lawrence: The Story of a Marriage*. New York: Simon & Schuster, 1994.

Meyers, Jeffrey. *D.H. Lawrence: A Biography*. New York: Vintage, 1992.

———. "D. H. Lawrence and Homosexuality." *D. H. Lawrence: Novelist, Poet, Prophet*. Ed. Stephen Spender. New York: Harper & Row, 1973. 135–46.

Mitchell, Stephen A. *Hope and Dread in Psychoanalysis*. New York: Basic Books, 1993.

Morrison, Andrew. *Shame: The Underside of Narcissism*. Hillsdale, N.J.: Analytic P, 1989.

Ruderman, Judith. *D. H. Lawrence and the Devouring Mother: The Search for the Patriarchal Ideal of Leadership*. Durham, N.C.: Duke UP, 1984.

Ryals, Clyde de L. "D. H. Lawrence's 'The Horse-Dealer's Daughter': An Interpretation." *Critical Essays on D. H. Lawrence*. Ed. Dennis Jackson and Fleda Brown Jackson. Boston: G. K. Hall, 1988. 153–69.

Smalley, Barbara M. "Lawrence's 'The Princess' and Horney's 'Idealized Self.'" *Third Force Psychology and the Study of Literature*. Ed. Bernard J. Paris. Rutherford, N.J.: Farleigh Dickinson UP, 1986. 179–90.

Spezzano, Charles. *Affect in Psychoanalysis: A Clinical Synthesis*. Hillsdale, N.J.: Analytic P, 1993.

Stern, Daniel. *The Interpersonal World of the Infant*. New York: Basic Books, 1985.

Stolorow, Robert and George Atwood. *Contexts of Being: The Intersubjective Foundations of Psychological Life*. Hillsdale, N.J.: Analytic P, 1992.

Storch, Margaret. *Sons and Adversaries: Women in William Blake and D. H. Lawrence*. Knoxville: U of Tennessee P, 1990.

Weiss, Daniel A. *Oedipus in Nottingham: D. H. Lawrence*. Seattle: U of Washington P, 1962.

Williams, Linda Ruth. *Sex in the Head: Visions of Femininity and Film in D. H. Lawrence*. Detroit: Wayne State UP, 1993.

Worthen, John. *D. H. Lawrence: The Early Years 1885–1912*. Cambridge: Cambridge UP, 1992.

Wurmser, Léon. *The Mask of Shame*. Baltimore: Johns Hopkins UP, 1981.

CHAPTER 8

Shame in Japan
and the American South:
Faulkner's Absalom, Absalom!

Philip Collington

I love my country enough to want to cure its faults and the only
way that I can cure its faults within my capacity, within my own
vocation, is to shame it.
                                        —William Faulkner (*Nagano* 125)

In one of this century's pioneering studies of shame, Helen Merrell Lynd
identified William Faulkner as an author particularly interested in this
complex psychological phenomenon. She called his 1932 novel, *Light in
August*, "a study in shame" in which "it is the small details that probe
the depths of pain" (Lynd 41–42). These details include depictions of
specific social transgressions that become massive narcissistic injuries,
and indelible personal incongruities based on race or class.

Faulkner demonstrated an interest in shame throughout his career,
but nowhere are his insights more apparent than in *Absalom, Absalom!*
This 1936 masterpiece is pervaded with motifs of hiding and retreat,
ranging from a scolded boy hiding in a cave to the Confederate army on
the run from the North. Léon Wurmser points out that hiding is "intrinsic to and inseparable from the concept of shame" because *shame* comes
from the Indo-European "*kam/kem*: 'to cover, to veil, to hide'"
(Wurmser 29). Lynd writes that individuals experience shame when
these defenses break down and "peculiarly sensitive, intimate, vulnerable aspects of the self" are unexpectedly exposed (Lynd 27–28). Yet
instead of covering, veiling, or hiding vulnerable aspects of his country,
Faulkner exposed the "baseness" of Southern racism to the rest of the
world (*Nagano* 126). In *Absalom, Absalom!* he traces the rise and fall

of a dynasty beginning in the 1830s—when Thomas Sutpen appears "out of nowhere" and constructs an enormous mansion on the outskirts of Jefferson, Mississippi—and ending in 1909 when it burns to the ground (5).[1] An intensely conformist society, Jefferson never fully welcomes this "poor white" upstart into its midst. Almost every character associated with Sutpen spends the novel fleeing censure by members of shaming communities, in spite of desperate attempts to gain acceptance and integration.

Using the self psychology of Heinz Kohut—which provides a model for investigating shame-prone behavior in adults—this paper will re-examine Ruth Benedict's influential assertion that Japan is a shame culture whereas America is a guilt culture. During a trip to Japan, Faulkner argued the opposite: that the two countries share similar histories, social systems, and individual psychological traits. Notorious for contradicting himself, Faulkner, in his depictions of shame in *Absalom, Absalom!*, problematizes his conflation of these two societies, as well as Benedict's facile distinctions between Eastern shame and Western guilt.

In August 1955, Faulkner travelled to Japan at the invitation of a group of Japanese professors, and at the request of the U.S. Department of State, which was eager to improve U.S.-Japanese relations (Karl 904–19). During a series of seminars and public lectures held in Nagano Prefecture and Tokyo, Faulkner acted as a kind of cultural ambassador—drawing parallels between Japan and the American South that were flattering to his hosts but that oversimplified his works and perpetuated social stereotypes. For example, he summed up differences between Europe and the East: "the French is a culture of rationality; the British have a culture of [insularity] [sic], the Italians, a culture of the five senses. As I understand it, the Japanese, the Chinese, is a culture of intellect" (*Nagano* 10). He went on to compare the Southern aristocrats to their Japanese equivalent, the *samurai*—erstwhile defenders of the peasantry and agricultural traditions, whether cotton- or rice-farming (*Nagano* 86). Both Japan and the South were defeated nations—in a sense, defeated by the same nation, industrial America (185–88).[2] Like Japan, the South had been conquered, had endured occupation, had undergone massive reconstruction, and as a result encouraged collective behavior as a form of defense: "We have to be clannish just like the people in the Scottish highlands, each springing to defend his own blood whether it be right or wrong" (192). One significant link between Japan and the South was the emphasis their "old tradition[s]" placed on decorum, courtesy, and respect toward elders (85, 144–45). Faulkner admired Japan for its long history: "The westerner's tradition is not much older than his grandfather, but the oriental tradition goes back past a hundred grandfathers" (22). Grandfathers are revered throughout

Faulkner's works because they provide a family link with the Old South; in Jefferson, even the pigeons can trace their "descendants" back to 1833, the year Sutpen arrived (23). Finally, both Japan and the South were experiencing racial controversies, as the reluctance of many Japanese to integrate Korean immigrants or intermarry with members of the Burakumin caste—euphemistically described in the seminars as "people in Japan who are set aside in segregated villages"—was analogous to Southern resistance to the desegregation of public schools and interracial marriages (*Nagano* 166–70).[3]

As one of Faulkner's biographers has observed, these jolting analogies resulted in "a rather severe bending of two different cultures" (Karl 915). Many of Faulkner's embarrassing comments bring to mind a well-known Japanese proverb, "*Tabi no haji wa kakisute*" or "Shame is discarded on a journey" (Takashima 270). To be fair, he was indefatigably polite, answering questions on matters about which he admittedly knew very little. Robert A. Jellife points out that the informal nature of the meetings encouraged Faulkner to speak "more freely and more intimately than he might have felt disposed to do in other circumstances" (*Nagano* vi–vii). He likely would not have spoken so freely at home, and when asked to clarify his earlier comments on the English, French, and Japanese, Faulkner backpedalled: "They were just generalizations. Of course, that's not a complete summation of any one culture. It's reducing it to what might be called a workable typification, just for discussion, for talk" (*Nagano* 116).

So while these caveats warn us not to take his impromptu comments as authoritative, Faulkner's fanciful transformation of "the samurai tradition into a Southern one" does shed interesting light on *Absalom, Absalom!* (Karl 908). Beginning with his "workable typification," this paper will address the questions: If shame is discarded on a journey, then is shame present at home? Is the American South, like Japan, a shame culture? Is either?

In *The Chrysanthemum and the Sword*, Benedict argued that there are fundamental differences between America and Japan. America is a typical guilt culture, which "inculcates absolute standards of morality and relies on men's developing a conscience" through internal sanctions such as religion (222). Guilt for sins or social transgressions can be purged by confession and atonement. On the other hand, shame cultures like Japan rely on external sanctions such as ridicule or ostracism to discourage undesirable behavior. Once made public, shame can never be purged. However, as Benedict notes, "So long as [a person's] bad behavior does not 'get out into the world' he need not be troubled" (223). Of course, Americans experience shame for "gaucheries which are in no way sins" (222), but the Japanese do not experience guilt: "Shame, they say, is the root of virtue. A man who is sensitive to it will carry out all the rules of good behaviour. . . . Shame has the same place of authority in Japanese ethics that . . . the avoidance of sin [has] in Western ethics" (224). This forms the basis of the oft-discussed group ethics of the Japanese—the enormous importance of conformity and of being accepted by peers—that is so often contrasted with Western individualism. The most devastating punishment for a Japanese child is derisive laughter: "All his life ostracism is more dreaded than violence. He is allergic to threats of ridicule and rejection, even when he merely conjures them up in his own mind" (288). Fear of ridicule, "not an absolute standard of virtue," is inculcated in a Japanese child (287).

According to Kohut's self psychology, shame occurs in individuals when others fail to admire the narcissistic displays that emanate from a grandiose self left over from early childhood.[4] A pre-Oedipal child does not differentiate fully between self and others; these objects are perceived as an extension of the self (i.e., as *selfobjects*). The archaic self is bipolar: at one pole, a child craves responses from a *mirroring selfobject*—verbal praise, cuddling, or even a smile. At the other pole, the child strengthens the developing self by merging with, and later imitating, an *idealized selfobject*—a seemingly omnipotent parent, older sibling, or role model. Initially, then, a Western child resembles his/her stereotypical Japanese counterpart, craving acceptance and imitating others. But these selfobjects are gradually internalized and depersonalized: mirroring ones become self-esteem; idealized ones become the child's conscience and values. A healthy, mature individual thus achieves a certain degree of autonomy and self-sufficiency. However, inadequate selfobject responses, or interruptions in the psychological weaning away from selfobject dependence, cause a person to remain chronically dependent on others in order to maintain a cohesive self. Unable to cope with *narcissistic injuries*—personal setbacks, insults, or unempathic responses— such a person "responds to actual (or anticipated) narcissistic injury either with shamefaced withdrawal (flight) or with narcissistic rage (fight)" (Kohut, "Thoughts" 637). Massive injuries cause *fragmentation*, or the breakup of the self; but a person can avoid this by using preventive attacks, defined as "the active (often anticipatory) inflicting on others of those narcissistic injuries which he is most afraid of suffering himself" (638).

In other words, when elements of a narcissistically perceived environment are unexpectedly uncooperative toward an individual with a shaky self-structure, he or she experiences shame and is impelled to choose between a fight or flight reaction. Helen Block Lewis—who defines the *self* as "a perceptual product . . . [which] depends on feedback" to maintain its structural integrity—also holds that shame is a "narcissistic" reaction, "an experience in which a source in the field [i.e., the environment] seems to scorn, despise or ridicule the self" (*Shame* 33–39). Lewis describes the fight reaction as "humiliated fury," and the fending off of further injury through preventive attacks as "turning the tables"; the flight reaction is more passive: "One could 'crawl through a hole,' or 'sink through the floor' or 'die' with shame" (*Shame* 41–42).

Whereas Lewis's etiology of shame is environmental, Gerhart Piers sees it as arising out of internal tension. An individual's ego fails to live up to the ego ideal, which punishes failure with the unconscious fear of abandonment, "death by emotional starvation" (26–29). Incompatibilities between Piers, Kohut, and Lewis may have been overstated, as Piers defines the "ego ideal" as the "*core of narcissistic omnipotence*" created through "*positive identifications* with the parental images" during an individual's formative years (26, his italics). In other words, the ego ideal is field dependent. Piers's process of identification with "the loving, the reassuring parent [and], the parent who explicitly and implicitly gives the permission to become like him [or her]" bears a strong resemblance to Kohut's concept of individual mergers with mirroring and idealized selfobjects (Piers 26). As Andrew P. Morrison points out, Kohut effectively repudiated Piers's theory, replacing the metapsychological concept of the *ego ideal* in which internalized aspirations are "byproducts of encounters with highly cathected objects" with a more experience-near concept, the *ideal self*: "the representation of the individual's personal and subjectively experienced aspirations with regard to the self" (Morrison, "Shame" 73). Yet Kohut's "new" construct may merely have been politically motivated hair-splitting done to distance his emerging self psychology from established object relations theories (Morrison, *Shame* 71–76). In effect, then, whether shame is caused by failure to impress (1) a thoroughly internalized metapsychological construct (Piers), (2) a narcissistically perceived selfobject (Kohut), or (3) an independent other (Lewis), the net result is devastation. The hypersensitive, grandiose self craves approbation from—but is rebuffed by—internal, semi-internal, or external sources; and possible reactions fall onto a spectrum of shame-related affects ranging from depression, to fragmentation, to narcissistic rage.[5]

While many of Faulkner's characters display volatile shame-prone behavior, Thomas Sutpen exemplifies a potentially dangerous variant of this: the narcissistic personality disorder. Only officially recognized as a mental disorder in the last decade—largely due to the influence of Kohut's writings—its symptoms are listed in the American Psychiatric Association's *Diagnostic and Statistical Manual of Mental Disorders.* People with this disorder are "preoccupied with fantasies of unlimited success" and experience "envy for those whom they perceive as being more successful than they." They suffer from fragile self-esteem, and show off because of "an almost exhibitionistic need for constant attention and admiration." If the desired responses are not forthcoming, they react with shame or rage. Finally, interpersonal relations are marred by a lack of empathy toward others, and a high degree of interpersonal exploitativeness. Friendships are formed for personal profit, and in love relationships, "the partner is often treated as an object to be used to bolster the person's self-esteem" (*Diagnostic* 349–51; see also Berman 20–21).

As an adult, Sutpen is ambitious, hypersensitive to slights, exploitative, and he shows off compulsively—racing carriages, holding shooting competitions and wrestling with his own slaves. His sister-in-law, Rosa Coldfield, complains, "he came here and set up a raree show which lasted five years and Jefferson paid him for the entertainment by at least shielding him to the extent of not telling their womenfolks what he was doing" (12). Phil Mollon describes shame-prone adults as displaying "a compelling need . . . to evoke mirroring responses from others" (274). Sutpen spends the greater part of his life attempting to enter Jefferson's planter aristocracy in order to gain respect, and avoid "unempathic attention" (Mollon 274). However, it is not easy to transplant oneself from one group to another, as he finds out.[6]

Raised in the mountains of West Virginia, thirteen-year-old Sutpen is initiated into a society divided by class and race when his family "tumbled head over heels back to Tidewater by sheer altitude, elevation and gravity" (180). During this descent, Sutpen's mother (likely his original mirroring selfobject) dies, and the unempathic "laughter and jeers" of "strange faces" instill in the young outsider feelings of self-consciousness about his family's lopsided cart, his unwed sister's pregnancy, and his father's "mountain drinking manners" (181–84). At Tidewater, they move into a shack on the periphery of a wealthy planter's property, where Sutpen discovers that "down-looking" plantation society will not admit his "poor white" family (179).

One day, when sent by his father to deliver a message to the owner, Pettibone, Sutpen knocks at the front door of the mansion. But instead of responding empathically to the boy (such as listening to the message or inviting him inside), Pettibone's butler tells him to go around back to the servants' entrance, scorning him with "mellow loud and terrible laughing" (186–89). Barefoot and wearing hand-me-down garments, Sutpen is outraged that a "monkey nigger" (189) would be his social superior, wearing a fancy butler's uniform and shoes (Brown 132). Already acutely self-conscious, Sutpen receives from this butler a devastating narcissistic injury that causes his self to fragment: "he seemed to kind of dissolve" (186). Initially, Sutpen reacts with shame-faced withdrawal: "He didn't even remember leaving. All of a sudden he found himself running and already some distance from the house, and not toward home. . . . He went into the woods. He says he did not tell himself where to go: that his body, his feet, just went there" (188). He crawls into a cave where he yearns for an idealized selfobject to repair his shattered self-esteem: "if there were only someone else, some older and smarter person to ask. But there was not, there was only himself" (189).[7] What ensues is a kind of internal debate between two introjected personalities. The voice of his idealized father recommends that he "[whup] one of Pettibone's niggers" (187), whereas Sutpen's own voice suggests, "I can shoot him" (190).

After much debate, however, Sutpen decides to imitate a new and more successful idealized model. With slaves to serve him lemonade and fan him while he swings in a hammock, Pettibone represents an attractive alternative to the mountain culture of poverty and violence. Resolved to become a plantation owner himself, Sutpen runs away to Haiti and plans his "design," an elaborate preemptive strike to beat rich Southerners at their own game: "You got to have land and niggers and a fine house to combat them with" (192). His subsequent behavior resembles Kohut's "variant of narcissistic rage wherein the dominant propelling motivation is less the revenge motif and more the wish to increase self-esteem" (*Restoration* 194). Sutpen wants to heal the blow to his self-esteem caused by the "balloon face" of the butler. By idealizing and imitating a successful model, he too will become a wealthy slave owner, for if the "laughter which the balloon held barricaded and protected [Pettibone]," it could protect Sutpen too (189–90). By converting the passive experience of being turned away from the door, into the active one of being the house owner who closes the door, Sutpen can control this narcissistically perceived environment—he will own the "balloon faces" that shame.[8]

Yet even when Sutpen returns to Jefferson from Haiti with a whole wagonload of slaves, the images of hiding and retreat persist. Rosa calls him a man "who fled here and hid, concealed himself behind respectability." She continues: "He sought the guarantee of reputable men to barricade him. . . . Then he needed respectability, the shield of a virtuous woman, to make his position impregnable" (9–10). Picking up where Rosa leaves off, Shreve proposes that Sutpen conceived of his wife and children as a fortress: "[Ellen] not only would consolidate the hiding but could would and did breed him two children to fend and shield both in themselves and in their progeny the brittle bones and tired flesh of an old man against the day when the Creditor would run him to earth for the last time and he couldn't get away" (145–46). Philip M. Weinstein argues that sanctuary, refuge, and protection are critically important to the "unbearably assaulted self" of characters in Faulkner's early fiction (173–74). While a sanctuary can be a physical place, Weinstein argues that the most effective protection is afforded by relationships "of shared and generous feeling" such as that enjoyed by Quentin and Shreve at Harvard (187). Kohut would agree that friendships or love relationships provide effective sanctuary for embattled selves through "mutual (self-esteem enhancing) mirroring and idealization" (*Restoration* 122). Sutpen, however, exploits other people and is not interested in mutuality. His design, not individual relationships, becomes "the sanctuary he can never abandon" (Weinstein 185). For example, he explains how he abandoned his first wife and child when he discovered she had mixed blood and would thus be unwelcome in Southern plantation society: "'I found that she was not and could never be . . . adjunctive or incremental to the design which I had in mind, so I provided for her and put her aside'" (194).

Shreve's invocation of a "Creditor" suggests an arbiter of human behavior, like the wrathful God of Western guilt culture, or the Devil that would claim this Southern Faustus's soul (Ragan 75). Yet Faulkner makes a point of showing that it is, in fact, a shaming community of humans who "catch [Sutpen], run him to earth" (25). When Sutpen mysteriously obtains four wagonloads of furniture for his new mansion, the town vigilance committee assumes that he has stolen the items and arrests him (33–35). Then, when this "public enemy" marries into a local family, invited guests boycott the wedding and a mob throws rotten vegetables at the bride and groom (39–45). Throughout the novel, Sutpen is subjected to "external sanctions" commonly attributed to shame cultures (listed in Singer 63–65): he is accused of sorcery (especially by Rosa), ostracized, slandered, intimidated, incarcerated, and has his property destroyed.

The novel presents four generations of fugitives associated with Sutpen and his design, all of whom are pursued by shaming communities: the French architect, Henry Sutpen, Wash Jones, Goodhue Coldfield, Miss Rosa, Charles Etienne de Saint Valéry Bon, and Jim Bond. Although the French architect is not retreating from a narcissistic injury, his flight is juxtaposed with Sutpen's to highlight aspects of Sutpen's character. Living in intolerable conditions at the Hundred, the architect, in his "formal coat and his Paris hat," experiences the incongruity of being *other*—surrounded by naked mudcaked slaves (28). The architect flees because he is too rich to live in a tent: Sutpen fled because he was too poor to live in a mansion. After several days of pursuit, he is tracked by Sutpen's dogs and slaves to his hiding place: a cave similar to that of Sutpen's childhood retreat (206). The architect also flees after discovering that Sutpen does not intend to pay him for his work—an example of

Sutpen's interpersonal exploitativeness. Instead of perceiving others as independent centers of volition, Sutpen views them as extensions of himself, instruments of self-fulfilment in a narcissistically perceived environment (Kohut "Thoughts," 655–56). He buys, sells, and mates slaves like "wild stock," and uses them like a pack of hounds to track game and men alike (48). He also treats women like animals. In his wedding proposal to Rosa, "[he] held out [his] hand and said 'Come' as you might say it to a dog" (135), and he insults Wash Jones's pregnant granddaughter, "'Well, Milly; too bad you're not a mare too. Then I could give you a decent stall in the stable'" (229).

In a vivid example of shame-faced withdrawal, young Henry Sutpen witnesses his half-naked father wrestling slaves in the barn and plunges out "screaming and vomiting" (20–22). Ellen's interruption of this midnight spectacle shames participants and audience alike: "'I know you will excuse us gentlemen,' Ellen said. But they were already departing, nigger and white, slinking out again as they had slunk in" (21). Later, Sutpen and his two sons go to war, not to defend the South, but to avoid making a decision about Charles's proposal to his own half-sister, Judith. Henry says, "'Maybe the war will settle it and we wont need to!'" (273). However, the war does not settle it, and when confronted by Henry, Sutpen denies that Charles is his son. Confounded, Henry retreats to a "lonely place" in the woods, analogous to the caves of Sutpen and the French architect (283–84). But when Henry discovers that Charles has mixed blood and keeps an octoroon mistress, he turns this passive indecision into active violence. Only after Charles's explosive (and suicidal) taunt, "I'm the nigger that's going to sleep with your sister," does Henry shoot his brother—not because incest is wrong, but because interracial marriage is socially inappropriate (285–86).[9] After the murder, Henry becomes a fugitive, journeying through a series of unspecified locations where he attempts to discard his shame. But when he returns home in 1909, shame returns to haunt him in the form of Rosa—who storms the Hundred armed with a rusty hatchet that links her revenge to Wash Jones's murder of Henry's father with a rusty scythe fifty years before.

Wash Jones also lacks a cohesive self, displaying chronic dependence on selfobjects. In a situation analogous to Sutpen's early life at Tidewater, Wash lives with his granddaughter Milly in a dilapidated shack on Sutpen's Hundred, where the slaves wear better clothing and scorn his poverty: "he walked always in mocking and jeering echoes of nigger laughter" (226).[10] Wash compensates for his depleted self-esteem by merging with his hero, mimicking Sutpen's attitudes and behavior and hoping to be admitted into the protective house. Adamowski argues that Wash worships Sutpen as a god, and "exceeds even the boy Sutpen in his idealization of a planter" (147). But when Sutpen seduces Milly and then insults her, Wash's self is shattered by this selfobject betrayal. Wash sees "his whole life shredded from him and shrivel away like a dried shuck thrown onto the fire" (233). In a frenzy of narcissistic rage, Wash murders Sutpen, Milly, and her newborn child. Then, when a group of men arrive to arrest him, Wash realizes that there is no escape: "if he ran he would be fleeing merely one set of bragging and evil shadows for another, since they (men) were all of a kind throughout all of the earth . . . [he] could never escape them" (232). Shame cannot be discarded on a journey, so he charges into the blazing guns of the posse.

Like Wash Jones, Goodhue Coldfield is marginalized by a shaming community. A Methodist and an abolitionist, he is never fully accepted by his fellow Jeffersonians and becomes a veritable pariah when the Civil War begins. Refusing to support the Confederate army, he closes his store and barricades his family in his house. Mr. Compson explains that this retreat is not motivated by guilt over a specific transgression, but by a sudden feeling of overwhelming incongruity: "he seemed to change overnight" (64). Lynd argues that shame is caused by a sense of incongruity and inappropriateness, as when a "discrepancy appears between us and the social situation" (34–35). Acutely conscious of social status yet stubbornly moral, Coldfield would be a prime candidate for discomfiture in either a guilt or a shame culture: "[his] only companion and friend seems to have been his conscience and the only thing he cared about his reputation for probity among his fellow men" (47). When neighbors loot his store, his symbol of "fortitude and abnegation," he reacts to this massive narcissistic injury by retreating into the attic where he dies of starvation three years later (66).

Another major example of retreat involves Coldfield's daughter Rosa, who spends forty-three years barricaded in her house nursing a grudge against Sutpen, or, more accurately, against a narcissistically perceived nightmare vision of the man. As a child, Rosa is deprived of mirroring selfobject responses: her mother dies during childbirth; her older sister Ellen lives at Sutpen's Hundred; and her surrogate mother, "the aunt," is as faceless and unempathic as she is nameless. Rosa's anger at being denied contact with empathic-mirroring faces causes her to develop a fixation in which she sees only a person's face (especially its color), instead of the whole person. For example, one of her earliest memories (age three) is of the "ogre-face" of the man who stole away her older sister, Ellen, and of the pallid faces of his family peering out of a carriage driven by a "wild negro" and pulled by "wildeyed horses." The vision is particularly disturbing because Sutpen's face is "exactly like the negro's save for the teeth" (16). Instead of smiling at her sister, Ellen's face is "transmogrified into a mask looking back with passive and hopeless grief . . . in a kind of jeering suspension" (47–48). Later in life, Rosa especially despises the inscrutable quality of Sutpen's illegitimate daughter Clytie's "sphinx face," which Rosa repeatedly calls a "coffee-colored face" (109–10)—scornful of her mixed blood (Ragan 57). Rosa's fixation with faces recalls Sutpen's obsession with the "balloon face" of Pettibone's butler. Rosa never experiences empathy; instead, faces mock and frighten, conceal secrets from her, or reveal such family secrets as her brother-in-law's miscegenation to the world.

Rosa buttresses her weak self-esteem through a series of idealized selfobject mergers with her seemingly omnipotent father and aunt. She imitates their lack of forgivingness. Rosa's father never forgave her for her mother's death, and her aunt never forgave the town for ruining Ellen's wedding. She also imitates their tendency to flee their problems or responsibilities. Her aunt abandons her to elope with a mule-trader, and her father locks himself in the attic. Thus when the adult Rosa's unstable self is shattered by Sutpen's indecent proposal "that they try it first and if it was a boy and lived, they would be married," she retreats back to Jefferson and the sanctuary of her childhood home (228). However, instead of dying in "impregnable solitude" as her father had done in the attic (70), Rosa turns her passive retreat into active revenge by sharing her story with Quentin and then returning to the scene of the outrage to assault Clytie and witness the destruction of Sutpen's Hundred in 1909.

In this way, Rosa presents yet another shame- and rage-prone Southerner whose hypersensitivity to slights manifests itself on several occasions. She is more humiliated by Wash Jones's indiscretion in front of the neighbors—"yelling of blood and pistols in the street before my house" without first discarding his tobacco cud—than upset at the news of her niece's fiancé's death. She converts this humiliation into an outburst of furious epithets, calling Wash a "brute" several times (107–8). Ashamed of her poverty, initially she would rather steal vegetables from her neighbors' gardens, than receive baskets of food from them (138). Later, she retaliates for the humiliation of receiving charity by returning the dishes soiled, an extraordinary breach of Southern etiquette (Ragan 91–92). Rosa perceives her environment narcissistically, and all these events—her father's isolated death, her aunt's elopement, Charles's murder, her neighbors' charity, even Wash's "poor white" manners—are experienced as malicious attacks directed at her personally.[11]

The motifs of shame and flight pervade each different narrator's version of events, in a novel where distinguishing narrative bias is of paramount importance (Matthews 115–61; Ryan 295–312). The omniscient narrator, Mr. Compson, Quentin, Shreve, even an elliptic letter written by Charles Bon—each provides examples of this rhetoric of retreat. The most vivid instances, however, are provided by Rosa who describes experiencing a "dream state in which you run without moving from a terror in which you can not believe, toward a safety in which you have no faith, held so not by the shifting and foundationless quicksand of nightmare but by a face which was its soul's own inquisitor" (113–14). For Rosa, the inquisitor face belongs to Clytie who—like the balloon face that haunts Sutpen—penetrates right to the core of Rosa's self, becoming an internalized face that shames. Having chosen a life of impoverished spinsterhood over marriage to the biggest landowner in Jefferson, Rosa becomes the talk of the town. She dreads her neighbors' scornful gossip, as suggested by the imaginary song that echoes in her head: "Rosie Coldfield, lose him, weep him; found a man but failed to keep him" (137). Erik H. Erikson distinguishes between "visual shame," precipitated by the faces of others, and "auditory guilt," precipitated by the internal voice of the superego (253). Yet Rosa's internal song does not reveal guilt, nor is it sung by her superego. The unempathic others that cause shame can be both real or imagined: gossiping neighbors or taunting internal voices; scornful faces without or the inquisitor-face within. This blurring of external and internal sanctions problematizes the distinction between guilt and shame.

Despite Rosa's insistence on expelling the "skeleton" from her family closet through her narration to Quentin (8), rhetoric itself is used as a kind of retreat as she uses layers of words to protect herself from painful truths. For example, after being abandoned by her father, Rosa becomes the county's "poetess laureate," turning her personal grief into public odes to the Confederate army (6). Quentin's and Shreve's flamboyant storytelling also protects them from painful truths, as the narrator explains: "It too was just that protective coloring of levity behind which the youthful shame of being moved hid itself, out of which Quentin also spoke . . . that best [kind] of ratiocination which after all was a good deal like Sutpen's morality and Miss Coldfield's demonizing" (225). Whether they are hiding from demons of family, race, incest, or history, they conceal themselves behind the very words that reveal their shame. The novel's retreat motif does more than simply delineate character: it structures the major events of the novel, as well as their narration.

Shame filters down through the generations of Faulkner's novel. For example, Charles Etienne de Saint Valéry Bon, Sutpen's grandson, is rejected by white Jeffersonians for being one-sixteenth black, but is not allowed to integrate into black communities either. After he is savagely beaten at a "negro ball," he is urged to run away by Grandfather Compson: "once you are among strangers, people who dont know you, you can be whatever you will" (164–65). In other words, his shame could be discarded on a journey. Yet instead of fleeing, Charles Etienne marries a "coal-black and ape-like woman," flaunts her before the locals, and barricades himself like a hermit in his cabin—a defiant marriage and siege that echo Sutpen's early years in Jefferson. Charles Etienne has not discarded his shame; his shamelessness is a kind of reaction formation, "a defence against shame rather than its absence" (Moore and Fine 182). Like Sutpen, Charles Etienne does not gain acceptance by a community through his marriage, and he remains an outcast (166–69). His son, Jim Bond, is also scorned by Jeffersonians such as young Quentin Compson because Jim has mixed blood and is mentally challenged (173–74). At the close of the novel, this great-grandson of Sutpen and last of his line is rejected by Rosa, "'You, nigger! . . . You aint any Sutpen'" (297). When the Hundred burns to the ground, he howls and haunts the ruins of his ancestor's home despite the sheriff's men's attempts to chase him away: "They couldn't catch him and nobody ever seemed to make him go very far away" (301).

The experiences of such myriad characters, taken collectively, suggest that the Faulknerian South is populated with shame-prone individuals. Indeed, the Confederate army is described primarily in retreat, "swept onward not by a victorious army behind it but rather by a mounting tide of . . . lost battles"—losses caused by incompetent generals promoted by an "absolute caste system" (276). This is not a "shamed" culture in retreat; rather, the ignominy of the defeated army is the sum total of individual disappointments. For example, Sutpen— the braggart colonel and best shot in Jefferson—must admit to Wash that he was "unable to penetrate far enough behind the Yankee lines to cut a piece from [Lincoln's] coat tail as I promised you" (223). Charles Bon's letter to Judith describes the soldiers as hollow men—"scarecrows"—reduced to looting Southern smokehouses (102–04).

Faulkner's novel suggests that these defeats are caused ultimately by the South's economic dependence on slaves (such as Sutpen's "herd of wild beasts" [10]) to cultivate plantations built on land swindled or stolen from the indigenous people (Sutpen's hundred acres were purchased from the Chickasaw chief Ikkemotubbe for one Spanish coin). In 1909, Quentin still suffers from the "disease" caused by his ancestors' actions: "his very body was an empty hall echoing with sonorous defeated names. . . . He was a barracks filled with stubborn back-looking ghosts still recovering, even forty-three years afterward" (7). Quentin's narration of the novel's events to Shreve suggests a kind of guilt-culture confession (Ragan 69; Hlavsa 63). However, Shreve cannot "shrive" or forgive him because Quentin does not suffer from feelings of guilt for something he has done, but shame for something he *is*—a Southerner, a Jeffersonian, a Compson, and possibly (because of his love for his sister Caddy) an incestuous "reincarnation" of Charles Bon.[12] When Quentin tries to avoid hearing Rosa's narration of the novel's early events, his father orders him to stay and listen because "she considers you partly responsible through heredity for what happened to her and her family" (8). This recalls an English proverb, "Shame in a kindred cannot be avoided" (qtd. in Lynd 54).

In a 1953 study, Milton B. Singer raised a number of questions about the dichotomy of shame versus guilt cultures. First of all, fear of shame can itself be internalized, becoming a sanction indistinguishable from guilt (65–67). Shame is not always precipitated by an external audience; the contrary is suggested by the internal faces that scorn Sutpen and Rosa. Some internal faces represent the idealized selfobjects of childhood, which, when "divested of the personality features of the object," become a mature adult's conscience and values (Kohut, *Analysis* 51). Yet Sutpen never dissociates his values-system from specific faces, whether his father's, Pettibone's, or the butler's. Calvin S. Brown suggests that Faulkner borrowed the idea for balloon faces from a popular comic strip in which the "Katzenjammer Kids" would copy their faces onto balloons and tie them so they appeared to peer over fences or hedges "in order to avert suspicion while they themselves were off performing some sort of devilment" (Brown 113). However, Sutpen's balloon represents the butler's face, not his own. Having projected onto others the internalized faces that inhibit behavior, Sutpen can act shamelessly. Race becomes his "ruse" as he blames his own "devilment" on, and conceals it behind, the jeering balloon faces. The butler made him do it.

Secondly, Singer notes that political and cultural biases prompted anthropologists to develop the shame/guilt dichotomy in the 1920s and 1930s in order to differentiate "progressive" Western cultures—characterized by guilt and the Oedipus complex—from non-European shame cultures that were considered "static, industrially backward, without absolute moral standards and dominated by 'crowd psychology'"; in short, primitive and pre-Oedipal (Singer 59–61). As late as 1950, Erikson writes of the "'shaming' used so exclusively by some primitive peoples" (253), and in 1971 Lewis comments on the persistent prejudice "of treating shame as a lower order of morality than guilt" (*Shame* 22). Yet there is nothing static or backward about the archaic processes that Kohut identified in his adult patients, and Faulkner intuited in his characters. Sutpen's exploitation of women *is* in accordance with a complex moral code—however racist, irrational, or misogynous—prescribing a racially pure wife and men-children to protect him from shame (Davis 185). Furthermore, Sutpen is a rugged individual who nevertheless conforms blindly to the racist code of plantation society—an example that undermines the dichotomy of individual versus collective behaviour in guilt and shame cultures (Singer 60). Finally, while Japan does rely heavily on external sanctions, its people are anything but primitive adherents to "situational ethics" (Dower 124–27).[13]

Absalom, Absalom! also problematizes many of the generalizations about the South that Faulkner made in Japan. Such images as Sutpen and his sons hiding in the war, or defeated Grays looting in their own land, tarnish the myth of the heroic Confederate soldier. Faulkner's South was not defeated by the power of the North so much as by its own social corruption. Unlike postwar Japan in its "economic miracle," the South did not endure defeat and reconstruction very well: Sutpen's plantation is reduced to a knick-knack store, and the "bulwark" of his progeny is destroyed (146).[14] Cleanth Brooks points out that the Old South was a paternalistic culture that emphasized the importance of family. Yet Sutpen is no successful patriarch: he abandons his first wife (Eulalia), alienates a second (Ellen), repels a possible third (Rosa), and indirectly causes the deaths of four of his five children. And finally, as Brooks also suggests, the aristocratic tradition of the antebellum South is somewhat exaggerated. Sutpen is ostracized by a "league of Jefferson women . . . [who] agreed never to forgive him for not having any past" (40) when in fact, most Southern aristocrats were of "plebian origins" (Brooks 169–74 and sources cited there). Their history extended back no further than one or two grandfathers; for example, Pettibone is a "*nouveau-riche*" with a "mean past" (Adamowski 146).

If Faulkner painted with broad strokes when comparing cultures on his visit to Japan, he produced more subtle portraits of individuals who make up Southern communities in *Absalom, Absalom!* His inductive literary explorations of group psychology support Singer's assertion that the most accurate way to psychoanalyse a culture is through a "psychoanalysis of a sample of individuals" (90). *Absalom, Absalom!* presents just such a sample.[15] Although its characters experience shame, Jefferson is not a shame culture. Their injuries spring from a variety of specific individual experiences that do not support sweeping cultural categories.

As Douglas Miller points out, in the 1940s and 50s, Faulkner "was viewed primarily as a sociologist or regional historian and only secondly as an artist" (209)—a misconception partially confirmed by the nature of many questions he fielded on his trip. In his parting "Impressions of Japan," Faulkner concentrated on individual faces he had seen during his trip. He explained that, although the scenery was beautiful, he preferred to look at faces and "speculate on what's behind those wrinkles, what's behind that expression, what that life could have been that that face shows" (*Nagano* 110–11). His questioners persisted in their misconception of Faulkner the sociologist/historian, demanding to know whether Japanese faces were "more interesting than other faces?" Faulkner replied that "it's only incidental that the face is Japanese or Scandinavian. It's the face, the life, the same life, the anguish, the same anguish" (111). He was not erasing differences between cultures, however, merely sticking to what he did best. His greatest talent consisted in the creative depiction of the individual faces that make up, not a shame culture, but cultures whose members are on the run from shame.

NOTES

An earlier version of this paper was delivered to the Canadian Comparative Literature Association at Carleton University, Ottawa, in May 1993. The author is grateful to Joseph Adamson (McMaster), T. H. Adamowski (Toronto), and Stephen Collington (Tokyo) for their many helpful suggestions, and acknowledges the Social Sciences and Humanities Research Council of Canada for financial support during the paper's composition.

1. All italics from the novel have been omitted.

2. Faulkner distinguishes the traditions and history of his "country," the South, from those of America's industrialized Northern states (*Nagano* 192–94). For an alternative view of Faulkner's novel as a more inclusive description of the "American dream," see Brooks 178–83.

3. Despite social, linguistic and cultural differences, neither the Koreans nor the Burakumin belong to a different *race* from the Japanese (De Vos 3–4). Yet in 1945, "First- and second-generation Koreans resident in Japan . . . were denied full citizenship and subjected to every conceivable form of discrimination—their treatment being very similar to that accorded blacks in the United States, despite the fact that many Koreans could pass physically for Japanese" (Dower 285). Similarly, the Burakumin differ from majority Japanese only in their status as social "outcasts" who work in taboo trades and live largely in poverty. As Benedict points out, "caste has been the rule of life" throughout Japan's history (57); to this day majority Japanese eschew intermarriage with these "invisible" minorities (De Vos and Wetherall 6–7).

4. Kohut's most important formulations of self psychology are his two monographs: *Analysis* and *Restoration*. More accessible introductions to self psychology can be found in his *Seminars* and his influential article "Thoughts." For useful summaries of Kohut's evolving theories, see Bacal 225–73; Baker and Baker 1–9; and Eagle 175–85. For discussions of various methodological applications of self psychology to literature, see the introductions to books by Berman 1–55; Bouson 11–24; and Layton and Schapiro 2–7.

5. As Morrison points out, Kohut rarely used the term "shame" but it is a concept that pervades his writings as they evolved over a twenty-five-year period (*Shame* 77). I have oversimplified a complex issue here, and the reader is directed to Morrison's thoughtful discussions of shame within self psychology (*Shame* 67–85 and "Shame" 71–90). While theories differ in the metapsychological details, there is much common ground surrounding the concept in psy-

choanalytic and in common parlance. The *Oxford English Dictionary* definitions of "shame" coincide with several processes already discussed. Definition one, "the painful emotion arising from the consciousness of something dishonouring, ridiculous or indecorous in one's own conduct or circumstances," coincides with Lynd's noncompliant field or Kohut's concept of narcissistic injury caused by unempathic responses. That shame arises from a consciousness of wrongdoing recalls Piers's demanding ego ideal, or the Japanese child's internalized fear of derisive laughter. Definitions two, "fear of offence against propriety or decency operating as a restraint on behaviour," and three, "disgrace, ignominy, loss of esteem or reputation," characterize shame as a powerful external sanction on behavior such as that attributed to shame cultures by Benedict. The judgmental aspects of definition four, "what is morally disgraceful or dishonourable; baseness in conduct or behaviour," coincide with Faulkner's condemnation of racial prejudice as the "shame" of the South (*OED* s.v.). Such pejorative connotations may have delayed shame's emergence as a legitimate area of psychoanalytic inquiry until the 1950s.

6. Rosa's complaint complicates notions that the South represented a monolithic culture with a consensus about acceptable behavior. Instead, Faulkner's Jefferson is composed of many distinct communities—planter aristocrats, merchants, Methodists, abolitionists, "poor whites," slaves, and so forth. A process of social Balkanization further subdivides the region's inhabitants: Southerners are divided into "countrified" provincials such as Henry Sutpen from Mississippi versus "Frenchified" sophisticates such as Charles Bon from New Orleans (Ragan 43); aristocrats into old adherents to the "code of gentlemanly conduct" such as Grandfather Compson (Ragan 10–11) versus upstart "backwoodsmen grown prosperous" such as Sutpen (Jenkins 180); vigilantes into daytime "vigilance committees" versus the night-riding forerunners of the Ku Klux Klan (Ragan 65–66); slaves into "house negroes" versus "field negroes" (Brown 81, 107); blacks into all-black versus creoles, quadroons, and octoroons; and white laborers into "white trash" such as Wash versus mountain men such as Sutpen's father. While there is some overlap, most of these groups espouse incompatible views and are as rigidly segregated as distinct nations. Furthermore, communities are divided along gender lines: for example, into the mirroring audience of men who admire Sutpen's performances and boost his self-esteem versus as the unempathic audience of "womenfolks" who censure such displays.

7. In an early short-story version of this episode, "The Big Shot," Sutpen's prototype, Martin, ran "into the woods and hid there all day, lying on his face in a ditch" (Faulkner, "Big" 508)—behavior that recalls Erik H. Erikson's discussion of shame as expressed in the urge "to bury one's face, or to sink . . . into the ground" (252).

8. John N. Duvall points out that Sutpen merges with three such models—Pettibone, the Haitian planter, and Grandfather Compson—during the execution of his "design" (106–7). For a different perspective on the origins of Sutpen's shame, see Adamowski 138–46, and Cobley 432–34.

9. Henry rationalizes the question of incest, "'But kings have done it! Even dukes!'" (273); and just before the shooting, Charles taunts his half-brother, "So it's the miscegenation, not the incest, which you cant bear" (285). In this way,

the Faulknerian South seems to display a fundamental characteristic of shame cultures, that undesirable acts are avoided "not because they are evil but because they are . . . inappropriate" (Benedict 287). Yet Henry's indecision stems from personal, not societal, pressures. For detailed psychoanalytic investigations into Faulknerian incest, see Irwin passim and Jenkins 200–19.

10. Wash's humiliation in this regard would have been particularly acute. To be regarded as socially inferior to slaves, especially *by slaves*, was a particular affront to white Southerners, as suggested by Sutpen's reaction to Pettibone's butler. In *Gone with the Wind*, published the same year as Faulkner's novel, Margaret Mitchell describes an exchange between Stuart Tarleton and Jeems over the servant's mockery of a neighbor who cannot afford to buy a "nigger" cook:

> There was frank contempt in Jeems' voice. His own social status was assured because the Tarletons owned a hundred negroes and, like all slaves of large planters, he looked down on small farmers whose slaves were few.
>
> "I'm going to beat your hide off for that," cried Stuart fiercely. "Don't you call Abel Wynder 'po white.' Sure he's poor, but he ain't trash; and I'm damned if I'll have any man, darky or white, throwing off on him." (Mitchell 19–20)

After the war, Scarlett O'Hara has a similar reaction to a group of "negroes" who laugh at her poverty from a passing carriage: "How dared they laugh, the black apes! . . . What devils the Yankees were to set them free, free to jeer at white people!" (Mitchell 579).

11. For more detailed examinations of Rosa's character and narrative, see Geoffroy 313–21, Wagner-Martin 1–13, and sources cited there.

12. Like Quentin, Faulkner repeatedly refers to the "internal sickness" of slavery that caused the South's defeat (e.g., *Nagano* 48–49). Douglas T. Miller describes Faulkner's contradictory attitudes toward Southern history as a vacillation between condemnation of the "sin of slavery" (such as in *Absalom, Absalom!* and at Nagano) and rhapsodic nostalgia for the South's lost "code of personal dignity, courage, honor and integrity" (Miller 204–6). For insightful perspectives on race and racism in the novel, see Davis 179–238, and Jenkins 177–219.

13. For a Japanese perspective on Benedict's "superficial views concerning shame," see Doi 48–57 and sources cited there.

14. There is, of course, no critical consensus about the degree to which the rise and fall of the Sutpen dynasty represents the general course of Southern history (Karl 547–48). Michael Millgate writes that "the fatal flaw in Sutpen's design [is] precisely that flaw of man's inhumanity to man inherent in the recent history and structure of the South, a flaw represented not only by slavery itself but by other and surviving forms of racial and social intolerance" (158).

15. The views of Faulkner and Singer seem to represent a kind of 1950s *Zeitgeist*; in a 1955 lecture, for example, Donald Winnicott also stated that "the basis of group psychology is the psychology of the individual" (146).

WORKS CITED

Adamowski, T. H. "Children of the Idea: Heroes and Family Romances in *Absalom, Absalom!*" *Mosaic* 10.1 (1976): 115–31. Rpt. in *William Faulkner's Absalom, Absalom! A Critical Casebook.* Ed. Elizabeth Muhlenfeld. New York: Garland, 1984. 135–55.

Bacal, Howard A. "Heinz Kohut." *Theories of Object Relations: Bridges to Self Psychology.* Bacal and Kenneth M. Newman. New York: Columbia UP, 1990. 225–73.

Baker, Howard S. and Margaret N. Baker. "Heinz Kohut's Self Psychology: An Overview." *The American Journal of Psychiatry* 144.1 (1987): 1–9.

Benedict, Ruth. *The Chrysanthemum and the Sword: Patterns of Japanese Culture.* 1946. Rutland, VT: Tuttle, 1985.

Berman, Jeffrey. *Narcissism and the Novel.* New York: New York UP, 1990.

Bouson, J. Brooks. *The Empathic Reader: A Study of the Narcissistic Character and the Drama of the Self.* Amherst: U of Massachusetts P, 1989.

Brooks, Cleanth. "On *Absalom, Absalom!*" *Mosaic* 7.1 (1973): 159–83.

Brown, Calvin S. *A Glossary of Faulkner's South.* New Haven, Conn.: Yale UP, 1976.

Cobley, Evelyn. "Desire and Reciprocal Violence in *Absalom, Absalom!*" *English Studies in Canada* 13.4 (1987): 420–37.

Davis, Thadious M. *Faulkner's "Negro": Art and the Southern Context.* Baton Rouge: Louisiana State UP, 1983.

De Vos, George A. *Japan's Outcastes: The Problem of the Burakumin.* London: Minority Rights Group Report, 1971.

——, and William O. Wetherall. *Japan's Minorities: Burakumin, Koreans, Ainu and Okinawans.* Updated by Kaye Stearman. London: Minority Rights Group Report, 1983.

Diagnostic and Statistical Manual of Mental Disorders. Third edition, revised. Washington, DC: American Psychiatric Association, 1987.

Doi, Takeo. *The Anatomy of Dependence.* 1971. Trans. John Bester. Tokyo: Kodansha, 1987.

Dower, John W. *War without Mercy: Race and Power in the Pacific War.* New York: Pantheon, 1986.

Duvall, John N. *Faulkner's Marginal Couple: Invisible, Outlaw, and Unspeakable Communities.* Austin: U of Texas P, 1990.

Eagle, Morris. "Theoretical and Clinical Shifts in Psychoanalysis." *American Journal of Orthopsychiatry* 57.2 (1987): 175–85.

Erikson, Erik H. *Childhood and Society.* 1950. 2nd ed. New York: Norton, 1963.

Faulkner, William. *Absalom, Absalom! The Corrected Text.* 1936. Ed. Noel Polk. New York: Vintage, 1990.

——. "The Big Shot." 1930. *The Uncollected Stories of William Faulkner.* Ed. Joseph Blotner. New York: Random, 1979. 504–25.

——. *Faulkner at Nagano.* Ed. Robert A. Jelliffe. 1956. Tokyo: Kenkyusha, 1962.

Geoffroy, Alain. "Through Rosa's Looking-Glass: Narcissism and Identification in Faulkner's *Absalom, Absalom!*" *Mississippi Quarterly* 45.3 (1992): 313–21.

Hlavsa, Virginia V. "The Vision of the Advocate in *Absalom, Absalom!*" *Novel: A Forum on Fiction* 8.1 (1974): 51–70.

Irwin, John T. *Doubling and Incest/Repetition and Revenge: A Speculative Reading of Faulkner.* 1975. Baltimore: Johns Hopkins UP, 1980.

Jenkins, Lee. *Faulkner and Black-White Relations: A Psychoanalytic Approach.* New York: Columbia UP, 1981.

Karl, Frederick R. *William Faulkner: American Writer.* New York: Weidenfeld, 1989.

Kohut, Heinz. *The Analysis of the Self.* New York: International Universities P, 1971.

——. *The Kohut Seminars on Self Psychology and Psychotherapy with Adolescents and Young Adults.* Ed. Miriam Elson. New York: Norton, 1987.

——. *The Restoration of the Self.* New York: International Universities P, 1977.

——. "Thoughts on Narcissism and Narcissistic Rage." *The Psychoanalytic Study of the Child* 27 (1972): 360–400. Rpt. in *The Search for the Self.* Vol. 2. Ed. Paul Ornstein. New York: International Universities P, 1978. 615–58.

Layton, Lynne and Barbara Ann Schapiro, eds. *Narcissism and the Text.* New York: New York UP, 1986.

Lewis, Helen Block. *Shame and Guilt in Neurosis.* New York: International Universities P, 1971.

——. "Shame and the Narcissistic Personality." *The Many Faces of Shame.* Ed. Donald L. Nathanson. New York: Guilford P, 1987. 93–132.

Lynd, Helen Merrell. *On Shame and the Search for Identity.* New York: Harcourt, 1958.

Matthews, John T. *The Play of Faulkner's Language.* Ithaca, N.Y.: Cornell UP, 1982.

Miller, Douglas T. "Faulkner and the Civil War: Myth and Reality." *American Quarterly* 15.2 (1963): 200–209.

Miller, Susan. *The Shame Experience.* Hillsdale, N.J.: Analytic P, 1985.

Millgate, Michael. *The Achievement of William Faulkner.* 1963. Lincoln: U of Nebraska P, 1978.

Mitchell, Margaret. *Gone with the Wind.* 1936. New York: Avon, 1972.

Mollon, Phil. "Self-Awareness, Self-Consciousness, and Preoccupation with Self." *Self and Identity: Psychosocial Perspectives.* Ed. Krysia Yardley and Terry Honess. Toronto: John Wiley, 1987. 273–85.

Moore, Burness E. and Bernard D. Fine, eds. *Psychoanalytic Terms and Concepts.* The American Psychoanalytic Association. New Haven, Conn.: Yale UP, 1990.

Morrison, Andrew P. "Shame and the Psychology of the Self." *Kohut's Legacy: Contributions to Self Psychology.* Ed. Paul E. Stepansky and Arnold Goldberg. Hillsdale N.J.: Analytic P, 1984. 71–90.

——. *Shame: The Underside of Narcissism.* Hillsdale N.J.: Analytic P, 1989.

Oxford English Dictionary. 1971. Compact Edition. 3 vols. Oxford: Oxford UP, 1987.

Piers, Gerhart. "Shame and Guilt: A Psychoanalytic Study." Piers and Singer 15–55.

Piers, Gerhart and Milton B. Singer. *Shame and Guilt: A Psychoanalytic and a Cultural Study.* 1953. Revised ed. New York: Norton, 1971.

Ragan, David Paul. *Annotations to Faulkner's* Absalom, Absalom! New York: Garland, 1991.

Ryan, Heberden W. "Behind Closed Doors: The Unknowable and the Unknowing in *Absalom, Absalom!*" *Mississippi Quarterly* 45.3 (1992): 295–312.

Singer, Milton B. "Shame Cultures and Guilt Cultures." Piers and Singer 59–100.

Takashima, Taiji. *Kotowaza no Izumi: Fountain of Japanese Proverbs.* 1981. Tokyo: Hokuseido, 1986.

Wagner-Martin, Linda. "Rosa Coldfield as Daughter: Another of Faulkner's Lost Children." *Studies in American Fiction* 19.1 (1991): 1–13.

Weinstein, Philip M. "Precarious Sanctuaries: Protection and Exposure in Faulkner's Fiction." *Studies in American Fiction* 6.2 (1978): 173–92.

Winnicott, D. W. "Group Influences and the Maladjusted Child: The School Aspect." *The Family and Individual Development.* 1965. Rpt. London: Routledge, 1993. 146–54.

Wurmser, Léon. *The Mask of Shame.* Baltimore: Johns Hopkins UP, 1981.

CHAPTER 9

Depression, Shame, and Reparation: The Case of Anne Sexton

Hilary Clark

> I wish to enter her like a dream,
> leaving my roots here on the beach
> . . . .
> and walk into ocean,
> letting it explode over me
> and outward, where I would drink the moon
> and my clothes would slip away,
> and I would sink into the great mother arms
> I never had . . .
> —Anne Sexton ("In Excelsis")

In one of her last poems, Anne Sexton looked forward to her own death as a return to an oceanic mother—enveloping and infinitely nurturing. Sexton's relationship with her own mother was always highly ambivalent. Anger toward the distant, shaming mother, along with a desire to return to her, recover her love, haunt much of Sexton's work. The mother's loss marks the poetry as both a work of mourning and a brave attempt to transcend shame (Wurmser 293–94).

In this paper I will explore the function of poetry in Sexton's life, a life marked by depression, agoraphobia, addictions, and frequent suicide attempts. This life has been recounted by Diane Wood Middlebrook in her absorbing book *Anne Sexton: A Biography*, which moves from Sexton's childhood through her adult life as wife and mother, psychiatric patient, and Pulitzer Prize–winning poet, to her suicide in 1974. Sexton's writing gave meaning and structure to her life; it is probable that without her poetic practice, she would have been permanently hospitalized, or would have killed herself long before she did. I will explore how writing poetry was therapeutic for Sexton—how the creative process itself, over and above the fame and public identity her poetry brought her, helped her to overcome deep shame, a radical sense of unlovability (Wurmser 92–93). Although, as Jeffrey Berman puts it, "[s]uicide was so much part of Sexton's everyday life and art that she seems to have constructed her personal and artistic identity around it," the making of poetry for some years provided her with another, more positive identity.

I will begin by reviewing accounts of depression, and will then consider the link between women's depression and shame, tracing issues of mourning and shame in Sexton's life and art. I will consider briefly one of Sexton's best-known poems, "The Double Image," in order to determine the role, for Sexton, of poetry in dealing with an insistent guilt and shame associated with her roles as daughter and mother. In *The Death Notebooks*, published eight months before her suicide, Sexton attempted one last time to find some reconciliation with her mother and motherhood; I will thus conclude with a discussion of shame and maternal reparation in the short sequence entitled "The Death Baby" from this final work.

DEPRESSION

Freud's article "Mourning and Melancholia" is crucial to the tradition of psychoanalytic thinking on depression. Melancholia, the traditional term for depression, is characterized by a "lowering of self-regarding feelings to a degree that finds utterance in self-reproaches and self-revilings, and culminates in a delusional expectation of punishment" (Freud 244). Freud argues that melancholia is similar to mourning in that both involve feelings of loss. However, although melancholy involves a mourning for a lost object, mourning is not necessarily melancholia; it only becomes so when the mourner turns the ambivalent anger felt for the lost object inward onto the ego, in a narcissistic identification with the lost object (243–46). This identification incorporates the lost object, "devour[s]" it (250) in order to recover and preserve it. Yet at the same time there is a fear of this object. As Melanie Klein puts it, "in both children and adults suffering from depression, . . . [there is a] dread of harbouring dying or dead objects (especially the parents) inside one and an identification of the ego with objects in this condition" ("Psychogenesis" 121). Sexton's "The Death Baby" illustrates this identification in a most striking manner.

What is the object that the depressive both loves and hates? Object relations theory, focusing on the crucial impact of early attachments, points to the mother as this ambivalently desired object. In this view, the relationship with the mother is crucial to the child's emerging sense of self: interacting with her, the child gradually gains a sense of having an inside and an outside, of being a unit, as D. W. Winnicott puts it (*Human Nature* 67–68). Through introjection this unit takes "good" objects into itself, through projection expels "bad" objects (Hinshelwood 125). In Melanie Klein's theory of the paranoid and depressive positions, in the former position the infant defends against anxiety by splitting objects—and self—into good and bad, the mother being split into good breast and bad breast. This splitting is the infant's defense against its anxiety or frustration at the mother's absences or tardiness in supplying demands (Klein, "Notes" 177–81).

In the depressive position, however, the infant begins to identify with the mother as a whole object, feeling guilt over having harmed her in fantasy: "[C]onfronted with the psychical fact that its loved objects are in a state of dissolution—in bits" (Klein, "Psychogenesis" 124), the ego needs to save them, and itself, from disintegration. Through identification with a whole object, the ego affirms its own integrity and value—seeking to overcome its own fragmentation by putting the loved object back together, bringing the dead back to life.

According to Klein, the depressive position is a normal stage in the development of identity. Indeed, Winnicott (following Klein) emphasizes the value of depression as presupposing a capacity for guilt. The experience of guilty concern for an other, involving the recognition that the other is *other*—not self—opens the possibility of compassion ("The Value of Depression" 71–76), an escape from narcissistic wounding or shame. Depression involves ambivalence, certainly; it also involves a need to reconcile conflicting feelings of love and hate (74–75) and to overcome disintegration—the cognitive experience of shame (Nathanson 209–11).

CREATIVITY AND REPARATION

In Kleinian theory, the guilt associated with the mingling of love and aggression in the depressive position leads to the need to make reparation to the object, recover it: guilt is "at the point of transformation of destructiveness into constructiveness" (Winnicott, "Aggression, Guilt and Reparation" 89). Such reparation can be achieved through creativity—art and play.

Following Klein, Julia Kristeva in *Black Sun* sees depression as involving an "*impossible mourning for the maternal object*" (9, her italics), an internalized object felt to be dead, in pieces, gone. This loss is experienced as a breakdown in signification: the depressive loses a sense of the power of the signifier, having difficulties with thinking and speaking, "concatenating" signs (42). Depression is marked by "asymbolia," as the depressive seeks to return mutely to the lost object—the mother—and beyond this to nondifferentiation and death (16–21). Kristeva argues that depression is alleviated when the sufferer begins to articulate signs again, to engage in the process of creation: through this process, he or she is able to reconstruct the object while at the same time realizing and accepting its loss. As such, the process of creation reenacts the process of normal mourning, lifting the sufferer out of narcissistic self-hatred. In a similar way, Wurmser affirms that shame is transcended through creative acts, which are "attempts to overcome profound woundedness . . . [and] despair" and "reach . . . out to others: the primary audience to whom the creative work is directed, whom one wants to love and to be loved by" (293).

Thus artistic creation can be a process of healing. Reentering the intersubjective field of signs, communication, the sufferer enters the "field of the Other" once again (Lacan 246). In Kleinian terms, this process of healing is a process of reparation, mending the damaged object, making amends to it—"restoring the wholeness of the mother's body" (Laplanche and Pontalis 389). In the child's play and the adult's art, the mother, and accordingly the damaged, fragmented self, is made whole again, at least temporarily. In slightly different terms, the creative process—in its "pattern of repeated dissolution and reorganization, proceeding in parallel with unconscious splitting and reintegration"—affords the artist (and, one would imagine, the child playing) the means of mastering trauma (Rose 110). The process reenacts the splitting or disintegration effected by trauma and shame, but in a controlled way, as part of a movement toward reintegration of the self.

The depressive drive to create, then, defends against excessive anxiety: "It appears that the desire for perfection is rooted in the depressive anxiety of disintegration, which is thus of great importance in all sublimations" (Klein, "Psychogenesis" 125), in art and play. The depressive affect, argues Kristeva in the same vein, "can be interpreted as a defense against parcelling . . . reconstitut[ing] an affective cohesion of the self" (19). Thus, however painful and potentially deadly depression can be, it can be a precondition of healing, of restoring psychic wholeness.

WOMEN, DEPRESSION, AND SHAME

It is generally agreed that at least twice as many women as men suffer from depression (Nolen-Hoeksema 3). One could argue as well that women are more prone to feelings of shame than men are, as shame is experienced by those who feel helpless, powerless, lacking in control over their environment: "Women's greater sociability and lesser aggression, taken together with their second-class status in the world of power, increase their tendency to the experience of shame" (Lewis, "The Role of Shame" 29). (One might add that when women display more aggression than is expected of them, and take on a more public role, they open themselves to charges of shamelessness, which can lead to more shame.) Helen Block Lewis has argued that "[s]hame is an inevitable human response to loss of love . . . [it is] the empathetic experience of the other's rejection of the self . . . in which one accepts the loss of the other as if it were a loss in the self" (30–32). Women are particularly vulnerable to shame and depression when relationships fail—or when they experience diminishment of self, silencing, within a relationship.

The social construction of femininity thus encourages a dependence upon others for self-validation; as Lewis puts it, women are somewhat more field-dependent than men ("The Role of Shame" 7) and hence more vulnerable to shame. For the daughter, the primary other is the mother. As Nancy Chodorow has suggested, girls do not detach themselves from their mothers as fully as boys do, largely because under patriarchy mothers are socialized to encourage their daughters' dependence more than their sons' (96–99).

Imagine, then, the consequences for a girl whose mother is consistently inaccessible or shames her daughter, physically or verbally abusing her. If we accept the accounts of depression above, then we can expect that the daughter will mourn, turning her anger inward and blaming herself, feeling shame at rejection by a loved other. Inadequately mothered, the daughter may seek as an adult to be mothered and may be unable to nurture her own children adequately. This was certainly the case for Anne Sexton: she had trouble accepting her role as mother, because her own needs as a daughter had not been adequately fulfilled by her own mother, Mary Gray Staples Harvey. She would play a game with her daughter Linda, in which they reversed roles, Linda being mother and Anne being "nine," seeking cuddles and affection. Naturally, this reversal of roles or blurring of boundaries frightened the girl: "[T]o me the game aroused over and over all my fears of losing my mother" (Linda Sexton 60), fears that also arose when the older Sexton went into trancelike states. Thus the cycle of deprivation and mourning will begin again, in the next generation, unless the need to be mothered is finally articulated and resolved in therapy—and sometimes, as in Sexton's poetry, in art.

The process of restoring the lost object through creative work is particularly crucial in healing female depression and shame. Artmaking or creative play can function as a process of mourning through which the daughter is reconciled with the mother's loss. In the articulation of signs, art breaks the narcissistic mirror of shame—the devastating image of unlovability—and thus serves as a defense, however tenuous, against self-hatred and identification with death.

ANNE SEXTON'S POETRY:
REPARATION AND THE LURE OF DEATH

The case of Anne Sexton confirms the link between feminine depression, shame, and inadequate parenting. And it shows particularly clearly the role of art in reconstructing the lost mother, or at least in making sense of maternal shame.

Anne Sexton was born in Newton, Massachusetts, in 1928, the youngest of three daughters in a well-to-do family. According to biographer Diane Wood Middlebrook, the parents did not have a close, loving relationship with their daughters: "Gaining their parents' attention seemed to require ingenious strategies on the children's part. . . . They vied with one another for praise, particularly from their elusive mother" (10). The father travelled extensively for his prosperous wool business; he began to drink heavily and behave unpredictably, apparently making passes at his daughters while drunk, and often disappearing for days at a time. The emotional unpredictability of the mother, who also drank heavily, was apparently even more disturbing. Middlebrook quotes Sexton's older sister Jane as saying, "'Daddy was either drunk or he was sober. . . . But you never knew, with Mother, when she was going to be horrible or nice. The minute you thought you knew where you were, she'd turn on you'" (13). Particularly disturbing were Sexton's memories of enduring her mother's intrusive genital inspections in the interests of "cleanliness" (59). The girl was without the privacy and predictable emotional nurturing that children require; it is no wonder that she grew up to struggle with shame and depression, unresolved feelings of unlovability, as she came to experience the pressures of mothering her own daughters.

"What does the baby see when he or she looks at the mother's face? . . . [O]rdinarily, what the baby sees is himself or herself" (Winnicott, "Mirror-Role" 112). Lacking a "good-enough mother" who would reflect back a loved self, consolidate an identity, Sexton turned to a substitute mother, her unmarried great-aunt Anna or Nana, her mirror or "twin" as she called her. With Nana she formed an "intense bond" (Middlebrook 15)—an erotically close relationship of naps taken together, back rubs, and whispered stories—until she was a teenager. Then this second mother withdrew into a breakdown. She did not recognize the girl when she visited, crying out "'You're not Anne!'" (16)

and calling her "horrible and disgusting" (16). (As well, Sexton's father did not spare the girl verbal abuse, calling her teenage acne "disgusting" [14] and declaring himself unable to tolerate her presence at the dinner table.)

Obviously the narcissistic wounds ran deep; as Wurmser puts it, "[t]he most radical shame is to offer oneself and be rejected as unlovable" (92). Sexton's parents were guilty of convincing their youngest daughter that she was thoroughly unlovable. As a teenager, she developed a depressive's low self-esteem, blaming herself for Nana's breakdown and eventually seeking acceptance in the conventional feminine career of wife and mother. But when her own daughters were very young (two years old and an infant), Sexton became ill with crippling anxiety and depression—mirroring Nana's illness as a way of asserting her neediness and recovering her lost love. As she said, "'I'd much rather get back to Nana before she was sick than to get well. That's the entire goal. If I were really sick I could get back to Nana'" (quoted in Middlebrook 16). Indeed, Sexton's neediness was boundless; even at the end of her life, she could write: "I want mother's milk,/ . . . / I want nipples like shy strawberries/ for I need to suck the sky" ("Food," *Complete Poems* 488). Her numerous suicide attempts were bids to return to, identify with, the dead mother: "She should be entered skin to skin,/ and put on like one's first or last cloth . . ." ("The Consecrating Mother," *Complete Poems* 555).

Over her life, then, Sexton struggled with her illness (exacerbated by heavy drinking and an addiction to sleeping pills). However, she managed to have a stellar career as a poet, publishing eight books of poetry and seeing one play produced. She won the Pulitzer Prize in 1967 for her book of poems *Live or Die*. She became famous for her charismatic public readings, and for her daring "confessional" poetry focusing on feminine sexuality and madness. It was Sexton's analyst, Dr. Martin Orne, who suggested that she write about her experience of mental illness in order to help other sufferers (Middlebrook 42), and she fastened on this idea, offering up her early poems to her doctor. This intensive formal activity—eroticized under the supervision of the male analyst, and later the guidance of a succession of male mentors (and sometimes lovers)—helped her consolidate an identity as a poet and as a woman. It helped her to work through and control, at least partly, the shame of early rejections, and feelings of guilt over her inability to live up to ideals of motherhood and daughterhood.

However, Sexton remained agoraphobic, feeling too vulnerable to leave the house or travel except in the company of trusted companions (Middlebrook 127–28), and having to drink heavily before performing in public. It seems she still wanted to hide, avoid exposure; the shame ran too deep. Yet Sexton was also quite "shameless" in not particularly seeking to hide her numerous extramarital affairs with poets, and in cultivating a sexy persona in her public performances, blowing kisses to the audience and unbuttoning herself as she read (Middlebrook 278, 395). This is no paradox if we understand shamelessness to be a defense against acute shame (Wurmser 263), a temporary escape from self-hatred.

Thus poetic or creative activity saved Sexton's life—at least for a time—helping her reintegrate a broken, shamed self. Issues of guilt and shame mark a number of Sexton's poems, one of the best known being "The Double Image": here, the poet explores her relationship with her mother, Mary Gray Harvey, and her youngest daughter, Joy. In this poem, Margaret Honton claims, "[t]he first words on the subject of mother-daughter relationships that Anne Sexton spells out are *blame, debt,* and *guilt* (100). The speaker blames herself for her baby daughter's illness and extended stay with her grandmother: "Ugly angels spoke to me. The blame,/ I heard them say, was mine" (*Complete Poems* 36). The speaker sees her own ensuing suicide attempt as an act of expiation ("I let the witches take away my guilty soul" [36]) but also as a new source of self-blame; she is now responsible, it seems, for her mother's cancer:

> . . . my mother grew ill.
> She turned from me, as if death were catching,
> as if death transferred,
> as if my dying had eaten inside of her.
> . . . .
> On the first of September she looked at me
> and said I gave her cancer.
> They carved her sweet hills out
> and still I couldn't answer. (38)

These feelings of "not being able to answer" reinforce the speaker's desire for death, the feeling that she does not deserve to have her daughter, her "splendid stranger," back home with her once again. However, her feelings of guilt have the virtue of bringing on a certain clarity, a fierce self-analysis:

> And I had to learn
> why I would rather
> die than love, how your innocence
> would hurt and how I gather
> guilt like a young intern
> his symptoms, his certain evidence. (39–40)

And she gathers shame as well. In "The Double Image," the mirroring portraits of mother and daughter emphasize issues of shame: the speaker is reminded how like her mother she is—a mother who rejects her daughter, who has her daughter's portrait painted in lieu of understanding and forgiving her suicide attempt; in turn, the speaker feels she has rejected her own daughter. Turning for love to a mother who is a "mocking mirror" (40), the daughter sees reflected back a shameful, disintegrating self: "I rot on the wall, my own/ Dorian Gray" (41).

Are the speaker's feelings of guilt and shame resolved in "The Double Image"? Not entirely. The poem's ending is problematic, as, addressing her daughter Joyce, the speaker acknowledges her narcissistic motives in wanting a daughter:

> I needed you. I didn't want a boy,
> only a girl . . .
> . . . .
> I, who was never quite sure
> about being a girl, needed another
> life, another image to remind me.
> And this was my worst guilt; you could not cure
> nor soothe it. I made you to find me. (41–42)

Unable to find a confirming self-image in her mother's face as "mocking mirror," the speaker admits that she wants her daughter to fulfil this role of reflecting back to her an image of someone loved and valued, a cherished mother—hence making her a little more "sure/ about being a girl," her own mother's daughter.

There *are*, in the poem, glimpses of the child Joy as truly other, as more than her mother's mirroring image, as when the little girl, a stranger returning home, asks her mother's name (41). While the speaker sees her relationship with her daughter in terms of her relationship with her own mother, inviting a sense of inevitable repetition of guilt and shame across the generations, one might conclude that her daughter Joy will fare somewhat better than she did—largely because the poem itself, as an act of self-distancing, has allowed the speaker to analyze her own feelings of guilt and shame, and their relation to her narcissistic needs. This is a first step toward true reparation, toward loving her daughter and her mother as others, rather than as images of herself.

Years later, like Anne Sexton in "The Double Image," Linda Gray Sexton would attempt, in writing *Searching for Mercy Street*, an act of both exorcism and reparation, seeking to restore her mother as loved *other*:

> From the perspective of starting the fifth decade of my life, I now understand my mother's life as a woman. . . . Perhaps I understand Mother better because I have forgiven her, and perhaps that forgiveness comes at this time of my life because I can finally empathize with what she endured and with the ways in which she both failed and triumphed. . . . I cast my feelings into "Language"—the shared medium in which Mother and I reveled—to find freedom. (301)

For both Anne Sexton and her daughter Linda, it was in "Language"— writing, art—that the lost mother could be sought as a whole person, beyond the shames of past mothering. As Linda Sexton concludes her memoir, "it no longer seems a crime to admit, 'I have been her kind'" (300).

As Anne Sexton's health and sanity deteriorated (a decline hastened by her addictions), her poems became less controlled, less effective in distancing shame and holding death at bay. In *The Death Notebooks*— published in 1974, the year of her suicide—Sexton quite theatrically flaunts her fascination with death. While in much of Sexton's poetry on suicide, "wish and fear are often functionally identical" (Hume George 77), in *The Death Notebooks* the wish for death is stronger than fear. Diana Hume George argues that the sequence "The Death Baby" in this book "provide[s] a poetic analogue for the hypothesis Freud outlined in 'Beyond the Pleasure Principle'" (78): that "the aim of all life is death" (Freud cited in Hume George 74), a return to an earlier, inanimate state of things. "The Death Baby" works out this overwhelming drive toward death within the context of the mother-infant relationship. The needs to be mothered and to mother, and the frustration of these needs, are linked here to imagery of fragmentation and dismembering, imagery rehearsing the final disintegration of identity in death. Deep shame is evoked in this imagery, a shame experienced as an undoing or disorganization of the self (Nathanson 209–11) and its boundaries.

"Dreams," the first poem in "The Death Baby," is a fantasy of dismembering. The speaker's sister "at six/ dreamt nightly of my death" (*Death Notebooks* 354); this dream springing from sibling aggression conveys the speaker's infancy, a time of unmet needs:

> I was an ice baby.
> I turned to sky blue.
> My tears became two glass beads.
> My mouth stiffened into a dumb howl. (354)

Lacking love and recognition, the infant turns into ice, an "ice baby" with two frozen tears; that is, it becomes as emotionally unresponsive as its caretakers, unable to express its anguish. The infant's "sky blue" tinge suggests a lack of oxygen. Is it holding its breath out of rage? Or, besides emotional sustenance, is even oxygen being withheld from the child? Now the infant is deliberately laid in the refrigerator and "'turned as hard as a Popsicle'" (354). Unable to cry or feed or breathe, it becomes food for others, cold food; it is "put on a platter and laid/ between the mayonnaise and the bacon" (354)—ready to be made into a sandwich, perhaps, for a parent made an ogre by the child's rage. There are nasty foods in the fridge that might also be projections of this rage (Klein, "Notes" 183–84): a "milk bottle hiss[es] like a snake," "tomatoes vomit . . . up their stomachs," and "caviar turn[s] to lava" (354). All of these objects are ejecting their contents, releasing pent-up pressure—something the frozen infant with its "mouth stiffened in a dumb howl" is unable to do.

Then, shamefully, the infant in the sister's dream is not only food but *dog* food:

> I was at the dogs' party.
> I was their bone.
> I had been laid out in their kennel
> like a fresh turkey.
> . . . .
> At first I was lapped,
> rough as sandpaper.
> I became very clean.
> Then my arm was missing.
> I was coming apart.
> They loved me until
> I was gone. (355)

The image of being food for dogs to devour suggests the extreme vulnerability of the infant, "laid out" like a sacrificial victim under the tongues and greedy gaze of more powerful beings. As well, the emphasis on dismemberment conveys particularly forcefully the depressive's sense of shame, the desire to disappear under the gaze of the other. Ironically, this annihilating eye is characterized as a loving one ("They loved me until/ I was gone"), while the self's disintegration is perceived as a form of purification: the shamed self is so dirty and despicable that it must disappear piece by tiny piece in order to "become very clean." The very short lines and repeated simple sentence structure in this poem reinforce the idea of fragmentation—the poem's sense, like the self, getting smaller and smaller until "gone."

The second poem in the "Death Baby" sequence, "The Dy-dee Doll," evokes the aggressive play of children noted so often by Melanie Klein in her case studies:

My Dy-dee doll
died twice.
Once when I snapped
her head off
and let it float in the toilet
and once under the sun lamp
trying to get warm
she melted. (355)

The broken child wreaks vengeance, transferring her aggression against the bad mother onto a female doll. (That the Dy-dee doll is a baby doll [Hume George 82] suggests that the child is also displacing aggression onto herself.) The toy must be killed, not once but twice for good measure; and as in "Dreams," aggression is expressed in an image of dismemberment. The doll is decapitated, with this gesture enacted in the line break ("I snapped/ her head off"). Like the unloved child who owns her, the doll is cold and "tr[ies] to get warm"—with disastrous results. She melts and "dies" in a grotesque caricature of maternal love, "her face embracing/ her little bent arms."

In "Seven Times," the next poem in the sequence, the appeal of suicide becomes more apparent:

I died seven times
in seven ways
letting death give me a sign,
letting death place his mark on my forehead,
crossed over, crossed over. (356)

The speaker sees her suicide attempts—seven of them, an apocalyptic number—as a baptism into death. Death is personified as a priest baptizing a candidate, "plac[ing] his mark on [her] forehead." This is a baptism into death, as in the Christian rite, but there is no new life on the other side of this passage. The speaker is marked with the sign of the cross; she is crossed over (out)—marked for deletion; she is crossing over (passing into death).

The death wish in "Seven Times" involves a desire to return to a lost maternal nurturing, a lost mother-daughter intimacy. In her past brushes with death, the speaker "held an ice baby/ and . . . rocked it/ and was rocked by it"; similarly, contemplating suicide now, the speaker nurtures death, while mother death rocks and comforts her. This mutual rocking is explored more fully in "Baby," the final poem in the sequence. For the moment, at least, the act of writing the poem displaces the melancholic's death-drive into mourning.

Ironically, in their movement toward embracing death, the "Death Baby" poems also record a movement from destructive hatred and aggression to the beginnings of compassion and love. In this development lies the possibility of overcoming narcissism and shame. The sequence as a whole, I would argue, traces a process of reparation, a mending of the shamed self and the object, the mother, broken by the child's aggression (Winnicott, "Aggression, Guilt and Reparation" 89). The sequence begins, as we have seen, with aggressive fantasies of dismemberment, but in "Seven Times"—despite the strong death-drive expressed—we find a developing emphasis on maternal care in the poem's imagery of rocking. This maternal gesture is central to the next poems, "Madonna" and "Baby." Guilt over aggression toward the loved object leads to a need to show care and concern. In "Madonna" and "Baby," the speaker enacts this need in the imagery of rocking, even as her death-wish continues to grow.

> My mother died
> unrocked, unrocked.
> Weeks at her deathbed
> seeing her thrust herself against the metal bars,
> thrashing like a fish on the hook . . .
> ("Madonna," *Complete Poems* 356)

Sexton's mother died painfully of cancer in 1959. Significantly, it was the breast—that "sweet hill" ("The Double Image"), source of maternal nourishment—that was first afflicted with cancer. The bad breast hated by the child is now a cancerous stomach tumour, "big as a football" (356). However, the child's love and concern are also evident, as the mother's and daughter's roles are reversed: the dying mother is a baby in a crib (a hospital bed with bars), while the daughter wants to mother her, "take her in [her] arms somehow/ and fondle her twisted grey hair" (356). Yet the daughter still wants to be mothered herself, "wanting to place [her] head in [her sick mother's] lap" (356). Ultimately, however, she cannot "soothe" or rock the mother, just as the dying mother is unable (and has always been unable) to nurture her. "My mother died/ unrocked, unrocked"; despite the speaker's guilty attempts to make amends, in the end reparation is not entirely successful. Like the all-suffering Madonna of Christian art, the mother has made the ultimate sacrifice already:

> With every hump and crack
> there was less Madonna
> until that strange labour took her.
> Then the room was bankrupt.
> That was the end of her paying. (356–57)

We might say that in her painful death, a "strange labour," the mother has given birth—to her daughter's "bankruptcy." In dying, that is, she has stolen away her daughter's chance to "pay," to work through her guilt, and hence to get well again. She may no longer be the mocking, rejecting mother of "The Double Image"; nonetheless, in her suffering and dying she is lifted up, reconfirming her daughter's guilt and shame: ". . . and me low at her high stage, letting the priestess dance alone" (356).

Rocking, nurturing, attempts at reparation—these notions are linked in the "Death Baby" sequence. In "Baby," the final poem, the image of rocking is insistent. As in "Seven Times," the "ice baby" being rocked is now death (whereas in the first poem, "Dreams," the *speaker* was the ice baby). In rocking the ice baby, then, the speaker is both nurturing herself and embracing death.

> Death,
> you lie in my arms like a cherub,
> as heavy as bread dough.
> . . . .
> I rock. I rock.
> You are my stone child
> with still eyes like marbles. (357–58)

Conventional representations of the Madonna and Child are exploited in this as in "Madonna." The death baby is a "cherub," an angel with "milky wings" and "[h]air the color of a harp" (357). The "stone child" and the mother-madonna rocking it form a "pietà," the traditional representation of Mary grieving over the dead Christ: "We are carved, a pietà/ that swings and swings" (358). Rocking a dead child, the speaker is rocking death itself. This links maternal nurturing with death rather than with life, a link that Sexton forged early in her experience of motherhood.

Yet these references to maternal nurturing are small positive signs, however recast in terms of warning:

> Beware. Beware.
> There is a tenderness.
> There is a love
> for this dumb traveler
> waiting in his pink covers.
> . . . .
> Hand me the death baby
> and there will be
> that final rocking. (359)

In their "final rocking," the mother and her death baby "plunge back and forth/ comforting each other" (358). Ironically, it is only in acknowledging death, the death or loss of the other, that the speaker is finally freed to mother, to show care and concern—and go some way toward overcoming shame.

What is the role of these poems written shortly before Sexton's suicide? The poem "Baby" is centered on an obvious death-wish; however, it manages this wish by means of aesthetic form, exercising control, through its formal play, over the trauma and shame of rejection and loss. As Ernst Kris puts it, art is a "controlled regression," a "controlled use of primary process" by the ego with the aim, not of private emotional expression but of "establishing contact with an audience" (197–98, 167). "Death,/ you lie in my arms like a cherub" (*Death Notebooks* 15): drawing on poetic devices of personification and metaphor, Sexton performs both a defensive distancing and a dramatic act of communication. [In personification, death—the dead object harbored within—is projected outside the self as Death; and in metaphor (here, simile) Death is displaced from a "grim reaper" to an innocent object, a cherub or angel baby.] Also striking among the poem's formal devices is the repeated refrain, "I rock. I rock," which is picked up in the final two lines: ". . . there will be/ that final rocking" (359). The repeated image of maternal rocking is enacted in the soothing and predictable returns of this poetic refrain. These returns—rather like the "fort-da" of the child in Freud's "Beyond the Pleasure Principle," who seeks through play both to reenact his mother's absence and to bring her back (14–16)—offer a form of control over ambivalence toward the mother, a reintegration of the split self (Rose 124) countering the disintegration and (self-) mutilation evoked earlier in "Dreams" and "The Dy-dee Doll."

Thus it is in poetic composition itself—as a process of mourning, reattachment—that the baby is soothed, death deferred, decomposition held at bay. As Sexton said once, referring to long conversations with Sylvia Plath (over martinis at the Ritz) about their suicide attempts, "Suicide is, after all, the opposite of the poem" (Middlebrook 107). Unfortunately, Sexton's view, at the end of "The Death Baby," of the "final rocking" with death as an overcoming of brokenness and shame in a final union with the lost, loved (m)other, makes death look very attractive—a "consummation devoutly to be wished," as Hamlet puts it.

Death, then, is both courted and deferred in Sexton's poetic creation. In the "Death Baby" sequence, Sexton records a fatal disintegration while at the same time seeking to make reparation to the mother and heal the shamed self, mourning and managing her losses in the rocking of poetic rhythms and in a controlled craziness of imagery. Although the mother and the self have been broken and invaded by death, aesthetic form (represented, in "Baby," by the pietà, Mary cradling the dead body of Christ) lifts up the broken object and the self crucified with grief and shame, and briefly makes them whole again.

CONCLUSIONS

For Anne Sexton each poem functioned as a temporary stay of self-execution. In poetry she found a vocation and an identity, an "authentic social presence that was not wife, lover, or mother" (Middlebrook 40). Establishing a poetic identity and reputation, she shut her ears to the terrible words, "You're not Anne," once uttered by Nana. Sitting at her typewriter, composing in impersonal typescript, Sexton worked and reworked her childhood experiences of suffering and shame, gaining aesthetic and emotional distance in the process. Further, she generalized this suffering in such a way that a wide range of women could recognize their own lives in it, at a time (the sixties and early seventies) when the women's movement was gathering force.

When Sexton was unable to write—when, under the influence of prescribed medication, she was "down" from her "creative manias" (Middlebrook 231), or when her addictions became too severe—she would disintegrate, take overdoses, and enter the hospital. Composition was for Sexton a form of controlled mania that lifted her out of her depressive self-hatred, timidity, and shame, an "upper" that could quickly tip over into "shameless" behavior. For Sexton, the activity of composition held shame and shamelessness in balance, freeing her briefly from a narcissistic dependence on the love and approval of others. Unfortunately, narcissistic needs are never far from creative work; the mirror of loving attention and scornful rejection is rarely broken. In the end, no longer writing fully realized, controlled poems but rather "anguished appeals for attention" (Middlebrook 379–80), Sexton took her own life.

Like play for children, then, aesthetic creation can be a means of managing shame; it allowed Anne Sexton "to master, if only temporarily, anxieties that might otherwise overwhelm the self" (Berman). Art makes sense of loss and shame. Although, for Sexton, poetry could not finally counter an intense drive toward death, her case demonstrates that creativity can, at least for a time, enable the shamed self to mourn loss and to restore the loved object—and in doing so, to be whole again.

WORKS CITED

Berman, Jeffrey. "Anne Sexton and the Poetics of Suicide" (from a manuscript in progress).

Block Lewis, Helen. "The Role of Shame in Depression over the Life Span." Block Lewis, ed. *The Role of Shame in Symptom Formation*. Hillsdale, N.J.: Lawrence Erlbaum, 1987. 29–50.

Chodorow, Nancy. *The Reproduction of Mothering: Psychoanalysis and the Sociology of Gender*. Berkeley: U of California P, 1978.

Freud, Sigmund. "Beyond the Pleasure Principle." *Standard Edition of the Complete Psychological Works of Sigmund Freud*. Vol. 18. Trans. J. Strachey. London: Hogarth P, 1957. 3–64.

———. "Mourning and Melancholia." *Standard Edition*. Vol. 14. 243–58.

Hinshelwood, R. D. *A Dictionary of Kleinian Thought*. London: Free Association Books, 1989.

Honton, Margaret. "The Double Image and the Division of Parts: A Study of Mother-Daughter Relationships in the Poetry of Anne Sexton." Diana Hume George, ed. *Sexton: Selected Criticism*. Urbana, Ill.: U of Chicago P, 1988. 99–116.

Hume George, Diana. "Beyond the Pleasure Principle: The Death Baby." *Sexton: Selected Criticism*. 73–96.

Klein, Melanie. "Notes on Some Schizoid Mechanisms" and "The Psychogenesis of Manic-Depressive States." *The Selected Melanie Klein*. Ed. Juliet Mitchell. Harmondsworth, U.K.: Penguin Books, 1991. 176–200; 116–45.

Kris, Ernst. *Psychoanalytic Explorations in Art*. New York: International Universities P, 1952.

Kristeva, Julia. *Black Sun: Depression and Melancholia*. Trans. Leon Roudiez. New York: Columbia UP, 1989.

Lacan, Jacques. "From Interpretation to Transference." *Four Fundamental Concepts of Psychoanalysis*. New York: Norton, 1981. 244–60.

Laplanche, J. and J. B. Pontalis. *The Language of Psychoanalysis*. Trans. D. Nicholson-Smith. New York: Norton, 1973.

Middlebrook, Diane Wood. *Anne Sexton: A Biography*. Boston: Houghton Mifflin, 1991.

Nathanson, Donald. *Shame and Pride: Affect, Sex, and the Birth of the Self*. New York: Norton, 1992.

Nolen-Hoeksema, Susan. *Sex Differences in Depression*. Stanford, Calif.: Stanford UP, 1990.

Rose, Gilbert. *Trauma and Mastery in Life and Art*. New Haven, Conn.: Yale UP, 1987.

Sexton, Anne. *The Complete Poems*. Boston: Houghton Mifflin, 1981. Excerpts from *The Complete Poems of Anne Sexton*. Copyright © 1981 by Linda Gray Sexton and Loring Conant, Jr., Executors of the Will of Anne Sexton. Reprinted by permission of Houghton Mifflin Company. All rights reserved.

Sexton, Linda Gray. *Searching for Mercy Street: My Journey Back to My Mother, Anne Sexton*. Boston: Little, Brown, 1994.

Winnicott, D. W. "Aggression, Guilt and Reparation" and "The Value of Depression." *Home Is Where We Start From.* Ed. Clare Winnicott. New York: Norton, 1986. 80–89; 71–79.

———. *Human Nature.* New York: Schocken Books, 1988.

———. "Mirror-Role of Mother and Family in Child Development." *Playing and Reality.* New York: Basic Books, 1971. 130–38.

Wurmser, Léon. *The Mask of Shame.* 1981. Northvale, N.J.: Jason Aronson, 1994.

CHAPTER 10

"Quiet As It's Kept": Shame and Trauma in Toni Morrison's The Bluest Eye

J. Brooks Bouson

A complicated shame drama and trauma narrative, Toni Morrison's *The Bluest Eye* focuses attention on the plight of Pecola Breedlove, an African-American girl who is the victim of inter- and intraracial shaming and who is severely traumatized by her physically abusive mother and sexually abusive father. If Morrison seems intent on using her fiction to gain *temporary* narrative mastery over the shame-laden traumas she describes, she also wants to involve her readers emotionally in her work. Her writing "demands participatory reading," as she has remarked. "The reader supplies the emotions. . . . He or she can feel something visceral, see something striking. Then we (you, the reader, and I, the author) come together to make this book, to feel this experience" (Tate 164).

Morrison's story of Pecola and her wish for blue eyes grew out of a conversation Morrison remembered having as a girl with one of her elementary school friends, who told Morrison that she knew that God did not exist because her prayers for blue eyes had gone unanswered (Ruas 95). Morrison recalls how she felt "astonished by the desecration" her friend proposed and how she, for the first time, experienced the "shock" of the word "beautiful." Recognizing the implicit "racial self-loathing" in her friend's desire, Morrison, twenty years later, found herself still wondering how her girlhood friend had learned such feelings. "Who told her? Who made her feel that it was better to be a freak than what she was? Who had looked at her and found her so wanting, so small a weight on the beauty scale?" ("Afterword" 209–10).

Morrison began working on *The Bluest Eye*, which was published in 1970, first as a story in 1962 and then as a novel in 1965, a time when there was public focus on the issue of racial beauty. bell hooks, remarking on how the Black Power movement of the 1960s "addressed the issue of internalized racism in relation to beauty," observes that the "Black is beautiful" slogan "worked to intervene and alter those racist stereotypes that had always insisted black was ugly, monstrous, undesirable" (173, 174). Morrison, who was in part responding to the 1960s black liberation movement in *The Bluest Eye*, recalls that the "reclamation of racial beauty" made her question why racial beauty was not "taken for granted" within the African-American community, why it needed "wide public articulation to exist." Coming to recognize the "damaging internalization of assumptions of immutable inferiority originating in an outside gaze," Morrison, in *The Bluest Eye*, set out to describe "how something as grotesque as the demonization of an entire race could take root inside the most delicate member of society: a child; the most vulnerable member: a female" ("Afterword" 210).

In dramatizing "the devastation that even casual racial contempt can cause" ("Afterword" 210), Morrison's *The Bluest Eye* explores the chronic shame of being an African American in white America. *The Bluest Eye* reveals that the shame experience, as recent psychoanalytic investigators have explained, is at once interpersonal and internal, involving not only the individual's feelings of inferiority and inadequacy in comparison to others but also the individual's deep inner sense of being flawed or defective or of having failed to meet the expectations of the "ideal self." At the core of shame, writes Léon Wurmser, is the "conviction of one's *unlovability*" because of an inherent sense that the self is "weak, dirty, and defective" (*Mask* 92, 93). In the classic shame scenario, in which the "eye is the organ of shame par excellence," the individual feels exposed and humiliated—*looked at* with contempt for being inferior, flawed, or dirty—and thus wants to hide or disappear (Wurmser, "Shame" 67). Fear of visual exposure, as Wurmser explains, leads to the wish to "disappear as the person" one has shown oneself to be, or "to be [seen as] different" than one is (*Mask* 232). In presenting the lives of the Breedloves, *The Bluest Eye* dramatizes "shame-vulnerability"—that is, "a sensitivity to, and readiness for, shame"—and "shame anxiety," which is "evoked by the imminent danger of unexpected exposure, humiliation, and rejection" (Andrew Morrison 14; Wurmser, *Mask* 49). And Morrison's novel also depicts the affects and defenses that accompany the shame situation: the self-loathing and self-disgust, the searing or numbing, paralyzing pain of shame-humiliation, the wish to conceal the self, and the deep rage, which is often expressed in the "attack other" script as the reactive desire to shame and humiliate others (see Nathanson 360–73).

Described by Donald Nathanson as a work that provides a "prolonged immersion in the world of shame" (463), *The Bluest Eye*, in the peripheral story of Soaphead Church, points to an important cultural source of racial shame in the mid-to-late-nineteenth- and early-twentieth-century biosocial myth of racial degeneration: that is, the view that blacks are biologically inferior and belong to a degenerate race, and that under certain conditions, they can revert to a more primitive—if not degraded and bestial—state.¹ A West Indian with light-brown skin, Soaphead comes from a family that "married 'up'" and thus lightened the family complexion, and he has been affected by his family's racist ideas. Anglophiles who were proud of their mixed blood and convinced of their superiority, they hoped "to prove beyond a doubt De Gobineau's hypothesis that 'all civilizations derive from the white race, that none can exist without its help, and that a society is great and brilliant only so far as it preserves the blood of the noble group that created it'" (168). Acting out a countershaming strategy, the narrative contests this racist notion by describing Sir Whitcomb, who introduced the "white strain" into the family, as a degenerate type—as a "decaying British nobleman, who chose to disintegrate under a sun more easeful than England's" (167). Similarly, Elihue Whitcomb, who is later known as Soaphead Church, is referred to as one of the flawed members of the family in whom the "original genes of the decaying lord" become expressed (168).

Despite his "noble bloodlines," Soaphead sinks into a life of "rapidly fraying gentility," and he comes to take comfort in the label "misanthrope" (171, 164). A shame-obsessed and shame-driven individual who has internalized his family's racist ideas, Soaphead has a "disdain of human contact," for he finds other people disgusting and contaminating (165). Abhorring "flesh on flesh"—he is overwhelmed by body and breath odors, disquieted by the body's "natural excretions," such as skin crusts, ear wax, blackheads, and moles—he molests little girls, for their bodies are not so offensive to him (166). Indeed, with little girls, "it is all clean," and there isn't any "nastiness" or "filth," and he doesn't feel "dirty" afterwards (181). Soaphead, as the narrative describes him, is "what one might call a very clean old man" (167). Because Soaphead projects his fear of his own racial contamination—that is, his own inherited blackness—onto others, contact with people other than little girls produces in him "a faint but persistent nausea," and he feels that "decay, vice, filth, and disorder" are "pervasive" (164, 172).

"It is not necessary to create a Gobineau-like hierarchy of races as victims," writes Sander Gilman, to observe that blacks "have been singled out with uncommon frequency" to serve the "function of the Other in the West" (130). In the history of the representation of African Americans one can uncover the "age-old associations of the black with corruption and disease," and blacks also have been associated not only with "pathology" but also with "psychopathology" (132). The image of the "dangerous Other"—who is at once "ill and infectious," "damaged and damaging"—serves "as the focus for the projection of anxiety concerning the self" (130). The power of such "ever-receding images should not be underestimated," writes Gilman. "They remain impressed on a culture as on a palimpsest, shaping and coloring all of the images that evolve at later dates" (239). And indeed, Joel Kovel, in his psychosymbolic analysis of white racism, comments that few groups "have suffered the appellation of filthiness" so much as blacks. In aversive white racism where there is a sense of disgust at the dirtiness of black bodies and black people, Kovel finds "a quintessential fantasy of Otherness—for the black body from which the white ego flees is his own body" (82, xlv).[2] African Americans, in other words, have served as the container for white shame—that is, for projected fears and anxieties that the self is defective and dirty; moreover, the darker-skinned and poor black has become the "dangerous Other" for lighter-skinned and middle-class blacks in the African American community.

In contemporary America where, as Morrison has described it, "blackness is itself a stain," racist codes remain pervasive ("Introduction" xviii). Like Soaphead, who has internalized the belief in the superiority of the white and the inferiority of the stained black race, the "poor and black" Breedloves have internalized the contempt and loathing directed at them from the shaming gaze of the humiliator—that is, the white culture—and thus they believe that they are "relentlessly and aggressively ugly" (38).

> It was as though some mysterious all-knowing master had given each one a cloak of ugliness to wear, and they had each accepted it without question. The master had said, "You are ugly people." They had looked about themselves and saw nothing to contradict the statement; saw, in fact, support for it leaning at them from every billboard, every movie, every glance. "Yes," they had said. "You are right." (39)

In what Morrison describes as the "woundability" of Pecola Breedlove ("Afterword" 210), *The Bluest Eye* dramatizes an extreme form of the shame-vulnerability and shame-anxiety of African Americans in white America. Morrison also depicts the intergenerational transmission of shame in her novel, showing how is it passed down from parent to child. For not only does Pecola's mother shame her, but Cholly Breedlove, when he rapes Pecola, acts out a shame drama as he projects his deep-rooted feelings of humiliation and rage—his self-loathing and self-contempt—onto his daughter. And in the response of members of the African-American community—who end up collectively scapegoating Pecola—the novel reveals how humiliated individuals can temporarily rid themselves of their shame by humiliating others. Indeed, the "ugly" Pecola becomes the ultimate carrier of her family's—and her African-American community's—shame.

The Bluest Eye, then, is a complicated shame drama. And it also is a trauma narrative, for Pecola, as Morrison has aptly described her, is "a total and complete victim," and she is a victim not only of racial shaming but also of her "crippled and crippling family" (Stepto 17; "Afterword" 210). In a relentless way, *The Bluest Eye* depicts the progressive traumatization of Pecola—who is rejected and physically abused by her mother, sexually abused by her alcoholic and unpredictably violent father, and ultimately scapegoated by members of the community. In her novel Morrison reveals that, as some investigators of trauma have argued, trauma can result not only from a "single assault" or "discrete event," but also from "a constellation of life's experiences," a "prolonged exposure to danger" or a "continuing pattern of abuse" (Erikson 457). The novel also shows how "inevitably" destructive incest is to the child (Herman, *Father-Daughter Incest* 4). Ultimately, "the damage done" to Pecola is "total," and she steps "over into madness" (*Bluest Eye* 204, 206). Her self damaged beyond repair, Pecola retreats from real life and converses with her alter identity, her only "friend": that is, she ends up living permanently in the dissociated world of the severely traumatized individual.

Aware that the traumatic, shame-laden subject matter of her novel is potentially disturbing to the reader, Morrison, in the opening words of Claudia's narration—"*Quiet as it's kept, there were no marigolds in the fall of 1941*"—entices the reader by invoking the intimate "back fence" world of "illicit gossip." In Morrison's description, the opening phrase—"*Quiet as it's kept*"—is "conspiratorial": "'Shh, don't tell anyone else,' and 'No one is allowed to know this.' It is a secret between us and a secret that is being kept from us. . . . In some sense it was precisely what the act of writing the book was: the public exposure of a private confidence." If the publication of the book involved exposure, the writing of *The Bluest Eye* "was the disclosure of secrets, secrets 'we' shared and those withheld from us by ourselves and by the world outside the community." Underlying the conspiratorial whisper was the assumption that the teller of the story was about to impart "privileged information." "The intimacy I was aiming for," Morrison remarks, "the intimacy between the reader and the page, could start up immediately because the secret is being shared, at best, and eavesdropped upon, at the least. Sudden familiarity or instant intimacy seemed crucial to me. I did not want the reader to have time to wonder, 'What do I have to do, to give up, in order to read this? What defense do I need, what distance maintain?'" ("Afterword" 212–13).

By foregrounding the flowers and backgrounding the shameful fact of incest—"*We thought . . . it was because Pecola was having her father's baby that the marigolds did not grow*"—Morrison protects the reader "from a confrontation too soon with the painful details," but also provokes the reader "into a desire to know them." The opening, as she describes it, "provides the stroke that announces something more than a secret shared, but a silence broken, a void filled, an unspeakable thing spoken at last." By "transferring the problem of fathoming" to the readers, "the inner circle of listeners," the novel justifies the "public exposure of a privacy." If readers enter into the "conspiracy" announced by the opening words, "then the book can be seen to open with its close: a speculation on the disruption of 'nature' as being a social disruption with tragic individual consequences" in which readers, "as part of the population of the text," are "implicated" ("Afterword" 213–14). And by breaking the narrative "into parts" that have to be "reassembled," Morrison attempts to lead her readers "into an interrogation of themselves for the smashing" of the Pecolas of this world ("Afterword" 211). Despite Morrison's complaint that "many readers remain touched but not moved" by Pecola's story ("Afterword" 211), *The Bluest Eye*, as we shall see in our analysis of the critical conversation surrounding the novel, not only has provoked feelings of shame or by-stander's guilt in readers, but it also has induced critic after critic to enact the trauma-specific and antishaming roles of advocate or rescuer, or to become unwitting participants in the shame drama of blaming and attacking the other in their critical responses to the novel.

In writing about the Breedlove family and Cholly's incestuous rape of Pecola, Morrison risks traumatizing readers, and she also sets up potential shame conflicts in them as she openly appeals to their active curiosity by positioning them as eavesdroppers and voyeurs, as onlookers onto a shameful family secret. If a mature sense of shame—that is, the recognition that some phenomena are "intrinsically private" and must be "protected by limited access"—shields the "private sphere from exposure" and safeguards the individual in moments of "increased vulnerability," it is also the case that "family privacy" has served to conceal the fact that the family provides "a dangerous hiding place for family violence and sexual abuse" (Schneider 41, xv, 55; Mason 30). In her strategic public exposure of the incest secret, Morrison breaks the taboo on looking and thus risks shaming her readers. For just as those who are exposed feel shame, so observers of shaming scenes can feel shame. Indeed, "Shame, by its nature, is contagious. Moreover, just as shame has an intrinsic tendency to encourage hiding, so there is a tendency for the observer of another's shame to turn away from it" (Lewis 15–16).

Speaking the unspeakable, Morrison's *The Bluest Eye* is permeated with shame and trauma. But it also uses narrative structure and aesthetic design not only to fascinate and impress readers—and thus to counteract shame—but also to partially defend against the horrors it is assigned to uncover. If an early version of the novel presented the fragmented narrative of Pecola, the shamed trauma victim—for *The Bluest Eye* was originally the story of Pecola and her family narrated in the third person "in pieces like a broken mirror"—Morrison, finding that "there was no connection between the life of Pecola, her mother and father," introduced Claudia as an "I"-narrator and thus provided in the narrative someone to "empathize" with Pecola and also to "relieve the grimness" of the narrative (Ruas 97). But for Morrison, despite her careful structuring of the novel, there remained a problem in the "central chamber" of the narrative.

> The shattered world I built (to complement what is happening to Pecola), its pieces held together by seasons in childtime and commenting at every turn on the incompatible and barren white-family primer, does not in its present form handle effectively the silence at its center: the void that is Pecola's "unbeing." It should have had a shape—like the emptiness left by a boom or a cry. ("Afterword" 214–15)

In narratively building a "shattered world" around the "void" of Pecola's "unbeing," Morrison calls attention to the careful design and structure of the novel. But she also, while depicting the incestuous rape of Pecola, partly denies the horrors she sets out to describe. That Morrison chooses to narrate the rape from the father's point of view and that she herself has described the rape as an "awful" thing and yet as "almost irrelevant" (Tate 164) is suggestive, given the fact that "[d]enial, avoidance, and distancing" are common responses to incest (Herman, "Father-Daughter Incest" 182).[3] Thus, the rape scene is the emotional center of the novel and yet it is oddly muted as the narrative proliferates, telling stories—including the tragic and sympathetic stories of Pauline, the complicit mother, and Cholly, the violating father—around the empty center of the text, the "void" of the silenced and backgrounded incest victim.

From the outset of *The Bluest Eye*, readers are aware that part of Morrison's agenda, as she describes the victimization and shaming of Pecola, is to dialogically contest the idealized depiction of American life described in the Dick and Jane primer story:

> Here is the house. It is green and white. It has a red door. It is very pretty. Here is the family. Mother, Father, Dick, and Jáne live in the

green-and-white house. They are very happy. See Jane. . . . She wants
to play. Who will play with Jane? . . . See Mother. Mother is very nice.
Mother, will you play with Jane? Mother laughs. . . . See Father. He is
big and strong. Father, will you play with Jane? Father is smiling. . . .
Here comes a friend. The friend will play with Jane. (3)

Morrison explains that she uses the Dick and Jane primer story, with its
depiction of a happy white family, "as a frame acknowledging the outer
civilization," and then she runs together the words of the primer story—
"Hereisthehouseitisgreenandwhite" (4)—because she wants "the primer
version broken up and confused" (LeClair 127). Through this "broken
up" and "confused" discourse—which is found in the opening frame
narrative and, as the narrative progresses, is used to head the chapters
focusing on Pecola and those who traumatize her—Morrison signals the
increasingly fragmented world of the trauma victim. Morrison's stark
reversals of the idealized discourse of the Dick-and-Jane primer story
also communicate to readers the intense, but highly controlled, feelings
of anger that drive the narrative. Thus the chapters of the novel that are
headed with the primer descriptions of Jane's idealized "green and white
house" and her "happy" family introduce readers to the decaying storefront dwelling where the "ugly" Breedloves live; the chapters that begin
with primer accounts of the dog and cat tell pointed stories of animal
abuse; the chapters headed with primer descriptions of the "very nice"
mother and "big and strong" father who "smiles" at his daughter
describe the mother's physical and the father's sexual abuse of Pecola;
and the chapter headed with the primer passage describing Jane's play-
ful "friend" relates Pecola's conversation with her only "friend," her
dissociated alter self. Part of the novel's explicit agenda is to assess the
"why" and the "how" of Pecola's plight. Although Claudia, the narrator, insists that she takes "*refuge in* how" (6), the narrative is driven by
the desire to elucidate the "why" of the Breedloves' story and to indict
the cultural—and also family—forces that lead to the destruction of the
vulnerable and shame-sensitive Pecola.

While the story of Pecola—who suffers from profound shame-anxiety, feels unlovable and ugly, and thus acts out the defensive hiding and
withdrawal behavior characteristic of shame-vulnerable individuals—is
at the center of the text, *The Bluest Eye*, through the interconnected
experiences of Pecola and Claudia, enacts a complicated shame drama.
If Pecola's characteristic body language fits Donald Nathanson's
description of the "purest presentation of the affect shame-humiliation"—the eyes are averted and downcast, the head droops, and the
shoulders slump (see 134–36)—and if Pecola so internalizes white contempt for her blackness that she wishes to be invisible or desires to have
blue eyes so that others will love and accept her, Claudia, in contrast,

gives expression to the anger experienced by the shamed individual, the desire to flail out that signals an attempt to rid the self of shame (see Andrew Morrison 13–14).

Unlike Pecola, who is the passive and utterly shamed victim, Claudia questions why people look at little white girls and say "Awwwww" but do not look at her that way. "The eye slide of black women as they approached them on the street, and the possessive gentleness of their touch as they handled them" (22–23) anger her. Unlike Pecola who dreams of having blue eyes, Claudia responds with rage when she is given a blue-eyed, yellow-haired, pink-skinned baby doll as a "special" gift. "I had only one desire: to dismember it. To see of what it was made, to discover the dearness, to find the beauty, the desirability that had escaped me, but apparently only me" (20). According to the official culture—the world of adults, shops, magazines, and window signs—girls treasure such dolls, but Claudia defiantly pokes at the doll's glass eyes, breaks off its fingers, and removes its head.[4] "I destroyed white baby dolls," she recalls. "But the dismembering of dolls was not the true horror. The truly horrifying thing was the transference of the same impulses to little white girls. The indifference with which I could have axed them was shaken only by my desire to do so. To discover what eluded me: the secret of the magic they weaved on others" (22).

Claudia's reactive rage is evident in her response not only to interracial but also to intraracial shaming. When the white Rosemary Villanucci rebuffs Claudia and her sister, Frieda, Claudia wants to "poke the arrogance" out of Rosemary's eyes and "make red marks on her white skin" (9). Claudia feels the "familiar violence" rise in her when she witnesses the little white girl, who lives in the house where Pauline Breedlove works as a housekeeper, call Mrs. Breedlove "Polly," even though Pecola herself calls her mother "Mrs. Breedlove" (108). And Claudia's angry reaction to Maureen Peal reveals the force of intraracial shaming within the African-American community. A "high-yellow dream child with long brown hair braided into two lynch ropes that hung down her back" (62), Maureen Peal enchants everyone at the school: the teachers smile at her when they call on her in class; black boys do not trip her in the hallways nor do white boys stone her; white girls readily accept her as their work partner, and black girls move aside when she wants to use the sink in the girls' washroom. Claudia and Frieda, in an attempt to recover their equilibrium, search for flaws in the much-admired Maureen. They secretly refer to her as "Meringue Pie"; they are pleased when they discover that she has a dog tooth; and they smile when they learn that she was born with six fingers on each hand and had this flaw surgically corrected. When Claudia, who is assigned a locker next to Maureen, thinks of the "unearned haughtiness" in Maureen's eyes, she plots "accidental slammings of locker doors" on Maureen's hand (63). And yet, despite her jealousy, Claudia is "secretly prepared" to be Maureen's friend, and over time Claudia is "even able to hold a sensible conversation" with Maureen without visualizing Maureen falling off a cliff or without "giggling" her way into what she thinks is "a clever insult" (63–64).

But ultimately Maureen pronounces judgment on Pecola, Claudia, and Frieda—insisting that she is "cute" and that the three girls are "[b]lack and ugly." While Claudia and Frieda are temporarily "stunned" by the "weight" of Maureen's shaming remark, they also recover themselves enough to reactively and publicly shame Maureen by shouting out the "most powerful" chant in their "arsenal of insults"—"Six-finger-dog-tooth-meringue-pie!" Pecola, in contrast, enacts the classic withdrawing and concealing behavior of the humiliated individual as she folds into herself, "like a pleated wing." Pecola's visible pain and shame at the public exposure of her inner sense of defectiveness antagonizes Claudia, who would prefer that Pecola assume a defiant antishame posture. "I wanted to open her up, crisp her edges, ram a stick down that hunched and curving spine, force her to stand erect and spit the misery out on the streets. But she held it in where it could lap up into her eyes" (73–74). And yet Claudia also identifies, in part, with Pecola's shame as she sinks under "the wisdom, accuracy, and relevance" of Maureen's taunt. If Maureen is "cute," Claudia recognizes, then she is somehow "lesser," unworthy. Claudia can destroy white dolls, but she is unable to destroy "the honey voices of parents and aunts," or the "obedience" found in the eyes of her contemporaries, or the "slippery light" in the eyes of teachers when they encounter "the Maureen Peals of the world." Despite this, Claudia also recognizes that Maureen Peal is "not the Enemy and not worthy of such intense hatred." Instead, the "*Thing* to fear" is what makes Maureen—but not Claudia, Frieda, or Pecola—"beautiful" (74).

The "Thing" Claudia learns to fear is the white, racist standard of beauty that members of the African-American community have internalized, a standard that favors the "high-yellow" Maureen Peal and denigrates the "black and ugly" Pecola Breedlove. Yet Claudia also partially internalizes this white standard over time. For the same Claudia who once dismembered white dolls and wanted to axe little white girls becomes ashamed of her own rage—her desire to hurt little white girls and hear their "fascinating cry of pain." When she comes to view her "disinterested violence" as "repulsive"—and she finds it repulsive because it *is* disinterested—her "shame" flounders about "for refuge" and finds a "hiding place" in love. "Thus the conversion from pristine sadism to fabricated hatred, to fraudulent love," remarks Claudia.

Although Claudia later learns to "worship" Shirley Temple—a popular figure she once responded to with "unsullied hatred"—this change is "adjustment without improvement" (23, 19, 23). Indeed, as *The Bluest Eye* reveals, because the standard of beauty—that is, the idealized version of the black self—is based on whiteness, the Pecolas and Claudias of the world cannot help but feel ashamed. For shame "is a reflection of feelings about the whole self in failure, as inferior in competition or in comparison with others, as inadequate and defective" (Andrew Morrison 12).

If the ultimate "Enemy" that shames and traumatizes African Americans is the racist white society, there are also more immediate and intimate enemies within the African-American community and family. Unlike Claudia, who is shame-sensitive but also uses defiance to defend herself against the pain of shame, Pecola suffers from an extreme and destructive form of chronic shame-vulnerability and shame-anxiety. Focusing on both the cultural and familial sources of Pecola's profound and crippling shame, *The Bluest Eye* reveals how Pecola's parents transmit to their daughter their own sense of inferiority and defectiveness, their own "ugliness."

Pecola's mother, Pauline—whose sense of defectiveness is intensified by her "crooked, archless foot" that causes her to limp (110)—ultimately transfers to her daughter her own "general feeling of separateness and unworthiness," and her own borrowed ideas about beauty that lead inevitably to "self-contempt" (111, 122). For as a young married woman, Pauline goes to the movies, and after she absorbs "in full"— that is, internalizes—the racist beauty standards conveyed in films, she is "never able . . . to look at a face and not assign it some category in the scale of absolute beauty" (122). Pauline identifies with white movie stars—she even affects a Jean Harlow hairstyle—but then, when she loses a front tooth, she resigns herself *"to just being ugly"* (123). Adding to Pauline's feeling of inferiority is the fact that she is also subjected to intraracial shaming, for when she first moves to the North she discovers that Northern blacks are *"[n]o better than whites for meanness"* and that they can make her feel *"just as no-count"* as whites (117).

Pauline's feeling that she is "ugly"—that is, inferior and defective— is reinforced during the shame-drama of Pecola's birth. When Pauline is about to deliver Pecola, she overhears the white doctors at the hospital refer to black women like her as animals, that is, as racially degenerate: *"They deliver right away and with no pain. Just like horses."* When the birth pangs begin, Pauline moans *"something awful"* to let the doctors know that delivering a baby is *"more than a bowel movement."* Shamed by the doctors who treat her as an object of contempt, Pauline unconsciously equates her child with excrement: that is, with something dirty and disgusting. And the fact that Pauline describes her new-born baby as "ugly"—"*Head full of pretty hair, but Lord she was ugly*"—suggests that from the outset Pauline projects her own sense of "ugliness" onto her daughter (124–25, 126).

Employing a classic "attack other" shame defense, Pauline does express contempt for the white family she works for during her first steady job as a housekeeper, describing them as "dirty," which is how poor African Americans are perceived by whites: "*None of them knew so much as how to wipe their behinds. I know, 'cause I did the washing. And couldn't pee proper to save their lives. . . . Nasty white folks is about the nastiest things they is*" (119–20). And yet when Pauline works for the well-to-do Fishers, she becomes "what is known as an ideal servant, for such a role filled practically all of her needs" (127). That is, only when Pauline embraces her black shame by assuming the inferior role of the ideal servant at the home of the white Fishers is she able to meet the goals of her ideal self and win the white approbation she desires. In the Fisher household, unlike in her "dingy" storefront dwelling, Pauline finds "beauty, order, cleanliness," and when Pauline acts as the representative of the Fishers, the creditors and service people—who would normally humiliate her—respect her and are even "intimidated" by her (127, 128). While Pauline dotes on the little white Fisher girl, she neglects and physically abuses Pecola, transferring to her daughter her deep-rooted contempt for her own blackness. Trying to make Pecola respectable, she teaches her fear of being a clumsy person, of being like her father, of being unloved by God—that is, fear of being inadequate and defective. And she beats into Pecola "a fear of growing up, fear of other people, fear of life" (128).

Like Pauline, Cholly Breedlove transfers his own chronic shame—his own feelings of humiliation and defeat—to his daughter. Not only is Cholly "[a]bandoned in a junk heap by his mother, [and] rejected for a crap game by his father," but he also is subjected to the racist insults that are "part of the nuisances of life" (160, 153). In a central scene of interracial shaming, Cholly is utterly humiliated when he is forced, during his initial sexual encounter as an adolescent, to perform sexually for two white hunters. The fourteen-year-old Cholly is "terrified" when he is discovered by two white men carrying long guns while he is "newly but earnestly engaged in eliciting sexual pleasure from a little country girl" (42). When one of the white men, who shines a flashlight on the scene, commands Cholly to "'Get on wid it. . . . An' make it good, nigger, make it good,'" Cholly hates the girl, Darlene, not the white men. While he simulates lovemaking, he almost wishes "he could do it—hard, long, and painfully," because he hates Darlene "so much" (148). Paralyzed by shame, he either obsesses over this episode or feels a "vacancy in his head" afterwards. Rather than hating the white men, he cultivates his hatred of the girl. "Never did he once consider directing his hatred toward the hunters. Such an emotion would have destroyed him. They were big, white, armed men. He was small, black, helpless. His subconscious knew what his conscious mind did not guess—that hating them would have consumed him, burned him up like a piece of soft coal, leaving only flakes of ash and a question mark of smoke." Thus he despises Darlene, for she has witnessed "his failure, his impotence" and he was unable to protect her (150–51).

Seeking comfort but unwilling to reveal his shame to Blue—an older man the boy Cholly views as a father-surrogate figure—Cholly runs away to find his real father. Yet when he finally encounters his father, and his father asks whose "boy" he is, Cholly doesn't say, "I'm your boy," because that sounds "disrespectful." Cholly is devastated when he is brutally rejected by his belligerent father—"[G]et the fuck outta my face!" he shouts at Cholly in a "vexed and whiny voice" (156). When the traumatically rejected and abandoned Cholly subsequently loses control and soils himself "like a baby," he feels exposed to the humiliating gaze of others; the literally dirtied and helpless Cholly imagines that his father will see him and "laugh" and, indeed, that "[e]verybody" will "laugh." Fearing shameful visual exposure, the mortified Cholly, "[i]n panic," takes flight: "Cholly ran down the street, aware only of silence. People's mouths moved, their feet moved, a car jugged by—but with no sound. . . . His own feet made no sound." Temporarily numbed and paralyzed by shame, Cholly conceals himself under a pier near a river, and he remains "knotted there in fetal position, paralyzed, his fists covering his eyes, for a long time. No sound, no sight. . . . He even forgot his messed-up trousers" (157). Shame, as Wurmser remarks, is the "*affect of contempt* directed against the self—by others or by one's own conscience. Contempt says: 'You should disappear as such a being as you have shown yourself to be—failing, weak, flawed, and dirty. Get out of my sight: Disappear!'" To be exposed as one who fails someone else's or one's own expectations causes shame, and to "disappear into nothing is the punishment for such failure" ("Shame" 67).

If as an adolescent Cholly is deeply traumatized and shamed at the disgraceful exposure of his self as weak and contemptible, as an adult even a "half-remembrance" of the episode with the white hunters, "along with myriad other humiliations, defeats, and emasculations, could stir him into flights of depravity that surprised himself—but only himself" (42–43). Cholly, who has the "meanest eyes in town" (40), lives in a chronic state of humiliated fury, and he vents his anger on "petty things and weak people" (38), including members of his own family. Cholly defends himself by assuming the defiant posture of the "[d]angerously free" man, who is "[f]ree to feel whatever he felt—fear, guilt, shame, love, grief, pity. Free to be tender or violent, to whistle or weep. . . . Free to take a woman's insults, for his body had already conquered hers. Free even to knock her in the head, for he had already cradled that head in his arms." The fact that the "dangerously free" Cholly has retaliated against white men—Cholly is "free to say, 'No, suh,' and smile, for he had already killed three white men" (159)—reveals that he has attempted to rid himself of his unendurable shame by attacking and destroying those who have shamed him. As Silvan Tomkins observes, "Depending upon the intensity and depth of humiliation, and the feelings of helplessness which grip him, the individual will struggle to express his humiliation, to undo humiliation, to turn the tables on his oppressor and at the extreme to destroy him to recover his power to deal with intolerable humiliation" (296).

A broken, bitter man who flaunts his shame, Cholly ends up as the utterly degraded, and thus socially ostracized, individual when he puts his family "outdoors." "[T]hat old Dog Breedlove had burned up his house, gone upside his wife's head, and everybody, as a result, was outdoors. Outdoors, we knew, was the real terror of life." While people could drink or gamble themselves outdoors, "to be slack enough to put oneself outdoors, or heartless enough to put one's own kin outdoors— that was criminal" (16–17). An object of contempt and disgust, Cholly, in his defiant display of shameless behavior—his shamelessness serving as a defense against his deep-rooted shame-anxiety—catapults himself "beyond the reaches of human consideration": "He had joined the animals; was, indeed, an old dog, a snake, a ratty nigger" (18). Contempt by others, as Wurmser remarks, is a type of aggression that degrades the individual's value, "equating him particularly with a debased, dirty thing—a derided and low animal." The humiliated person is "shunned," "sent into solitude," "discarded from the communality of civilized society" (*Mask* 81, 82). It is also interesting that the communal shaming of Cholly repeats racist discourse by describing Cholly as a degenerate type—as someone who has reverted to an animal state.

That "contempt" is a "'cold' affect," a form of aggression that wants to "eliminate the other being" (Wurmser, *Mask* 81, 80), is evident in the ritualized quarrels that occur in the Breedlove marriage. To Pauline, her fights with Cholly give "substance" to the dull sameness of her life (41). Wearing the antishame mask of Christian respectability, Pauline views herself as an "upright and Christian woman, burdened with a no-count man, whom God wanted her to punish," and she pleads with Jesus to "help her 'strike the bastard down from his pea-knuckle of pride.'" If Pauline's Christian pride and retaliatory fantasies are reaction formations against her deep-seated shame, Cholly's "inarticulate fury," which he vents on his wife, signals his attempt to express and temporarily rid himself of his shame-rage. "Hating her, he could leave himself intact" (42). Pauline and Cholly beat each other "with a darkly brutal formalism." "Tacitly they had agreed not to kill each other. . . . There was only the muted sound of falling things, and flesh on unsurprised flesh" (43).

What Pecola learns from her parents—that like them she is "ugly"—is confirmed by the hostile gaze and insulting speech of others. Pecola's ugliness makes her "ignored or despised at school, by teachers and classmates alike," and when a girl wants to especially insult a boy, she simply accuses him of loving Pecola, a taunt that provokes "peals of laughter from those in earshot" (45, 46). To Geraldine, who teaches her son "the difference between colored people and niggers"—"[c]olored people" like her are "neat and quiet" while "niggers" are "dirty and loud" (87)—Pecola is an object of disgust and contempt.

In the deliberately staged encounter between Pecola and Geraldine, *The Bluest Eye* focuses attention on the connection between class and shame in the African-American community. Geraldine is identified by the narrator as one of the "brown girls," who have internalized white, middle-class standards of beauty and behavior, and who, in developing "high morals" and "good manners," have lost their "funkiness," that is, their passion and spontaneity (82, 83). Donning the mask of middle-class respectability perhaps, in part, in an effort to disassociate themselves from the shaming racist and sexist stereotype of the "oversexed-black-Jezebel"—a pervasive stereotype that views African-American women not only as connoting sex but also as instigators of sex (Painter 209–10)—the "plain brown" women walk with their "behind[s] in for fear of a sway too free," and they give their bodies to their husbands "sparingly and partially" (84, 83, 84). Geraldine, a middle-class "brown" woman, shuns Pecola, who embodies the shame and stigma of black poverty. Pointing to the class differences among black people, the narrative describes Geraldine's perception of Pecola, viewing the underclass Pecola through Geraldine's black, middle-class—and shaming—gaze.

When Geraldine looks at Pecola—who has a torn and soiled dress with a safety pin holding up the hem, muddy shoes and dirty socks, and matted hair where the plaits sticking out on her head have come undone—she feels that she has "seen this little girl all of her life" (91). Geraldine's revulsion toward poor blacks like Pecola—whom she sees as dirty and subhuman—reveals her internalization of the racist idea of black degeneracy. To Geraldine, such children "were everywhere. They slept six in a bed, all their pee mixing together in the night as they wet their beds. . . . Tin cans and tires blossomed where they lived. They lived on cold black-eyed peas and orange pop. Like flies they hovered; like flies they settled" (92). That the "affective roots" of prejudice, as Donald Nathanson remarks, involve "dissmell and disgust" (133) is also apparent in this passage. Linked to the "phenomenology of interpersonal rejection," dissmell is a primitive mechanism by which individuals keep at a distance those people that they define "as too awful or too foul to get near" (124). Moreover, the "purpose or function of contempt seems to be to instill in the other person a sense of self-dissmell or self-disgust and therefore shame at self-unworthiness" (129). When Geraldine contemptuously pronounces Pecola a "nasty little black bitch" (92), her shaming words reinforce Pecola's fear of exposure and rejection and intensify her feeling that she is ugly, dirty, and defective.

Similarly, in the vacant gaze of the white store owner, Mr. Yacobowski, Pecola senses racial contempt. "He does not see her, because for him there is nothing to see." In his "total absence of human recognition—the glazed separateness"—Pecola senses his distaste. "The distaste must be for her, her blackness. . . . [I]t is the blackness that accounts for, that creates, the vacuum edged with distaste in white eyes" (48–49). After Pecola purchases three Mary Jane candies from Mr. Yacobowski, she attempts to soothe herself. Outside his store, she "feels the inexplicable shame ebb" and takes temporary refuge in anger. "Anger is better. There is a sense of being in anger. A reality and presence. An awareness of worth. It is a lovely surging." But when she recalls Mr. Yacobowski's eyes, her shame "wells up again." Attempting to overcome her inner feelings of defectiveness, she imagines that to eat the Mary Jane candy is to "eat the eyes" of, indeed is to "eat" and to "[b]e," Mary Jane—the blond-haired, blue-eyed white girl pictured on the candy wrapper (50). To incorporate and thus "be"—that is, merge with—the idealized Mary Jane is to be an object of admiration, not contempt, and to turn the shaming or ostracizing gaze of others into a look of approval and acceptance.

In a pivotal episode, which purposefully and with didactic intent brings together the "ugly" black Pecola and the "high-yellow" Maureen Peal, Morrison underscores the pain and rage of intraracial shaming. When Claudia, her sister, Frieda, and Maureen Peal notice that there is some commotion going on in the schoolyard playground and stop to investigate, they discover that a group of blacks boys is "circling and holding at bay a victim, Pecola Breedlove." "[T]hrilled by the easy power of a majority," the boys "gaily" harass Pecola with an extemporaneous, insulting verse: "Black e mo. Black e mo. Yadaddsleepsnekked." What gives the first insult "its teeth" is their "contempt for their own blackness." Repeating what has been done to them and attempting to rid themselves of their own deeply rooted sense of racial shame and self-loathing, they humiliate Pecola. Their "exquisitely learned self-hatred" and "elaborately designed hopelessness" become expressed in their angry, insulting speech, and they dance a "macabre ballet" around Pecola, "whom, for their own sake, they were prepared to sacrifice to the flaming pit" of their scorn (65).

Responding passively to her public shaming, the crying Pecola edges around the circle of boys. The taunting stops when an angry Frieda and Claudia intervene. But the rescue of Pecola is short-lived. When Maureen Peal, who initially seems friendly to Pecola, asks if Pecola has, indeed, ever seen a naked man, Pecola becomes "agitated" and remarks that no girl's father would appear naked in front of his daughter "unless he was dirty"—that is, shameful and debased (71). Retorting that she asked Pecola about a naked man and not her father, Maureen insists that Pecola has, in fact, seen her own father naked. If Maureen's words suggest that there is already community suspicion about the possibility of sexual abuse in the Breedlove family, Pecola's physical response to Maureen's accusation is also suggestive. Enacting the characteristic hiding or concealing behavior of the shamed individual, "Pecola tucked her head in—a funny, sad, helpless movement. A kind of hunching of the shoulders, pulling in of the neck, as though she wanted to cover her ears" (72). But when Maureen taunts Claudia by calling her "black" (73), Claudia, unlike Pecola who responds passively to Maureen's insults, flails out angrily and defiantly at the humiliator, giving physical expression to Pecola's unexpressed rage. Claudia also takes on the role of the protector-rescuer in this scene. Yet it is telling that when Claudia swings at Maureen, she misses and instead hits Pecola in the face. Despite her enactment of the protector's role, Claudia, as this scene reveals, also shares at some deep level the community impulse to victimize Pecola: that is, to rid herself of her own shame by scapegoating the utterly vulnerable Pecola.

In the plight of Pecola Breedlove, *The Bluest Eye* dramatizes what Wurmser describes as the "theme" of unlovability—"the triad of weakness, defectiveness, and dirtiness" that occurs in the classic shame situation (*Mask* 98). Feeling unloved by her parents and "ugly" in the gaze of others, Pecola defends herself by withdrawing. "Concealed, veiled, eclipsed," she hides behind her "mantle" of ugliness, "peeping out from behind the shroud very seldom, and then only to yearn for the return of her mask" (39). The "goal of hiding as part of the shame affect," as Wurmser explains, is "to prevent further exposure and, with that, further rejection, but it also atones for the exposure that has already occurred" (*Mask* 54). That Pecola, who is terrified by her parents' physical violence, wants to "disappear" is also suggestive. "If it is appearance (exposure) that is central in shame, disappearance is the logical outcome

of shame," writes Wurmser (*Mask* 81). Indeed, "[s]hame's aim is disappearance. This may be, most simply, in the form of hiding; . . . most
archaically in the form of freezing into complete paralysis and stupor;
most frequently, in the form of forgetting parts of one's life and one's
self; and at its most differentiated, in the form of changing one's character" (*Mask* 84). Pecola's attempt to bodily disappear also marks the
beginning of her experiences of depersonalization: that is, her "estrangement from world and self" that Wurmser describes as symptomatic of
shame anxiety (*Mask* 53). Pecola "squeezed her eyes shut. Little parts of
her body faded away. . . . Her fingers went, one by one; then her arms
disappeared all the way to the elbow. Her feet now. Yes, that was good.
The legs all at once. It was hardest above the thighs. She had to be real
still and pull. . . . The face was hard, too. Almost done, almost. Only her
tight, tight eyes were left" (45).

Pecola, who is unable to make her eyes disappear, spends hours
looking at herself in the mirror, "trying to discover the secret" of her
"ugliness." And she prays for a miracle—she prays for blue eyes—
because she believes that if God grants her blue eyes, she will no longer
be ugly, and thus her parents might not "do bad things" in front of her
"pretty" blue eyes (45, 46). Because "[l]ove and power are vested in the
gaze," writes Wurmser, to "seek forever with the eye and not to find
leads to shame." Pecola's wish for blue eyes recalls Wurmser's description of the "magic eye," the use of "eye power" and looking in an
attempt to attract the "beckoning, admiring" gaze of the absent mother
and thus undo, "by magic expression, the wound of basic unlovability"
(*Mask* 94, 95, 94). Feeling utterly flawed and dirty, Pecola rejects her
African-American identity when she imagines that she can cure her
"ugliness"—that is, her shame and basic unlovability—only if she is
magically granted the same blue eyes possessed by little white girls.

In the story of Pecola, *The Bluest Eye* depicts not only the interpersonal and internalized shaming of racism but also the horrors of father-
daughter incest. But although *The Bluest Eye* depicts the shameful family secret of an incestuous rape, it also is caught up in a form of denial.
Indeed, Morrison has described the rape as "almost irrelevant," insisting that she wants readers to "*look* at" Cholly and "see his love for his
daughter and his powerlessness to help her pain." Cholly's "embrace,
the rape," in Morrison's words, "is all the gift he has left" (Tate 164).
If Morrison, in writing the novel, found herself thinking the "unthinkable" as she worked out the incest secret that lies buried at the heart of
The Bluest Eye (Bakerman 39–40), she also ran into difficulties as she
felt the need to provoke reader sympathy for Cholly, despite his incestuous rape of his daughter.

By insisting that the "pieces of Cholly's life" can be rendered "coherent only in the head of a musician" who can connect together the various fragments of Cholly's life (159), the narrative invites readers to focus on the connection between Cholly's fragmented trauma narrative and his rape of Pecola: that is, to understand Cholly's rape of Pecola the reader must understand Cholly's traumatic sexual initiation as an adolescent. The fact that Morrison chose to tell the rape from Cholly's point of view and the fact that Morrison's narrative, in part, endorses Cholly—for he is, in Morrison's own description, one of her "salt tasters," a "fearless" and "lawless" character (see Stepto 19–20; Tate 164–65)—suggests the hidden way in which the novel positions readers not only with the humiliated victim but also with the humiliator, the shamed, enraged father who projects his own shame onto his daughter and thus acts as an unwitting agent in the white society's humiliation of this vulnerable girl. And if Morrison wants to elicit reader sympathy for Cholly, she also risks shaming her readers as she breaks the taboo on looking and positions her readers as voyeurs of the incest scene.

When Cholly sees Pecola—who assumes the permanent posture of the shamed, traumatized individual with her "hunched" back and her head turned to one side "as though crouching from a permanent and unreceived blow"—he wonders why she looks "so whipped" and why she isn't happy. Feeling accused by the "clear statement of her misery," he wants "to break her neck—but tenderly." "What could a burned-out black man say to the hunched back of his eleven-year-old daughter? If he looked into her face, he would see those haunted, loving eyes. The hauntedness would irritate him—the love would move him to fury. How dare she love him? . . . What was he supposed to do about that? Return it? How?" (161)

Cholly initially responds to the misery of his shamed daughter with anger, and he also sees her as an object of contempt and disgust. "His hatred of her slimed in his stomach and threatened to become vomit." But then, when Pecola scratches the back of her calf with her toe—which is what Pauline did the first time Cholly saw her many years before—the "timid, tucked-in look" of her scratching toe reminds him of the tenderness he once felt toward his wife. Sinking to his knees, he crawls toward Pecola, catches her foot in his hand, nibbles at the back of her leg, and then digs his fingers into her waist. Despite the "rigidity of her shocked body, the silence of her stunned throat," he wants "to fuck her—tenderly," and yet the tenderness does "not hold." "His soul seemed to slip down to his guts and fly out into her, and the gigantic thrust he made into her then provoked the only sound she made—a hollow suck of air in the back of her throat. Like the rapid loss of air from a circus balloon." Afterwards, Cholly again feels "hatred mixed with tenderness" as he looks at the unconscious body of his daughter lying on the kitchen floor (162–63).

The Bluest Eye presents a disturbing account of Cholly's rape of Pecola and then partially denies what it has described by insisting in the closure that Cholly loved Pecola even though his "touch was fatal," for the "love of a free man is never safe" (206). While some critic/readers of The Bluest Eye have remarked on the "raw horror" of the rape scene or have described the rape as a "tremendous and overwhelming act of paternal violence" or have insisted that Cholly's act is "diabolical" (Miner 88; Holloway 44; Jones and Vinson 30), others have followed the text's directives by partially denying what Cholly has done or by attempting to exonerate him. Because Cholly has been socially conditioned to view himself as an "object of disgust," he "can do nothing other than objectify Pecola," argues one commentator, and hence he exploits his daughter "because his own exploitation makes it impossible to do otherwise" (Byerman, "Beyond Realism" 59). "At least . . . he wanted to touch his daughter. Pauline Breedlove responds to the rape by beating Pecola, an act not much less brutal than Cholly's," in the view of another commentator (Carmean 24). Although most readers would be unwilling to "forgive Cholly for his crime against his daughter," remarks another commentator, many understand the "why and how" of the rape, which is "a terribly tragic manifestation of a severely skewed upbringing" (Portales 504). If Morrison's treatment of the rape is said to foreground the reader's "awareness of the complexity of judgment and feeling" (Dittmar 139), it is also the case that some critics/readers appear to identify with Cholly's violent act and condemn Pecola. "A profound expression of love, the rape is also an exercise of power and freedom, a protest against an unjust and repressive culture," argues one critic who also claims that while the defeated and ultimately mad Pecola is "someone to be pitied," her "ignorance" and "passivity" merit the reader's "contempt" (Otten 21, 24). Such readers repeat the text by partially denying the horror of Pecola's plight, and they also, in exonerating Cholly and scapegoating Pecola, inadvertently become caught up in the shame drama presented in the novel.

If, in the rape scene, Pecola is silenced, earlier she poignantly asked, "[H]ow do you get somebody to love you?" (32). Pecola, who feels that she is unlovable, craves the affection of her father only to be raped by him. The utterly helpless and vulnerable daughter and the embodiment of her father's self-contempt and loathing, the shamed Pecola becomes the target of her father's humiliated fury. He does to her what has been done to him and thus, when he rapes Pecola, he inflicts on her his own feelings of exposure, powerlessness, narcissistic injury, and humiliation. Pecola's fainting depicts not only the "somatic reactions" that occur in extreme states of shame—which include physiological responses such as "fainting, dizziness, rigidity of all the muscles"

(Wurmser, *Mask* 83)—but also the physical and mental paralysis experienced by the trauma victim.[5]

Raped by her father and then severely beaten by her mother, Pecola seeks out help from Soaphead Church, a child molester who advertises himself as a spiritualist and psychic reader. When Pecola asks Soaphead Church for blue eyes, he finds her request "the most fantastic and the most logical petition" he has ever received, and he wants the power to help the "ugly little girl asking for beauty" and desiring to "rise up out of the pit of her blackness" (174). In his letter to God, Soaphead insists that he has "caused a miracle," that he has given Pecola cobalt blue eyes. "No one else will see her blue eyes. But *she* will," remarks Soaphead (182). And, indeed, Pecola ends up living permanently in the dissociated world of madness where she talks to her alter identity—her "friend"—about her magical blue eyes. The traumatically shamed Pecola believes that others are fascinated with, and envious of, her blue eyes. But she is, in fact, the subject of gaze avoidance by her mother, who looks "drop-eyed" at her daughter. As Pecola remarks to her alter "friend," "Ever since I got my blue eyes, she look away from me all of the time. Do you suppose she's jealous too?" Similarly, members of the community look away from the shamed outcast, Pecola, socially ostracizing her with their gaze avoidance. "Everybody's jealous. Every time I look at somebody, they look off" (195). Only in her mad world is Pecola someone special, a black girl with the blue eyes of a white girl.

While Claudia and her sister Frieda are initially Pecola's allies despite their "defensive shame"—for they feel "embarrassed for Pecola, hurt for her, and finally . . . sorry for her"—other members of the community pronounce Cholly a "dirty nigger" and insist that the pregnant Pecola carries "some of the blame" for what has happened to her (190, 189). Members of the community, who treat Pecola as the subject of shaming gossip, are "disgusted, amused, shocked, outraged, or even excited" by Pecola's story. Her baby, they remark, is "'[b]ound to be the ugliest thing walking,'" and they feel it would be "'better off in the ground'" (190, 189–90). But when Claudia thinks about the baby that everyone wants dead, she feels "a need for someone to want the black baby to live—just to counteract the universal love of white baby dolls, Shirley Temples, and Maureen Peals" (190). Intent on changing the course of events, Claudia buries the bicycle money she earned from selling seeds and plants the marigold seeds, hoping that God will be impressed enough with her sacrifice so that he will produce a miracle and save Pecola's baby.

But the baby, which is premature, dies, and the permanently damaged Pecola is socially ostracized. "She was so sad to see. Grown people looked away; children, those who were not frightened by her, laughed outright." And Claudia, whose marigolds never grow, ends up avoiding Pecola who spends her days "walking up and down, up and down, her head jerking to the beat of a drummer so distant only she could hear" and who, with her bent elbows and her hands on her shoulders, flails her arms "like a bird in an eternal, grotesquely futile effort to fly" (204). Pecola, who absorbs the "waste" that others dump on her, ultimately becomes the scapegoat for the entire community as they project their own self-loathing and contempt—their own stain of blackness—onto the vulnerable, ostracized Pecola. "All of us—all who knew her—felt so wholesome after we cleaned ourselves on her. We were so beautiful when we stood astride her ugliness. . . . And she let us, and thereby deserved our contempt. We honed our egos on her, padded our characters with her frailty, and yawned in the fantasy of our strength" (205).

Morrison's "impetus" for writing *The Bluest Eye*, as she recalls, "was to write a book about a kind of person that was never in literature anywhere, never taken seriously by anybody—all those peripheral little girls" (Neustadt 88). By indicting the community for their scapegoating of Pecola, Morrison also wanted to prompt her readers to recognize their own participation in the smashing of the Pecolas that surround them. Part of Morrison's intent, as she explains, was to peck away at the "gaze that condemned" Pecola, but she also wanted to "avoid complicity in the demonization process Pecola was subjected to," and thus she did not want to "dehumanize the characters who trashed Pecola and contributed to her collapse" ("Afterword" 210, 211). Yet despite Morrison's intent, we can find evidence in the critical conversation surrounding *The Bluest Eye* of how the novel involves its readers in a drama of blame-assessment, which, at times, veers into a variation of the blaming and attack-other transactions that sometimes occur in the shame scenario.

Although it has been claimed that "to read *The Bluest Eye* looking to assign blame" is to "miss the point" (Kuenz 430), critics, again and again, have attempted to determine who is responsible for Pecola's plight. Pecola has been described as a character whose "innocence and tragedy" are presented to readers and as "the epitome of the victim in a world that reduces persons to objects and then makes them feel inferior as objects" (Rosenberg 442; Davis 14). But she also has been characterized as a "scapegoat without benefit of martyrdom, a hopeless rather than tragic character" and as a "grotesque Messiah," a character who is "sacrificed so that others may live with the perversions of society" (Otten 24; Byerman, "Intense Behaviors" 452). Pecola has also been described as possibly a "participant and not simply victim, victim and at the same moment participant" in the rape, and as a character who is "responsible, in the final analysis, for what happens to her" because she fails to recognize that she must define a life for herself (Gibson 29; Samuels and Hudson-Weems 15). And yet the victimizing father has often been judged as not fully responsible for his life or actions.[6] Representative of this view is the remark that Cholly, the "victim of earlier, more blatant oppressions," has "struggled throughout his life against a society that treats him, intentionally or not, without compassion or sympathy" and hence, "almost everything that Cholly does, he does as a reaction to forces and pressures around him" (Portales 499, 503). In yet another common reading, blame is displaced from Cholly onto the black community or the white culture. "Pecola seems less a victim of her father than of a whole community, which has allowed itself to become debased by the dominant culture and alienated by adopting its norms" (Göbel 131). Similarly, the black community "must share the blame for Pecola's diminishment," for Pecola has "been made a scapegoat by a neighborhood of people who themselves live their own unnatural lives under the gaze of the dominant culture" (Bjork 53). If Morrison, herself, has sometimes been implicitly condemned for writing a novel that is "mired in the pathology of Afro-American experience" (Dittmar 140), the blame and shame also often attaches to Morrison's readers. "No one is indicted for Pecola's destruction," remarks one critic, "but then in another way we all are" (Demetrakopoulous 36).

"To read the book . . . is to ache for remedy," writes an early commentator on *The Bluest Eye* (Dee 20). This points to yet another common response to the novel, which has provoked a variety of rescue fantasies in its critic/readers. Pecola "might have been saved if someone had cared enough to nurture her spirit," writes one commentator, and although it is "too late" for Pecola, Claudia may be rescued as she is prompted "to transcend the enervating image imposed on minorities, to derive strength and momentum from Pecola's sad example, and to develop a strong self-image, a whole" (Carmean 27, 30). Claudia, in the view of such critic/readers, "has survived to tell her and Pecola's story," and her story "serves as a point of departure in her own search for an authenticating self"; moreover, Claudia creates a tale that, "by negative example, offers corrective possibilities" (Bjork 54; Harris 15). Readers of Morrison's tale also may undergo a form of rescue. It has been argued that Morrison, by her "foregrounding of the unstable and constructed nature of knowledge, and of the collaborative processes which guide it, affirms the possibility of positive change." Thus while Morrison's characters "may not participate in such change," readers who assemble the text may be empowered, for the novel, by enacting ways readers "produce and re-produce ideology," reminds them that they "can take charge" of their future (Dittmar 142).

The fact that *The Bluest Eye* can prompt readers to such a variety of responses—to engage in a rescue fantasy or to participate in the drama of blame assessment or to recognize their own guilty and shameful participation in the smashing of the Pecolas of American society—points to the powerful way Morrison works on her readers' emotions. Repeatedly critics have remarked on the emotional impact of this novel. *The Bluest Eye* has been described as a work that can make readers feel "helpless and afraid" (Dee 20) or as a work that uses "obscenity" to shock the readers' "sensibilities," and that urges readers to see the "destructive absurdity" of American life and to recognize that "the real horrors are still loose in the world" (Byerman, "Intense Behaviors" 456–57). By "exposing the contrast between the ideal and the real," Morrison's objective narrator offers the reader "no escape from her anger at the dissolution of black lives" (Bjork 32). In *The Bluest Eye*, writes another, Pecola is "too vulnerable and uncomprehending to be angry at what happens to her. It is Morrison who is angry, and the careful form of the novel intensifies rather than deflects the reader's sense of that anger." Indeed, the "coherence of Morrison's vision and the structure which parses out its logic into repeating patterns offer the reader no solace, no refuge from Morrison's anger" (Hedin 49, 50). But to other critics/readers, although Morrison is angry, her narrative provides the reader "solace" and her voice is "regenerative, even in the face of the despair inscribed in the novel's cyclical structure and wrenching plot" (Dittmar 146).

In writing *The Bluest Eye*, Morrison recalls that one of the problems she confronted was language. "Holding the despising glance while sabotaging it was difficult. The novel tried to hit the raw nerve of racial self-contempt, expose it, then soothe it not with narcotics but with language that replicated the agency I discovered in my first experience of beauty. Because that moment was so racially infused (my revulsion at what my school friend wanted: very blue eyes in a very black skin; the harm she was doing to *my* concept of the beautiful), the struggle was for writing that was indisputably black" ("Afterword" 211). In *The Bluest Eye*, Morrison explores black self-contempt—the sense of the self as racially stained, as "dirty" and "nasty" to use descriptions that recur in the text—but in a rich and beautiful language and in a carefully shaped narrative. Using verbal beauty to counteract shame and narrative design as a way of gaining artistic mastery and control over the shame-laden, traumatic subject matter of her novel, Morrison, in *The Bluest Eye*, explores the woundedness of African Americans, and she does this in an idealized art form that conveys but also contains intense feelings of anger, shame, and pain.

NOTES

1. In *Degeneration, Culture, and the Novel*, William Greenslade remarks, "By the mid-nineteenth century racial biology had mapped out a 'science of boundaries between groups and the degenerations that threatened them when those boundaries were transgressed'. . . . In contrast to industrious 'historic races' of northern Europe, certain races were cast as degenerate types. The biologist Cuvier identified the negro race as 'the most degraded human race whose form approaches that of the beast.' Within the ideology of progress, it was imperative to establish a hierarchy of racial difference. 'The savage races are without a past,' said F. W. Farrar in 1861. 'The highest places in the hierarchy of civilisation will assuredly not be within the reach of our dusky cousins,' was the view of T. H. Huxley in 1865. For the major race theorist of the nineteenth century, Comte de Gobineau (1816–82), such was the necessity of keeping the races apart, that miscegenation and race-mingling would inevitably lead to degeneration and the extinction of civilisation. For many race theorists, including Robert Knox and Charles Kingsley in Britain, the degenerate races were best off dead" (21–22).

Nancy Stepan, in "Biological Degeneration: Races and Proper Places," discusses the interest of racial biologists in the idea of racial types and their "proper places." "On the basis of analogies between human races and animal species, it was argued that races, like animal types, tended to be confined to definite localities of the earth." Not only did races have ties to particular geographical places, but movement out of their designated places "caused a 'degeneration.'" A common theme "sounded in the typological theory of racial degeneration" was "the degenerations caused by the movement of freed blacks into the geographical and social spaces occupied by whites and into the political condition of freedom" (99).

A "major concern" of American racial biologists was the "proper place" of blacks in the Americas, observes Stepan. "Most racial theorists in the United States shared, by the 1840s and 1850s, the typological orientation of the European scientists." It was argued, for example, that "though Negroes fared well in the hotter, southern latitudes of the United States, north of forty degrees latitude they steadily deteriorated." After the Civil War and the freeing of the slaves, the "old belief that freed blacks were, of all blacks, the 'most corrupt, depraved, and abandoned element in the population,' was . . . given a biological rationale." "Freedom was an unnatural environment which removed constraints and plunged the Negro into 'natural' and innate excesses and indulgence of the racial appetites." Given freedom, blacks returned "to their primitive state of savagery and sexuality, revealing the ancient features of the race by a process of reversion" (99–100, 101, 102).

2. The "nuclear experience" of "aversive" white racism, writes Kovel, "is a sense of disgust about the body of the black person based upon a very primitive fantasy: that it contains an essence—dirt—that smells and may rub off onto the body of the racist" (84). Kovel roots racist aversion in a "bodily fantasy about dirt, which rests in turn upon the equation of dirt with excrement: the inside of the body turned out and threatening to return within. And within this nuclear fantasy,

black people have come to be represented as the personification of dirt" (89–90). Treating the black as "other," the white racist assigns hated or impure aspects of the self onto the black. "It is precisely this process of purification that creates the need to see another as the exemplar of impurity and to treat him as if he were exactly that" (91). Thus, a "central theme" in white racism "from a subjective standpoint," according to Kovel, is the "fantasy of dirt and purification" (xlv).

For an interesting analysis of the role played by the "discourse of dirt and defilement" in the Clarence Thomas Supreme Court confirmation hearings, see Kendall Thomas, "Strange Fruit," 376–86.

3. Judith Herman's description, in *Father-Daughter Incest*, of the repeated recovery and suppression of the incest secret beginning with Freud reveals the power of such defensive denials. Freud, the "patriarch of modern psychology," became aware of the "incest secret" in the early part of his career during his study of hysteria. When Freud's patients—"women from prosperous, conventional families"—confided that they had been sexually abused in childhood, he believed them and in his *Studies on Hysteria*, published in 1896, he announced that the origin of hysteria was childhood sexual trauma. But he was uncomfortable with the implications of this—that incest was "endemic to the patriarchal family." Consequently, he "refused" to publicly identify *fathers* as sexual aggressors, and he falsified his incest cases by identifying governesses, nurses, maids, and children of both sexes as the offenders (9). Then within a year, Freud "repudiated" his seduction theory, insisting that "his patients' reports of sexual abuse were fantasies, based upon their own incestuous wishes." "To incriminate daughters rather than fathers was an immense relief to him," writes Herman. And for many years after Freud's disavowal of the seduction theory, "clinicians maintained a dignified silence on the subject of incest" (10).

The fact of incest was "discovered" a second time by social scientists who, beginning in 1940, conducted surveys of sexual behavior (12). Yet while sexologists like Alfred Kinsey and his associates "dared to describe a vast range of sexual behaviors in exhaustive detail," they apparently felt "the less said the better" on the topic of incest even though "they had accumulated the largest body of data on overt incest that had ever appeared in the scientific literature" (17). And if in the 1970s incest was rediscovered a "third time" by the women's liberation movement, there also coexisted the pro-incest apologists who portrayed themselves as "an embattled minority, gamely challenging obsolete social and religions conventions," and who argued not only that incest was harmless but also that it was a way to liberate the sexuality of children (18, 23, 23–26). See also Herman, *Trauma and Recovery* 10–20, 28–32.

4. It is possible that when Morrison wrote this scene she was remembering and responding to media reports on the response of African-American children to white and black baby dolls. "During the early fifties," recalls Susan Bordo, "when *Brown v. the Board of Education* was wending its way through the courts, as a demonstration of the destructive psychological effects of segregation black children were asked to look at two baby dolls, identical in all respects except color. The children were asked a series of questions: which is the nice doll? which is the bad doll? which doll would you like to play with? The majority of black children, Kenneth Clark reports, attributed the positive characteris-

tics to the white doll, the negative characteristics to the black. When Clark asked one final question, 'Which doll is like you?' they looked at him, he says, 'as though he were the devil himself' for putting them in that predicament, for forcing them to face the inexorable and hideous logical implications of their situation. Northern children often ran out of the room; southern children tended to answer the question in shamed embarrassment [note that both of these are shame responses]. Clark recalls one little boy who laughed, 'Who am I like? That doll! It's a nigger and I'm a nigger!'" (262–63).

5. As Judith Herman observes, "When a person is completely powerless, and any form of resistance is futile, she may go into a state of surrender. The system of self-defense shuts down entirely. The helpless person escapes from her situation not by action in the real world but rather by altering her state of consciousness. Analogous states are observed in animals, who sometimes 'freeze' when they are attacked. . . . A rape survivor describes her experience of this state of surrender: 'Did you ever see a rabbit stuck in the glare of your headlights when you were going down a road at night. Transfixed—like it knew it was going to get it—that's what happened.' In the words of another rape survivor, 'I couldn't scream. I couldn't move. I was paralyzed . . . like a rag doll'" (*Trauma and Recovery* 42).

Similarly, shame anxiety, according to Wurmser, can have a "freezing" or "numbing" quality and be "accompanied by a profound estrangement from world and self" (*Mask* 53). Wurmser links the depersonalization seen in some shame patients to physical trauma. "This general affect denial and affect repression, motivated by shame, reflects early traumatization of a very severe (emotional or physical) kind—typically in severely abused or neglected children—and the ensuring broad affect regression, well studied by Krystal" (*Mask* 175).

6. Elizabeth Hayes reports that "many college-age readers are more outraged by Pauline's failure to protect Pecola than by Cholly's brutal rape of his own child. . . . They angrily condemn Pauline as unnatural, a monster, horrible, while they merely shake their heads over Cholly's devastating abuse. This response is yet another example of the 'blame the mother' syndrome so common in our post-Freudian culture, a response Morrison does not share" (176–77).

WORKS CITED

Bakerman, Jane. "The Seams Can't Show: An Interview with Toni Morrison." Taylor-Guthrie, *Conversations* 30–42. (Rpt. *Black American Literature Forum* 12.2 [Summer 1978]: 56–60).

Bjork, Patrick. *The Novels of Toni Morrison: The Search for Self and Place within the Community.* New York: Lang, 1992.

Bordo, Susan. *Unbearable Weight: Feminism, Western Culture, and the Body.* Berkeley: U of California P, 1993.

Byerman, Keith. "Beyond Realism: The Fictions of Toni Morrison." *Toni Morrison: Modern Critical Views.* Ed. Harold Bloom. New York: Chelsea, 1990. 55–84. (Rpt. *Fingering the Jagged Grain: Tradition and Form in Recent Black Fiction.* Athens: U of Georgia P, 1985. 184–216).

————. "Intense Behaviors: The Use of the Grotesque in *The Bluest Eye* and *Eva's Man.*" *CLA Journal* 25.4 (June 1982): 447–57.

Carmean, Karen. *Toni Morrison's World of Fiction.* Troy, N.Y.: Whitston, 1993.

Davis, Cynthia. "Self, Society, and Myth in Toni Morrison's Fiction." *Toni Morrison: Modern Critical Views.* Ed. Harold Bloom. New York: Chelsea, 1990. (Rpt. *Contemporary Literature* 23.3 [Summer 1982]: 323–42).

Dee, Ruby. "Black Family Search for Identity." *Critical Essays on Toni Morrison.* Ed. Nellie McKay. Boston: G. K. Hall, 1988. 19–20. (Rpt. *Freedomways* 11 [1971]: 319–20).

Dittmar, Linda. "'Will the Circle Be Unbroken?': The Politics of Form in *The Bluest Eye.*" *Novel* 23.2 (Winter 1990): 137–55.

Demetrakopoulos, Stephanie. "Bleak Beginnings: *The Bluest Eye.*" *New Dimensions of Spirituality: A Biracial and Bicultural Reading of the Novels of Toni Morrison.* Karla F. C. Holloway and Stephanie A. Demetrakopoulos. Westport, Conn.: Greenwood, 1987. 31–36.

Erikson, Kai. "Notes on Trauma and Community." *American Imago* 48.4 (Winter 1991): 455–72.

Gibson, Donald. "Text and Countertext in Toni Morrison's *The Bluest Eye.*" *LIT: Literature Interpretation Theory* 1 (1989): 19–32.

Gilman, Sander. *Difference and Pathology: Stereotypes of Sexuality, Race, and Madness.* Ithaca, N.Y.: Cornell UP, 1985.

Göbel, Walter. "Canonizing Toni Morrison." *AAA: Arbeiten aus Anglistik und Amerikanistik* 15.2 (1990): 127–37.

Greenslade, William. *Degeneration, Culture and the Novel: 1880–1940.* Cambridge: Cambridge UP, 1994.

Harris, Trudier. *Fiction and Folklore: The Novels of Toni Morrison.* Knoxville: U of Tennessee P, 1991.

Hayes, Elizabeth. "'Like Seeing You Buried': Persephone in *The Bluest Eye, Their Eyes Were Watching God,* and *The Color Purple.*" *Images of Persephone: Feminist Readings in Western Literature.* Ed. Elizabeth Hayes. Gainesville: UP of Florida, 1994. 170–194.

Hedin, Raymond. "The Structuring of Emotion in Black American Fiction." *Novel* 16.1 (Fall 1982): 35–54.

Herman, Judith Lewis. *Father-Daughter Incest.* Cambridge, Mass.: Harvard UP, 1981.

————. "Father-Daughter Incest." *Post-Traumatic Therapy and Victims of Violence.* Ed. Frank Ochberg. New York: Brunner/Mazel, 1988. 175–95.

————. *Trauma and Recovery.* New York: HarperCollins/BasicBooks, 1992.

Holloway, Karla. "The Language and Music of Survival." *New Dimensions of Spirituality: A Biracial and Bicultural Reading of the Novels of Toni Morrison.* Karla Holloway and Stephanie Demetrakopoulous. Westport, Conn.: Greenwood, 1987. 37–47.

hooks, bell. *Outlaw Culture: Resisting Representations.* New York: Routledge, 1994.

Jones, Bessie and Audrey Vinson. *The World of Toni Morrison.* Dubuque, Iowa: Kendall/Hunt, 1985.

Kovel, Joel. *White Racism: A Psychohistory.* 1970. New York: Columbia UP, 1984.

Kuenz, Jane. "*The Bluest Eye*: Notes on History, Community, and Black Female Subjectivity." *African American Review* 27.3 (1993): 421–31.

Lewis, Helen Block. *Shame and Guilt in Neurosis.* New York: International Universities P, 1971.

LeClair, Thomas. "The Language Must Not Sweat: A Conversation with Toni Morrison." Taylor-Guthrie, *Conversations*, 119–28. (Rpt. *New Republic* 184 [21 March 1981]: 25–29).

Mason, Marilyn. "Shame: Reservoir for Family Secrets." *Secrets in Families and Family Therapy.* Ed. Evan Imber-Black. New York: Norton, 1993. 29–43.

Miner, Madonne. "Lady No Longer Sings the Blues: Rape, Madness, and Silence in *The Bluest Eye*." *Toni Morrison: Modern Critical Views.* New York: Chelsea, 1990. 85–99. (Rpt. *Conjuring: Black Women, Fiction, and Literary Tradition.* Ed. Majorie Pryse and Hortense Spillers. Bloomington: Indiana UP, 1985. 176–91).

Morrison, Andrew. *Shame: The Underside of Narcissism.* Hillsdale, N.J.: Analytic P, 1989.

Morrison, Toni. "Afterword." 1993. *The Bluest Eye*, 209–16.

———. *The Bluest Eye.* 1970. New York: Penguin/Plume, 1994.

———. "Introduction: Friday on the Potomac." *Race-ing Justice, En-gendering Power: Essays on Anita Hill, Clarence Thomas, and the Construction of Social Reality.* Ed. Toni Morrison. New York: Pantheon, 1992. vii–xxx.

Nathanson, Donald. *Shame and Pride: Affect, Sex, and The Birth of the Self.* 1992. New York: Norton, 1994.

Neustadt, Kathy. "The Visits of the Writers Toni Morrison and Eudora Welty." Taylor-Guthrie, *Conversations*, 84–92. (Rpt. *Bryn Mawr Alumnae Bulletin* [Spring 1980]: 2–5).

Otten, Terry. *The Crime of Innocence in the Fiction of Toni Morrison.* Columbia: U of Missouri P, 1989.

Painter, Nell. "Hill, Thomas, and the Use of Racial Stereotype." *Race-ing Justice, En-gendering Power: Essays on Anita Hill, Clarence Thomas, and the Construction of Social Reality.* Ed. Toni Morrison. New York: Pantheon, 1992. 200–214.

Portales, Marco. "Toni Morrison's *The Bluest Eye*: Shirley Temple and Cholly." *Centennial Review* 30.4 (Fall 1986): 496–506.

Rosenberg, Ruth. "Seeds in Hard Ground: Black Girlhood in *The Bluest Eye*." *Black American Literature Forum* 21.4 (Winter 1987): 435–45.

Ruas, Charles. "Toni Morrison." Taylor-Guthrie, *Conversations*, 93–118. (Rpt. *Conversations with American Writers.* New York: McGraw-Hill, 1984. 215–43).

Samuels, Wilfred and Clenora Hudson-Weems. *Toni Morrison.* Boston: Twayne, 1990.

Schneider, Carl. *Shame, Exposure, and Privacy.* 1977. New York: Norton, 1992.

Stepan, Nancy. "Biological Degeneration: Races and Proper Places." *Degeneration: The Dark Side of Progress.* Ed. J. Edward Chamberlin and Sander Gilman. New York: Columbia UP, 1985. 97–120.

Stepto, Robert. "Intimate Things in Place: A Conversation with Toni Morrison." Taylor-Guthrie, *Conversations*, 10–29. (Rpt. *Massachusetts Review* 18 [1977]: 473–89).

Tate, Claudia. "Toni Morrison." Taylor-Guthrie, *Conversations*, 156–70. (Rpt. *Black Women Writers at Work*. Ed. Claudia Tate. New York: Continuum, 1983. 117–31).

Taylor-Guthrie, Danille, ed. *Conversations with Toni Morrison*. Jackson: UP of Mississippi, 1994.

Thomas, Kendall. "Strange Fruit." *Race-ing Justice, En-gendering Power: Essays on Anita Hill, Clarence Thomas, and the Construction of Social Reality*. Ed. Toni Morrison. New York: Pantheon, 1992. 364–89.

Tomkins, Silvan. *Affect, Imagery, Consciousness*. Vol. 2: *The Negative Affects*. New York: Springer, 1963.

Wurmser, Léon. *The Mask of Shame*. 1981. Northvale, N.J.: Aronson, 1994.

———. "Shame: The Veiled Companion of Narcissism." *The Many Faces of Shame*. Ed. Donald Nathanson. New York: Guilford, 1987. 64–92.

CHAPTER 11

Unmasking Shame in an Expository Writing Course

Jeffrey Berman

I refuse to be labeled a victim, a survivor, or a degenerate. I will
be an avenger.

—Nick

Shame was one of the powerful emotions emerging in an expository
writing course I taught at the University at Albany in the fall of 1995.
The course was an experiment in personal writing and self-disclosure.
Like most English professors, I have taught a variety of writing courses
even though, in the highly specialized world of academia, "writing" is
not my specialty. Assigned to teach a section of expository writing, I
wondered whether my students could write about their lives with the
insight, honesty, and rigorous introspection that my psychoanalytic literary criticism students regularly do in their diaries.

   Since the mid-1970s, these students have been writing weekly
diaries in which they apply psychoanalytic theory to their lives. The
diaries are the "laboratory" part of the course, allowing students to pur-
sue the Delphic oracle's injunction, "Know thyself." These ungraded
diaries enable students to compare their feelings and experiences to
those of fictional characters and, in the process, identify problematic
aspects of their lives. By writing about vexing personal conflicts and
hearing their diaries read anonymously to the class, they often experience significant breakthroughs in their lives. In their evaluations at the
end of the semester, students single out the diary component as the most
valuable part of the course, and nearly all say that writing is therapeutic. Although writing about personal problems is sometimes painful, students feel better about themselves, particularly when they realize that
others are struggling with similar issues.

Convinced of the importance of expressive writing, I wrote *Diaries to an English Professor*, published in 1994. The book explores the major personal struggles students write about year after year, including divorce, eating disorders, suicide, and sexual abuse. Given the pervasiveness of these problems and the secrecy surrounding them, I wondered whether students in an expository writing course would also benefit from writing and talking about personal issues.

The students enrolled in my section of expository writing assumed it would resemble the English Department's catalog description, which would fit most expository writing courses:

> English 300 is for experienced writers who wish to work on such skills as style, organization, logic, and tone. Practice in a variety of forms: editorials, letters, travel accounts, film reviews, position papers, and autobiographical narrative. Classes devoted to discussions of the composing process and to critiques of student essays. Intended primarily for juniors and seniors. S/U graded.

A believer in truth-in-advertising, I wrote my own course description and distributed it to each of the nineteen students on the first day of the semester:

> Although we will discuss a wide variety of literary forms, we will emphasize personal, exploratory, and expressive writing. Several of the assignments will be based on my new book, *Diaries to an English Professor*. As you will discover, the book consists of the introspective diaries that University at Albany students have written over the years in my literature-and-psychoanalysis courses. These diaries are often highly personal, self-analytic, and self-disclosing. I'm interested in the extent to which you identify and empathize with the students in my book and how you write about your own lives. There are, to be sure, important differences between ungraded, anonymous diaries and S/U graded, formal essays; consequently, each of you will need to determine how personal you wish to be in your writings. When we discuss your writing in class, typically we will know your name; but if the writing under discussion might make you feel uncomfortable, then you can choose to remain anonymous to your classmates (though I will obviously need to know your name so that I can give you credit for your writing).

I informed them that all were to submit an essay every week, regardless of whether it would be discussed in class. The minimum writing requirement was forty acceptable pages, typed, double-spaced. The class would meet every Tuesday evening for three hours and would be run as a workshop. About once every three weeks, each student would bring twenty copies of his or her essay to class, at which time it would be read and discussed. I would usually give students a specific assignment, but they would have considerable freedom in the way they handled each assignment.

THE RISKS OF PERSONAL WRITING

I knew from the beginning that the experiment in personal writing and self-disclosure was fraught with peril. I could foresee at least three potential problems. First, would the students engage in constructive criticism? It was essential for everyone to be as compassionate and open-minded as possible when discussing essays on sensitive and controversial subjects. Students would be willing to engage in self-disclosure only if they trusted and respected their audience—and trust and respect are not easily established in a large university perceived to be impersonal. If classmates did not respond empathically to an essay on shame, would the writer feel doubly shamed?

Second, would the students tolerate my own criticisms of their writing? Is it helpful to correct grammar when a person might be writing about alcohol addiction, anorexia, or depression? Students in my literature-and-psychoanalysis course write diaries on the most intimate subjects, but I never correct or grade this writing. English 300, however, is a writing course, whose primary goal is to improve students' writing skills. It is well known that writers improve not only by writing but by having their work criticized. Mine was hardly a traditional writing course: students were to write about their lives—their most private feelings, experiences, and conflicts. Though I did not assign a grade to an essay beyond judging whether it was acceptable, I did feel compelled to discuss grammar, organization, voice, tone, and the other elements of writing. Would students be able to accept my criticisms of their writing without feeling that I was making a judgment of their lives?

Third, although I emphasized that they did not have to be personal in their writings, would students feel manipulated into self-disclosure; and, if so, might they become at risk? Could writing about suicide trigger suicide? Of the over one thousand students who have taken my literature-and-psychoanalysis course, none has ever intimated, in diaries or course evaluations, that he or she felt at risk as a result of the course. Their diary identities, however, remain safely anonymous to classmates. But in the expository writing class, students might sign their names to an essay discussed in class and later regret it. I believe writing promotes health—indeed, I teach a graduate course called "Writing and Healing." Nevertheless, would I help or harm my expository writing students by encouraging self-disclosure?

These issues concerned me throughout the term. I had no intention at the beginning of the semester to write about the course, but toward the end of the semester I wondered whether other teachers and students might be interested in the results of our experiment. Two weeks before the term ended I asked my students for permission to use their writings for an essay on expressive writing. Following the University at Albany Human Institutional Review Board guidelines, I told my students that their participation in the research project was voluntary and that they would not be asked for permission to use their writings until after they had completed the course. They could make whatever factual changes they wished to preserve anonymity. Additionally, I promised them that before I submitted my essay for publication, I would send each of them a copy of that section containing his or her writings. Students could withdraw permission if they felt uncomfortable with the way I used their writings.

All nineteen students gave me permission to use their writings, but I shall focus here on one student, Nick. Though he never uses the word "shame," his writings explore a frightening childhood event that produced intense feelings of humiliation, powerlessness, violation, depression, and rage—essential elements of shame. Nick was taking a calculated risk in gradually disclosing this experience, one which he was willing to take only at the end of the semester, when he felt secure enough with his classmates to reveal a secret that he had shared only with his immediate family.

Nick's writing is important not only for the story he tells but for the way he tells it and for its impact on his classmates. I cannot capture in a brief essay the dynamics of Nick's class—the ways in which students, slowly and tentatively at first, then more self-assuredly, came to trust and support each other, developing a bond that made possible remarkable self-disclosures. Nevertheless, readers will see how Nick opens up to his classmates and responds to their acceptance of him. This gradual self-revelation stands at the center of Nick's story. Shame is probably the most unspeakable of emotions, for unlike guilt, which reflects pain arising from an act or thought, shame involves the violation of the self. Nick's writings dramatize the unmasking of shame—expressing the inexpressible. The process of writing leads to nothing less than the reclaiming of the self. In several of his essays, Nick uses the metaphor of a "barrier" to describe how this childhood event has isolated him from his contemporaries. In the following pages, we will see how Nick lets down this barrier, allowing his readers a glimpse into his life.

In quoting from Nick's writings, I have not changed a word nor a punctuation mark. There are occasional grammatical, spelling, and typographical mistakes. These errors are minor, as when he misspells the name of Robert Louis Stevenson's tormented hero, Dr. Jekyll. (Even though I pointed out the correct spelling on an early essay, Nick persisted with the misspelling on a later essay.) I have not bracketed these errors with the customary "sic" and have resisted the temptation to make silent emendations. I would remind anyone inclined to judge these errors harshly that Nick had no idea his essays would be published someday. Nick is a good writer striving to become a better one, and in rereading his writings he now wishes to rewrite them. Throughout the semester he was extremely critical of his own writing and insisted that I be "tough" on his prose. He was, in fact, less interested in my praise than in my criticism. He was also one of the most rigorous critics of his classmates' prose, though he was always fair and balanced in his comments.

GETTING TO KNOW EACH OTHER

For the first writing assignment, which I modified from Scholes and Comley's *The Practice of Writing*, I sought to encourage the students to introduce themselves to each other:

> Part 1: Draw up a chronology of ten important events in your life, ranging from birth to the present. For each event, write a paragraph on its significance. Such events may include your first day in school, the birth or death of a relative, your first love experience, a particular success or failure, a serious illness, a memorable college experience, an event that shaped your career plans, etc. Provide enough factual material for the details of your life to be known to another person, and enough psychological material to make your biography interesting. The chronological events should focus on the past but also suggest the kind of person you are now and how you might be in the future.
>
> Part 2: After you have drawn up this chronology, exchange it with a classmate. Your classmate will read your chronology, interview you for additional material, and get to know the salient details of your life. You will do the same with your classmate, interviewing him or her for additional information. Your classmate will go home and write a biography of you, using your material as a basis for the biography. Just as your classmate is writing a biography of you, so will you be writing a biography of him or her.

Nick's first biographical event was striking and mysterious:

> *At the age of fifteen, a brother, my twin, was taken from my family and me. He was taken by a series of events that are senseless and to this day not fully understandable, and are all the more painful because of this. He was dead upon his 2:54 PM arrival at an upstate New York hospital, on August 17, 1982. He had been in a car accident with a family relative, one who was called Uncle, but who was really our Mother's cousin. He was close to our family, like an "Uncle." He took Stephen and I skiing, and to the movies; he gave us rides to places we'd be embarrassed to be dropped at by our parents; he was our friend. Is it fortunate or unfortunate that during that summer I spent less time with*

*both Stephen and John, in running and training for my fall cross coun-
try season? That's a question that will haunt me forever.*

*The details behind the accident are many and strange. They
include Stephen's unannounced trip, a few blocks across town, to my
"Uncle's"; their decision to go for a drive in the country in John's MG;
the discovery that Stephen was behind the wheel when the accident
occurred; his death, and John's (my "Uncle's) survival of the accident;
the signs of sexual abuse found on the scene and on Stephen's body;
and the general lack of information for the family when they declined
to press charges to avoid public disgrace. These last few details are the
most upsetting. We will never know the facts behind this senseless accident. And it may seem strange to one looking at this from the outside
that charges were not pressed, but you must understand, 1982 held
much different reactions to sexual abuse than 1995. I don't know if my
parents did the best they could have done for the family, but they did
the best they could at the time with the knowledge they had.*

*I'll never fully understand the depth of this accident's effect on me,
though I've spent the last five years trying to. In it's most obvious
effects, it has shut me down emotionally and to some degrees mentally.
I spent my high school years in a daze, separated from those around
me by a barrier that I erected. At twenty eight, I'm just beginning to be
able to look over that barrier, but I have not yet knocked it down
entirely. This event hasn't just shaped me and my life. Unfortunately,
it has defined it, by causing me to live in separation from the world
around me. It has eclipsed any and all events that preceded it in my life
and colored any events that followed it.*

Nick begins the second biographical event by noting that he looks
back at his high school years with no fondness whatsoever. "I never
knew who knew about the family scandal, and I tried not to think
about it, but at the back of my head, I felt as though everyone knew."
None of the many academic and athletic awards Nick received in high
school meant anything to him, nor did he allow anyone to come close
to him.

College was much better for Nick than high school, and his other
eight biographical events are more positive than the first two. In college
he was initiated into the "wonderfully many and diverse worlds of
music, art, film, photography, creativity, sex, friendship, politics,
drugs, and fashion." He formed close friendships; studied film, photography, and journalism; and traveled and studied abroad. Upon
returning from Europe, he completed college and moved to the South-
east, where he found employment. Feeling lonely and depressed, he
returned to upstate New York and fell in love with a woman whom he
married. He has learned about himself through her. "In her eyes I see
myself as hero and villain, the two extremes, Dr. Jeckyl and Mr. Hyde.

I now realize that it is only through another that one can see anything of himself."

Nick closes his biographical sketch by observing that the love and support he now receives from his parents and wife have allowed him to move forward to a new phase of his life:

> *I'm getting on, trying to move past the pain of my past and enjoy the me that I slowly discover. It's a wondrously slow and challenging process to see yourself as who you really are, beyond just the image you see in the mirror, and the one that exists in your mind, but the you that walks and talks and lives with others, and works and walks the dogs and shops for groceries. To this aim I have returned to school to become an English teacher; the career I have wanted for the past six years, but was afraid to pursue. As a returning student, I'm getting to live the cliche, "I wish I had known then, what I know now." For I do know now, the things I need to know, and the things I still need to learn. I have realized that it's the process of this learning that is life. Everyday we all come a little bit closer to catching ourselves peeking into the mental mirror. One day soon I'll be able to look at myself full-on and like what I see.*

Nick gave his ten chronological events to his classmate Ellen, who, combining his words with her own, proceeded to write his biography. Though she does not devote much attention to the psychological damage he suffered following his brother's death, she empathizes with his loss:

> *If the pain of losing a brother wasn't bad enough, the strange and upsetting details to the incident, and the fact that he would never know the truth behind the accident were. Nick could only wonder about why Stephen was driving the car, and why there was evidence of sexual abuse. Charges were not pressed in order to avoid negative public attention. It's no wonder that Nick would erect such a barrier that would keep him from getting close to people. How frightening the idea of letting someone in must have been to someone who had just lost his best friend.*

In reading Ellen's thoughtful biographical sketch of Nick—I did not have access to his ten chronological events, which were to be turned in at the end of the semester—I was puzzled by the reference to sexual abuse. I wrote the following comment on her essay: "All of this is very mysterious—too mysterious, I think. I would omit the detail about sexual abuse or develop it further." I don't know if Nick's classmates were as curious about this enigmatic event as I was, but in the following weeks I found myself buried beneath an avalanche of essays and soon forgot about it.

WRITING ABOUT DEPRESSION AND SUICIDE

Nick did not refer to this subject again until the middle of the semester, when I asked the class to read the chapter in *Diaries to an English Professor* called "Suicide Survivors" and write an essay on one or more of the following questions:

1. What are your feelings about suicide? Do you think a person has the right to take his or her own life? Do others have the right or obligation to prevent suicide?

2. Do you know anyone who has attempted or committed suicide? How did that attempted or completed suicide affect you?

3. Were you able to identify with any of the diarists in the chapter? If so, which ones? Why?

4. Have you ever seriously thought about suicide? If so, when? Did you ever tell anyone you were feeling suicidal?

5. How did you feel about my discussion of my friend Len's suicide? Did it change your impression of me? If so, how? In general, how do you feel about a teacher's self-disclosure?

6. Did you find yourself strongly agreeing or disagreeing with anything I wrote in the chapter? Please be specific.

7. Have you ever written about suicide before? Do you like or dislike this writing assignment? Was this a relatively easy or difficult subject to write on? Did this assignment put you at risk?

Focusing more on depression than on suicide, Nick opens his five-page essay with a haunting personification developed at great length:

> *Depression is a strange dark beast that slowly and quietly invades a mind. There, it grows, feeding off its host, turning thoughts black and tasty, assuring its own survival. In the beginning, few thoughts come or go that have not been nibbled on by its sharp and rotting teeth. Its greasy, dirty fingers then begin to touch and violate all. It stirs up the vicious cycle of apathy breeding pessimism, giving rise to melancholy. The animal gets stronger. It stretches and tests its power. Eventually it takes over. It cultivates its own nourishment. Its growing season is short, dark and howling. Before long every thought is a dismal one; joyous memories are mauled and twisted out of shape; what was once optimism is beaten into hopelessness. Eventually a door is slammed shut on the dwindling light at the end of the tunnel and the candles of the past, that had lighted the way and given strength, are turned blood red, the color of lies and hate and betrayal. Nothing that was or is can be seen clearly, but only through the dimness of depression's smoky, foul breath.*

Nick reveals later in the essay that in his mid-twenties he suffered from depression resembling the gloom he experienced earlier in his life. Nothing in his life—not reading, biking, talking with friends, or work— brought him pleasure. Looking in front of the television screen for hours, he saw only the reflection of his life, years highlighted with loss, betrayal, isolation, and torment. He again alludes to Stevenson's novel of the divided self but without mentioning his reactions upon learning of his twin brother's death:

> *The more I searched for the worthiness in me and my life, the more I saw the past loss, hate, and betrayal; the more I felt I was weak, lazy, and wrong in every decision presented to me. I brutally dissected my past, invalidating any bit of good that was there as superficial and irrelevant to the situation at hand. I second-guessed every decision I had made, and judged that all were the wrong ones. I indicted myself as the sole cause of all my misery. I began to dislike myself more and more, until I truly hated what was in me as if it were something independent and tangible, a monstrous me within the shell of an innocent and overwhelmed me. I was hating and hurting the Mr. Hyde within my Dr. Jeckyl. I decided it was time to destroy the monster. The only question that remained was: could I still save the man, were the two that separable?*

Without disclosing the reasons for his depression, Nick observes that the most powerful deterrent to suicide during this period in his life was his family. They loved him for the positive traits that he did not always see in himself. Slowly he emerged from his depression, realizing that he could learn to live with the monster, a self-integration Stevenson's tormented character never achieves. Nick ends the essay by giving credit to therapy; he is confident about "fight[ing] off the monster I have been working so hard to keep at bay" should it spring upon him again.

"A LIE COVERING UP A MUCH MORE PAINFUL TRUTH"

Nick's next essay was a revelation, one which proved to be a turning point for him and the class:

> *The time has come to confess to a lie; that, and to share something few know about me. I'm not sure why I feel I must share this but I've felt it coming out since I began to write the first essay for this class. It was there that the lie began. Now, it will end. This essay is an experiment for me, an experiment in self-acceptance and emotional control. So in the spirit of introspection, acceptance, empathy, and admission to the truth, here goes . . .*
> *The first entry in my chronicle of ten life shaping events was a lie. Unfortunately, it's a lie covering up a much more painful truth. It's not*

a good lie, but it's the best I could come up with at the time. There was no twin brother; there was no car accident and there was no death. There was only me and John, a family relative, who was also a child molester. I was the child. The dates are true to the best of my recollection, and the results you read were the true end results. Though, the end has not yet been reached. I couldn't chronicle ten events in my life without this one because it has defined who I am. I also couldn't admit it to a bunch of strangers on our second day of class. Now, I am ready.

I was sexually abused, cunningly and systematically, for what seemed like years. I'm not sure how long the abuse went on. My heart says years; my head says it might not have been that long. I will never know. My feelings and reactions read like a textbook case in abuse. My silence was won through naive trust and bribery. I said nothing to no one. I'm still hesitant to speak of the abuse to others for fear that they will think less of me, the victim.

But I am no longer a victim. I gave up that role a long time ago. I don't handle pity too well, either my own or others'. The acceptance of this event in my life has been difficult. Initially I just ignored it. I didn't block it out as many do; I simply didn't let it affect me. This worked for ten years or more. It worked well enough for me to actually forgive my uncle, enough that I thought about telling him this in person. I never did, however. As I went through the various stages of acceptance, I developed two sides: one sensitive and empathic to everyone's emotional difficulty, and another, devoid of all emotion when it came to self. Unfortunately the inhuman side seems to dominate when problems arise with those closest to me.

Several years ago I began battling with depression. It seemed to come out of nowhere, and I'll probably never know the true cause behind it. I began to wonder. As I sunk deeper and deeper, I looked back on my life for the first time and blamed the abuse from years ago on my present situation. I realized that everyday of my past had been altered just a bit by this sick and selfish man. As I further retraced my path, I wondered what would have been. I became furious. I felt that a monster had been created within the man I should have been. How could someone take another's life and twist it so out of shape, then fade into the distance? My anger rose to new heights. I lay in bed one night and planned how I could get away with killing my abuser. I seriously thought about taking his life. I have since considered blackmail, harassment, and legal battle; I still haven't ruled out physical violence. It seems to me now that sexual abuse was not the reason for my depression, but depression was the catalyst which prompted me to deal with sexual abuse.

The death of a twin, a part of me, was the only suitable disguise I could find for my ugly past. The real death was that of my innocence and childhood. A huge piece of me was sliced out on the day John first decided that I would be his little sex toy. As the days became years, my mind compensated for what had been killed. I wish I could explain what that kind of abuse does to a young boy and the man that follows, but I haven't yet reached that point of understanding myself. Right now every hard fought answer comes surrounded in question.

I continued to visit my uncle regularly after the abuse started. I didn't understand what was happening. He was an adult and my friend; why would he involve me in something bad, hurtful? At times I even thought that in some strange way he was doing something for me. I just couldn't understand how. I blindly trusted him, as only a child could. Several years of his manipulation and abuse later, my father and brother showed up at his house unannounced. The truth exploded out into the world. What they found, I can never imagine from their perspective. There was their son and brother naked on the bed of their trusted relative. It is only by fate and my father's restraint that John lived.

What followed for me was a summer of conflicting emotion and confusion. I gave a statement to the police, then I was cut out of the proceedings. My parents tried to shelter me, to save me from this bomb that had been dropped into our life. I don't think they knew that this had been going on for several years and that anything for me would be easier than continuing the abuse. I never admitted to them its duration for fear of their disappointment that I didn't come to them for protection. They asked me if I thought I needed counseling, but I said no. I was a teenager, all I wanted to do was move on. In the end, my parents dropped all charges against John in order to protect me from the publicity that it would generate in the small town. I immediately put the days of abuse behind me.

Thirteen years later it still amazes me that I was the victim of sexual abuse at the hands of a man who was old enough to be my father. Whenever I think about it, my mind becomes so paralyzed with conflicted emotion that I have to put it aside. Only once in the past was I able to write about it. It was almost two years ago. I wrote a letter with the hopes of releasing some of the emotions that were devastating me at the time. I can't bring myself to edit the original emotion of the letter. It's not eloquent and it's not pretty:

25 February, 1994
You dirty sick bastard. . . . Many years ago you took something from me that I can never really get back . . . ever. . . . My innocence and youth. Can you imagine how that feels??? To have part of yourself missing . . . I doubt you can. I doubt you even really know what I'm talking about or maybe even who I am. Let me refresh your memory . . .

Many years ago you were caught in bed with a little boy!!! That may not even clarify things because I'm sure there was more than one. But who cares who I am . . . you will never know who I am, so I'll appoint myself as spokesman for all the children you may have abused and molested, and all the children that other sick bastards just like you rape and fuck up for the rest of their lives.

First of all let me say that I hope you have lived a horrible, tortured, guilt ridden life and that you regret your acts daily. I hope you sincerely want to die. I hope nightly you wake up screaming and sweating thinking of all the evil that's inside you. If you have forgiven yourself, reconsider because what you did is so inexcusable to me or any other normal person. I hope your life has been ruined by your actions (if it hasn't, give me some time and I'll ruin it by mine). I want you to live in HELL every day that you are on this earth, and when you die I'll feel a bit better because I'm sure then you'll truly be where you deserve to be with others like you.

You took the youth, innocence, adolescence, and life from a child. A CHILD. What the FUCK were you thinking? . . . And to think for a time I forgave you and felt that you didn't mean to do what you did. That you were sick, that you had good intentions at heart, that you didn't want to hurt me. Where the fuck have I been? I'll tell you where. . . . With my head in the sand afraid to hurt the loved ones around me by bringing this horrible incident in my life back up. I did that because I wasn't ready to deal with the anger deep within me, but now that my mind and my life are at a point to be ready, I welcome the anger and I try to bring it out. I'm no longer worried about hurting any of my loved ones, because I know they would want me to be rid of the hurt I feel. I was going to face you in person (and I still may) but I am truly afraid of what I'd do to you. I want to tear you apart and watch you suffer and plead. I want to pound you around that house of yours, so I can drive down that street and not have to hide my eyes when I pass it. I want to hold my head up and get the weight off that's been holding it down for so many years. To do that I want to knock your head off.

You victimized a boy because you knew you would have power and control, but now I have the control, and I'm sure you never considered what the boy might do to you twenty years later. You never thought of one single thing except your sick, perverted desires. Of yourself. You never gave one second of consideration to the young boy who's dick you had in your hand as often as you could get it there. What in HELL did you think would become of that situation? That it would go on forever, that it would just end without a trace and everyone would be okay? The entire time you were molesting me I feared being caught most of all. In my young mind I thought I was doing something wrong. Well FUCK that!!! I did nothing, except not turn you in. If I had only known. . . . You didn't think of my family, of my friends, of my life and what this would do to it, of how I'd be affected at twenty-seven years old, of how this would potentially eat at me forever and fuck up my life. You selfish, sick, perverted, piece of shit, worthless bastard!!!!!

You should dread every knock at the door and every phone call, because you never know where I might choose to approach you . . . at work (do your friends and co-workers know what you've done in your past??) . . . at home (do your neighbors know??) . . . in the street . . . I haven't decided myself. All I know is that you are no longer off the hook as far as I'm concerned. I don't know what you have suffered on account of your actions, but it's not enough. Nothing is enough! What I do know is that I want your life ruined. I want you to live in tortured hell for the rest of your life. I want to take from you so you know how it feels, and I want you to know that you deserve everything you get. I'm going to release all the anger and hurt that I've suppressed for years. Release it and move on with my life, putting my head back together and putting you as far behind me as is possible, but . . . I WILL NEVER FORGIVE YOU!!!!!

Don't misinterpret this as a threat of physical violence, because I don't think I'm like that. I've never struck anyone in anger (but if I do, rest assured that it WILL be you.) I'd love to pound the shit out of you. I'd love to dominate you like you did me. I'd love to be in the control position and hurt you over and over, but that's not in me, at least yet. All I want is to completely ruin your life . . . forever. . . .

> *Very Sincerely,*
> *Nick*

After I wrote this letter, I wrote nothing more for over a year: no journal, no letters, no nothing. Words stopped coming. It is only within the past six months that I have again turned to my computer keyboard for the consoling that only it knows how to give. I find that in my time away, the thinking I have done has moved me to a new level of awareness. I am getting closer to knowing myself as who I am. I can embrace my past and be thankful for the inner strength it has given me. I am finally starting to like the person that looks back at me from the bathroom mirror.

It has taken me over ten years to reopen the inner box that has held all these emotions tight. It feels good. Depression is behind me for now, and I see a million goals ahead. Everyday I grow and learn. My battle with the past is not won yet, nor will it ever be. I will always continue to fight to regain the unknown but tragically missed piece of me that was taken away so many summers ago. But only recently have I been able to turn and fight head on instead of turning to flee. I have found that the enemy is not so strong when you can actually see it.

My heart goes out to any and all in this class who may be the victims of similar abuse.

Reading Nick's essay, I felt first shock and horror, then admiration. I had never read a student paper containing more shame, anger, and hurt, yet the writer expresses his feelings with power and eloquence. He tells us in the first paragraph that the essay is an experiment in self-acceptance and emotional control, and after reading the essay, with its righteous fury expressed in nearly flawless language, one can only agree that the experiment is a success. Writing about himself with remarkable objectivity and detachment, he acknowledges a lie designed to conceal a terrible truth; now ready to reveal that truth, he also confesses to his own dark impulses. What makes the essay more authentic is the furious emotion within the unedited journal entry, written nearly two years earlier. The contrast between Nick's past rage and present composure is striking. Recognizing that he will probably never be able to forget or overcome entirely the psychological effects of sexual abuse, he nevertheless demonstrates the progress he has made. In expressing the shame he has experienced for so many years, Nick is able to confront and, to a large extent, exorcise his inner demon.

NARCISSISTIC INJURIES

Though I did not realize it until after the course was over, when I had the opportunity to study his writings closely, Nick's description of shame recalls the traumatic injuries experienced by many nineteenth- and twentieth-century fictional characters. For example, *Frankenstein*, *Wuthering Heights*, and *Great Expectations* portray characters who are victimized by crimes committed against them in childhood. These crimes awaken within the Creature, Heathcliff, and Pip, respectively, feelings of intense shame, a response to the perception that the self is radically defective or deficient. The narcissistic injuries experienced by these characters produce shattered identities, heightened vulnerability, empathic disturbances, and massive rage.

The theme of the dark double pervading these and other novels about the divided self may be seen in Nick's metaphor of the "monster" threatening to destroy him. The death of his "twin brother" represents the split off part of the self. The victim's feeling of complicity is perhaps the most insidious aspect of sexual abuse of children. The violence committed against a child's body penetrates the spirit and produces unspeakable suffering.

For thirteen years Nick had concealed his shameful secret from everyone outside his immediate family. During the three months in which he was a member of English 300, he had carefully considered whether to open himself up to his classmates' and teacher's scrutiny. Writing about the experience, he unmasked his shame—and therein gambled that he would not expose himself to further humiliation.

OPPOSITION TO PERSONAL WRITING

Encouraging students like Nick to write about shameful feelings is bound to provoke strong criticism from educators. Some may believe that, by promoting personal writing, teachers abdicate their responsibility to train students in traditional academic discourse. David Bartholomae, an influential composition theorist, has argued recently that personal writing is a "corrupt, if extraordinarily tempting genre." Bartholomae calls such writing sentimental realism. "I don't want my students to celebrate what would then become the natural and inevitable details of their lives" (71).

Bartholomae's dismissal of personal writing in favor of traditional academic writing reflects in my view a false dichotomy. In an age that privileges theory, it is unfortunate that the personal has been banished. Too often personal writing is equated with solipsistic writing—as if writing about the self is an act of self-blindness. The repudiation of personal writing not only devalues a long and honorable tradition of autobiographical writing but also deprives students of the opportunity for self-discovery.

Other educators, like Ann Murphy, believe that teachers of personal writing may regard themselves as therapists and thereby endanger their students' health. She fears that students will unwittingly open a Pandora's box of problems. Susan Swartzlander and her colleagues also warn that students who were victimized in the past may become victimized again through personal writing.

WRITING ABOUT A PAINFUL SUBJECT

Much of the evidence against personal or expressive writing is anecdotal, but rarely do students have the opportunity to comment on the rewards and risks of such writing. In an effort to discover how my students felt about personal writing, I gave them the following assignment near the end of the course:

> Although there are differences between personal writing and psychotherapy, there are also important similarities. Both involve the process of self-discovery and the attempt to arrive at interpretations of experience. Both bring to the surface tensions, conflicts, and even traumas which, as a result of being expressed, may lead to cathartic relief.
>
> Choose one of the painful personal essays you have written in English 300 and then discuss whether you felt better or worse as a result of writing about it. Had you ever written about this experience before? Were you surprised by what you wrote? Would you have pre-

ferred to remain anonymous during our discussion of your essay? Was it useful to have another person read your essay? How did it feel to have your classmates or teacher respond to your essay?

Here is Nick's response:

I couldn't get through the semester without writing about my darkened past. Thoughts and visions welled up with each accumulated assignment. My life, my parents, my thoughts of depression and suicide; they all brought me back to the abuse I experienced as a youth. I couldn't avoid it any longer; the time was right to give my past the recognition it deserved in writing. At last, I welcomed the opportunity. The truth is that without me, my paper began writing itself almost three months ago.

As I watched the semester progress, I saw also the pattern of assignments develop. Read a chapter; write about it. I skimmed through Diaries to an English Professor *to see just what was in store for us. The first chapter I read in the first week of class was "Sexual Disclosures." I realized then that writing about my abuse would be inevitable if I was to remain true to who I am. After all the searching I have done for answers about sexual abuse and what it does to an individual, I couldn't cover it up again. I had to own up and face it. I felt guilty enough presenting the charade I had in the first assignment. I felt I had taken a step back in my hard and long fought march forward; I had watered down a past that made me uncomfortable. I had to show the truth of who I am. For who are we, and what is writing without honesty? The paper grew without me.*

I had no fear in writing my essay. In fact, the atmosphere of safety generated by the class made me comfortable with the thoughts I gave credence to. I knew I had a sympathetic non-judgmental audience for at least three hours, but probably beyond that. The worst that could happen was that my writing would be criticized. (That is also the best thing that could happen. God knows, I need it.) As many others in class have admitted, this is a support group of sorts. There are few places where you can admit to, even speak, the absolute truth without fear. One is the psychiatrist's couch, the other is a stranger's ear. Our classroom has elements of both. And as we have seen and read, admission is a big step toward healing.

As I wrote, I wrote for myself and for the class. This is the first group I could safely reveal my truth to. I had to take that step and more. I had to shine a light on a problem that is forever shrouded in haze. As a society, we are afraid of sexual abuse; not as afraid as we used to be, but afraid all the same. It is so ugly and brutal that no one wants to run the risk of further victimization by those around them when they admit their truth.

The truth of sexual abuse is that it leaves the victim with ambivalent feelings about themselves both physically and mentally. They share the blame with their abusers, and are sensitive to how the world sees them. The lines between abuser and abused can be very skewed in the mind of the victim. Thus it takes very little in the way of disapproval for them to re-silence the truth they so want to scream out. Any hint of disapproval or discrimination is a continuation of an abuse that will not end. After years of silence, fear and pain, I no longer worry about appearance and disapproval. I know who I am and accept that. The world's stare no longer keeps me silent. My opinion is if my words disturb you, you can dismiss them with your denial, pity, or blame; it makes no difference to me. The strong and open minded will embrace what I say and ask how it could be so. It is the latter that solve the problems of this world and change the future.

I refuse to be labeled a victim, a survivor, or a degenerate. I will be an avenger. I want to avenge the wrong that was done to me and millions of other children. My essay was one of the early steps in that quest, for until we can speak about abuse in concrete, non-judgmental terms, no one will come forward. The truth will remain locked in the minds of the abused, where it spins and turns like a rock in a jeweler's tumbler, losing its rough edges and original shape, only coming out when it's attractive to the eye and smooth to the touch. Abuse will perpetuate itself in millions of lives that could have been saved through empathy and self-understanding. There should be no stigma in being an abused child. Our world has enough illusion; let's face some cold, brutal reality for a change. Believe it or not, it's freeing.

Before I wrote my essay, I reread the letter I had written the year before. I loved it's anger. It was my first and most formal declaration of anger and hurt at the man who so altered my life at his whim. My anger hasn't changed since then, but it has become more refined. I am no longer afraid of it, but welcome it as a healthy emotion. As I understand more about myself, and how I have been shaped by sexual abuse, I feel more comfortable with my emotions. I still have not taken any actions against my abuser, and maybe never will. I now let my mind dictate my actions. I don't force issues and I don't turn away from them. When they come up, or bring me down, I face them and resolve them. Here I oversimplify the process greatly, for it has taken years for me to face some issues, and still more years for me to understand and deal with them.

My essay was one more step in the process of resolution. As abstract thoughts become ink on paper, they enter the world of the writer. For the first time, they can stare into my face, and I into theirs, instead of them staring out from within, while I see nothing. On the page thoughts become real; when spoken, still more real.

I value the opportunity this class has afforded me to examine my reality and share it with a few sympathetic strangers. It has also provided me with the impetus, safety and structure to write such an important essay (important to me, that is) without fear; the fear of losing control over the subject, and the fear of the judgment of my peers. It took me a long time of searching, not for the right words in the essay but the reason. Now it is out and I am better for that.

Especially intriguing is Nick's observation that both the worst and the best that could happen to his writing is that it would be criticized. Anyone reading his essays must be aware of how important language is to him, how he regards it as essential to his continued recovery. Language is both a defensive and offensive weapon to Nick: it holds in check dangerous emotions that threaten to overwhelm the self, and it is the instrument of choice to avenge past humiliations. Such writing serves many purposes, enabling one to express and purge toxic emotions, master intolerable fears, memorialize loss, avenge wrongs, create a lasting record of experiences, connect with readers, and unify a divided self.

WRITING AS THERAPY

Creative writers have long known the therapeutic benefits of self-expression, believing, as D. H. Lawrence did, that "One sheds one['s] sicknesses in books—repeats and presents again one['s] emotions, to be master of them" (*Letters*, 2: 90). Or as Sylvia Plath observed, "Fury jams the gullet and spreads poison, but, as soon as I start to write, dissipates, flows out into the figure of the letters: writing as therapy?" (*Journals*, 256). Writing is not always completely or permanently effective—Sylvia Plath committed suicide during the height of her creative powers—yet it is often helpful. The research psychologist James Pennebaker has shown in his book *Opening Up* that writing about one's problems not only makes one feel better but also strengthens the body's immune system. A growing number of scholars, including Alice Glarden Brand, Ira Progoff, Tristine Rainer, Jerome Bump, and Marian MacCurdy, have concluded that writing promotes healing both in and outside the classroom.

Ironically, though Nick wrote his essay on child sexual abuse expecting it to be discussed in class, I had to inform the students that new essays would not be read in class for the next two weeks because of a backlog of papers. When Nick heard me say this, he felt both relieved and disappointed—he later told me wryly that I had given him a "reprieve." As soon as I read his essay, however, I realized it would be valuable for the entire class to discuss it, and so I telephoned Nick and requested him to bring twenty copies the following week. I also asked him if he was willing to write a brief essay describing his feelings during the class discussion. He was eager to comply:

As I sat before class, I tried not to think about what I was about to do, to reveal about myself. Thoughts kept creeping back. Would everyone, in unison look up at me, horrified by my past? Would they gasp in horror? Would they slide their chairs a little bit further away? Would I break down and have to leave the room? Would I be unable to face them? Or would we be presented with an overwhelming and uncomfortable silence? Would they find my essay and my revelation to them extreme and inappropriate? As fast as my uncertainty piled up, I crushed it to the back of my mind. I had carried these thoughts and these papers too far not to give them their due.

Once in class, I nonchalantly dropped the stack of essays face down on the desk. In my mind the papers fell as if in a movie: an extreme close up as the papers fall in very slow motion, filling the screen and crushing the viewer; they fall as a single stack, landing on the desk, with an overwhelming and deep thump; they compress slightly as they hit, then bounce and settle into place, each slightly askew. The deed had been done, and my truth would be known. I could have turned back anytime, but I never considered it. Now there was no turning back; the class had the paper in their hands. Since the paper was held till last, I spent two hours unable to truly concentrate on the work at hand. I read and responded to what I could, the entire time thinking, "let's just get this over with." At last, that time came.

Everyone began to read. The silence grew thick and heavy like I was underwater. I tried to read along, but could not. I pretended to read; I read certain sentences, and I fidgeted in my seat. The lights hummed louder and louder. I couldn't look up for fear that anyone would look me in the eyes with anything resembling disapproval or, even worse, disgust. The only sound I heard was that of pages flipping louder and louder as the minutes slowly ticked away. What the hell had I done? Was I thinking clearly in deciding to do this? What had made me do it? I had to. . . . It seemed they would never stop reading. Finally, they did. All sat in silence, stunned, uncomfortable or both. Finally I looked up and tried to smile feebly as if to apologize for what I had done, what I had put them through. Again I wondered at the appropriateness of my confession to the class.

After an uncertain silence, the discussion began. To my relief, but not to my surprise, no one moved away from me and no one gasped. In fact I felt as if all took a step toward me in support and maybe amazement. The first comment was that the reader felt as if she had just witnessed a horrible accident, a second reader said she was on the verge of tears. As others confessed their horror, sickness, and disgust at my abuser, I felt my lips raised into a sincere and heartfelt smile. I wondered about the appropriateness of my expression. I figured that I should try to look sincere and serious about such an event in my life. I tried to suppress the smile, but it flowed through my body. It came for two reasons.

For the first time in my life a roomful of twenty people all knew who I was, and what I'd been through in my life. I had momentarily dropped the barrier that I have so carefully erected over the years. The class seemed to understand. They expressed understanding for the past I have shown them, and the past I have not. They tried to understand more; they asked questions; they wanted to know. In trying to understand me and empathize with me, the class has helped me take one more step toward understanding and accepting myself. I had to smile at the open acceptance I felt after my admission of such a horrible event.

My smile also came from my sense of accomplishment as a writer. As all know I am my own harshest critic, but for a few minutes I was happy with something I had written. It had affected. It had an effect. My writing had taken on life before my eyes. Today, I would rewrite much of the essay, and I realize its content probably had more effect than its style. But it did have life, independent of me, for a short time. For the first time in my life, I felt a rush of adrenaline from a page of prose. It recommitted me to the life of the writer. Although I still would not label myself as a writer, I felt like one for awhile.

As my smile grew, I felt guilty and overjoyed at the classes responses. I was sorry that I had hurt them so, but glad that they could feel empathy deeply enough to hurt. I had no idea what to expect, but I couldn't have asked for a better response from the class. I knew that all were on my side, and had vividly glimpsed, however fleetingly, a painful piece of my life.

It would be false to say that I feel better as a result of the class. Twenty years of scarring doesn't heal that easily. I do feel that I have taken steps forward. I know now that there are twenty people who can either accept me or not based on the truth of who I am, with no falsity. It's hard to admit to something that I have kept in the dark for so long, but it feels freeing to be able to.

RESPONDING TO EXPRESSIVE WRITING

One of the course's biggest surprises was that although it seemed odd at first to correct comma splices or faulty subject-verb agreement in a personal essay, students expected and welcomed grammatical criticisms. Two students, including Nick, complained during the middle of the semester that I was not being rigorous enough in my class criticisms—a complaint I took seriously and tried to rectify. It is true that in discussing the more wrenching essays, we spoke more about content than form, and in a few cases, as with Nick's essay on sexual abuse, we talked almost entirely about how we felt while reading it. But I always made technical corrections on my own copy, which I returned to the students the following week.

Different teachers have different styles when reading student essays;

my own style is to circle every grammatical, spelling, and typographical error. This strategy may become counterproductive, especially if a teacher's tone becomes angry or impatient, but I believe most students want to improve their writing. When students realize that others take their work seriously, they, too, take their work seriously.

More important than my technical comments on student essays are the affirming, validating ones. Effective teaching is affective teaching; intellectual and emotional development go hand in hand. I praise my students' writing in order to be what Heinz Kohut calls a "mirroring selfobject," that is, an extension of themselves, and thus to help them realize their potential. It is seldom hard to find something to praise in their personal essays, whether it is their willingness to confront a challenging subject, their emotional openness, or a felicitous phrase. I always thank students for sharing personal information with me. Corny as it may seem, sometimes I pen a happy face at the bottom of an essay to indicate how touched I am by it. Whenever I come across an essay that I think other people might like to read, I encourage the writer to share the contents with them.

At the bottom of Nick's essay on his close relationship to his father and mother, for example, I urged him to send a copy to them. Sometimes I suggest, as tactfully as possible, that the writer has not yet fully succeeded in conveying an idea or feeling to the reader. When Nick mentioned in his essay on depression that he had been in therapy and that he had reached insights about himself, I wrote in the margin: "Do you want to share any of these self-revelations with the reader? I think it would be helpful. Otherwise, the reader remains at a distance from you."

A THERAPEUTIC MODEL OF TEACHING

I realize that my model of teaching approaches a therapeutic one in affirming self-esteem, empathy, and personal development. In the words of one student,

> *I feel as though I know each of you to some extent, and vise versa, but there is some level of distance. We may talk about the intimate details of our lives in the classroom, but once outside of class we would most likely not call each other and "hang out." Actually, this class really is similar to my idea of a group therapy session. We talk about our problems, feel better and more connected, and then use the knowledge we have gained to help us in our other relationships. The classroom acts as a practice session of sorts in preparation for the real game, life. We work through the rough "spots," and then take our improved selves to the world. I suppose, although have no idea, that the relationship*

between a patient and his/her therapist is quite intimate, while maintaining a proper amount of distance. This is what this class is like for me, the perfect balance between distance and intimacy.

Both the teacher-student relationship and the therapist-patient relationship involve relational situations in which affective and cognitive issues are discussed from a variety of theoretical perspectives. As Lad Tobin points out, "most writing teachers know that therapeutic models can help explain and explore the teacher-student relationship, but because they find this comparison threatening they publicly deny it" (29). Self-discovery, which is so central to discussions of literature, writing, and psychotherapy, implies the willingness to change and grow. For all their obvious differences, Wendy Bishop notes, the humanities teacher and therapist both aim for empowerment.

Lest I be misunderstood, I must point out that I am careful not to "psychoanalyze" my students or their writing. I am neither trained nor inclined to offer clinical interpretations, and if I did, my students would surely experience them as inappropriate and intrusive. At no point in the semester did Nick or his classmates seek advice or counseling from me. Our class discussions inside and outside the classroom were generally limited to issues involving writing. Teachers need to observe professional boundaries and avoid playing the role of "prophet, saviour and redeemer" (Freud 50n). In this way, the problems associated with personal writing by Murphy and Swartzlander can be avoided.

"WAS I TOO HONEST?"

A colleague to whom I showed an early version of this essay made the intriguing observation that the class resembled the Catholic tradition of the confessional but without either absolution or confidentiality. I was surprised by how many people declined confidentiality when their highly personal essays were discussed in class. Some students who chose to remain anonymous noted that although classmates would probably guess their identity, they were still willing to disclose aspects of their lives.

I suspect that it was not only trust that enabled students to self-disclose but also the realization that they would never see each other again after the semester ended:

Letting a complete stranger read my most private thoughts about my parents divorce (among other things) made me feel vulnerable. Will they laugh . . . will they condemn? I am a very insecure person how can I trust these people? Every time I made copies, I would say "f@#$ it" *they don't know me. Will I realize the class probably knows more about me than any of my close friends do. I don't talk about my parent's divorce with my friends. So who cares I have to trust these strangers for a couple of months and they have to trust me. I feel we are a strong class, maybe because we know each others weakness'. Were we too honest . . . was I too honest? It doesn't matter I have only a few classes left I probably won't see most of the people in this class ever again.*

GENDER ISSUES

Because there were so few men in the class—only four—it is difficult to generalize about the role of gender in expressive writing. Based upon the introspective diaries students write in my courses on literature and psychoanalysis, women tend to be more self-disclosing than men, and they write about certain subjects that men rarely write about, such as eating disorders. Are women's shame issues deeper than men's? Is it harder for female students to feel that the classroom is a safe place for self-exposure of the kind Nick undertook? There are many important research questions for the future, including the extent to which the teacher's gender, age, and theoretical approach influence the form and content of student writings.

FINDING A SAFE PLACE

The unmasking of shame can be devastating as well as empowering, and one of the risks of personal writing is that students can never predict their teacher's or classmates' reactions to an essay. To my knowledge, no one ever felt humiliated by a response to an essay, though some (including Nick) were apprehensive before class discussion. To reduce this anxiety, I told the students that those who did not wish to disclose, anonymously, a personal experience to their classmates had the option to disclose it to me alone. They could thus "try out" an essay on me and then, if they felt secure, submit it to their classmates. Those who exercised this option often revised an essay before showing it to their classmates. The revisions revealed not only an improvement in the quality of prose but also greater emotional control.

THE IMPACT OF NICK'S ESSAY ON HIS CLASSMATES

Nick's essay on sexual abuse turned out to be liberating for several students, inspiring them to write about painful or shameful experiences that they had never revealed before. Nick's self-disclosure emboldened a male student to write about the sexual abuse he also encountered as a child, and in his next essay, he paid textual tribute to Nick:

> *When the paper on sexual disclosure Nick wrote was given to the class, I would have bet money I was the first person to read it. If I can remember correctly I was the only one who did not comment on it. I could not. I was so moved and so upset that any words I would have said would have never come out the way I wanted them to. I feel now I can say those words. The paper Nick wrote dredged up feelings from my past that I was not ready to deal with. It brought to light memories that have been eating me up for years. For the first time in my life I was able to transfer those memories from my mind to paper. Dealing with this issue was, for me, taking a step in reclaiming who I am. It is probably one of the biggest I will ever take. What Nick did I will never forget. I believe in my heart that I was not the only one Nick helped through helping himself. For me, however, it is the most I have ever learned from someone I have never really known. Thank you.*

Nick's essay encouraged another student to write about the most traumatic event in her life, her boyfriend's suicide:

> *After reading Nick's essay on the "truth," I decided that it was time for my own revelation. I sat down at the computer, but I couldn't write anything. I must have begun to re-write twenty times. Finally, two nights ago I was alone in my apartment. I just began typing and I finally finished six hours later. I had to take breaks to wipe the tears, blow my nose and wash my face. I was so emotionally drained that I went to sleep at 10 o'clock and slept for fourteen hours.*

Others shared agonizing personal experiences with their classmates. One woman wrote about the terror she experienced when she was date-raped at a party: the worst part of the experience, she said, was the fear that she would be disowned by her strict parents. A Latino man wrote about the shame he experienced when, upon moving into an all-white community, his parents received a petition from neighbors, demanding that they leave. A woman wrote a letter to her father expressing indignation over his constant belittling of her when she was younger. An alarming number of students wrote about their anguish growing up with alcoholic parents. Other students wrote about experiences with which they still could not come to terms. Witness this opening paragraph of an essay on abortion:

> *—was the day I killed my baby. Or, you could say it was the day I terminated my pregnancy. For me, both sentences mean the same thing. For others, it is a never ending debate between the respect for human life and the respect for human choice. I have to admit now that this is*

the first time that I have ever written about this event and I am not sure
if I am ready. However, I know that if I let this opportunity (this class)
go by, I may regret it for the rest of my life.

The students discovered the truth of Shoshana Felman's and Dori
Laub's observation in their book *Testimony* that one must have a witness in order to recover from a traumatic experience. Students bonded
and formed a close classroom community. In the words of one woman:

I am still completely astounded by the revelations that you, my fellow
class members, have shared. I can honestly state that I know more
about the lives of students in this course than I do about many of my
"closest friends." We are no longer acquaintances; we have become an
extended family that can be considered both diverse and unified.

AN EXTENDED FAMILY

The bond created among the members of the class did indeed resemble
that of an extended family. Most of the students were nineteen or twenty
years old, but two women were older, one in her fifties, the other in her
sixties. These two women wrote poignant essays about their families,
including the death of a husband and a child, and their presence in class
created a feeling of intergenerational connection. I always encouraged
students to view experience from as many perspectives as possible,
including both a child's and parent's. The students came to feel not only
that the family was an appropriate subject for an essay but that the class
itself was a kind of family. As in all families, tensions and "sibling rival-
ries" sometimes emerged but never became problematic.

THE TEACHER'S SELF-DISCLOSURES

As students came to trust each other, they revealed more about their
lives, and these self-disclosures encouraged others to reciprocate. I suspect that one reason students were willing to open up about their lives
was because they followed my own lead. I am highly self-disclosing in
my writing and teaching, and I have never felt that appropriate self-disclosure undermines a teacher's authority. Quite the opposite: when students realize that their teachers are human beings, able to acknowledge
hopes and fears, they often do their best work. As a student, I worked
hardest for those teachers who were willing to share aspects of their lives
with their class.

Research on self-disclosure indicates that the ability to reveal one's
feelings to another person promotes close relationships (Mikulincer and

Nachshon). Research also demonstrates that self-disclosure encourages reciprocity: "as one individual discloses more intimate information, his or her partner (often a confederate) also discloses more information" (Miller and Kenny, 713). I believe that self-disclosure in the classroom fosters the exchange of points of view. During class discussions I talk about my experiences as a son, husband, and father, especially those experiences that have proven to be cautionary tales. When discussing shame, for example, I share with my students the mortification I experienced when I came up for tenure in the late 1970s and was told that my scholarship was "deficient"—a criticism that called into question not only my worth as a scholar but my identity and self-esteem.

I also believe it is important to explore the complex link between our personal and professional selves. In *Diaries to an English Professor*, I discuss the devastation I felt when, on Labor Day, 1968, my mentor and closest friend called me to say that he had just swallowed an overdose of sleeping pills. His suicide filled me with feelings of anguish, guilt, and anger. In retrospect, I can see how much of my teaching, research, and writing has been an effort to work through this loss. Reading the "Suicide Survivors" chapter of my book encourages students to write about their own painful experiences and share them with classmates. In the process, they often reach insights that initiate the healing process. I believe that teachers can talk about themselves in ways that open dialogues with their students. Getting personal in the classroom can be a healthy antidote to our current preoccupation with theory.

EVALUATING THE COURSE

How did the students finally evaluate the course? What precisely did they learn from it? Would they recommend it to a friend? In an effort to answer these and other questions, I asked everyone to fill out an anonymous multiple-choice questionnaire and return it on the last day of the semester. Consisting of eighty-five questions, the evaluation form asked them to rank the strengths and weaknesses of the course, the degree of improvement of their writing, and the rewards and risks of personal writing and self-disclosure in the classroom.

All seventeen students who turned in the form judged the course successful, sixteen grading it an "A" and one a "B." When asked to describe what they liked most about the course, they listed (in order of decreasing importance) the opportunity to learn more about themselves, improve their writing, and learn more about their classmates. A large majority felt that the course required more work than others, that their writing improved a great deal more than it would have in a traditional writing course, and that they did not feel manipulated into self-disclosure.

Fourteen students said that it was painful to write about divorce, eating disorders, suicide, and sexual abuse. Only two had written on these subjects before this class. When asked whether writing or reading about painful subjects made them feel at risk, which I defined as "feeling anxious, panicky, depressed, or suicidal—feelings that were serious enough to warrant clinical attention," fifteen responded in the negative on the questionnaire; the remaining two were not sure. All but one agreed that writing about painful subjects brought therapeutic relief. They believed that such writing brought them new insights, made them feel better, enabled them to feel less isolated, and helped them to master fears.

I also asked them whether the course heightened their emotional intelligence, which Daniel Goleman defines as self-awareness, impulse control, persistence, zeal, motivation, empathy, and social deftness. All responded affirmatively. There was almost unanimous agreement that the course heightened their self-understanding, understanding of classmates, connection with classmates, and connection with me.

Nearly all of the students were surprised by the degree of self-disclosure throughout the semester. Interestingly, although most considered themselves to be average self-disclosers, they rated their classmates as high self-disclosers. Sixteen students believed that their classmates' self-disclosures encouraged their own self-disclosures. When asked whether they preferred high, average, or low self-disclosing teachers, they were divided; but, in perhaps the most telling answer of all, all seventeen believed that the ability to disclose personal information about oneself contributes to health and well-being. They also indicated that they had become more self-disclosing and trusting of others as a result of the course.

I was, of course, delighted with the results of the questionnaire. All indicated that they would recommend the course to a friend and that there should be other courses like this one. It was apparent that many students regarded the course as a transformative experience.

"THE JURY IS STILL OUT"

And yet one successful experiment in personal writing and self-disclosure does not guarantee future results. The number of students in the class was small, and two students did not turn in questionnaires. Would the results have been similar if the course were graded? Half the students believed it would be problematic to grade a course on personal writing, even though their answers were virtually identical when asked first to assign a letter grade to their own work and then to predict what my letter grade would be.

Would another class of students have the same experiences and results, whether taught by me or by someone else? This is the crucial question—one that can be answered only through future experiments. As a student observed at the close of the semester,

> Writing and therapy are similar in that they get at the roots of the unconscious. There is a support system with a good therapist; there may or may not be one in a group such as a college writing class. Is the classroom a safe environment for personal disclosure? In my thinking, the jury is still out.

For the experiment to be successful, teachers must scrupulously observe the following safeguards. They must, first, impress upon everyone in the class the necessity to be sensitive to and respectful of classmates' feelings; second, they must themselves be as empathic and nonjudgmental as possible; third, they must not coerce or manipulate students into involuntary self-disclosure; fourth, they must avoid playing the role of therapist, confessor, or clergyman; fifth, they must respect boundaries between self and other; and finally, they must be able to make appropriate referrals if students become at risk.

Teachers must also be able to acknowledge, without guilt or defensiveness, their own shame experiences. Morrison's clinical observation has important pedagogical implications:

> [T]he shame of patients is contagious, often resonating with the clinician's own shame experiences—the therapist's own sense of failure, self-deficiency, and life disappointments. Painful countertransference feelings may thus be generated in the analyst/therapist, feelings that he or she, like the patient, would just as soon avoid, feelings that not infrequently lead to a collusion, preventing investigation of the shame experience. (6)

I have never taught a course on shame in literature, but if I did, I would encourage my students to write personal essays relating fictional characters' lives to their own. I would also invite them to explore shame from a variety of theoretical perspectives: psychoanalytic, feminist, historical, reader-response. The aim of such a study would be to examine the various masks of shame and to come to terms with the painful past. Unmasking shame evokes intense resistance, as Léon Wurmser has noted, and it is the students themselves, not the teacher, who must decide when if at all to disclose their fears to others. Judging from my students' experiences, I believe that the writing or literature classroom is an appropriate setting to unmask shame and, through insight and empathy, achieve self-acceptance.

I realize that relatively few teachers will be interested in having students write on personal topics and that there is strong institutional opposition to this practice. In an age where teachers fear lawsuits almost as much as they fear violence, there are few incentives to narrow the distance from their students. The questions I hear most often from colleagues reflect their anxiety over involvement. "What happens if you come across a student who is at risk?" "What do you do if a student is depressed?" "How do you know a student won't commit suicide in your class?" These are legitimate questions, especially since, according to a 1991 CDC study, more than a quarter of American high school students seriously consider committing suicide each year.

My experience is that students become at risk, not by revealing their problems, but by concealing them. The signs of suicide are generally not difficult to recognize. They include making threats like "I won't be around here much longer" or "You won't have to bother with me anymore," prolonged depression, dramatic changes of behavior or personality, giving away prized possessions, withdrawal from family or friends, and abuse of alcohol or drugs. All teachers regardless of whether they encourage expressive writing should be able to recognize these signs and, when they come across someone who is at risk, respond appropriately. Responses include recommending that a student visit the counseling center or, in extreme situations, telephoning the campus crisis center or police (something I have never had to do). Once or twice a year a student will ask me for the name of a therapist, and I always comply. I believe that teachers' fears that their students will become emotionally dependent upon them are greatly exaggerated. Teachers can be caring without becoming caretakers.

In closing, I want to let Nick have the last word, for it is his story, after all, that I have presented to you. Evaluating the course at the end of the semester, he writes:

> I have thoroughly enjoyed every session of this class. It's not very often that one can sit around with a group of intelligent peers and discuss such sensitive and important topics. I only wish there had been more time: time to discuss the issues in depth, time to discuss the writing in depth, time to learn about each other in depth. But you can't accomplish everything in three hours a week.
>
> As for me, I'm not a person that joins well with others. I feel more comfortable at the fringes watching everyone like a hawk, and avoiding their gazes as quickly and deftly as possible. I won't fool you and tell you that now I'm different and you're all my new best friends and role models. You're not . . . but you can be proud that you have entertained me, perplexed me, taught me, helped me, supported me and constantly surprised me. That's impressive for such a small group that I had such

small hopes for. More importantly you have taught me to reserve judgment on people until I have at least some of the facts. That discovery of the unknown value and respectability of people has cracked open a door on a new world where I just may see myself a bit clearer.

NOTE

I am grateful to Professors Joseph Adamson, Hilary Clark, Randall Craig, Jerome Eckstein, Marian MacCurdy, and Steve North for their valuable comments on this essay. My deepest gratitude goes to Nick and his classmates, who entrusted their writings—and thus parts of their lives—to me.

WORKS CITED

Bartholomae, David. "Writing with Teachers: A Conversation with Peter Elbow." *College Composition and Communication* 46.1 (1995): 62–71.

Berman, Jeffrey. *Diaries to an English Professor.* Amherst: U of Massachusetts P, 1994.

Bishop, Wendy. "Writing Is/ And Therapy? Raising Questions about Writing Classrooms and Writing Program Administration." *Journal of Advanced Composition* 13.2 (1993): 503–14.

Brand, Alice Glarden. *Therapy in Writing.* Lexington, Mass.: Lexington Books, 1980.

Bump, Jerome. "Innovative Bibliotherapy Approaches to Substance Abuse." *The Arts in Psychotherapy* 17 (1990): 355–62.

Felman, Shoshana and Dori Laub. *Testimony.* New York: Routledge, 1992.

Freud, Sigmund. *The Ego and the Id. Standard Edition of the Complete Psychological Works of Sigmund Freud.* Vol. 19. London: Hogarth P, 1961.

Goleman, Daniel. *Emotional Intelligence.* New York: Bantam Books, 1995.

Kohut, Heinz. *How Does Analysis Cure?* Ed. Arnold Goldberg. Chicago: U of Chicago P, 1984.

Lawrence, D. H. *The Letters of D. H. Lawrence.* Vol. 2. Ed. George J. Zytaruk and James T. Boulton. Cambridge: Cambridge UP, 1981.

MacCurdy, Marian. "From Image to Narrative: The Politics of the Personal." *Journal of Teaching Writing* 13.1–2 (1995): 75–107.

Mikulincer, Mario and Orna Nachshon. "Attachment Styles and Patterns of Self-Disclosure." *Journal of Personality and Social Psychology* 61.2 (1991): 321–31.

Miller, Lynn and David Kenny. "Reciprocity of Self-Disclosure at the Individual and Dyadic Levels: A Social Relations Analysis." *Journal of Personality and Social Psychology* 50.4 (1986): 713–19.

Morrison, Andrew. *Shame: The Underside of Narcissism.* Hillsdale, N.J.: Analytic P, 1989.

Murphy, Ann. "Transference and Resistance in the Basic Writing Classroom: Problematics and Praxis." *College Composition and Communication* 40.2 (May 1989): 175–87.

Pennebaker, James. *Opening Up*. New York: Avon, 1992.

———. "Self-Expressive Writing: Implications for Health, Education, and Welfare." *Nothing Begins with N*. Ed. Pat Belanoff, Peter Elbow, and Sheryl Fontaine. Carbondale, Ill.: Southern Illinois UP, 1991. 157–70.

Plath, Sylvia. *The Journals of Sylvia Plath*. Ed. Francis McCullough. New York: Dial P, 1982.

Progoff, Ira. *At a Journal Workshop*. New York: Dialogue House, 1975.

Rainer, Tristine. *The New Diary*. Los Angeles: J. P. Archer. 1978.

Scholes, Robert and Nancy Comley. *The Practice of Writing*. New York: St. Martin's P, 1981.

Swartzlander, Susan, Diana Pace and Virginia Lee Stamler. "The Ethics of Requiring Students to Write about Their Personal Lives." *Chronicle of Higher Education* 39 (17 February 1993).

Tobin, Lad. *Writing Relationships*. Portsmouth, N.H.: Boynton/Cook, 1993.

United States Center for Disease Control. "Attempted Suicide among High School Students—United States, 1990." *Morbidity and Mortality Weekly Report* 40.37 (1991): 633–35.

Wurmser, Léon. *The Mask of Shame*. Baltimore: Johns Hopkins UP, 1981.

NAME INDEX

SUBJECT INDEX